America the Beautiful

Part 1: America from 1000 to 1877

Charlene Notgrass

America the Beautiful
Part 1: America from 1000 to 1877
by Charlene Notgrass

ISBN 978-1-60999-038-1 (hardcover)

Unless otherwise noted, scripture quotations taken from the
New American Standard Bible, Copyright 1960, 1962, 1963, 1971, 1972, 1973,
1975, 1977, 1995 by the Lockman Foundation Used by permission.

Lesson and Family Activities by Bethany Poore

Cover design by Mary Evelyn McCurdy
Interior design by Charlene Notgrass

Printed in the United States of America

Notgrass Company
975 Roaring River Rd.
Gainesboro, TN 38562

1-800-211-8793
www.notgrass.com
books@notgrass.com

Table of Contents
Part 1

Introduction

When God created the land we call America, He sculpted and painted a masterpiece. America is a land of prairies and mountains, lakes and rivers, deserts and bayous. People created in God's image have lived here for many centuries. Using the intelligence God placed in their hearts and minds and the strength He gave their bodies, these people have found many ways to use the plants, animals, rocks, and minerals He has provided in abundance.

America the Beautiful is first a book of history, but it is also a book of geography. All human history happens in a place. American history has happened along America's coastlines, on its prairies, between its mountains, beside its lakes, upon its rivers, and within its forests.

Thirty Units in Chronological Order

Each unit in *America the Beautiful* is about a certain time period in American history. In Unit 1, we learn about America before 1492. In Unit 30, we learn about things happening in the 21st century. The units in between are in chronological order.

Five Types of Lessons

To give children a comprehensive understanding of America, lessons in this course are divided into five types:

Our American Story — A lesson about major events in the time period of the unit.

God's Wonders — A lesson describing an amazing creation God placed in America.

An American Landmark — A lesson about an important site in American history.

An American Biography — A lesson focusing on a person who lived at the time being studied.

Daily Life — A lesson telling how certain people lived and worked during the period.

The Purpose of *America the Beautiful*

My heart's desire is that the children and parents who study *America the Beautiful* will be in constant awe of what God has created in America, both the physical place and the people whom God in His wisdom caused to live here. By learning about what God made, we learn about Him:

> For since the creation of the world His invisible attributes,
> His eternal power and His divine nature,
> have been clearly seen, being understood through what has been made . . . .
> Romans 1:20

The Native Americans who lived in America when Europeans first arrived were here because God wanted them to be here. We live in America today because God wants us to be here.

> He made from one man every nation of mankind to live on all the face of the earth,
> having determined their appointed times and the boundaries of their habitation,
> that they would seek God, if perhaps they might grope for Him and find Him,
> though He is not far from each one of us; for in Him we live and move and exist . . .
> Acts 17:26-28

As people created in the image of God, we are living history every day in a place God made. Our responsibility is to conduct ourselves according to the will of the One who made us. Americans are a richly blessed people. Like every person who has ever lived (except Jesus), we Americans are sinners in need of grace. Our history has many beautiful stories and some stories that are not so beautiful. We have done many things right, but not everything. *America the Beautiful* emphasizes the wonderful things that God has done and the positive things that we Americans have done, while being honest about some of our biggest shortcomings, including treatment of Native Americans and African Americans.

When your student comes to the conclusion of the study, I hope that he or she will look back on America's story with:

- gratitude for what God has created here,
- awe at what people made in His image have done with the gifts He gave us, and
- a realization of their personal responsibility to do God's will while living in this amazing place we know as *America the Beautiful*.

Charlene Notgrass

How to Use
America the Beautiful

Notgrass Company provides you as a parent with tools that help your children learn from a Biblical worldview. We create curriculum that is as easy to use as a textbook but with the richness of a unit study. When we wrote *America the Beautiful*, we created a variety of tools for you and your children to use. You can use any or all of these resources as you see fit.

Basic *America the Beautiful* Curriculum Package

The basic curriculum package for *America the Beautiful* includes:

America the Beautiful, Part 1 — A book with seventy-five lessons, designed to be completed in a semester. It begins with the way life was in America before Europeans discovered it and continues through the first years after the Civil War.

America the Beautiful, Part 2 — A book with seventy-five lessons, designed to be completed in one semester. It begins with America's expansion into the lands west of the Mississippi River after the Civil War and continues to modern times.

We the People — A collection of original letters, poems, songs, stories, and other writings from American history.

Maps of America the Beautiful — A book with maps drawn especially to accompany the curriculum. Students will often look at a map while reading a lesson in *America the Beautiful*. They will also do activities on the maps.

Timeline of America the Beautiful — A timeline of American history designed specifically to include facts learned in *America the Beautiful*. As they go through the lessons, students will add events to their *Timeline of America the Beautiful*.

America the Beautiful Answer Key — Answers to the timeline and vocabulary assignments included at the end of some lessons, plus answers for the activities in the optional *Student Workbook* and the questions and quizzes in the *Lesson Review*.

Additional Products

To make this curriculum a rich experience and to make it usable with children from grade five through grade eight, we offer three additional products:

America the Beautiful Student Workbook — A book of puzzles and other handwork activities which review information learned in the daily lessons. These are designed for younger students and for students whose learning style fits these types of activities.

America the Beautiful Lesson Review — A book of daily questions, literature review questions, and weekly quizzes, designed for older students. We expect that students will use either the *Student Workbook* or the *Lesson Review*, but your student can complete both if you prefer.

America the Beautiful Literature Package

- *The Sign of the Beaver* by Elizabeth George Speare (Units 4-5)
- *Amos Fortune, Free Man* by Elizabeth Yates (Units 6-7)
- *Brady* by Jean Fritz (Units 9-10)
- *Bound for Oregon* by Jean Van Leeuwen (Units 12-13)
- *Across Five Aprils* by Irene Hunt (Units 14-15)
- *Little Town on the Prairie* by Laura Ingalls Wilder (Units 16-17)
- *All-of-a-Kind Family* by Sydney Taylor (Units 19-20)
- *Blue Willow* by Doris Gates (Units 21-22)
- *Homer Price* by Robert McCloskey (Units 25)
- *Katy* by Mary Evelyn Notgrass (Units 29-30)

Note: These literature titles can be purchased from Notgrass Company as a package or individually. You can also obtain them from some other source, such as the library. You can use any unabridged edition of the books.

How to Use *America the Beautiful, Part 1 and Part 2*

These two volumes are the core of the curriculum. They give you and your child all of the information you need in order to use *America the Beautiful* on a daily basis.

These two volumes are divided into fifteen units each for a total of thirty units. Your child can study Part 1 during one half of the school year and Part 2 during the other half. Each unit has five lessons. If a student reads one lesson a day, he or she will cover five lessons in a week.

At the beginning of each unit, an introductory page gives an overview of the unit, a list of the lessons, and a list of what additional books the student will be using while studying that particular unit. Students should always read the unit introductions.

Following the unit introduction are five daily lessons, one to be read each day. Students can read these on their own or you can read the lessons aloud. The lessons are richly illustrated. The student's learning experience will be greatly enhanced if he or she is encouraged to examine the illustrations closely. Many are historical photographs and historical illustrations. Many are from the Library of Congress and from the National Park Service. They have been carefully selected to be an integral part of the learning experience.

At the beginning of each lesson is a lesson heading with the title of the lesson, the lesson number, and the lesson category (i.e., Our American Story, God's Wonders, An American Landmark, An American Biography, or Daily Life). In many lessons there is a map number (or numbers) beside the lesson number. The student should get in the habit of looking for this number each day. When a map is indicated in the heading, the student should open *Maps of America the Beautiful* so he or she can find places on the map while reading through the lesson.

At the end of each lesson is a list of four to six activities. Students are not necessarily expected to complete all of these activities. You may choose which activities you wish to assign. Subjects of the activities vary from day to day, but they include:

- Thinking Biblically assignments
- Creative writing assignments
- Vocabulary assignments
- Family activities (one per week)
- Literature assignments from *We the People* and the ten books in the literature package
- Assignments in *Timeline of America the Beautiful*
- Assignments in *Maps of America the Beautiful*
- Assignments in the *America the Beautiful Student Workbook* or the *America the Beautiful Lesson Review*

How to Use *We the People*

At the end of many daily lessons, students will be given a short assignment to read in *We the People*.

How to Use *Maps of America the Beautiful*

Students will look at a particular map while reading many of the lessons and will write or color in the book when assigned.

How to Use *Timeline of America the Beautiful*

The student will write one entry in *Timeline of America the Beautiful* after most lessons. To enhance learning, the student can read a few events already printed in the timeline before and after filling in the new entry each day.

How to Use the *America the Beautiful* Literature Package

We have carefully chosen the literature to go along with the lessons. Each book is broken into daily reading assignments, which are included in the end-of-lesson activities for the appropriate unit. *Across Five Aprils* is a good book for a parent to read aloud, since it deals with harsh realities of the Civil War.

How to Use the *America the Beautiful Student Workbook*

Students using the *Student Workbook* will complete Activity 1 after reading Lesson 1 and continue completing each daily activity through Lesson 150.

How to Use the *America the Beautiful Lesson Review*

Students using the *Lesson Review* will complete the questions for Lesson 1 after reading Lesson 1 and continue this way through Lesson 150. After finishing a book in the literature package, the student will answer questions on the book. At the end of each unit, the student will take a quiz.

Using a Three-Ring Binder Notebook for End-of-Lesson Activities

We recommend that each student have a three-ring binder notebook to use only for *America the Beautiful*. He or she will keep in this notebook the Bible study, creative writing, and vocabulary written work completed from the end-of-lesson activities.

Enjoying the Weekly Family Activities

One day per week a family activity is included in the list of activities at the end of one lesson. Projects include art, crafts, recipes, games, and parties. The instructions for the family activities are found in the back of *America the Beautiful Parts 1 and 2*. We recommend reading the instructions and gathering the supplies early each week and then completing the activity either on the day it is assigned or on another day that is convenient for your family. Our family has long enjoyed a family night once each week. You could do your family activity on a family night so that more family members could take part in the fun and learning.

Like all components of the *America the Beautiful* curriculum, the family activities are optional. We offer them as extra learning experiences. You, the parent, are the best one to decide if you are able to schedule time to complete them. Your supervision is required for your child's safety. See box at right.

Parental Supervision Required

The *America the Beautiful* family activities are designed for parental involvement. Please review the activity and discuss with your child what he or she may do alone and what he or she needs your supervision to do. The family activities in this book include the use of sharp objects, the oven and stove, and a few Internet research suggestions. Notgrass Company cannot accept responsibility for the safety of your child in completing these activities. You are responsible for your child's safety.

Please Note: Be careful. Some children may be allergic to recipe ingredients or craft supplies.

How Much Time Does It Take to Complete Each Lesson?

This curriculum has one hundred and fifty lessons and is designed to be completed in one school year. Since a typical school year has about one hundred and eighty days, the student completes one lesson on most school days. However, some families may choose to spread the curriculum out over a longer period of time.

Depending on how many activities you assign, most students will need forty-five minutes to an hour and a half to complete one lesson. More time will be needed on the day you do the family activity.

What Supplies Will My Student Need?

Students will need a pencil, colored pencils, notebook paper, and a three-ring binder, plus the materials needed to complete the family activities. These materials are listed on the individual family activity instruction pages.

What Ages Can Use This Curriculum?

The curriculum is designed for students in grades five through eight. With parental help and supervision, younger children can participate in many activities and can benefit from hearing the lessons read aloud.

How Can I Use *America the Beautiful* with Different Ages?

Parents know best what their children are capable of accomplishing. *America the Beautiful* is designed to be flexible. A variety of activities is included in each lesson. A parent may require an eighth grader who is academically gifted to read the daily lessons, read every book in the literature package on his own, complete worksheets in both the student workbook and the lesson review book, and complete every assignment at the end of each lesson. On the other hand, a parent with an academically-challenged fifth grader may decide simply to read aloud each lesson from *America the Beautiful*, talk about the map that goes with it, copy the timeline entry into *Timeline of America the Beautiful* with the student watching, and read aloud the selections from *We the People* and the books in the literature package.

If you have more than one child in grades five through eight, you may enjoy reading the lessons aloud as a group. Afterwards, you can give each child different assignments, depending on his or her age and skill level. If you have carefully observed your child and prayed about the direction to take, then you can look back at the end of the school year and know that the goal of completing *America the Beautiful* has been accomplished.

Suggested Activities Per Grade

On the next page is a suggested guide for choosing activities by grade. However, please keep in mind what other curricula you are trying to complete this year and adjust these suggestions accordingly. Feel free to adjust your goals after you have used the curriculum for a few weeks.

Suggested Activities Per Grade

Grade 5	Grade 6	Grade 7	Grade 8
Parent reads lessons aloud from *America the Beautiful.*	Parent reads lessons aloud from *America the Beautiful.*	Student reads lessons from *America the Beautiful.*	Student reads lessons from *America the Beautiful.*
Parent reads assignments aloud from *We the People.*	Parent reads assignments aloud from *We the People.*	Student reads assignments in *We the People.*	Student reads assignments in *We the People.*
Student completes activities in *America the Beautiful Student Workbook.*	Student completes activities in *America the Beautiful Student Workbook.*	Student completes questions in *America the Beautiful Lesson Review* and takes quizzes.	Student completes questions in *America the Beautiful Lesson Review* and takes quizzes.
Student completes assignments in *Maps of America the Beautiful.*	Student completes assignments in *Maps of America the Beautiful.*	Student completes assignments in *Maps of America the Beautiful.*	Student completes assignments in *Maps of America the Beautiful.*
Student writes daily entries in *Timeline of America the Beautiful.*	Student writes daily entries in *Timeline of America the Beautiful.*	Student writes daily entries in *Timeline of America the Beautiful.*	Student writes daily entries in *Timeline of America the Beautiful.*
Parent or student reads books from literature package.*	Parent or student reads books from literature package.*	Student reads books from literature package.*	Student reads books from literature package.*
Parent chooses two activities per week from Bible Study, Vocabulary, and Creative Writing activities.	Parent chooses three activities per week from Bible Study, Vocabulary, and Creative Writing activities.	Parent chooses four activities per week from Bible Study, Vocabulary, and Creative Writing activities.	Student completes all Bible Study, Vocabulary, and Creative Writing activities at the end of each lesson.
Family completes weekly Family Activity.	Family completes weekly Family Activity.	Family completes weekly Family Activity.	Family completes weekly Family Activity.

* We recommend *Across Five Aprils* as a family read-aloud.

Some Reminders So You Will Not Feel Overwhelmed

Remember that God gave you your children and your daily responsibilities. A homeschooling mother who has one child can complete more *America the Beautiful* activities than a homeschooling mother who has seven children and an elderly grandparent living in her home. God will use the efforts of both of these mothers. God does not expect you to do more than you can do. Be kind to yourself. He knows exactly what you and your children need this year. Remember that out of all the parents in the world to whom He could have given your children, He chose you. He is the one who put your family together. He knows what He is doing. Relax and trust in His choice. God created our beautiful country. God created you. He created your children. Relax and remember that this is the day that the Lord has made. Rejoice and be glad in it!

We are here to help you. When you need encouragement, send us an email (books@notgrass.com) or give us a call (1-800-211-8793).

Acknowledgements and Dedication

I am grateful to my husband Ray who has served as the editor-in-chief of *America the Beautiful*. For thirty-six years I have been blessed with my own personal human encyclopedia, concordance, and dictionary; his name is Ray Notgrass. Ray has shared with me his own vast personal knowledge of American history, along with his research skills. He was a servant leader during this project, taking on many responsibilities to give me time to complete a project he believed in as much as I did. He and I worked together to create the *Timeline of America the Beautiful*. Together we have explored America for all these years, beginning with our honeymoon trip to the Chattanooga Choo Choo and the Lookout Mountain battlefield.

I am grateful to our son John. A few years ago the two of us were driving home from a homeschool convention in Virginia. We talked excitedly about a concept for a new American history for children in grades five through eight. We had the idea for a study that emphasized a different aspect of America on each day of the week. That idea has now grown into *America the Beautiful*. I also appreciate the work he has done researching, proofreading, and correcting. He has guided this project through the printing process. John is a wonderful detail guy and he has put those talents to work. He also oversaw compilation of the index. I am grateful for John's wife Audra. She has helped research photographs, proofread, and tested activities. She has been a wise sounding board. I am also grateful to Audra for giving birth to our first grandson Avery John on January 26, 2011!

I am grateful to our daughter Bethany who has lovingly and excitedly selected the books students read as they study *America the Beautiful*. She also chose the selections students read in *We the People*, wrote the introductions to each of them, and did the book's graphic design. Bethany wrote *Maps of America the Beautiful* and drew each map. She created the Thinking Biblically, Creative Writing, and Vocabulary assignments. Bethany designed and wrote the Family Activity for each unit. She has been such an encourager. I am grateful for her husband Gregory Poore, too. Even with his many responsibilities as a full-time graduate student, he was a good sport and willing guinea pig who helped test many of her great family activities.

I am grateful to our daughter Mary Evelyn who used her creative abilities to design each of the *America the Beautiful* covers. She wrote and designed the *America the Beautiful Student Workbook* and *America the Beautiful Lesson Review*. Her presence in our office cheers me each time she is here. I am grateful, too, for Nate McCurdy, Mary Evelyn's husband and our newest Notgrass Company partner. Nate did a great job helping with his first curriculum project. He has proofread, researched, tested activities, and given wise counsel. We admire our newest partner and newest child-in-law.

I am grateful, too, for my mother. Night after night on the phone, she has wanted to know how the curriculum is coming. Thanks, Mother, for your kind interest and support.

I am grateful to God who created this wonderful place, America the Beautiful. He gave me much to write about. He has guided me in this project, while taking care of these precious people and of me.

I dedicate *America the Beautiful* to God
and to these precious loved ones.

America Before the Arrival of Europeans

One of the first lessons people learn in American history is that Christopher Columbus discovered America in 1492. But what was America like before that? In our first lesson, we learn about God's Wonders that He placed in America—wonders that were here in 1492.

Maine in the Fall

In the second lesson, we find out about the first immigrants who came to America and about the lifestyles of the Northwest Coast and California Indians. We finish the week learning about lifestyles of Indians living in the Plateau, Great Basin, Southeast Woodlands, and Northeast Woodlands.

Lessons in Unit 1

Lesson 1 – God's Wonders: God Created America the Beautiful
Lesson 2 – Our American Story: The First Immigrants to America
Lesson 3 – Daily Life: Natives of the Plateau and the Great Basin
Lesson 4 – Daily Life: Natives of the Southeast Woodlands
Lesson 5 – Daily Life: Natives of the Northeast Woodlands

Books Used in Unit 1

- *Maps of America the Beautiful*

- *Timeline of America the Beautiful*

- *We the People*

Oregon Coast

God Created America the Beautiful

O beautiful for spacious skies,
For amber waves of grain,
For purple mountain majesties
Above the fruited plain!

America! America!
God shed His grace on thee,
And crown thy good with brotherhood
From sea to shining sea!

Imagine America the Beautiful in 1492. It is an immense land with green forests, golden plains, and purple mountains. Billions of animals amble across, burrow beneath, and soar above the land, while billions more swim in its rivers and streams. The mighty Mississippi River flows southward from the northern forests to the Gulf of Mexico. The world's two largest oceans lie on either side of the land, the Atlantic to the east and the Pacific to the west. A few hundred miles inland from the Atlantic, the Appalachian Mountains rise toward the sky; and a few hundred miles from the Pacific, the Rocky Mountains ascend to heights of thousands of feet.

God put swamps, bayous, and marshes in America. He made vast deserts, and He placed just the right plants and animals here. He filled the Great Lakes and thousands more lakes and ponds with water and with life. He created the perfect routes for birds, butterflies, fish, and animals to use when they migrate each spring and fall.

Along the Atlantic Coast

Humpback whales, right whales, and swordfish swim in the Atlantic. Bottle-nosed dolphins play nearby. Walruses lounge on the rocky northern coast, while gray seals play along the sandy beaches to the south. Manatees nibble at water plants in coastal waters and nearby rivers, while American alligators crawl and swim nearby. The American crocodile hunts its prey in the far south. Sea turtles come ashore to lay eggs to begin a new generation.

American Alligator

American Crocodile

Humpback Whale

Gray Seal

Bottle-Nosed Dolphins

Green Sea Turtle

Manatee

Walrus

Right Whale

Across the Land

Herds of North American bison and packs of wolves roam over almost the whole land that will one day become the continental United States. Black bears rob beehives and search for insects and berries nearly everywhere. Caribou herds munch on lichens, shrubs, and grasses across the north from near the Atlantic to the Rocky Mountains. Elk range across the land's midsection on both sides of the Mississippi River. Pronghorn antelope abound in the central region between the Mississippi River and the Rocky Mountains. Jaguars stalk their prey across the entire southern half of the country from sea to shining sea. The mountain lion hunts in places as diverse as the northeast, the far north, the Florida peninsula, lands near the Pacific Ocean, and the country's center.

From north to south, bald eagles fly high over waterways,

Gray Wolf

Caribou

Jaguar

North American Bison

American Black Bear

swooping down to catch tasty fish. The ivory-billed woodpecker flies over the Southeast; while the prairie chicken eats leaves, seeds, and insects in America's broad central grasslands.

In and Near the Pacific Ocean

Killer, pilot, and gray whales swim along the Pacific coast. Sea mammals such as elephant seals, sea otters, harbor seals, and sea lions live on and near the beaches. The waters teem with shellfish including abalone, clams, mussels, and Pacific oysters.

Salmon return from the Pacific and swim to the stream of their birth so they can lay their eggs before they die. Bears of the Pacific northwest feast on the salmon. Mule deer graze in

California Condor

Mountain Lion

Gray Whale

Sea Otter

places farther inland. Gigantic California condors, with a wingspan of up to nine and a half feet, soar above.

Look at each picture in this lesson. Think about God filling the land, waters, and skies with these and many thousands of other creatures. He painted a masterpiece when He created America the Beautiful. As you come to know this great land, you will be able to identify with the psalmist:

O LORD, how many are Your works!
In wisdom You have made them all;
The earth is full of Your possessions.
Psalm 104:24

Activities for Lesson 1

Thinking Biblically – Look in your Bible in Genesis 1. In your notebook, make a list numbered 1-6 and write beside each number what God made on that day. Next to each item on your list, write one thing that people in America can enjoy that was made on that day of Creation.

Map Study – Complete the assignments for Lesson 1 on Map 1 "America the Beautiful" in *Maps of America the Beautiful*.

Literature – Read the Introduction on page vii and "America the Beautiful" on page 1 in *We the People*.

Creative Writing – Choose one of the animals pictured in this lesson and write a descriptive paragraph about its appearance in your notebook. Title your paragraph, "God Made _____."

Student Workbook or Lesson Review – If you are using one of these optional books, complete the assignment for Lesson 1.

Bald Eagle

Killer Whale (also called Orca)

Elephant Seal

Sea Lion

Bears Hunting Salmon

The First Immigrants to America

God created Adam. He took one of Adam's ribs and formed a wife for him. Adam named his wife Eve, because she was the mother of all the living (Genesis 2-3). Adam and Eve had children. Many descendants were born to this family. Eventually the people became very evil, and God was sorry that He had made them. God sent a great flood to destroy the wicked; but He saved eight people, Noah and his family (Genesis 6-9). Noah's sons and their wives began to have children. Eventually, some of Noah's descendants decided to build the Tower of Babel (see drawing at right). God was not pleased with what they did, so He confused mankind's language and the people scattered over the earth (Genesis 11).

Drawing of People Building the Tower of Babel

Noah's Descendants Come to America

We don't know how or when, but sometime after the flood, some of Noah's descendants came to America. These immigrants might have come to North America by crossing a land bridge through the Bering Sea between Russia and Alaska. Notice the photograph of walruses swimming in the Bering Sea below. One problem with that theory is that there is no land bridge there now! Maybe they walked across ice. Another theory is that people came to America on boats, perhaps from islands in the Pacific.

Walruses in the Bering Sea

Although we don't know exactly how or when they came, we do know that by the 1400s, people with similar physical characteristics were scattered across North and South America and on the islands nearby. These people lived in groups. Some lived in extended family groups, some in tribes, and others in confederations of several tribes.

7

Early immigrants to America were created in the image of God. Because of this, they were intelligent and creative. They used their God-given abilities to figure out ways to live and work together. Some tribes searched for plant foods, some hunted or fished, and some farmed. Some tribes did a combination of these. These Native Americans created cultures filled with games, music, and art. They held festivals. They loved and cared for their families.

Like other humans, these people did right sometimes and wrong sometimes. In some years, tribes lived in peace and traded goods with other tribes; at other times, the tribes fought wars.

Native American Regions in the Lands That Became America

A few tribes had beliefs that were similar to God's teachings in the Bible. For example, the Cherokee believed in one God they called Ye ho waah, which is similar to the Hebrew YHWH. The Ottawa taught precepts that were similar to the Ten Commandments.

Just as the nature of daily life in Europe or Africa or Asia depended on where a person lived, the same was true in America. The native customs were influenced by the geography God had created around them, the weather He sent, and the plants and animals He placed in their environment. Daily life in the mountains was different from life on the prairies. Life in cold climates was different from life in hot climates. The culture of a particular tribe depended on its history and the ways of life in other tribes living nearby. Sometimes people from two or more tribes joined together to form a new tribe.

Natives who lived within each of the ten regions of America shown on the map above shared similar lifestyles. Read the names of the regions aloud. In the first two units of *America the Beautiful*, you will learn about natives in each region, except the Great Plains, Arctic, and Subarctic. These are in later lessons. In today's lesson, we begin with those who lived in the Northwest Coast region and in California. Keep in mind that just as Americans today move from place to place and change their ways of life, the same was true for Native Americans. Though people have lived in America for many centuries, these lessons will tell mainly about how natives lived at the time they first met Europeans.

Natives of the Northwest Coast

Northwest Coast natives lived from southern Alaska to northern California. This region has coastal mountains and dense wet forests and is home to many animals. The people here lived in extended family groups who had common ancestors. Among the natives of the Northwest Coast were the Chinook, Tlingit, Haida, Nootka, and Wasco.

Tlingit Man

Some Northwest Coast natives traveled on the ocean in large cedar dugout boats with painted designs. Some boats held as many as sixty people. Many, like the Tlingits, were known for their woodcarving. See the Tlingit man at right. Many natives of the Northwest Coast created beautiful art. Examine the Chinook petroglyph (rock painting), Tlingit turned basket, and Haida painting below.

The Chinook people of the Northwest Coast were involved in trade. Natives who lived farther east in the Plateau and Great Plains regions traded with the Chinook, who provided them with cedar wood, dried salmon, horn carvings, fish oil, furs, seashells, and seal oil. The Chinook used the Columbia River as a trade route. They took words from local

Chinook Petroglyph

Tlingit Turned Basket

Art from the Haida People

languages and developed a trade language, which peoples all along the Northwest Coast used. Notice the Chinook man at right.

People of the Northwest Coast were born into classes. Some were nobles, some were common people, and others were slaves. Slaves were people who had been captured in war and people who were in debt, as well as the children born to them.

Chinook Man

Beach Villages

Northwest Coast Indians built villages on beaches. They faced their large, cedar plank homes toward the Pacific Ocean. House fronts were decorated with painted carvings. Grandparents, aunts, uncles, and cousins lived together, but each mother and father had a separate section for themselves and their children.

Food from the Sea and Forests

Most Northwest Coast natives got their food from the sea. They ate cod, flounder, halibut, herring, salmon, seals, and sea lions. Some hunted for whales. Natives fished in streams and rivers, too. Some hunted for bear, deer, elk, and mountain goats. They ate fresh meat and fish in warm weather and they dried meat and fish to eat in the winter.

Bird Heads, Otter Fur, and Goat Hair

Both men and women wore clothes made from woven plant fibers. Northwest natives made rain hats and headdresses from plants also, but sometimes they made headdresses from feathers and bird heads! For warmth they wore sea otter robes and blankets. The Nootka tribe wove dog and mountain goat hair into their clothing. Notice the clothing and head coverings of the Chinook, Wasco, and Nootka men on this page. The Wasco and Nootka men are dressed in traditional clothing, while the Chinook man wears a European style.

Wasco Man   *Nootka Man*

Tribes of the California Region

Many distinct Native American tribes lived in the California region. Over one hundred languages were spoken there. Some tribes traded with one another. At times they used shells as a form of money. Most California tribes traveled by log or reed rafts. Some made dugout canoes. Notice the Hupa dugout canoe on page 11. The Chumash tribe made boats from planks of wood. They were the only Native Americans to make boats that way.

The California peoples made beautiful baskets of many shapes and sizes. They used bark, grass, reeds, and roots to make baskets that they used for baby carriers, games, and containers. See the basket cradle below; it is from the Wintun tribe. California natives also made objects from antlers and stone. Notice the antler spoons below. They are from the Yurok tribe.

Hupa Canoe

Yurok Antler Spoons

Huts and Sweathouses

The California peoples lived in small villages. Various tribes built different kinds of homes, but the most common type was a cone-shaped hut about eight feet across, like the one on page 12. They built these huts with poles which they covered with brush, grass, reeds, or a type of bulrush. Also common was a dome-shaped hut built over a pit and covered with earth. Another type of home was a lean-to, covered with bark and built with a slanted roof. In some tribes only women and children slept in the huts. Men slept, worked, and socialized in sweathouses, like the one pictured on page 13. These were built of redwood planks and rocks.

The Acorn Diet

Abundant food grew in the California climate, so natives could gather most of their food without having to farm. Their main food source was acorns from oak trees. The natives gathered, dried, and washed the acorns and then ground them into flour. They made soup, mush, and bread from acorn flour. The photograph at right below shows several caches where natives stored acorns in California's Yosemite Valley. A cache is a secure place where provisions are stored.

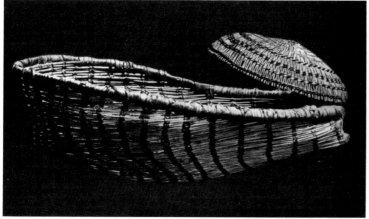
Wintun Basket Cradle

Acorns Stored in the Yosemite Valley of California

11

Notice the California natives beside their cone-shaped hut.

Berries, Birds, Bugs, and More

California natives gathered berries, bulbs, greens, nuts, roots, and seeds in addition to acorns. They roasted grasshoppers and boiled caterpillars and grubs. The California peoples used bows and arrows to hunt deer, ducks, geese, swans, and small mammals. Rabbit meat was a favorite. They used nets to catch ducks, geese, and swans.

Tribes living along the coast of the Pacific Ocean hunted for seals, sea lions, and sea otters. They gathered shellfish along the shore. California natives fished. They used hooks, lines, nets, and spears. Sometimes they built small dams called weirs to trap fish. Notice the Hupa fisherman at left.

Skins, Bark, Feathers, Fibers, and Furs

Natives of California made clothes from animal skins and shredded bark. They used plants to make hats and hairnets and feathers to make headbands and crowns. Feathers or fur from rabbits and sea otters kept them warm in winter. Most people went barefoot, though some wore ankle-high

A Hupa Man, 1923

moccasins or yucca plant sandals. Many wore shell jewelry.

God created the Northwest Coast and California tribes and decided where and when they should live. As Paul taught the people of Athens:

Yurok Sweathouse, c. 1923

And He made from one man
every nation of mankind
to live on all the face of the earth,
having determined their appointed times
and the boundaries of their habitation.
Acts 17:26

Activities for Lesson 2

Thinking Biblically – At the top of a blank piece of paper, copy Acts 17:26 from your Bible. Below the verse, make a chart showing the names of the members of your family, their birthdates, and all the places they have lived. You many want to include your grandparents as well. Ask your parents for help to make sure you have all of the information correct. Post the chart in a prominent place (such as your refrigerator door) so that everyone in your family can be reminded that God has "determined their appointed times and the boundaries of their habitation."

Map Study – Complete the assignments for Lesson 2 on Map 4 "Native Peoples of North America" in *Maps of America the Beautiful*.

Vocabulary – Look up each of these words in a dictionary: descendant, immigrant, confederation, dense, cache. In your notebook, write each word with its definition.

> **Please note:** In the vocabulary assignments, we have used simple forms of the vocabulary words. In some lessons, a vocabulary word appears in a different form from the form used in the vocabulary assignment. For example, in this lesson the word descendant is used in its plural form descendants. In other cases a verb might appear in the past tense in the lesson. Keep this in mind when you look back in a lesson to find vocabulary words.

Literature – Read "Indian Child Life, Part 1" in *We the People*, page 2.

Student Workbook or Lesson Review – If you are using one of these optional books, complete the assignment for Lesson 2.

Natives of the Plateau and the Great Basin

Mount Hood

The Cascade Mountains extend from southern British Columbia in Canada into Washington and Oregon. Mount Hood, pictured at left, is part of the Cascade chain. Plateau tribes lived between the Cascade Mountains and the Rocky Mountains. South of the Plateau region is the Great Basin, where a few tribes lived as nomads. Nomads travel from place to place in search of food.

Natives of the Plateau

Native Americans in the Plateau region were divided into many tribes, including the Klamath, Yakima, Nez Perce, Kalispel, Cayuse, Kootenai, Klikitat, Spokane, Walla Walla, and Salish (also called Flathead).

Plateau tribes created many beautiful and useful objects. Some used marsh plants to weave soft bags which they decorated with elaborate designs. They made intricate baskets. Below is an example of a Klamath basket. Some tribes also made basket hats. Notice the variety of traditional crafts in the photograph of the Yakima woman at right.

Plateau tribes used parts of animals to create objects they needed. Some made animal horns into cups. Notice the Flathead woman at center right on page 15. She is using a

Klamath Basket

Yakima Woman

14

horn cup to dip water from a stream. Some tribes made leather baskets. The Kootenai man below is in an elk hide canoe. Other tribes also built canoes. Notice the Nez Perce man at right in his pole-guided canoe.

Nez Perce Man in a Pole-Guided Canoe

Kootenai Man in an Elk Hide Canoe

Moving Villages

Plateau villages had five or six houses. Four to six families lived together in each house. To build a cold weather house, Plateau builders dug a pit and placed a large post in the center. They made a cone shape by placing poles around the pit and attaching them to the center post. They covered this cone with mats made of bark, sagebrush, grass, and packed dirt.

In warm weather, villagers moved from place to place, depending on where they found food. Summer houses were made of basswood and mats.

Hunting, Gathering, Fishing, and Digging

The Plateau Indians did not farm. Instead, they hunted, fished, and gathered food from plants. They picked blackberries and huckleberries and dug for roots and bulbs such as bitterroot, camas, wild carrots, and wild onions. At right, a Plateau woman uses a hand scythe to gather piyake roots into a leather basket.

Flathead Woman Using Horn Cup to Dip Water

Plateau Woman Gathering Roots

Plateau natives hunted for bear, deer, elk, jackrabbits, mountain sheep, and pronghorn antelope. They caught various fish, but mainly salmon. They caught fish with nets, traps, and long spears. Sometimes they stood on riverbanks to fish and sometimes on platforms they had built beside the banks. They ate fish fresh and they dried fish to eat in the winter. Plateau natives cooked in tightly-woven baskets. They filled them with water and added heated stones.

Shredded Bark, Deerskin, and Fur

Plateau men wore deerskin clothing, while the women wore clothing made from shredded bark. Fur robes kept them warm in winter. Western Plateau natives went barefoot. In the eastern Plateau, they wore bison or deer-skin moccasins.

Raven Blanket, from the Nez Perce tribe, wears a feathered war bonnet with ermine fur streamers.

A Flathead (or Salish) Tribesman

The Spokane tribe lived in the Plateau region. At left is a Spokane chief and at right are members of the tribe.

Klikitat Man, 1910

Kalispel Man, 1910

Kalispel Couple, 1861

Nez Perce Man, 1905

Cayuse Man

Some tribes in this region compressed their babies' heads to make them have a peak on top. Those other tribes called the Salish people "Flatheads," because the Salish did not compress the heads of their children.

Examine the pictures of Plateau natives on pages 14-17. Notice their clothing, jewelry, hair decorations, and head coverings. Examine the intricate designs of their beadwork. Notice the baby in its ornate baby carrier.

Klamath Woman, 1923

Yakima Woman and Baby

Nez Perce Man, 1910

Natives of the Great Basin

The Great Basin is a desert region west of the Rocky Mountains and east of California. Most of the land is low in elevation. Death Valley, the lowest place in North and South America, is in the Great Basin. Small numbers of nomadic tribes lived there, including the Paiute, Shoshone, Ute, Washoe, and Chemehuevi.

In the Great Basin region, families of parents, children, grandparents, aunts, uncles, and cousins traveled together, hunting for firewood, food, and water. Some families joined with others to hunt together or to spend the winter together. Great Basin Indians made baskets. They also made bows, arrows, and clubs to use in hunting. Some wove hunting nets and others made duck decoys from duck skins.

Ute Woman and Baby, 1916

Shoshone Chief Washakie, Early 1900s

Paiute Man, 1924

Paiute Man, 1924

Most natives of the Great Basin lived in huts made from willow poles. They covered them with brush, grass, or reeds. See a home of the Chemehuevi at right. The photo was taken around 1924.

Great Basin Home Built by a Chemehuevi

Reptiles, Grubs, and More

For their food, the peoples of the Great Basin hunted for birds, lizards, rabbits, rodents, and snakes. They searched for berries, nuts, seeds, and grubs. These tribes also dug in the ground to find insects, reptiles, and small mammals. They made long, hooked tools out of sticks and used them to pull animals out of their burrows.

Yucca, Skin, and Bark

Like the tribes of the Plateau, men's clothing was made of deerskin and women's was made of shredded bark. Notice the women below. Though most natives of the Great Basin

Paiute Women in Basket Hats

Ute Chief Ouray and Chipeta, 1880   Washoe People, 1866

wore no shoes, some wore sandals made of yucca or the skin of deer or rabbit. Look at the photographs of Paiute, Shoshone, Ute, and Washoe people on pages 18-20.

Try to imagine what life was like for the people of the Plateau and Great Basin before Europeans arrived in America. Like us, they were dependent on God. He provided them with everything they needed for food, shelter, and clothing. As the Psalmist said:

> They all wait for You,
> To give them their food in due season.
> Psalm 104:27

Activities for Lesson 3

Thinking Biblically – Read Psalm 104:21-28. In your notebook, write a prayer thanking God for providing you with food.

Map Study – Complete the assignments for Lesson 3 on Map 4 "Native Peoples of North America" in *Maps of America the Beautiful*.

Literature – Read "Indian Child Life, Part 2" in *We the People*, page 3.

Alta Washakie,
a Shoshone Girl

Creative Writing – In your notebook, write a paragraph detailing how one of your favorite foods gets to you. For example, how does ice cream go from milk in the cow to your cone? Or how do potatoes get from the farm to your plate? Try to include all of the steps in the process.

Student Workbook or Lesson Review – If you are using one of these optional books, complete the assignment for Lesson 3.

Natives of the Southeast Woodlands

Before Europeans arrived, much of eastern America was covered with dense forests. Woodlands Indians lived there. The Woodlands Indians are divided into the Northeast Woodlands tribes and the Southeast Woodlands tribes.

The geography of the Southeast Woodlands region is varied. It includes rolling hills in Kentucky and Tennessee, flat delta land by the Mississippi River, swamps and

Southeast Woodlands natives traveled on and lived near rivers.

bayous in the deep South, coastal regions near the Atlantic and the Gulf of Mexico, and mountains along the border between Tennessee and North Carolina. Many rivers and streams flow through these varied landforms. Southeast Woodlands natives rode their dugout canoes in these waters, using poles or paddles to propel them along. It was along these waterways that they built their villages.

Over one hundred tribes lived in the Southeast Woodlands, including the Alabama, Caddo, Catawba, Cherokee, Chickasaw, Choctaw, Coushatta, Creek, Natchez, Timucua, Yamasee, and Yuchi. Florida's Seminole tribe is another well-known Southeast Woodlands tribe, but it did not form until after Europeans came to America. Sometimes Southeast tribes went to war with one another, while at other times they lived in peace.

Individuals in some Southeast Woodlands tribes, like the Natchez, were born into a particular class, like priests, nobles, and commoners. In other tribes people treated one another as equals. Those tribes were organized with democratic ideals. Both men and women were leaders in some groups. Many people around the world trace their ancestry through their fathers, but individuals in many Southeast Woodlands tribes traced their ancestry through their mothers. Some tribes joined together to form confederacies. The Alabama, Creek, and Coushatta people were joined together in the Creek Confederacy.

After Europeans came to America, five Southeast Woodlands tribes adopted many European customs. These were the Cherokee, Chickasaw, Choctaw, Creek, and Seminole tribes. They joined together in 1859, calling themselves the Five Civilized Tribes. Notice the

Pushmata, a Choctaw, lived from 1764 to 1824.

European influence in the clothing of the Choctaw man pictured at left.

Mound Builders of the Southeast Woodlands

Earth mounds are scattered throughout much of the Southeast Woodlands region. Some of the mounds were used as burial grounds. It is likely that others were used as platforms for buildings. Mounds have been discovered in every southeastern state. See the designs of artwork found in mounds in Arkansas and Tennessee below. Many mounds have also been discovered in the Northeast Woodlands region. Lesson 5 tells about the mounds in the Northeast.

Archaeologists believe that some of these mounds are only a few hundred years old and that others are much older. Mound builders may have lived in the eastern United States during four different time periods. Archaeologists call these periods Poverty Point, Adena, Hopewell, and Mississippian.

The most recent mound building period was the Mississippian. It probably began around 800 and lasted into the time that Europeans began settling in America. The Natchez tribe of Mississippi continued to use mounds into the 1600s. Archaeologists believe that Natchez was part of the Mississippian culture that stretched along the Mississippi River from Cahokia, Illinois, to Natchez, Mississippi. These Mississippians had the most advanced native culture that has been discovered in America. The Mississippian culture declined in the mid-1500s for reasons that are unknown. Many of the tribes that the first European explorers met in the Southeast Woodlands, including the Creek and Choctaw, were likely descendants of Mississippians. Evidence shows that a group of natives migrated into Georgia about 1400. During the fifteenth century they built the Etowah Indian Mounds northwest of present-day Atlanta. The Etowah Mounds include three large mounds shaped like flat-topped pyramids. They are surrounded by a village area and a moat.

Design Found Inside a Mound in Tennessee

Homes, Villages, and Towns

Many Southeast Woodlands natives built homes and public buildings with sticks or cane which they covered with clay or mud. This building method is called wattle and daub. Other natives covered buildings with animal skins, reeds, palm fronds,

Pottery from Mounds in Arkansas

grasses, bark, or woven mats. Roofs were often thatch or bark. The Chickasaw built summer homes with open walls. After the Seminole tribe formed, they also used an open wall design. The open-sided Seminole homes, called chickees, were built on stilts (see photo at right). Some Seminoles still live in chickees.

Seminoles in Front of a Chickee

Most Southeast Woodlands structures were rectangular, but a few were circular. The Cherokee used both. They lived in rectangular houses in summer and circular houses in winter. The Caddo tribe stretched from the Red River Valley of Louisiana to the Brazos River Valley of Texas. (A river valley includes a river and the lowlands that surround it. The soil in river valleys is often especially fertile, making the areas good for farming.) The Caddos lived in cone-shaped homes made of poles covered with thatched grass. Their homes surrounded a temple mound.

In addition to villages, some Southeast Woodlands tribes built central towns surrounded by stockades or palisades. Look at the Florida village below. It has a public building in the center and homes around it. A palisade encircles the village.

The Creeks often had a ceremonial building in the center of their villages. Sometimes it sat atop a mound. Caddo villages also had a mound in the center.

Growing Food

Southeast Woodlands tribes grew crops, with women doing most of the farming. Their main crops were corn (also called maize), beans, and squash. These three crops were known in some places as "three sisters." Some tribes, including the Cherokee, grew three kinds of corn: one for roasting, one for boiling, and one for grinding into grain. Some tribes, like the Cherokee, Chickasaw, and Creek, celebrated a special Green Corn festival. The Cherokee gave thanks and forgave wrongs during the Green Corn festival.

Fortified Village of the Timucua Tribe of Florida

Other Southeast Woodlands crops included melons, pumpkins, sunflowers, and sweet potatoes. Some tribes, like the Choctaw, were such good farmers that they had more food than they needed and were able to use some for trade. They even developed a trade language that used simple words and signs.

Gathering Food

In addition to farming, natives gathered wild fruits, greens, nuts, roots, and stalks. The Calusa of south Florida did not need to raise crops because they were able to obtain abundant fish and shellfish. Other tribes also fished, using hooks, lines, spears, and traps.

Southeast Woodlands tribes also hunted for meat, using bows and arrows to kill deer, bears, and elk. They used darts shot through blowguns to kill small animals like rabbits, raccoons, squirrels, and turkeys. Natives made blowguns from cane stems and darts from wood and feathers.

Members of the Creek Tribe

Clothing and Appearance

In many Southeast tribes, both men and women wore deerskin clothing, including moccasins, when the weather was cold. In warm weather, the women of some tribes wore skirts made from plant fibers. Timucua women wore dresses they made from Spanish moss. Some leaders and priests wore feathered capes on special occasions.

Tattoos were popular among some tribes. Timucua men were tattooed from their heads to their ankles. The designs depended on their social status. Some men plucked out their hair. The Choctaw tribe flattened the heads of their boys. Notice the appearance of Southeast Woodlands natives illustrated on this page.

Leisure Activities, Art, and Crafts

Many tribes, including the Cherokee and Choctaw, played Indian stickball, a game like lacrosse. Residents of different villages competed against each other. Hundreds of participants played at the same time. Players could bite, hit, and stomp, so injuries were common. When the Choctaw played, their priests performed rituals to try to influence the game.

Southeast Woodlands natives were creative. They formed pottery, carved stone, created from metal, made shell necklaces, and wove

Cherokee Chief with Tattoos

A Chickasaw Youth

baskets. Baskets made by natives in Louisiana are pictured at right.

Like us, the people of the Southeast Woodlands are all the work of God's hand. As Isaiah wrote:

But now, O Lord, You are our Father, we are the clay,
and you our potter; and all of us are the work of Your hand.
Isaiah 64:8

*Baskets Made by Natives
Living in Louisiana*

Activities for Lesson 4

Map Study – Complete the assignment for Lesson 4 on Map 4 "Native Peoples of North America" in *Maps of America the Beautiful*.

Vocabulary – In your notebook, write your own definition for each of these words: archaeologist, fertile, palisade, status, ritual. Look in the lesson for clues for the meaning of the words. When you are finished writing your definitions, look in a dictionary for comparison.

Timeline – In *Timeline of America the Beautiful* next to 1400, write: Native American tribes migrate into what is now Georgia.

Literature – Read "Indian Child Life, Part 3" in *We the People*, page 4.

Student Workbook or Lesson Review – If you are using one of these optional books, complete the assignment for Lesson 4.

Natives of the Northeast Woodlands

Many different tribes lived in the Northeast region. They lived on lands in what are now twenty-four states. The languages of the Northeast Woodlands tribes are divided into two main language families. Throughout the world people speak thousands of languages. Those believed to have had a common beginning are called a language family. Many tribes of the Southeast Woodlands spoke a language of the Muskogean family, but the main language families of the Northeast were Algonquian and Iroquoian. Scholars believe that native tribes who spoke Algonquian lived in the Northeast before those who spoke one of the Iroquoian languages.

Read the chart of Northeast tribes on page 27 and look at the portraits of Northeast natives from several tribes. At right is a picture of two members of the Ojibwe tribe, which lived near the Great Lakes.

Ojibwe Men

Gathering Food

Southeast natives were mainly farmers who supplemented their diets with foods they found in their surroundings. Northeast Woodlands tribes, on the other hand, were mainly hunters and gatherers, who supplemented their diet with farming. One notable exception were the Delaware people of New Jersey. God created especially rich farmland in New Jersey, which is known as the "Garden State." The Delaware were primarily farmers. One farming discovery made by the Delaware is that wood ashes make good fertilizer.

The main meat of the Northeast Woodlands tribes was deer meat; but they also hunted bears, beavers, ducks, elk, geese, moose, partridges, rabbits, squirrels, and turkeys. Some tribes living in the western parts of the region hunted bison. The Northeast natives hunted creatively. They used bows and arrows, spears, traps, and clubs. Five clubs used by the Winnebago tribe are pictured on page 28. The traps some Northeast Woodlands natives used made heavy objects fall on their prey. Sometimes hunters used animal calls and disguises to lure animals. At other times they set fires to make the animals go in a certain direction.

Tribes of the Northeast Woodlands

Along and Near the Atlantic Ocean
Abenaki, Croatan, Delaware (or Lenni Lenape), Mahican, Maliseet, Massachusett, Micmac, Minisink (or Munsee), Mohegan, Mohican, Nanticoke, Nantucket, Narragansett, Nauset, Niantic, Nipmuc, Passamaquoddy, Pennacook, Penobscot, Pequot, Pocasset, Pocumtuc, Pokanoket, Poospatuck, Powhatan, Quiripi, Roanoke, Secotan, Susquehannock, Tuscarora, Tutelo, Unalachtigo, Wampanoag

Along and Near the Great Lakes
Cayauga, Dakota Sioux, Erie, Kickapoo, Laurentian, Menominee, Miami, Mohawk, Ojibwe (or Chippewa), Oneida, Onondaga, Potawatomi, Seneca, Sauk and Fox, Winnebago (or Ho-Chunk)

Along and Near the Ohio River
Ohio Valley Tribes, Shawnee

Along and Near the Mississippi River
Chickasaw, Dakota Sioux, Illini

Dakota Sioux

Wampanoag Chief

Potawatomi

Miami

Sauk and Fox Chief

Kickapoo

Seneca Chief

Fox Warrior

Winnebago

Shawnee

Ojibwe (Chippewa) Girl

Mohawk Chief

27

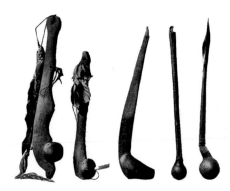

Clubs of the Winnebago Tribe

Northeast tribes also used harpoons, hooks, nets, and traps to catch fish from lakes, ponds, rivers, and streams. Those who lived near the Atlantic also gathered shellfish.

Northeast Woodlanders collected edible parts of wild plants. Some tribes gathered wild rice along the Great Lakes. Some tribes enjoyed blueberries and cranberries. Tribes living near maple trees collected sap and made maple syrup and maple sugar.

Villages of Longhouses and Wigwams

Like their southern neighbors, many Northeast tribes built villages beside rivers and streams. Others, however, cleared forest lands and built their villages in the clearings. Some Northeast Woodlands tribes lived in permanent villages and others were semi-nomadic, meaning that they lived in villages part of the time but also traveled to find food.

Some Algonquian tribes in New York built large, rectangular bark houses with rounded roofs of thatch. People who lived near Chesapeake Bay also built rectangular houses with rounded roofs. First, they pushed long, slim poles into the ground, forming two parallel rows. They pulled the tops of opposite poles together and tied them to form a rounded roof. They laid young saplings across the poles and then attached mats made from rushes or bark to the frame created by the poles and saplings. Two or three families lived together in these rectangular homes. Notice the Secotan village at right. These homes are in a style similar to those built near Chesapeake Bay.

However, the two main types of houses used by Northeast Woodlands tribes were longhouses and wigwams.

This Secotan village was near the Pamlico River in North Carolina. Its houses are in the style popular near the Chesapeake Bay, which lies about 125 miles north of the Pamlico River. This is how the village looked around 1600.

An Iroquoian Longhouse, a House of Five Fires

Iroquoian tribes lived in large communities of longhouses. The name Iroquoian is a French version of an Algonquian word, but the Iroquoians called themselves "Haudenosaunee," meaning "people building an extended house."

To build a longhouse, the Iroquois would first build walls and a roof out of wooden posts, beams, and tree saplings. Some groups built pointed roofs and others built rounded ones. A longhouse with a pointed roof is illustrated above. One with a rounded roof is illustrated below. The Iroquoians left holes in the roofs to let out smoke from their fires.

The Winnebago tribe lived in eastern Wisconsin and spoke a Siouan language. This structure does not have individual rooms. Perhaps it is a ceremonial building.

They often covered their longhouses with elm bark. They put a door in each end.

A long hall ran through the center of each longhouse. Rooms for individual families were along this passage. Along one wall of a family's room was a raised platform used for sleeping. Each family had its own small fire in the center of its room. To indicate the size of a longhouse, the Iroquoians called it a house of "six fires" or "ten fires." Notice that the Iroquoian house above has five fires. More rooms could be added to each end of a longhouse. Some houses were 400 feet long.

Wigwams were popular among the Algonquian-speaking peoples. Wigwam is an Algonquian word meaning dwelling. A wigwam was similar to a Chesapeake Bay home, but it was built as a circle instead of a rectangle. The first step was to place saplings in a circle and then bend and tie them into a dome shape, as illustrated at right. Coverings included mats, birch bark, and sometimes animal skins. Some villagers made pointed roofs instead of rounded ones. Wigwams are also illustrated on page 30.

The Wabanaki confederation of tribes that lived in New England lived in both wigwams and longhouses.

An Ojibwe Wigwam Under Construction

An Ojibwe Settlement with Cone-Shaped Wigwam

Moving from Place to Place

Algonquian communities often moved seasonally. They lived near their food sources—by their agricultural fields in summer and in forests filled with game in winter. Some tribes, like the Algonquian Pennacook tribe of New Hampshire and Massachusetts, moved to the seacoast in summer to fish and to gather shellfish. Northeast villages were connected by many footpaths. Natives also traveled in bark-covered canoes. See picture on page 26. Algonquians covered their canoes with birch and the Iroquoians covered theirs with elm. Birchbark canoes were lightweight so they could be carried from one stream to another.

These Penobscot wigwams were on display at the World's Columbian Exposition held in Chicago in 1893. The Exposition celebrated the 400th anniversary of Columbus discovering America. The wigwams are made of birch bark.

Art and Crafts

The Northeast Woodlands natives created beautiful objects. See the Algonquian deerskin mantle pictured below and the Iroquoian birch basket on page 31. Northeast tribes experienced cold winters, so they also made clothing from bear and beaver fur.

The Iroquoians of the Northeast made polished purple and white beads called wampum from whelk and quahog shells. The belts, sashes, and strings made from these beads are also called wampum. See top of page 31. Natives wore these to show status. They also used them as a type of money and recorded information on them. To record information, they arranged beads into pictographs, a type of writing that uses symbolic pictures instead of letters. When a tribe or council wanted to communicate with another tribe or council, it sent wampum. This made the communication official. Only certain tribesmen were able to read the messages created with

This Powhatan deerskin mantle is decorated with shells.

A Mohawk Wampum Belt

An Onandaga Wampum Belt

An Iroquoian Birch Bark Basket

wampum. Ojibwe natives drew pictographs on birchbark to keep tribal records.

Mound Builders of the Northeast Woodlands

Mound builders once lived in the Ohio River Valley. They left a mound near Peebles, Ohio, that is almost one-quarter of a mile long. The mound twists and turns in different directions and is called the Serpent Mound. Archaeologists believe it was built shortly before the birth of Jesus Christ. Another Ohio River Valley mound is the Alligator Mound in Granville, Ohio. Both are illustrated on page 32.

Archaeologists believe that Cahokia in Illinois was the largest settlement of the Mississippian cultural area mentioned in Lesson 4. See the illustrations below. People probably inhabited Cahokia from 700 to 1400 A.D. At its height around 1200, its population was perhaps 20,000 people. This would have made it one of the greatest cities in the world, perhaps larger than London, England, at the time. Evidence shows that Cahokia had rows of houses, open areas, and over 120 mounds. It was probably surrounded by large agricultural fields. Tourists can see what remains of this great city at the 2,200-acre Cahokia Mounds State Historic Site in Illinois. These mounds have been designated as a U.S. National Historic Landmark and as a World Heritage Site.

Mounds have also been discovered in Kentucky, Indiana, Iowa, Michigan, Minnesota, Missouri, New York, Virginia, West Virginia, and Wisconsin. In addition to earth mounds, American Indians built rock structures. Sometimes Northeast natives erected

At top is a drawing of Cahokia. At bottom is an artist's idea of people living there.

"Standing Stones," which are large rocks set into the ground. Early European settlers saw Algonquian tribes building cairns, which are piles of rocks that served as landmarks.

God loved the people of the Northeast Woodlands, just as He loves everyone. When Jesus died, He died for us all, as we learn in Revelation:

> . . . for You were slain,
> and purchased for God with Your blood
> men from every tribe
> and tongue and people and nation.
> Revelation 5:9b

Six Mounds from the Northeast Woodlands:
3 is the Serpent Mound; 4 is Cahokia;
6, at bottom right, is the Alligator Mound in Granville, Ohio

Activities for Lesson 5

Map Study – Complete the assignment for Lesson 5 on Map 4 "Native Peoples of North America" in *Maps of America the Beautiful*.

Timeline – In *Timeline of America the Beautiful* next to 1200, write: The Native American city of Cahokia, in what is now Illinois, has an estimated population of 20,000 people.

Literature – Read "Indian Child Life, Part 4" in *We the People*, page 5.

Family Activity – Make an Iroquoian Longhouse. Follow the instructions on page 417.

Student Workbook or Lesson Review – If you are using one of these optional books, complete the assignment for Lesson 5. If you are using the Lesson Review, take the quiz for Unit 1.

Spanish Explorers Come to America

During this unit we learn about Leif Eriksson and Christopher Columbus and their explorations in the New World. We find out about the earliest encounters between Native Americans and visitors from the Old World. Since some of those explorers entered the Southwest, we learn about the natives who lived in that region. This week we look at two American Landmarks: the Cliff Palace of Mesa Verde, built by ancestors of natives living in the Southwest, and St. Augustine, the first permanent European settlement in the land that became the United States of America.

Painting of Navajo Woman

Lessons in Unit 2

Lesson 6 – Two European Biographies: Leif Eriksson and Christopher Columbus
Lesson 7 – Our American Story: Native Americans Meet Spaniards
Lesson 8 – Daily Life: Natives of the Southwest
Lesson 9 – An American Landmark: The Cliff Palace of Mesa Verde
Lesson 10 – An American Landmark: St. Augustine, America's Oldest European City

Books Used in Unit 2

- *Maps of America the Beautiful*

- *Timeline of America the Beautiful*

- *We the People*

Leif Eriksson and
Christopher Columbus

When Native Americans living along the Atlantic coast looked east toward where the sun rose each morning, they probably wondered what was out there beyond the horizon.

This map shows the parts of the world that Europeans knew about in 1492.

They had canoes, but as far as we know they never tried to build large ships so they could sail east. They didn't know that if they sailed far to the east they would find Europe.

On the other side of the Atlantic, Europeans looked to the west and wondered what would happen if they sailed their ships across the ocean. They only knew about the parts of the world shown on the map at left. Many people knew that the world was round, but they did not know that if they traveled west, they would discover two continents lying between Europe and the Far East.

Finally, courageous Europeans set sail to find out. They discovered the land mass that we call North and South America. The first Native Americans known to have met Europeans were ones who lived near the Atlantic Ocean. Historians are unsure about exactly when that first meeting took place. Perhaps it was in 1492, but it might have happened around 1000 A.D.

The Vikings

The Vikings were a powerful force in Europe between about 800 and 1100 A.D. The Vikings are also called Nordic peoples. Their homeland is Scandinavia, which includes the modern countries of Norway, Denmark, and Sweden (find Scandinavia on the map above). At the beginning of this

A Viking Ship in Greenland

34

Vikings Row Toward the Coast of North America

period, many Europeans were believers in Jesus Christ; but the Vikings were not.

Vikings built ships and traveled great distances to trade and to explore. Fierce Viking warriors often attacked other Europeans. Eventually, they began to move into the areas they conquered. They established many cities, including York, England, and Dublin, Ireland. By the mid-800s, Viking explorers had discovered Iceland. From there, they explored further west. A good result of the exploits of the Vikings was their coming into contact with those who believed in Jesus. Soon many Vikings became believers.

Erik the Red and His Son Leif Eriksson

In 985 Erik the Red of Iceland sailed westward to Greenland. He settled there with his family. According to the Icelandic "Saga of Erik the Red," Erik's son, Leif Eriksson, traveled from Greenland to Norway shortly before 1000. In Norway King Olaf I taught Ericksson about Jesus; and he became a Christian. The king sent him back to Greenland to convert the settlers to Christ. The illustration at the bottom of page 34 shows a Viking ship in Greenland.

According to the saga, Eriksson headed toward Greenland but lost his way. Instead, he found a place with wild wheat, grapes, and a kind of tree thought to be a maple. Eriksson named the rich land Vinland. Many people believe that Vinland was on the eastern coast of Canada in North America. After Eriksson left there, he rescued a ship and received its cargo as a reward. Thus he came to be called Leif the Lucky.

Leif Eriksson eventually went to Greenland and taught the people about Jesus. One person who became a believer was his mother, Thjódhild (pronounced THYOHD-hild). She is given credit for guiding the construction of the first church building in Greenland.

Another Icelandic saga, "Tale of the Greenlanders," tells a different story about the first Viking in North America. In that story, Bjarni Herjólfsson saw North America about 986. Later, Leif Eriksson bought Herjólfsson's ship, sailed to North America himself, and established Vinland. In that saga, Eriksson and his crew built dwellings and stayed in Vinland a year or two. Look at the illustrations of Viking ships above and at right.

In 1960 Norwegian explorer and writer Helge Ingstad searched for evidence of Viking settlements

Leif Eriksson and his crew come ashore in Vinland.

along the coasts of New England and Canada. While at L'Anse aux Meadows in Newfoundland, Canada, a local man, George Decker, showed Ingstad some overgrown ridges. Helge and his wife, archaeologist Anne Stine Ingstad, led an international team of archaeologists as they excavated the area around these ridges. They found the lower stones of eight Viking buildings, a pin that was used to hold a Viking man's cloak, a stone oil lamp, three tools women used in making cloth or clothing, and many iron boat nails.

Perhaps L'Anse aux Meadows was Vinland or another Viking settlement. Its discovery gives evidence that Vikings spent time in North America. Perhaps Vikings met native peoples who lived in Canada or what became New England, as the illustration at right suggests.

Perhaps Vikings met natives of the Northeast Woodlands.

It was almost five hundred years before history records more Europeans coming to America. While it is possible that Vikings visited America around 1000, that meeting did not have the impact on the history of the world as did the encounters that began in 1492.

Christopher Columbus Looks for a Way to Sail to the Far East

In 1451 a boy was born in the seaport town of Genoa, Italy. His name in Italian was Cristoforo Columbo. In English he is called Christopher Columbus. His father was a wool weaver. The little boy grew up, became a sailor, and moved to Portugal.

Christopher Columbus became fascinated with the possibility that people could travel to the Far East by sailing west on the Atlantic Ocean. He tried to get the king of Portugal to sponsor a voyage that would prove this, but the Portuguese king refused. Finally, Columbus convinced King Ferdinand and Queen Isabella of Spain to sponsor his voyage (see picture at right).

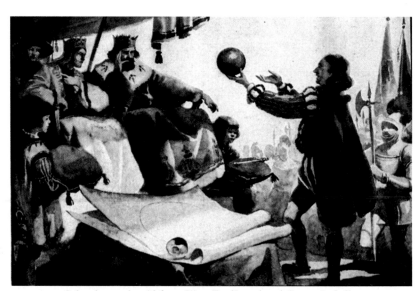
Columbus seeks aid from King Ferdinand and Queen Isabella.

Columbus Discovers America

Columbus prepares to sail from Palos, Spain.

Columbus and his crew left Spain on August 3, 1492 (see picture at left). They sailed in three small ships, the Niña, the Pinta, and the Santa Maria, pictured below. Like other ship captains of the time, Columbus kept a detailed ship's log. Columbus was a devout Catholic. The first words of his log are: "In the Name of our Lord Jesus Christ." His journal tells that he and his crew stopped in the Canary Islands off the western coast of Africa. From there he and his crew sailed into the unknown.

Finally on October 12, 1492, Columbus and his crew sighted land. It was one of the islands of the Bahamas, northeast of Cuba. Columbus and his crew went ashore. See the drawing at lower right. Since Columbus believed that the island was one of the Indies of the Far East (near China), he called the people of the island Indians. He didn't realize that he had discovered the "New World."

The Niña, the Pinta, and the Santa Maria

The coming of Europeans brought many changes for Native Americans. In his log Columbus wrote about wanting to convert the island natives to Christ. Some natives did indeed become believers in Jesus Christ. This was one good result of Europeans discovering North and South America. However, many Native Americans were hurt and many died. Great numbers of natives died because their bodies did not have immunity to European diseases. Others were killed by Europeans.

Columbus' Armor

Columbus came to America in the Middle Ages, when soldiers still wore metal suits of armor. Like other Europeans who came to America later, Columbus and his crew brought armor with them to the New World.

The illustration at left appeared in the 1886 book *Narrative and Critical History of America* by Justin Winsor. It is labeled "Christopher Columbus' Armor, from the Collection in the Royal Palace at Madrid, Spain." Sadly, the first Europeans to meet Native Americans were not only explorers, but also conquerors.

Columbus Comes Ashore in the Bahamas

Columbus and his crew explored islands in the area and returned to Spain in 1493 with the news of their adventures. When other Europeans learned about what Columbus had found, they wanted to travel there, too. Columbus himself returned three times. From 1493 to 1496, he explored the islands of the Caribbean Sea. During his journey of 1498-1500, he saw South America. During his final journey of 1502-1504, he sailed along the coast of Central America. Columbus died at age 54 in 1506.

Columbus' discovery in 1492 opened the way first for the Spanish and later for many other Europeans to come to America to explore and to settle. Columbus, like others throughout the ages, was fascinated by the seas God made. In Proverbs Solomon wrote:

> There are three things which are too wonderful for me,
> Four which I do not understand:
> The way of an eagle in the sky,
> The way of a serpent on a rock,
> The way of a ship in the middle of the sea,
> And the way of a man with a maid.
> Proverbs 30:18-19

Activities for Lesson 6

Thinking Biblically – Read Psalm 71:15-18 and Matthew 28:18-20. Imagine you were telling the good news about Jesus to someone who had never heard about Him. How would you explain it? Write this in four to six sentences in your notebook.

Map Study – Complete the assignments for Lesson 6 on Map 5 "Europe and the Western Hemisphere" in *Maps of America the Beautiful*.

Timeline – In *Timeline of America the Beautiful* next to 1000, write: Viking explorers land on the North American continent.

Literature – Read "Journal of Christopher Columbus" in *We the People*, page 6.

Creative Writing – Think about the attitude that Columbus and other Europeans had toward Native Americans. What were the good and bad things that happened because Columbus came to America? In your notebook, write one or two paragraphs giving your opinion.

Student Workbook or Lesson Review – If you are using one of these optional books, complete the assignment for Lesson 6.

Native Americans Meet Spaniards

Native Americans meet Spaniards who have come ashore in Florida.

Adventurers from Spain began coming to the newly-discovered islands they called the West Indies. Some explored beyond the islands. In 1510 Vasco Núñez de Balboa founded a successful colony at Darién in Central America. Three years later he led an expedition across the Isthmus of Panama and became the first New World explorer to see the Pacific Ocean. See his picture at right.

Though Balboa is known as the first European to discover the Pacific Ocean, other Europeans, like Marco Polo and merchants who traded in the Far East, had probably already seen the Pacific while visiting Asia. Ferdinand Magellan (who was Spanish, though born in Portugal) sailed west from Spain and led an exploration that circled the globe between 1519 and 1522. Magellan is pictured on page 40.

Vasco Núñez de Balboa

Amerigo Vespucci

Ferdinand Magellan

As mentioned in Lesson 6, many Spanish explorers were also conquistadors or conquerors. They began to conquer the lands they explored and to make war against the people who lived there.

Newly-Discovered Continents Named North and South America

Amerigo Vespucci, pictured above, was from Italy. He worked as a ship navigator. Most historians believe he first came to South America in 1499 as part of a Spanish expedition. He later made three other voyages. Vespucci wrote down his experiences and concluded that these lands the Spanish were exploring were not part of the Far East, but new lands. When Martin Waldseemuller, a German geographer and mapmaker, created a world map in 1507, he labeled the newly-discovered lands America in honor of Amerigo Vespucci. One thousand copies of the four-by-eight-foot map were published. In 2003 the Library of Congress purchased the only known surviving copy.

In *America the Beautiful*, we use the name America for the lands that became the United States of America. When talking about the American continents, we use the terms North America and South America.

Juan Ponce de León and the Fountain of Youth

Spanish monarchs began to appoint governors to rule places that Spain controlled in the New World. When Christopher Columbus sailed to the New World on his second voyage in 1493, thirty-three-year-old Juan Ponce de

North America

Central America

The West Indies, now called the Caribbean Islands

Isthmus of Panama

South America

León accompanied him. Ponce de León later served as Governor of the Caribbean island of Borinquen, which is now called Puerto Rico. He is pictured at right.

Juan Ponce de León

Governor Ponce de León heard stories told by Caribbean natives. They talked of Bimini, a legendary island north of Cuba, where there was a fountain of youth. The natives said that water from this spring could make people young again. Ponce de León believed the stories and asked the Spanish king for permission to find Bimini. He wanted to conquer it and begin a colony.

Ponce de León sailed north to find Bimini. On Easter Sunday, March 27, 1513, he saw land. He thought he had found Bimini, but he had really discovered a peninsula of North America. Ponce de León and his crew landed on the Florida coast, just south of 30 degrees latitude on April 2, 1513. See drawing below. Ponce de León named his discovery "Florida" because he first saw it during the Easter holiday season. In Spain Easter is called *Pascua Florida,* meaning flowery festival. Ponce de León and his crew tried to sail around the "island," but of course they could not. They returned to Puerto Rico in September.

Juan Ponce de León landed in North America in 1513.

Eight years later, in 1521, Ponce de León took two hundred people to form a colony on the west coast of Florida. Natives attacked the group and wounded Juan Ponce de León. He and the colonists sailed to Cuba where he died.

Hernando de Soto

Hernando de Soto, pictured at right, was born in Spain around 1500. At about fourteen years of age, he sailed to Darién in Central America. At first he worked for the Governor. Later he explored Central America.

When de Soto was about 30 years old, he traveled to Peru in South America under the leadership of the cruel Spanish conquistador Francisco Pizarro. (Pizarro had been with Balboa when he first saw the Pacific Ocean).

Hernando de Soto

While in Peru, de Soto and other Spaniards became wealthy by conquering the native Inca Empire and taking its treasures.

In 1537 Charles V, king of Spain and of the Holy Roman Empire, made de Soto Governor of Cuba and Florida. Two years later, de Soto and an army of about six hundred men landed on the western side of Florida and marched up its coast.

For four years, de Soto and his army marched 4,000 miles through the southeast area of North America searching for treasure. Here they met many Southeast Woodlands tribes. The army crossed the Savannah and Ocmulgee Rivers in what is now Georgia. They crossed present-day Alabama, which has established De Soto State Park to mark part of the area they explored. The Spaniards explored in the Appalachian Mountains of Tennessee

Native Americans of the Southeast Woodlands Meet de Soto

and probably passed through northern Mississippi, where a town named Hernando is now located in De Soto County.

De Soto and his army became the first Europeans to see the Mississippi River. They probably sighted it near what is now Memphis, Tennessee. The explorers then crossed the river into the area that is now Arkansas. They entered present-day Texas and Oklahoma before turning back to the east. Hernando de Soto died of a fever near the Mississippi River almost exactly four years after the expedition began. What was left of his army built barges which they floated down the Mississippi River. They entered the Gulf of Mexico and went on to Mexico, reaching it in September of 1543.

Hernando de Soto died after a four-year search for treasure. In Proverbs Solomon taught us what true treasure is:

> How much better it is to get wisdom than gold!
> And to get understanding is to be chosen above silver.
> Proverbs 16:16

Activities for Lesson 7

Map Study – Complete the assignments for Lesson 7 on Map 5 "Europe and the Western Hemisphere" in *Maps of America the Beautiful*.

Timeline – In *Timeline of America the Beautiful* next to 1507, write: A map is published in Europe that gives the name America to the land mass that includes North and South America.

Vocabulary – In your notebook, write a paragraph using all of these words: merchant, navigator, monarch, Governor, colony. Consult a dictionary if you need help with their definitions.

Creative Writing – How do you think a native in Florida would have described Ponce de León and his party of explorers? Look closely at the pictures in this lesson for ideas. In your notebook, write a paragraph as if you are a native living at that time who is describing the Spanish men to a friend who has not seen them.

Student Workbook or Lesson Review – If you are using one of these optional books, complete the assignment for Lesson 7.

Natives of the Southwest

At the same time that Hernando de Soto explored the Southeast, Spanish conquistador Francisco Vásquez de Coronado explored the lands of the Southwest, where he met tribes of the Southwest region. Coronado searched, not for a fountain of youth as Ponce de León had almost thirty years before, but for legendary cities of gold.

Coronado

From 1540 to 1542, Coronado, pictured at right, led his men across the Southwest trying to find the Seven Cities of Cíbola, which he had heard were filled with gold. When they found the Zuni tribe living in six or seven villages, Coronado was disappointed to find that their villages were not filled with gold. Zuni still live on the site of one of those original villages. Below is a picture of a Zuni village as it appeared in 1873.

Coronado continued to explore the Southwest, but he never found the cities of gold. Soon more Spanish soldiers moved into the Southwest, along with traders and missionaries.

The homelands of the Southwest Indians were the canyons, deserts, mesas, and mountains of New Mexico, Arizona, southern Texas, and small areas in southern Utah and southern Colorado. Most historical tribes still live in the region today. Read the chart of Southwest tribes on page 45. Many continue to keep their ancient traditions, and some have come to believe in Jesus Christ.

Pueblo Tribes

Several Southwest tribes are called Pueblo Indians. Pueblo is Spanish for village, but the word is mainly used for the people and for the homes they built. We will use the terms "Pueblo Indians" for the Pueblo tribes and "pueblo" to refer to the structures they built for homes.

A Zuni Pueblo, Photo Taken in 1873

The Hopi, Keres, Tewa, Tiwa, Towa, and Zuni were Pueblo Indians. Some tribes built their pueblos of adobe bricks, while others used stone and plaster. They made ceilings out of wooden beams and poles covered with brush and clay. Inside walls were often

Zuni women work under a food drying structure in front of their pueblo home.

whitewashed and sometimes they were decorated with geometric designs. Some homes had no windows. T-shaped doorways let in light. In the Hopi tribe, women built the pueblos and owned them. Pueblos could be as tall as five stories. People used ladders to climb from one level to another. Notice the pueblos pictured on these two pages.

Each pueblo housed several families. As many as 1,000 people could live in one pueblo, with each family having its own separate apartment. Pueblo Indians also built special rooms called kivas, which were used for religious ceremonies.

Some Southwest pueblos have been occupied for hundreds of years. The Acoma Pueblo was built

Two Tewa Girls Outside a Pueblo in 1900

Tribes of the Southwest
Arizona
Hopi, Keres, Papago (or Tohono O'Odham), Pima (or Akimel O'Odham), Yumans (including the Cocopa, Havasupai, Hualapai, Maricopa, Mojave, and Yavapai) and Yuma (or Quechan)
New Mexico
Tewa, Tiwa, Towa, and Zuni
Southern Texas
Coahuiltecan and Karankawa
New Mexico, Arizona, Southern Utah, and Southern Colorado
Apache and Navajo

around 1000, about the time of Leif Eriksson. See Acoma dancers at right. Acoma is thought to be the oldest settlement in America. The Hopi village of Oriabi in Arizona was built around 1100. New Mexico's Taos Pueblo was built around 1400.

Pueblo Snake Dance at Acoma Pueblo

Village and Nomadic Life in Other Southwest Tribes

The Pima tribe built villages beside rivers. With mud and brush, they made domed huts. The Mojaves who lived near the Colorado River built their thatch homes on stilts to protect them from flooding. The Cocopa tribe also lived along the Colorado River. They lived in homes made of brush and limbs in summer and in wattle and daub plaster houses in winter. The Hualapai ("People of the Tall Pine") live along the Colorado River in the Grand Canyon. They think of their homeland as the backbone of the Colorado River.

The Havasupai continue to live in the Grand Canyon beside Havasu Creek with its aquamarine-colored water. See picture at right. Havasupai means "blue water people." Their traditional dwellings were made of brush and sometimes covered with mud.

Homeland of the Havasupai

The Navajo built earth homes called hogans. One is pictured at left. These homes had wooden frames covered with clay. Navajo doors always faced east so they could welcome the rising sun. The Maricopa built similar homes, as did members of the Mojave tribe who did not live close to a river.

Apache homes were called wickiups. As seen at left, women built these cone- or dome-shaped huts. They put up poles and covered them with brush, grass, or reeds, and sometimes buffalo hides. Some women could build a hut in as little as two hours.

Some Southwest tribes were nomadic. Most of these tribes traveled on foot, but the Karankawa of what is now Texas used dugout canoes to relocate from one fishing spot to another during fall and winter. A Karankawa canoe held a whole family. These natives lived along the coast of the Gulf of Mexico in the fall and winter and about twenty-five

A Navajo Hogan

An Apache woman builds a wickiup.

46

miles inland in spring and summer. Karankawa women used thin poles, brush, and animal hides to make their huts.

Foraging and Farming

Favorite cooked foods among Southwest tribes were baked beans, corn balls, cornbreads of various kinds, hominy, and soups. The Southwest region has little rainfall, so natives had to be creative in both growing and finding food. All of the Pueblo tribes farmed, as did many other Southwest tribes. The word Navajo means planted fields or farmland. See photo below.

The Hopi continue to farm according to historic farming traditions. They plant corn, squash, and melons in fields that are watered by melting snow and the few summer rains. They tend terraced gardens, which they water by gravity-fed irrigation or by buckets. Some gardens have been in use since the 1200s. For hundreds of years the Hopi have planted beans in sand dunes and also tended fruit trees.

Some Southwest tribes irrigated while others did not. The Pima used wooden tools to dig irrigation canals for their crops. The Papago tribe did not irrigate their crops of corn, beans, and cotton, but they knew how to plant seeds so they could take advantage of the limited rainfall.

The Havasupai tribe ate mainly deer meat and the native agave plant, which they gathered. They hunted deer in winter and dried the meat to eat in the summer. Sometimes they also ate mountain goat or black bear meat.

The Hualapai grew squash, peaches, corn, and beans. Their main wild foods were cactus fruit and seeds of various grasses. They also gathered acorns, grapes, medicinal herbs, and walnuts.

Apache men hunted for antelope, buffalo, deer, and small animals. Apache women searched for fruit, nuts, and seeds. The Apache regularly ate corn, which they obtained through trade or theft.

Pueblo Gardens

The Coahuiltecan tribes gathered the fruit and pads of the prickly pear cactus. During summer they ate nothing else. In late summer and fall, they gathered mesquite beans, ground them into flour, and mixed them with other foods. During one special ceremony, the men ate the flour mixed with dirt.

Clothing, Hair, and Beauty

Pueblo Indians wove cotton to make clothing. They also wore fur, skins, and feathers. They sometimes wore ponchos. The nomadic Apache and Navajo tribes wore deerskin. The

Zuni Woman Wearing White Moccasins and White Strips Around Her Legs

Hopi Man Wears Headband and Bead Necklaces

Yuma Man with Hair Twisted into Rolls

Hopi Woman in Traditional Dress

Papago Woman

Tewa Girl

Maricopa wore leather capes. They and the Mojave also wore rabbit-skin robes to keep warm on cool nights. Some Zuni men wore kilts; Zuni women wore cotton dresses.

Southwest Indian footwear included sandals, moccasins, and boots. Some footwear was made from woven plant fibers and some from leather. Hopi and Zuni women painted their moccasins white for special occasions and wrapped white strips of deerskin around their legs, like the woman at left.

Zuni, Hopi, and Apache men often wore cloth headbands. See the Hopi boy on page 49 and the Hopi man at left. Apache women wore their hair long and loose or put it up in a bun. Many young Apache women placed a special ornament called a nah-leens in their hair. Apache men usually cut their hair at their shoulders.

Maricopa, Mojave, and Yuma men twisted their hair into several individual rolls, like the man at lower left. Sometimes they painted the rolls in bright stripes and wound them up in a coil. Sometimes they attached eagle feathers. Maricopa women wore straight hair with bangs. Many Mojaves painted their hair with white or yellow stripes.

Both male and female Navajos put their hair up into a tsiyeel, which is a bun shaped like a figure eight. Some Zuni men and women also wore their hair in that style, which the Zunis called a chongo. Hopi men wore the style, too. They called it a hömsoma. Married Hopi women wore two long pigtails, but unmarried women wore the squash blossom or butterfly whorl style. Hopi mothers wound their daughters' hair around a piece of wood to give it a round shape, like the girl at top right.

Male and female Apache wore shell necklaces, like the Apache girl is wearing below. During dances, they sometimes wore painted masks and feather crowns. Some tribes painted themselves for ceremonies. Mojaves wore facial tattoos, as did Maricopa women. Karankawa men were pierced and tattooed.

Creating and Performing

Pottery. The Hopi and Zuni were skilled potters. See a Zuni pot at the bottom of page 50. The Karankawa made coiled clay bowls and wide-mouth jars, decorated with tar dots and lines. The Maricopa were known for red clay pottery jars and bowls. Among the Navajo, pottery making was thought of as women's work. See the Tewa girl with a large jar on her head on page 48.

Baskets. The Pima wove intricate, water-tight baskets. The Maricopa traded their pottery for Pima baskets. The Apache were also skillful basket makers. Some of theirs took months to create. Antique Apache baskets are valuable today. Most were trays, but some were in the shape of jars. See Apache baskets on page 50. The Hopi also made fine baskets, as did the Papago. On page 48 is a Papago woman with a basket on her head.

Carving, Beadwork, and Jewelry-Making. The Karankawa fashioned tools from shells. The Zuni carved small fetish stones in the shapes of animals. They believed that the stones helped those who carried them. The Hopi also carved stone. They and other tribes carved beads. The Hopi made their beads from coral, shells, and turquoise obtained through trade. The Apache were skilled at beadwork. Among the Navajo, jewelry-making was men's work. See a Pueblo tribesman working with turquoise at right.

Weaving. The Hopi wove colorful blankets. Navajo women created beautiful rugs. Among the Tewa, it was men who did the work of weaving. Look at the Navajo weaver on page 50 and the Navajo man wearing traditional weaving at left.

Religious Arts. The Hopi and Tewa danced as part of their religion. Some Tewa dances were accompanied by a drum. See a Tewa priest with drum at left. Today the Hopi also create kachina dolls, which are tied to ancestor worship. The Navajo created paintings with colored sand. These depicted myths and were believed to heal.

A Hopi Boy with Headband

Apache Girl

Pueblo man uses drill to make turquoise jewelry.

Navajo Man Wearing Traditional Weaving

Tewa Priest with Drum

Trade, War, and Peace

Southwest tribes traded with one another. Pueblo Indians used trade routes into Mexico and to the coast of California to trade with other tribes.

Apache and Navajo tribes raided other tribes. The Apache did not believe in attacking openly because children and old people might be hurt. They believed it was brave to sneak in and steal things. The Mojave had frequent wars, especially with the Maricopa and the Pima. The Zuni fought mostly with the Apache and Navajo who raided them.

Hopi means peaceful person or civilized person. This tribe usually lived in peace unless others attacked or hurt them. God teaches all people to seek peace. As David wrote in Psalm 34:

Depart from evil and do good;
seek peace and pursue it.
Psalm 34:14

Navajo Weaver

Apache Baskets

Activities for Lesson 8

Thinking Biblically – In your notebook, copy Psalm 34:14, Psalm 4:8, and John 14:27. Circle the word "peace" in each verse.

Map Study – Complete the assignment for Lesson 8 on Map 4 "Native Peoples of North America" in *Maps of America the Beautiful*.

Timeline – In *Timeline of America the Beautiful* next to 1000, write: The Acoma Pueblo is built in what will later become New Mexico.

Literature – Read "The Mountain Chant: A Navajo Ceremony" and "The Coyote and the Turtle" in *We the People*, pages 7-8.

Family Activity – Make Navajo Flatbread. The recipe is on page 418.

Student Workbook or Lesson Review – If you are using one of these optional books, complete the assignment for Lesson 8.

Zuni Pottery

50

The Cliff Palace of Mesa Verde

Elaborate Native American villages lie in ruins on top of mesas and in the sides of cliffs in Arizona, Colorado, New Mexico, and Utah. Notice the photos of ruins below. These structures were built by ancestors of Indians currently living in the Southwest. The most spectacular ruin is the Cliff Palace in Mesa Verde National Park in Colorado.

Mesa Verde National Park

Yellowstone National Park was the first national park in America. It became a national park in 1872. It preserves geysers, hot springs, and other geothermal creations. In 1906 Mesa Verde National Park in Colorado became the first national park to preserve creations of man. Mesa Verde means green table and describes the geography of the area. Over 4,000 Native American sites lie within Mesa Verde National Park. The park preserves the best collection of cliff dwellings in North America, including the Cliff Palace. In addition to almost six hundred structures built into the sides of cliffs, the park also preserves structures built on top of mesas, like pueblos, brick towers, farming terraces, reservoirs, dams, and pithouses.

Ruins in Mesa Verde

The "White House" ruin in the Canyon de Chelley National Monument in Arizona is on Navajo land.

This 5-story, 20-room cliff dwelling in north central Arizona is called Montezuma's Castle because it was once thought to be of Aztec origin.

Ancient Pueblo Peoples

Hopi Pueblo, 1906

Archaeologists believe that ancestors of the Pueblo Indians probably built and occupied these mesas and cliffs from about 550 to 1300. These ancestors are sometimes called Anasazi, but a better term is Ancient Pueblo People (or Ancient Puebloans). Evidence shows that they lived and farmed mainly on top of the mesas for about six hundred years until the late 1100s. At first they lived in pithouses, and later they built adobe pueblos.

By about 1000, the Ancient Puebloans began to build stone homes two or three stories high with fifty or more rooms. Their earlier pottery had been gray with simple designs, but they later made white pottery decorated with black drawings. Over the next generations, the Ancient Puebloans developed greater skill, making carefully shaped stones and building fine straight walls. The 1906 photograph of a Hopi pueblo, shown above, reveals similarities with the ancient ruins.

Moving Down into the Cliffs

Around 1190, for some unknown reason the Ancient Puebloans began to build structures in cliffs under the mesa, while continuing to farm the tops. Most of the cliff structures in Mesa Verde National Park have one to five rooms, but one-fourth of them have more than five rooms; some have many more.

Ancient Puebloans built their cliff dwellings from sandstone that they cut into blocks about the size of a loaf of bread. They put them together with a mortar made of mud and water and added chinking stones to make them strong. Many stone walls were covered with earthen plasters of brown, pink, red, white, or yellow. They painted designs on many of these. Wooden beams were used to support ceilings. Each room was the right size for two or three people. Rooms were built toward the back of the cliff, with storage rooms at the far back. In front of the rooms were courtyards. Underneath some courtyards were kivas, which were likely used for ceremonies. The design of each cliff dwelling varied depending on the shape of each individual cliff opening.

Daily Life in the Cliffs

The residents of Mesa Verde threw their garbage down the slopes near their homes, thus archaeologists have been able to discover many details about how they lived. The residents kept turkeys and used their meat for food and their bones for tools. They made cloth and feather robes to stay warm. Ancient Puebloans obviously

A descendant of the Ancient Puebloans tends her indoor fire in 1889.

built fires in their homes, since walls and ceilings have been blackened by smoke. Notice the photo on page 52 of a descendant of Ancient Puebloans tending her fire.

The Ancient Puebloans did not use metal. They made tools from bone, stone, and wood, using stones from creeks to shape them. They had seashells and turquoise, so they must have traded with other tribes. During their first years at Mesa Verde, the Ancient Puebloans made fine baskets; but as they began to make better pottery, they did not put as much effort into their baskets. They stored grain in some baskets and carried water in others. To cook, they put food and water in a basket and dropped heated stones inside it. Ancient Puebloan black and white pottery was varied and beautiful. They made bowls, canteens, jars, ladles, mugs, and pots.

The Mancos River was the closest river, and it was several miles away. Nearby springs provided some water; but the Puebloans used various methods, like dams and drainage diversion systems, to catch and store the limited water that was available.

The Ancient Pueblo People Migrate South

For less than one hundred years, Ancient Puebloans built, repaired, remodeled, and lived in their cliff dwellings. Around the late 1270s, the people who lived in the Mesa Verde region began to migrate into New Mexico and Arizona. They had all left by about 1300.

The Cliff Palace

On December 15, 1888, two cowboys, Richard Wetherill and Charlie Mason, rode across the top of Mesa Verde through the snow looking for stray cows. The cowboys looked at a cliff across a canyon and saw something that looked like "a magnificent city." They called what they saw "Cliff Palace." See photos on this page. They are the first people of European descent known to have seen it. For almost twenty years, Wetherill and Mason explored the area, finding at least 182 more cliff dwellings.

From the top of the canyon, 120 stone steps descend one hundred feet before reaching the Cliff Palace. This structure has 150 rooms, twenty-one kivas, and seventy-five open areas. Its rooms

Views of The Cliff Palace

Cliff Palace   *Long House*

were for living, sleeping, working, and storing goods. It is believed to have been the home of about one hundred people.

The second largest cliff dwelling in Mesa Verde National Park is Long House, shown at left. It has a large open space that may have been used for dances and ceremonies. Spruce Tree House, shown on page 55, is the third largest cliff dwelling in the park. It has 129 rooms and eight kivas in a cliff alcove 216 feet wide and eighty-nine feet deep. About sixty to eighty people probably lived in Spruce Tree House. When local ranchers first discovered it, a tree grew in front of it all the way to the mesa top. According to legend, the ranchers climbed down the tree to enter the cliff dwelling. It is still called Spruce Tree House, though the tree was actually a fir and it was cut down by an early explorer. Residents of Spruce Tree House climbed up hand-and-toe-hold trails cut into canyon walls to reach their farmland on the mesa top!

Visitors to Mesa Verde can also tour Balcony House. It has 40 rooms, plus kivas and plazas. Another cliff dwelling in the park is Step House, which has evidence of Ancient Puebloans living there at two separate times, in the 600s and again in the 1200s.

A Cliff Dwelling in Mesa Verde National Park

Like the eagle, the Ancient Puebloans dwelt and lodged on cliffs. Near the end of the book of Job, God taught Job by asking him questions. God asked:

Is it at your command that the eagle mounts up and makes his nest on high?
On the cliff he dwells and lodges,
Upon the rocky crag, an inaccessible place.
Job 39:27-28

Activities for Lesson 9

Map Study – Complete the assignment for Lesson 9 on Map 3 "American Landmarks" in *Maps of America the Beautiful.*

Timeline – In *Timeline of America the Beautiful* next to 1190, write: Ancient Puebloans build the cliff dwellings of Mesa Verde.

Literature – Read "Mesa Verde Wonderland Is Easy to Reach" in *We the People*, pages 9-10.

Creative Writing – In your notebook, write a poem of 4-10 lines about the Ancient Puebloans of Mesa Verde.

Student Workbook or Lesson Review – If you are using one of these optional books, complete the assignment for Lesson 9.

Spruce Tree House

St. Augustine, America's Oldest European City

The Timucua tribe lived along the east coast of Florida in the 1500s. They fished and collected shellfish, gathered food in swamps and forests, and planted beans, corn, and squash. See the illustration of a Timucua village on page 23. In the 1560s, the Timucua were joined by Europeans, first the French and then the Spanish.

French Settlement of La Caroline

France wanted to enjoy some of the financial benefits Spain was gaining from the New World. The French parliament sent Jean Ribault to find a place for a permanent settlement. The colony had two purposes—to make money and to be a place of refuge for French Huguenots who were being persecuted in Catholic-dominated France. In 1562 Ribault put up a monument near the mouth of the St. Johns River on the northeast coast of Florida. A few hundred soldiers, aristocrats, and artists arrived in 1564.

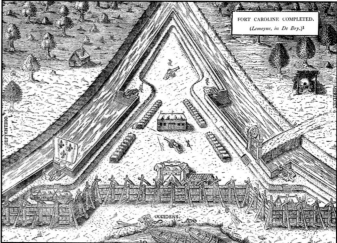

Top: Illustration of La Caroline Under Construction
Bottom: Fort Caroline Completed

The Timucua helped them build a village and a fort. See pictures above. They named the fort La Caroline after France's King Charles IX.

By this time, Spain was shipping gold and silver from Mexico and Peru to Europe. The Spanish were not happy that France had built a settlement on the Florida coast. They feared that French raiders might be hiding at La Caroline so they could attack Spanish ships and steal their treasures.

St. Augustine is Established

In 1565 Spain sent Admiral Don Pedro Menéndez de Avilés to establish a permanent Spanish settlement in Florida and to expel the French from La Caroline. Admiral Menéndez and six hundred soldiers and colonists arrived in Florida on August 28, 1565. It was the feast day of St. Augustine. Eleven

Preparing to Build at St. Augustine

days later they established a military base at a Timucuan village on Anastasia Island and named their colony St. Augustine. They used the Timucuan village council house as their first fort.

The French sent Jean Ribault to help protect La Caroline. Ribault tried to attack Menéndez, but was prevented by a hurricane. Later, Menéndez attacked La Caroline and was victorious over the French.

Menéndez led the new Spanish colony as they built St. Augustine. He established Catholic missions among the natives and explored the nearby area. In 1572 the colonists moved the town to its present location. Menéndez led the colony until his death in 1574. When his nephew Pedro Menéndez Marquez became its leader in 1576, St. Augustine had three hundred residents, mostly soldiers and their families.

The St. Augustine colony was important to Spain for three reasons. It guarded the route of Spanish treasure ships, it was a refuge for people who survived shipwrecks, and it salvaged the cargoes of wrecked ships. It became the center of Spanish power in North America.

A Short History of St. Augustine

Before 1600 St. Augustine endured Indian attacks, fires, a major hurricane, and an attack by English explorer Sir Francis Drake. In 1586 Drake made a map of St. Augustine before he and his crew burned it to the ground. In 1602 the Spanish considered moving St. Augustine or abandoning it all together, but they decided to keep it where it was. A new Governor, Mendez de Canzo, led the city well. The city added a horse-drawn grist mill, a hospital, a market, and a plaza. See photo at right.

After trying to take the city by force for many years, England received Florida through a treaty in 1763. When the English took control, only three or four people stayed in St. Augustine. Most

The Plaza in 1886

Castillo de San Marcos

residents went to Cuba and a few to Mexico. In 1784 Florida was returned to Spain. In 1821 it became part of the United States of America. During the Civil War, Florida became part of the southern Confederate States of America. Union forces captured St. Augustine in 1862.

St. Augustine Landmarks

Developer Henry M. Flagler promoted St. Augustine as a tourist attraction in the late 1800s and early 1900s. It became a fashionable place for wealthy tourists. Read about stereoscopic pictures in the box at right. Pictures like these helped Florida businesses; they made people want to visit for themselves.

Tourists coming to St. Augustine at that time could see:

Castillo de San Marcos. Between 1672 and 1695, the Spanish built a stone fort to protect St. Augustine. It is the oldest stone fort still standing in the United States. See photo above.

The Old City Gates. Fifteen hundred citizens of St. Augustine took shelter in Castillo de San Marcos in 1702 when an English force attacked the city. After that, the Spanish military and local residents built a wall around the city. Beyond it, they dug a moat. A

Stereoscopic Pictures

In the late 1800s, stereoscopes like the one pictured below were popular. Photographers traveled to famous and unusual places and to events to take pictures. To create a stereoscopic image, they took two photographs of the same scene from slightly different angles. When someone looked at the two photographs through a stereoscope, the image appeared to be three-dimensional (3-D).

Below is an example of a stereoscopic picture. It was part of a series called Gems of American Scenery. This image is identified as "Florida—the Oldest House in St. Augustine."

Wealthy people used stereoscopes to remember places they had seen and to find out about places they wanted to visit. People who couldn't travel used them to view places they would never be able to see in person.

The Library of Congress has thousands of stereoscopic photos in its collection. Many are included in *America the Beautiful*. When you see a photograph that is straight at the bottom and curved at the top, you will know that it is one of the two views in an historic stereoscopic photograph.

Stereoscope

Cathedral Basilica

drawbridge crossed the moat in front of the gates and was drawn up at night. The walls were carefully maintained for over one hundred years. The city gates still stand and a portion of the wall has been reconstructed at Castillo de San Marcos.

The Oldest House. Three blocks away from the plaza is "The Oldest House," which was built around 1706. Examine its stereoscopic picture on page 58.

Plaza de la Constitución. The Spanish colonial plaza, pictured on page 57, was home to the Government House, built in 1713. The Spanish colonial Governor lived here. Also on the plaza is the Cathedral Basilica of St. Augustine. The current Cathedral includes the parish church finished in 1797. It is one of the oldest Catholic structures in America. See photo above.

Hotel Ponce de Leon. Henry Flagler built the Hotel Ponce de Leon from 1885 to 1887. Famous artist Louis C. Tiffany designed its interior decor, which includes stained glass, murals, and mosaics. See photos below.

Interior and Exterior Views of Hotel Ponce de Leon

Alcazar Hotel—Henry Flagler's Alcazar Hotel opened in 1889. Its towers, spires, and roofs of red tile were designed to look like the royal palace in Seville, Spain. Its name is similar to an Arabic word meaning royal castle. It now serves as St. Augustine's City Hall and houses a museum. The Alcazar Hotel is pictured at right.

Natives of the Southwest have older permanent communities, but St. Augustine is the oldest permanent city in America settled by Europeans. It continues to be a popular tourist destination because of its history and the beautiful seashore God created nearby.

Alcazar Hotel

The people of St. Augustine built a gate to guard their city. See a photograph of it at right. Jesus taught about the gate we all need to enter to come to Him. He invites us to enter that gate. He said:

Enter through the narrow gate;
for the gate is wide and the way is broad
that leads to destruction, and there are
many who enter through it. For the gate is
small and the way is narrow that leads to
life, and there are few who find it.
Matthew 7:13-14

St. Augustine City Gates, Photographed During the Civil War

Activities for Lesson 10

Map Study – Complete the assignment for Lesson 10 on Map 3 "American Landmarks" in *Maps of America the Beautiful*.

Timeline – In *Timeline of America the Beautiful* next to 1586, write: Sir Francis Drake makes a map of St. Augustine before he and his crew burn the city.

Literature – Read "Florida Tourism Advertisement" in *We the People*, page 11.

Vocabulary – In your notebook, write each sentence below, filling in each blank with one of these words: persecute, refuge, salvage, parish, destination.

1. My friend moved to a different _____, so he goes to a different church.
2. During thunderstorms, our dogs find _____ under the front porch.
3. When we left on our trip, we were excited that St. Augustine was our _____.
4. I want to stand firm if anyone tries to _____ me for what I believe.
5. Dad sometimes goes to the junk yard to _____ anything useful he can find.

Creative Writing – Design a colorful, attractive flyer advertising St. Augustine to tourists. Include the special places you read about in this lesson.

Family Discussion – As you have dinner tonight, have each family member discuss what he or she believes would be the ideal family vacation.

Student Workbook or Lesson Review – If you are using one of these optional books, complete the assignment for Lesson 10. If you are using the Lesson Review, take the quiz for Unit 2.

English and French Settlers Come to America

This week we begin by learning about the first English settlers who came to live in America. The second lesson is our first American Biography. It teaches about Pocahontas, the Indian princess who helped the English settlers of Jamestown. In our God's Wonders lesson, we learn about the Great Lakes and the French who explored the lakes and traded with the nearby Indians. This week's American Landmark is Plymouth, Massachusetts, where the Pilgrims settled. We finish the week by learning about the settlement of more English colonies, including Massachusetts Bay, New Hampshire, Maryland, and Connecticut.

Pictured Rocks National Lakeshore
Beside Lake Superior

Lessons in Unit 3

Lesson 11 – Our American Story: English Settlements in Virginia
Lesson 12 – An American Biography: Pocahontas
Lesson 13 – God's Wonders: God Created the Great Lakes
Lesson 14 – An American Landmark: The Pilgrims Settle at Plymouth
Lesson 15 – Our American Story: The Massachusetts Bay, New Hampshire, Maryland, and Connecticut Colonies

Books Used in Unit 3

* *Maps of America the Beautiful*

* *Timeline of America the Beautiful*

* *We the People*

English Settlements in Virginia

Italian John Cabot moved to the seaport city of Bristol, England, around 1488. About the same time that Columbus sailed west to find a route to the Far East, Cabot was thinking about the same idea. In 1493 the news of Columbus' discoveries in the New World reached England.

Businessmen in Bristol agreed to sponsor Cabot on a venture to the Far East. England's King Henry VII authorized the expedition. In 1497 Cabot and a crew of

John Cabot sets sail from Bristol, England.

eighteen sailed west from Bristol on the *Matthew*. See illustration above. They sailed much farther north than Columbus and landed in northern North America, perhaps on Cape Breton Island in what is now Canada. They sailed along the coasts of New England, Labrador, and Newfoundland, the latter of which Cabot named as a "new-found-land." He claimed these lands for King Henry VII.

Among the discoveries made by Cabot were the rich cod beds along the northern coast of North America. English, French, Portuguese, Spanish, and Basque fishermen began fishing there, especially off Newfoundland. (Basques are an ancient ethnic group who still live in southwestern France and north central Spain.) Like his fellow Italian Columbus, Cabot believed he had sailed to Asia.

After the death of Henry VII, his son Henry VIII reigned in his place. During his reign, English explorers and fishermen continued to come to America. King Henry VIII did not directly affect American history, but his policies made a great impact in the long term. Henry VIII worked hard to improve ships and to build up the British navy. As European kings continued to fight to see who would be the main power in North and South America, a strong British navy would eventually prove to be important.

Queen Elizabeth I

Henry VIII's daughter Elizabeth came to the throne in 1558, after brief reigns by her brother Edward VI (1547-1553) and her sister Mary (1553-1558). Elizabeth I reigned until 1603. See her portrait at left. During her reign, she encouraged settlers to move to America. Since she never married, she was called the Virgin Queen. The English began to call much of the land near the Atlantic coast Virginia for Elizabeth.

The Lost Colony of Roanoke

English noble Sir Walter Raleigh was a close friend of Queen Elizabeth I. See his portrait below. In 1587 Raleigh sponsored a group of English men, women, and children to settle in America. That July, about one hundred colonists landed at Roanoke Island, off the coast of present-day North Carolina (at that time it was part of Virginia). The settlers built a fort on the island.

Sir Walter Raleigh

John White served as the Governor of Roanoke. On August 18, about a month after they arrived, Ananias Dare and his wife Elinor had a baby girl. Virginia Dare was the first child of English parents to be born in America. Elinor Dare was John White's daughter. Just nine days later, White left the settlers on the island and went back to England for supplies.

Notice the illustration below of the landing at Roanoke. Like many old maps, this one shows a sea monster. Find it in the lower left corner. An arrow points to the Roanoke settlement. Find the Indian villages of Secotan and Weapemeoc on the map. Secotan is pictured on page 28. Also nearby was the Pomeiock village. It is pictured on page 64. Notice how similar Pomeiock is to the Timucuan village near La Caroline, pictured on page 23. Another tribe that lived nearby was the Roanoke.

The Landing at Roanoke (Roanoke Island is marked with an arrow.)

At the time, England and Spain were in conflict. Spain was the dominant power, not only in North and South America, but also in Europe. The Spanish Armada, also known as the "Great and Most Fortunate Navy," was considered the most powerful navy in the world. In 1588 Spain tried to destroy the English fleet; but instead the English defeated the Spanish Armada. This defeat reduced Spain's power in Europe and in North and South America. The war also kept John White from being able to return to Roanoke until 1590.

When White returned, the settlers and their houses had disappeared. The only evidence

Palisaded Pomeiock Village Near the Roanoke Settlement

found were the letters CRO carved on a tree and the word "Croatoan" carved on a post of their wooden palisade. Croatoan was a friendly tribe of natives who lived near the settlement, but the clues did not help White solve the mystery. No evidence has ever been found that they died on the island. What happened to the settlers remains a mystery. The National Park Service operates the Fort Raleigh National Historic Site on Roanoke Island. It has archaeological excavations that show what remains of the fort.

Jamestown, First Permanent English Settlement

After the death of Queen Elizabeth I, King James VI of Scotland, pictured below, became King James I of England. James was the king who authorized the translation of the Bible known as the King James Bible. In 1607 a group of London businessmen formed the Virginia Company and obtained an official document called a charter from King James. Later that year, the company sent three ships to America. The ships brought only men and boys. The group of 104 included a blacksmith, a barber, a mason, a tailor, two bricklayers, several carpenters, laborers, gentlemen (men of high social standing), and a beloved Anglican priest, Robert Hunt. The Virginia Company instructed the men to make a settlement, find gold, find a water route to the Far East, and convert the natives to Christianity.

On May 14, 1607, these English settlers landed in Virginia near a river, which they called the James River after their king. They began to build, placing their settlement where it would be difficult for Spanish ships to fire upon it. They honored their king again by naming their new community Jamestown. The men built a wooden palisade in the shape of a triangle. Inside they erected a storehouse and several houses. All settlers

King James I

64

Building the Jamestown Settlement

participated regularly in religious services which Hunt led. At first, they met in the open and later they built a church. See the illustrations of Jamestown at left and below.

Native tribes sometimes attacked the settlement. At other times, they brought food to exchange for copper and iron tools. This food helped the colony survive, as did the able leadership of Captain John Smith, Sir Thomas Dale, and Thomas West de la Warr. De la Warr was called Lord Delaware; Delaware was named for him. You will learn more about Smith and his native friend Pocahontas in the next lesson.

Life in Jamestown was challenging for many years. Many of the settlers died. The Virginia Company sent additional settlers and supplies again and again. Other settlements were built along the James River. Jamestown settlers worked hard to make products to export. They tried making silk and glass and exporting tar, pitch, lumber, sassafras, and soap ashes. Lesson 12 will tell what they finally found that became a profitable business.

A New Government

In 1619 Virginia settlers began to select men to represent them in an assembly which met to make laws and decisions. The Virginia Company had ordered them to "establish one equal and uniform government over all Virginia." Like Parliament in England, the assembly had two houses. Members of one house were selected by the Virginia Company. The other was the House of Burgesses with members elected by settlers.

Africans Come to America

Also in 1619, the first Africans came to America. A Dutch slave trader stopped at Jamestown and traded the Africans he had on board for food provided by the settlement. These Africans may not have been owned by the Jamestown settlers. Instead, they might have been indentured servants, like many English men and women in Virginia and other English colonies later. An indentured servant served for a certain length of time, often for seven years. Afterwards, he became free and was usually given land and supplies so he could begin his own farm.

Ruins of Jamestown Church

Virginia Becomes a Crown Colony

In 1624 King James revoked the charter of the Virginia Company and it became a crown colony. People probably lived on the site of the Jamestown fort until the middle of the 1620s. However, most people moved into an area of Jamestown which was outside of the fort. They called this area New Town. Jamestown served as Virginia's capital until 1698.

Jamestown was the first permanent English settlement in America. Tourists can visit Jamestown Settlement, which has a museum teaching about life in colonial Jamestown. In 2007 people from America and Great Britain celebrated the 400th anniversary of the founding of Jamestown. England's monarch Queen Elizabeth II visited Jamestown during the celebration.

The first Africans in America did not get the chance to decide whom they would serve but were forced to serve settlers. As Christians we have an opportunity to choose to serve Jesus. That has great blessings, as Jesus said:

> If anyone serves Me, he must follow Me; and where I am, there My servant will be also;
> if anyone serves Me, the Father will honor him.
> John 12:26

Activities for Lesson 11

Map Study – Complete the assignments for Lesson 11 on Map 7 "The Thirteen Colonies" in *Maps of America the Beautiful*.

Timeline – In *Timeline of America the Beautiful* next to 2007, write: Queen Elizabeth II of England visits Jamestown to celebrate the 400th anniversary of the settlement.

Literature – Read "The Founding of Jamestown" in *We the People*, page 12.

Creative Writing – What do you think happened to the settlers at Roanoke? In your notebook, write three or four possible ideas.

Student Workbook or Lesson Review – If you are using one of these optional books, complete the assignment for Lesson 11.

Pocahontas

Captain John Smith

An Indian princess befriended Jamestown leader Captain John Smith. Her brief but influential life has made her one of the most famous people in American history.

Pocahontas Meets John Smith

Captain John Smith was not only a leader in Jamestown, he later explored the northeastern coast of America, including Maine and Massachusetts Bay. He named that area New England. He created a map of the coast from Penobscot Bay in Maine to Cape Cod in Massachusetts. John Smith was a deeply religious man who believed God worked in his life and believed God helped to save the settlements along the James River.

In his journal, Captain Smith told a story about being captured by local Powhatan Indians just a few months after he and the other settlers arrived at Jamestown. The name of the tribe and their chief were both Powhatan. Smith was treated to a feast at the home of Chief Powhatan and then he was forced to lie on stones. Men stood over Smith with clubs. Matoaka, the chief's daughter, rushed in and put Smith's head in her hands and laid her head on his. She pulled him to his feet. Chief Powhatan then proclaimed that he and Smith were friends. He made Smith a part of the tribe.

Matoaka Rescues Smith

This event may have been part of a common ceremony that the Powhatans performed, rather than an actual threat on Smith's life. Smith was about twenty-eight years old at the time and Matoaka was about twelve. See illustration at right.

Matoaka became a close friend to John Smith and a frequent visitor to Jamestown. She came with her fellow Powhatans, bringing food and furs to trade. Matoaka is best known by her nickname, Pocahontas.

Captain Smith and His Friend Pocahontas

Pocahontas and Other Powhatans

It means "playful one." Look at the drawings of Pocahontas above and at left.

Pocahontas Is Kidnapped

The Jamestown settlers hoped to convert Native Americans to Christianity and to educate them like Europeans were educated. They sent some English boys from the settlement to live with Native Americans, so these boys could learn their language and customs. Relations between the English and Indians were friendly for about a year after Smith's capture and release. However, over time both the natives and the English acted in ways that strained their relationship. In 1609 Smith was injured in an explosion and returned to England for treatment.

Powhatans later took some of the English hostage. Afterwards a member of the Patowomeckan tribe helped Englishman Samuel Argall capture Pocahontas. Argall held her for ransom and kept her prisoner on a ship. The ransom demand included corn, weapons that the Powhatan tribe had stolen, and English prisoners whom Chief Powhatan was holding. Chief Powhatan sent part of the ransom and requested good treatment for his daughter.

This painting shows Anglican priest Alexander Whiteaker christening Pocahontas, while her sister, brother, uncles, and others watch.

Pocahontas Comes to Faith While in Captivity

In 1613 Argall took Pocahontas to Jamestown and later to the nearby settlement of Henrico. While in Henrico, Pocahontas was taught about God and His Son, learned English, was christened, and took the name Rebecca. On page 68 is a painting of her christening. It hangs in the United States Capitol in Washington, D.C.

John Rolfe

John Rolfe was a settler who had left England on the *Sea Venture* in 1609 along with 149 other settlers. His ship was one of nine that carried a total of five hundred new settlers, including some women, one of whom was his wife. The *Sea Venture* was delayed because of a hurricane. The ship was destroyed but all its passengers were rescued. They spent several months in Bermuda. While there they built two new ships named the *Patience* and the *Deliverance*. Rolfe's wife gave birth in Bermuda, but the little girl died. The Rolfes named her Bermuda. Mrs. Rolfe died soon afterwards.

When Rolfe began his work in Virginia, he experimented with tobacco. The Spanish had learned about smoking tobacco from New World natives. Sir Walter Raleigh had made its use popular among the English. The English preferred tobacco grown in the islands of the Caribbean to that grown by Indians in Virginia. John Rolfe brought Caribbean tobacco seed to Virginia and tested it in Virginia soil. Both American settlers and people in England liked it. Tobacco exporting became an important source of money for the Virginia colony.

Pocahontas and John Rolfe began to care for one another. John Rolfe was a very devout man. For weeks he agonized about the decision to marry a Native American. He only wanted to marry her if it was God's will. He wrote a long letter to Sir Thomas Dale who was then serving as the colony's Governor. The letter spoke of his deep love for and devotion to Pocahontas. Pocahontas, who was still in captivity, was allowed to see two of her brothers. She told them of her love for John Rolfe. After the visit, Chief Powhatan gave her his permission to marry Rolfe.

Pocahontas Marries John Rolfe

On April 5, 1614, John Rolfe and Rebecca were married. See illustrations at right and on page 71. The marriage helped relationships between the settlers and the local Native Americans. John and Rebecca had a son, whom they named Thomas. He was the first recorded child born to an Englishman and a Native American.

The Rolfes Visit England

In 1616 the Rolfe family traveled to England with Sir Thomas Dale, other settlers, and some Native Americans. Rebecca was popular in England. She met her husband's

An Artist's Depiction of the Wedding of John Rolfe and Pocahontas

family and Sir Walter Raleigh. In London she was also reunited with her old friend John Smith.

As their ship headed home seven months later, Rebecca became ill. The ship docked at Gravesend, England, and Rebecca was taken ashore. Before she died, she told her husband, "All must die. 'Tis enough that the child liveth." Rebecca was buried in a nearby English churchyard. She was about 22 years old. A grieving John Rolfe returned to Virginia, leaving his young son in the care of a guardian. Rolfe married again but he died in 1622. Thomas Rolfe, son of John and Rebecca, came to America when he was 20 years old. Both his father and his grandfather Chief Powhatan had left him land. Today many Americans trace their ancestry back to John and Rebecca Rolfe.

Though Pocahontas was not able to bring permanent peace between English settlers and the native Powhatans, she played an important role in the first permanent English settlement in America. She helped them have food and helped the two peoples have times of peace with one another. The food and the peace helped give the struggling colony time to get established. Her fame has endured for over four hundred years. Look at the ways artists have imagined her in the illustrations in this lesson.

Portrait of Pocahontas

The United States Senate has a copy of this portrait. The original once hung in Booton Hall, the Rolfe family home in England. It is now in the National Portrait Gallery in Washington, D.C.

The caption on the portrait lists her name as Matoaka, tells her father's name, and tells of her conversion and christening, but mistakently says she was the wife of Tho. (an abbreviation for Thomas) Rolfe rather than John Rolfe.

At left: The Cover of a 1942 Storybook by Marion Gridley, Illustrated by Virginia Ullrich;
Center: A Page from The Story of Pocahontas; *At right: Pocahontas Paper Dolls*

The statue below was unveiled in Jamestown in 1922. The sculptor was William Partridge, a descendant of the Pilgrims in Massachusetts. In 1958 the state of Virginia presented a replica of the statue to the British people. It was placed on the grounds of St. George's Church in England where Pocahontas was buried.

Artist's Depiction of the Wedding of John Rolfe and Pocahontas

The Jamestown settlers who shared their faith with Pocahontas knew that Jesus loved this young native woman and that:

He Himself is the propitiation for our sins;
and not for ours only, but also for those of the whole world.
1 John 2:2

Activities for Lesson 12

Thinking Biblically – Copy 1 John 2:2 in your notebook. Underneath, write a prayer for people who do not know God.

Timeline – In *Timeline of America the Beautiful* next to 1614, write: Pocahontas (Rebecca) marries John Rolfe.

Vocabulary – Copy these words in your notebook, each on a separate line: influential, hostage, christen, export, guardian. Look up each word in the dictionary. Next to each word, write what part or parts of speech it is.

Creative Writing – In your notebook, write a letter from Pocahontas to her father as she might have written him while she was visiting England.

Pocahontas Statue in Jamestown

Family Activity – Create a Pocahontas Museum. See the instructions on pages 419-420.

Student Workbook or Lesson Review – If you are using one of these optional books, complete the assignment for Lesson 12.

God Created the Great Lakes

God created five giant lakes at the top of America. They are Lake Superior, Lake Michigan, Lake Huron, Lake Erie, and Lake Ontario. Together they are called the Great Lakes. About 20 percent of the world's fresh water is in these five lakes!

New France

The French did not send great numbers of settlers to America, though they did build some settlements in Canada. Most of the French who came to America were men. They explored, formed alliances with Native Americans, worked as fur traders, spread Catholicism among the natives, and built trading posts and forts. The French were the first Europeans to explore the Great Lakes. In 1608, just one year after the English arrived at Jamestown, Frenchman Samuel de Champlain led an expedition into the Great Lakes region.

By 1719 the French had built Detroit and Fort Michilimackinac in Michigan; Mobile in Alabama; Biloxi and Fort Rosalie

Full-Blooded Ojibwe, 1918

Ojibwe Wedding, 1870s

(later Natchez) in Mississippi; Kaskaskia in Illinois; and New Orleans in Louisiana. By 1763 the French controlled the areas around the Saint Lawrence River, the Mississippi River, and the Great Lakes.

Lake Superior

One of Champlain's crew members was Ètienne Brûlé. He probably explored Lake Superior in 1622. The name of Lake Superior comes from the French word *supérieur*, which means "upper lake." Not only is it the largest of the Great Lakes and the deepest, Lake Superior is the largest freshwater lake in the world. It covers 31,700 square miles. Its deepest point is 1,333 feet! Notice the pictures of Lake Superior at right.

Lake Superior's coastline includes beaches, forests, cliffs as high as 1,000 feet, sand dunes, and many bays. On the southeastern coast is Pictured Rocks National Lakeshore, with its tall sandstone rocks in many colors. God placed rich mineral deposits in the land around Lake Superior, including copper, nickel, iron, and silver. Lake Superior has many large islands, including Wisconsin's Apostle Islands.

Between Lake Superior and Lake Huron is the Saint Mary's River. The Saint Mary's has rapids that drop 21 feet before reaching Lake Huron.

The Ojibwe (or Chippewa) tribe lived in the western Great Lakes region near Lake Superior. They were one of the most powerful tribes in North America. Ojibwe are pictured on these two pages and on pages 26, 27, 29, and 30.

Views of Lake Superior

Arrowmaker, an Ojibwe, 1903

Lake Huron

The second largest of the Great Lakes is Lake Huron. It is the Great Lake with the most islands. Notice the islands in the picture of Lake Huron on page 74. Lake Huron was named for the Huron confederation of tribes that lived near the lake in Canada. Ètienne Brûlé learned to speak the Huron language and lived with them for many years. Jesuit missionaries from France settled on the shores of Lake Huron in 1638. The French bought furs from Native Americans in the Great Lakes region. The Huron became involved in the fur trade.

They taught the French how to live in the Great Lakes area. The Huron used snowshoes like those shown below to walk over deep snow.

Lake Michigan

South of Lake Superior is Lake Michigan. Its waters also flow into Lake Huron. Lakes Michigan and Huron are separated by the Straits of Mackinac. Look at the picture of Lake Michigan at right. It is the third largest of the Great Lakes, but it has more water than Huron because it is deeper. The name comes from *Michi-guma*, a Chippewa word which means "big water."

Jean Nicolet, one of the members of Samuel Champlain's crew, had good relations with Great Lakes natives. He explored Lake Michigan in 1634. He drowned in 1642 trying to save an Iroquois.

Lake Huron with Islands

Lake Michigan

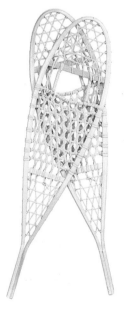

Sportsmen today still use Huron-style snowshoes.

Lake Erie

Connecting Lake Huron and Lake Erie are first the Saint Clair River, then Lake Saint Clair, and then the Detroit River. Lake Erie is the fourth largest Great Lake and the shallowest. French explorer Louis Joliet discovered this lake in 1669. It was named for the Erie Indians, who lived south of it. The peninsula in the photo of Lake Erie at right is Point Pelee, which is the southernmost point of Canada's mainland.

Lake Erie and Point Pelee

Rugged Coast of Lake Ontario

Lake Ontario

Between Lake Erie and Lake Ontario is the Niagara River. The Niagara River drops 326 feet before it empties into Lake Ontario. About half of the drop is at beautiful Niagara Falls. Though Lake Ontario is the smallest of the Great Lakes, it is still the fourteenth largest lake in the world. Champlain explored this lake in 1615. Its name may be an Iroquoian word that means "beautiful lake" or "sparkling water." Lake Ontario's shore has rugged rock formations, as you can see in the picture on page 74.

Mammals of the Great Lakes

Snowshoe Hare

River Otter

Mink

Muskrat

Raccoon

Red Fox

Animals In and Around the Great Lakes

God filled the Great Lakes with many fish. Around the lakes, He made habitats for a variety of animals. Great Lakes mammals include muskrats, red foxes, raccoons, mink, snowshoe hares, and river otters. See the photos above. Amphibians that live in the region include painted turtles, northern leopard frogs, and gray tree frogs. See the photos below.

Great Lake Amphibians

Painted Turtles

Northern Leopard Frog

Gray Tree Frog

Many bird species stop at the Great Lakes when they migrate south for the winter and north for the summer. Birds that spend all or part of the year near the Great Lakes include the Canada goose, common loon, least bittern, northern harrier, and great blue heron. See the photos at right.

Great is our God, who created the Great Lakes, the animals that live there, and the birds that visit it on their annual migrations. Look at the pictures of these creations and think of the amazing power of God. The Bible teaches us spiritual truths through the wonders God created. As Jeremiah wrote:

> Even the stork in the sky knows her seasons;
> and the turtledove and the swift and the thrush
> observe the time of their migration;
> but My people do not know the ordinance of the Lord.
> Jeremiah 8:7

Activities for Lesson 13

Thinking Biblically – Read these verses about birds: Genesis 1:20-22, Psalm 104:16-17, and Matthew 6:26.

Map Study – Complete the assignments for Lesson 13 on Map 2 "God's Wonders," Map 6 "Europe," and Map 8 "The Great Lakes" in *Maps of America the Beautiful*.

Timeline – In *Timeline of America the Beautiful* next to 1608, write: Samuel de Champlain leads an expedition into the Great Lakes region.

Vocabulary – In your notebook, write your own definition for each of these words: alliance, bay, rapids, shallow, rugged. Look in the lesson for clues to the meaning of each word. When you are finished writing your definitions, look in a dictionary for comparison.

Literature – Read "Great Lakes Poems" in *We the People*, page 13.

Student Workbook or Lesson Review – If you are using one of these optional books, complete the assignment for Lesson 13.

Birds of the
Great Lakes

Canada Goose

Common Loon

Least Bittern

Northern Harrier

Great Blue Heron

The Pilgrims Settle at Plymouth

In the early 1600s, the Church of England (also called the Anglican Church) was the official church of England. Some English believers, called Puritans, thought their church was corrupt and wanted to purify it. Other English believers wanted to separate from the Church of England. They were called Separatists. In 1608 a group of Separatists left England and went to the Netherlands (also called Holland), so they could worship God with more freedom than they had in England. One member of the Separatist group in Holland was William Bradford. He was the first person to use the term Pilgrims to refer to the people in their group of Separatists. While living in the Netherlands, the Pilgrims became afraid that their children would begin to speak Dutch (the language of the Netherlands) and follow Dutch customs. Separatist elder William Brewster and others decided to return to England on the *Speedwell,* and then go to America. Pilgrim John Carver made arrangements for the group's trip across the Atlantic.

Setting Sail on the *Mayflower*

On September 16, 1620, one hundred and two men, women, and children boarded two ships, the *Speedwell* and the *Mayflower.* Less than half were Pilgrims. The rest were sailors and adventurers. Their destination was the Virginia colony. The *Speedwell* leaked, so the travelers crowded onto the *Mayflower.* Notice the painting at right. After their voyage across the Atlantic Ocean, the sailors dropped anchor on November 21, 1620, near the modern city of Provincetown, Massachusetts. For the next month, they explored along Cape Cod.

Pilgrims Set Sail from Plymouth, England

Mayflower Compact

While still on the ship, all the men signed an agreement called the Mayflower Compact. It stated that their government would be one they established themselves and that each of them would obey the laws they made. The settlers would live by what the majority

Signing the Mayflower Compact

Landing of the Pilgrims

Pilgrims on Plymouth Rock

decided. The passengers elected John Carver to be their first Governor. The signing of the Mayflower Compact is illustrated at left.

The Pilgrims Begin a Settlement at Plymouth

The group went ashore near the western end of Cape Cod on December 21. At left is an illustration of rowers bringing a small group from the *Mayflower* to the land. Together the Pilgrims and other passengers built a settlement. They named it Plymouth after the English city they had left three months before. Plymouth was the first permanent English settlement in New England. According to one story, the passengers stepped out onto a large rock, which has come to be called Plymouth Rock, pictured below. The oldest written record of that story dates from the early 1700s. In 1880 the date 1620 was chiseled into a portion of what some believe to be the original Plymouth Rock.

December was a hard time to settle in New England. The Pilgrims had no buildings for shelter and no harvest. Many died that first winter. In May the *Mayflower* returned to England. Look at the picture of this event at the top of page 79.

Squanto, Friend of the Pilgrims

The Wampanoag tribe was one of the tribes of the Northeast Woodlands who spoke Algonquian. Around 1585 a Wampanoag woman gave birth to a little boy. He was called Squanto. When Squanto

78

was young, some people from Spain came to the area where Squanto's family lived. They captured Squanto and made him a slave. The Spanish took him to Spain, but he escaped and went to England where he learned English. In 1619 Squanto sailed back to America on an English ship. He served as the pilot for the ship's captain. Squanto ran away from the English ship and went back to his home. Sadly, the people in his village had died from a plague.

Mayflower *Returns to England, May 1621*

When the Pilgrims arrived in 1620, Squanto was living nearby. A Native American from Maine, who had learned English from fishermen, introduced Squanto to the Pilgrims. See picture at left below. Squanto became a friend to the Pilgrims. He was a great help, teaching them how to plant corn, how to fish, and how to survive in their new home.

In 1621 Plymouth Governor John Carver and Wampanoag Chief Massasoit signed a treaty. Squanto served as the interpreter. See picture at right below. The next year Squanto led William Bradford and other settlers on a trip around Cape Cod. Squanto got sick and died while they were on the trip. He was about thirty-seven years old.

Squanto's story was like that of Joseph in the Bible. The Spanish had done wrong to Squanto by capturing him and making him a slave, but God made good come of it. Squanto blessed the Pilgrims during his four short years back in his homeland. Today over 2,000 Wampanoag live in America. Another 2,000 Americans are part-Wampanoag.

Squanto Comes to Plymouth

Massasoit and Governor Carver

Pilgrims at Home

Pilgrims Going to Church

The First Years of the Plymouth Colony

John Carver died in April 1621. Plymouth residents elected William Bradford as their new Governor. That fall he invited Chief Massasoit and some of his tribesmen to a celebration. They thanked God for sustaining them through hard times. This is the historical beginning of our modern Thanksgiving. Bradford was elected Governor thirty times. Except for five years, he served from 1621 to 1656.

Bradford wrote *History of Plymouth Plantation, 1620-1647*. During those years the Pilgrims began farming and built a fort, several homes, and a meeting house. Slowly, they built a new life, as illustrated above. Also look at the picture on page 81.

Other Famous Pilgrims

Henry Wadsworth Longfellow, an American poet, made three original Plymouth residents, John and Priscilla Alden and Miles Standish, famous in his poem, *The Courtship of Miles Standish*. The poem is an imagined story, but it is based on real-life Pilgrims.

John Alden married Priscilla and became a partner with Miles (or Myles) Standish. Together Standish and Alden founded the town of Duxbury, Massachusetts, around 1627. John Alden lived longer than anyone who signed the Mayflower Compact. See illustrations at right.

Illustration of Longfellow's Poem

Visiting Plymouth, Massachusetts

If you visit Plymouth, you can see Plymouth Rock and climb aboard the *Mayflower II*, a life-sized replica of the Pilgrims' ship. You can also visit Plimoth Plantation, a reconstructed living history village where actors pretend to be individual settlers who lived in Plymouth. Plimoth is another way that the early settlers spelled Plymouth.

John and Priscilla Alden's Home in Duxbury

80

At the village, you can see animals and crops like the ones they raised, sit in the Pilgrims' church building, smell colonial food cooking, and feel like you have gone back to 1627. You can also see a recreated Wampanoag homesite.

Fort, Storehouse, and Homes of William Brewster, Governor Bradford, and Others

When the Plymouth settlers gathered with Native Americans at the first Thanksgiving, they expressed appreciation for what God had done for them. They knew:

The earth has yielded its produce;
God, our God, blesses us.
God blesses us,
That all the ends of the earth may fear Him.
Psalm 67:6-7

Activities for Lesson 14

Thinking Biblically – When William Bradford wrote about the history of the Pilgrims, he quoted from Psalm 107. Read this Psalm, thinking about what the words and promises meant to the Pilgrims.

Map Study – Complete the assignments for Lesson 14 on Map 3 "American Landmarks," Map 6 "Europe," and Map 7 "The Thirteen Colonies" in *Maps of America the Beautiful*.

Timeline – In *Timeline of America the Beautiful* next to 1621, write: Squanto helps the Pilgrims and Wampanoag make a treaty.

Literature – Read "Of Plimoth Plantation" in *We the People*, pages 14-15.

Creative Writing – Imagine that you are involved in starting a new colony like the Pilgrims. You are assigned the job of writing a compact for everyone to sign. Think of a name for your colony. In your notebook, title your document "[*Your Colony Name*] Compact." Write down ten things everyone in the colony must agree to obey.

Student Workbook or Lesson Review – If you are using one of these optional books, complete the assignment for Lesson 14.

The Massachusetts Bay, New Hampshire, Maryland, and Connecticut Colonies

After the success of the Jamestown colony, more English citizens settled in America. Settlers came from the Netherlands, too. This lesson will tell about early settlers in Massachusetts, New Hampshire, Maryland, and Connecticut.

Puritans Founded the Massachusetts Bay Colony in 1630

In the early 1600s, another group of English Protestants began thinking about settling in America. They were called Puritans. Puritans opposed corruption in the Church of England. They believed that English kings were worldly. Some believed that God would destroy England because of sin. Puritan colonists came to America to preserve their religion in case England was destroyed. They also wanted to be a light to the world.

Puritan Woman

During the 1620s, the British government authorized the Massachusetts Bay Company to settle and to do business in an area north of the Plymouth colony. The Plymouth colony had been controlled by businessmen in England. The Massachusetts Bay Company was to be controlled by settlers living in America.

John Winthrop, pictured on page 83, was chosen to be Governor of the Massachusetts Bay Colony. In 1630 he and over seven hundred Puritans left England for America. First,

Thatched Cottage in Salem

they came to the small settlement of Salem where a few Englishmen involved in a fishing enterprise were already living. An early Salem home is pictured at left.

From Salem the Puritans moved to Charlestown and finally to the mouth of the Charles River on the Shawmut peninsula. Later they named their settlement Boston, after the English town which had been home to some of them. Hundreds more settlers joined them.

John Winthrop and the Puritan settlers set up a government based on their beliefs. In this system,

Governor John Winthrop

citizens could vote, participate in decisions, and hold government offices, but only if they were male members of the Puritan church. The Puritans required people to work from the time the sun rose until it set. They required church attendance and told people how to dress. Notice the Puritan woman's clothing in the picture on page 82.

The Puritans wanted pure church members, pure worship, and pure church organization. In America they formed independent congregations and were called Congregationalists. They made the Congregational Church the colony's official church and would not let people with other beliefs hold meetings. When Quakers moved in, they were forced to leave. Lesson 18 has more information about the Quakers.

Massachusetts Bay settlers began to form towns that had a green, park-like area in the center. Around the green were homes. The settlers built their homes in close proximity. Beyond the homes were agricultural fields. Townspeople held town meetings in which every male had an equal voice in decisions. Through the years settlers spread out into other areas of New England, building the same style of towns and holding the same kind of town meetings. The tradition of free public schools supported with tax dollars began in Massachusetts. The town of Dedham, Massachusetts, claims to have started the first tax-supported free public school in America, but other towns also claim that distinction. See picture on page 84.

God created resources that met the needs of the Massachusetts Bay settlers and that they could use in trade. Most people were farmers. During long winters, the settlers made

implements for sale and for their own use. Businessmen sold ships, wagons, furniture made from area forests, and fish that had been caught in the Atlantic. They shipped these from Boston Harbor. Eventually Plymouth, the Massachusetts Bay Colony, other settlements, and Maine joined together to form the Massachusetts colony. Maine continued to be part of Massachusetts until 1820.

Thousands of Puritans migrated to New England over the next few years. In 1642 English Puritans became involved in a civil war, so immigration stopped for a time. Still, the population of New England grew. The area had safe drinking water and a healthy environment. Most Puritans brought their families with them or married and had large families after they came. By 1770 almost 120,000 Europeans lived in New England.

Statuary Hall in the U.S. Capitol has two statues from each state. One of Massachusetts' statues is of John Winthrop, first Governor of Massachusetts Bay. It is pictured at right.

Settlers Move to New Hampshire in 1623

In 1623 Scotsman David Thomson and two London fish-merchants, Edward and Thomas Hilton, led settlers to establish two fishing colonies in what is now New Hampshire. Thomson settled near what is now Rye, pictured on page 85. There he and his men set up a fishing operation. Eight miles away the Hiltons formed another fishing settlement at what is now Dover.

John Winthrop Statue in Statuary Hall in the U.S. Capitol

Rye, New Hampshire

Over the years other towns grew up nearby. New Hampshire became a royal province in 1679. In 1698 the area became part of Massachusetts, but it again became a separate royal province in 1741.

Settlers Come to Maryland in 1634

In 1632 George Calvert, a recent convert to Roman Catholicism, appealed to King Charles I for a charter to form a new colony. He wanted the colony to be a place where Catholics could worship in freedom. Calvert died before King Charles gave him the charter, but his son, Cecil Calvert, whose title was Lord Baltimore, organized a group of two hundred settlers to move to America. Cecil Calvert is pictured at right. Settlers bought a Native American village and formed the town of Saint Mary's in 1634. The colony was named Maryland for Queen Henrietta Maria, the wife of King Charles I. Notice the picture of the first Catholic mass in Maryland below. Almost one hundred years later the city of Baltimore, Maryland, was founded and named for Lord Baltimore.

Cecil Calvert, Lord Baltimore

The Dutch and English in Connecticut

Both the English and the Dutch moved into the land that became Connecticut. The Dutch began to explore the area in 1614. By 1633 Dutch settlers had bought land from the Pequot tribe to build a settlement. Later, some Englishmen built a stockade and trading post at Windsor. To protect their claims, the Dutch built a fort at Hartford.

In 1636 Thomas Hooker, a minister who had been living in the Massachusetts Bay Colony, led a group of about

First Catholic Mass in Maryland

one hundred settlers to Connecticut. Hooker is pictured at right. Three years later Connecticut settlers proclaimed the "Fundamental Orders of 1639" for the colony. This document may be the first written constitution for a government based on democracy anywhere in the world. Because of this, Connecticut is known as the Constitution State. In 1656 New Haven, Connecticut, became the first American city to have a public library that was owned by a city.

Thomas Hooker

Settlers to the Massachusetts Bay Colony and to Maryland were seeking religious freedom. We must always remember Who truly makes us free:

> So if the Son makes you free, you will be free indeed.
> John 8:36

Activities for Lesson 15

Thinking Biblically – Copy Galatians 5:13 in your notebook. Write a paragraph about how people can use freedom in the wrong way or in the right way.

Map Study – Complete the assignments for Lesson 15 on Map 7 "The Thirteen Colonies" in *Maps of America the Beautiful*.

Timeline – In *Timeline of America the Beautiful* next to 1656, write: New Haven, Connecticut, has the first public library owned by a city.

Vocabulary – Write five sentences in your notebook, using one of these words in each sentence: enterprise, pure, resources, province, mass. Check in a dictionary if you need help with their definitions.

Student Workbook or Lesson Review – If you are using one of these optional books, complete the assignment for Lesson 15. If you are using the Lesson Review, take the quiz for Unit 3.

Early Colonial Life in America

English settlers continued to move to America, as did immigrants from the Netherlands and Sweden. More new colonies formed during the 1600s. Someone who had been banned from Massachusetts Bay founded Rhode Island. King Charles II gave eight of his loyal subjects a tract of land called Carolina, which eventually divided into North and South Carolina. This week we learn about William Penn, who began Pennsylvania as a place dedicated to freedom. Our Daily Life lesson is about the first books written and printed in America. We finish the week with a look at Cape Cod, Nantucket, and Martha's Vineyard, three of God's Wonders He created along the Atlantic coast.

Commemorative Medal Honoring Dutch Explorer Henry Hudson

Lessons in Unit 4

Lesson 16 – Our American Story: The Rhode Island and Carolina Colonies
Lesson 17 – Our American Story: The Dutch and Swedes in America
Lesson 18 – An American Biography: William Penn, Founder of Pennsylvania
Lesson 19 – Daily Life: Printing Books in Colonial America
Lesson 20 – God's Wonders: God Created Cape Cod, Martha's Vineyard, and Nantucket

Books Used in Unit 4

- *Maps of America the Beautiful*

- *Timeline of America the Beautiful*

- *We the People*

- *The Sign of the Beaver* by Elizabeth George Speare

The Rhode Island and Carolina Colonies

English settlers moved to America for many reasons. Some, like the Pilgrims and Puritans of Massachusetts and the Catholics of Maryland, sought religious freedom. Virginia settlers, on the other hand, were part of a business venture. Even so, faith was important to many of those who moved to Virginia.

Rhode Island and Carolina were founded under different circumstances. The small colony of Rhode Island was founded in 1636 by a Puritan minister. Eight nobles founded Carolina in 1663.

Roger Williams Comes to America

Roger Williams had known Boston founder John Winthrop when they both lived in England. Williams came to Boston in 1631, and he was invited to be the minister of the Boston church. Williams believed the Puritans should break ties with the Church of England. The Boston church had not done so, therefore Williams refused the position. Williams served churches in Salem and Plymouth, but he continued to disagree with Puritan officials in Boston. Williams also believed settlers should pay Native Americans for their land and did not believe the government should punish people for religious failings.

In 1635 officials banished Roger Williams from Massachusetts. He escaped to Narragansett Bay, where he made friends with the Narragansetts and learned their language. In 1636 Williams bought land

Roger Williams

from them. He and some companions began the Providence settlement, which he named in thankfulness "for God's merciful providence unto me in my distress." Look at the pictures on this page and the next page.

Roger Williams and the Narragansetts had a relationship built on respect for each other.

Rhode Island Offers Freedom of Religion

In 1639 Williams came to believe in adult baptism by immersion. He was baptized and baptized others, forming the first Baptist church in America. The Providence settlement became a safe place for people from other colonies who were persecuted for their beliefs. Roger Williams wrote a declaration of the principle of religious liberty.

Soon other colonial leaders who believed in freedom of worship established settlements nearby. These communities joined together as one colony, which they called Rhode Island. One theory on the origin of the name Rhode Island is that the Dutch named it *Roodt Eylandt* which means red island, since part of the area's shore had red clay soil.

In 1663 the colony received a royal charter from England's King Charles II. The king gave the residents of Rhode Island more freedom to govern themselves than any other American colony. He authorized their continuing to give freedom of religion. The statue of Roger Williams shown at right is one of Rhode Island's two statues in the U.S. Capitol's Statuary Hall.

Roger Williams Statue in the U.S. Capitol's Statuary Hall

89

Carolina Settlers

Five hundred Spanish settlers came to what is now South Carolina in 1526, but stayed only a short time. French Huguenots (Protestants) tried to settle there in 1562 but also left

Northeastern North Carolina

quickly. Spanish settlers built the town of Santa Elena in 1566, but the Spanish finally left the South Carolina area for good after 1586.

As explained in Lesson 11, the first European settlers in North Carolina were those who tried to establish Roanoke in 1587. The earliest permanent settlement in North Carolina began almost seventy years later, when Virginians moved south to the area near Albemarle Sound around 1653. Find Albemarle Sound on the map at left. Find Virginia, too.

King Charles II Gives Carolina to Eight Proprietors

In 1663 King Charles II of England gave eight proprietors a large area south of Virginia. These proprietors were some of his most loyal subjects. The area King Charles II gave them included what is now North Carolina and South Carolina. The colony was named Carolina in honor of the king's father, Charles I. Carol is the French version of the name Charles.

At first the proprietors tried to establish a lifestyle similar to life in the Middle Ages, when settlers lived in distinct social classes. They divided Carolina into three districts: Albemarle, Claredon, and Craven. The Albemarle area was near Albemarle Sound. See map above. Claredon was in the area around Cape Fear, pictured at right. Both were in present-day North Carolina. Craven was in what is now South Carolina.

The northern and southern settlements were different because of Carolina's geography. As in

Cape Fear

all American colonies, the first settlements were near the Atlantic Ocean. The eastern area of North Carolina had thick forests and many swamps, like the one shown on page 91. Most settlements there were small. The people generally lived and worked on small farms. In South Carolina, the geography and climate allowed people to establish large plantations. By the early 1700s, Carolina was already dividing into distinct northern and southern regions.

The Founding of Charleston

One of the eight proprietors who received land in Carolina was Lord Anthony Ashley Cooper. In 1670 he founded Charles Town, now called Charleston, the first English settlement in what is now South Carolina. The town and area around it grew quickly. Most of the English settlers who came to Charleston were members of the Church of England. Other settlers included French Hugenots and people from New England who did not like the laws of the Puritans. Below is a map of early Charleston. Two early Charleston buildings are described in the box on page 92.

The eight proprietors and their descendants controlled Carolina until 1729 when they sold their rights to the English crown. At that time the area was officially divided into North Carolina and South Carolina. Both became royal colonies.

North Carolina Swamp

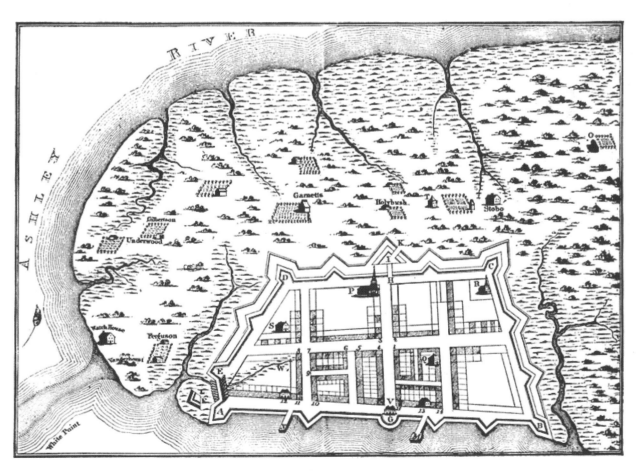

Map of Charleston

South Carolina settlers realized that their climate was well-suited for growing rice. The settlers established large rice plantations in the 1700s. England paid high prices for South Carolina rice, so South Carolina became one of the richest colonies in America. Since Charleston served as the colony's main port, it became one of the wealthiest cities in the colonies.

Solomon gave this warning about wealth in Proverbs:

He who trusts in his riches will fall,
But the righteous will flourish like the green leaf.
Proverbs 11:28

Activities for Lesson 16

Thinking Biblically – Roger Williams named his settlement "Providence" because God took care of him during a difficult time. Providence means God's guidance and care. Think of someone in the Bible whom God helped in a difficult time. In your notebook, write down his or her name and a one-paragraph description of how God cared for that person.

Map Study – Complete the assignments for Lesson 16 on Map 7 "The Thirteen Colonies" in *Maps of America the Beautiful*.

St. Michael's and Carolina Hall

St. Philip's, the first Anglican church building in Charleston, was built of wood in 1680. St. Michael's Church is built on the same site. Its cornerstone was laid in 1752. Inside the church, visitors can see the pew where President George Washington and Confederate General Robert E. Lee worshiped.

Carolina Hall (also called South Carolina Hall) was built in 1804. It is a club house for the South Carolina Society, begun in 1737 by French Huguenots. The Society once built schools for orphans and poor children. Today it gives scholarships.

Carolina Hall and St. Michael's

Timeline – In *Timeline of America the Beautiful* next to 1636, write: Roger Williams buys land from the Narragansetts and learns their language.

Literature – Read chapters 1-2 in *The Sign of the Beaver*.

Student Workbook or Lesson Review – If you are using one of these optional books, complete the assignment for Lesson 16.

The Dutch and Swedes in America

Henry Hudson

Spain, England, and France were not the only countries wanting to reap the financial benefits the New World had to offer. The Swedes and the Dutch began to lay claim to parts of America, too.

Henry Hudson Explores the Hudson River

In 1607 and 1608, Englishman Henry Hudson made two exploratory voyages searching for a northern water route to the Far East. See the illustration at left. Both expeditions were funded by an English company, and both times Hudson sailed from England on the *Hopewell*. After the English company withdrew its financial support, Hudson decided to try again, this time with funds from the Dutch East India Company. Hudson and his crew of both Dutch and English sailors sailed from Texel, a Dutch island, on the *Half Moon*. Again he sailed north, but Hudson faced the mutinty of his crew because of the cold, harsh weather. Hudson turned south and sailed along the Atlantic coast.

In September of 1609, Hudson entered New York Bay. For a month, he explored the Hudson River (a name given to it later in his honor), sailing as far as present-day Albany.

Many Native Americans lived in the Hudson River Valley when the Half Moon *sailed up the river in 1609.*

Look at the picture of the Hudson River on page 94 and at the illustration of Hudson's voyage at left. When Hudson returned to England, his crew and ship were captured by the English. Hudson was ordered not to sail again, unless he sailed for England.

The following year, Henry Hudson sailed for an English company in his new ship, the *Discovery*. They sailed north, as he again tried to find a

93

At left: In 1909 New Yorkers celebrated the 300th anniversary of Henry Hudson's exploration of the Hudson River. Stereoscope fans enjoyed looking at this photograph of a replica of the Half Moon, *which sailed during the celebration. New Yorkers celebrated the 400th anniversary in 2009. At right: The Hudson River Valley*

Hudson's mutinous crew puts him off the ship, along with his son and seven others.

passage to the Far East. This crew also mutinied, but this revolt was more serious. The crew forced Hudson and eight others, including his son, into a small boat. See illustration at left. Hudson and his loyal followers were never seen again.

Life along the Hudson River has changed dramatically since Hudson and his crew explored it in 1609. Notice photos at top and lower left.

New Netherlands

The Dutch East India Company began to trade guns, blankets, and tools for furs collected by local Indians. After 1614 Dutch settlers came to the Hudson River Valley. See below. They called the area New Netherlands. Peter Minuit served as the first Governor of New Netherlands.

New York City Along the Hudson River

New Netherlands Colonists

94

Dutch Settlers in Manhattan

In the early 1620s, persecuted Protestants in Belgium escaped to the Netherlands. In 1624 a few of these Belgian Protestants settled on Governor's Island in New York harbor. The next year, they moved to Manhattan Island. According to legend, Peter Minuit negotiated with local Canarsees and gave them goods worth sixty Dutch guilders in exchange for the island. See the picture at right. This Belgian/Dutch settlement on Manhattan Island was named New Amsterdam. See map and illustration below.

New Netherlands allowed various religions. It attracted Moravian, German, Portuguese, English, Swiss, and French settlers. In the 1640s, New Amsterdam's 450 citizens spoke eighteen different languages. The last New Netherlands Governor, Peter Stuyvesant, arrived in 1647. Though a harsh ruler, he helped modernize New Amsterdam with cobblestone streets, police, fire protection, a hospital, and a protective wall where Wall Street is now. An illustration of Peter Stuyvesant is on page 96.

England never recognized Dutch claims in America. In 1664 English troops invaded Manhattan Island. The residents there did not like Stuyvesant's policies, so they refused to fight against the British. England easily took control of New Netherlands. New Amsterdam was renamed New York after James, Duke of York, brother of King Charles II.

More Colonists of New Netherlands

Peter Minuit Buys Manhattan from the Canarsees

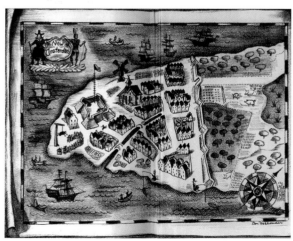
Map of New Amsterdam

New Amsterdam in 1641

At left: Peter Stuyvesant. At right: In this parade, children depict New Amsterdam settlers. Notice the boy in front with a pretend wooden leg. Stuyvesant lost a leg in a battle in 1644 and had a wooden leg decorated with silver. Notice that these two portrayals show Stuyvesant with the wooden leg on different sides.

The Dutch and English in New Jersey

Dutch settlers built a trading post around 1620 at what is now Jersey City, south of New York. Other Dutch settlements began in 1623 and in the early 1630s. Swedes began to settle in the area in 1638, but Governor Stuyvesant made them leave. See Stuyvesant above.

When the English took over New Netherlands, they named this area New Jersey. Jersey is the name of an island in the English Channel. King Charles II gave New Jersey to his brother James, Duke of York. James gave it to two nobles, Sir George Carteret and Lord John Berkeley.

Governor Johan Bjornsson ("Big Belly") Printz

Swedish and English Settlers in Delaware

The first European settlement in Delaware was Swanendael, built by Dutch settlers in 1631. It was soon destroyed by Native Americans. Later, Swedish settlers, led by former New Netherlands Governor Peter Minuit, bought land from natives. In 1638 they built a trading post at the site of present-day Wilmington. The area was called New Sweden. It attracted settlers from Finland, Denmark, and the Netherlands. Swedish Governor Johan Bjornsson Printz led New Sweden from 1643 to 1653. He had good relationships with Native Americans, who called the almost 400-pound man "Big Belly." See the illustration above. Under Printz, the Swedes built forts, houses, mills, and wharves. The Dutch captured Delaware in 1655, making it part of New Netherlands. After the English took control of New Netherlands, Delaware grew rapidly as American colonists and English settlers moved in.

Settlers of the Hudson River Valley and the rest of New Netherlands and New Sweden enjoyed the lands and waters that God created. David teaches:

The earth is the Lord's, and all it contains,
The world, and those who dwell in it.
For He has founded it upon the seas
And established it upon the rivers.
Psalm 24:1-2

Activities for Lesson 17

Map Study – Complete the assignments for Lesson 17 on Map 7 "The Thirteen Colonies" in *Maps of America the Beautiful*.

Timeline – In *Timeline of America the Beautiful* next to 1609, write: Henry Hudson explores New York Bay and the Hudson River.

Vocabulary – In your notebook, write each of the following words with its definition from the list below: financial, mutiny, legend, negotiate, modernize.

a. to discuss and compromise to arrive at a settlement of a matter
b. to bring to an up-to-date status
c. men in submission forcibly taking control away from their leader
d. relating to money
e. a story or myth that may be true or based on truth, though without conclusive evidence

Literature – Read "Flushing Remonstrance" in *We the People*, page 16, and chapters 3-5 in *The Sign of the Beaver*.

Student Workbook or Lesson Review – If you are using one of these optional books, complete the assignment for Lesson 17.

William Penn, Founder of Pennsylvania

By the end of the 1600s, Europeans lived in twelve English colonies along the Atlantic coast. The devout English Quaker William Penn founded the last colony formed in that century.

The Early Life of William Penn

William Penn, pictured as a young man at left, was born in London, England, on October 14, 1644. His mother was Dutch. His father was often away at sea, serving as an

The Young Aristocrat William Penn, Dressed in a Suit of Armor

admiral in England's navy. The Penns gave their son a classical education at a country grammar school. While still a child, William heard a missionary speak at a meeting of members of the Society of Friends. At that time, members of the Society of Friends were called Quakers by their enemies. Today the term Quaker is not considered derogatory.

In his mid-teens, William entered Oxford University. See picture below. At seventeen, he protested mandatory Anglican chapel and was expelled. His parents sent him to France where he enrolled in a French Huguenot university. He studied under a professor who taught that people should tolerate the religious beliefs of others.

William Penn as a Young Man

When William Penn returned to England in 1664, he was a tall, handsome, and athletic young man. He began to study at a respected London law firm. There he learned the legal basis for civil liberties, which are freedoms a government guarantees to its citizens.

William Penn While Studying at Oxford

After studying law, he served as his father's messenger to King Charles II. He became acquainted with both the King and his brother James, who later became King James II.

William Penn, Quaker Author

Penn Arrested

Penn started attending Quaker meetings and came to share their beliefs. In 1667 Penn and other attendees at one of these meetings were arrested. Since Penn looked like an aristocrat and not like a plainly-dressed Quaker, he was released. He insisted that he be treated the same as the others and went to jail. See the picture at left. While in jail, he began to write literature that encouraged freedom of conscience for individuals. He became a major writer for the Quaker movement.

Admiral Penn disowned his son, so William began living with various Quaker families. While living with wealthy Quaker Isaac Penington, Penn came to care about Gulielma Springett, the stepdaughter of his host. William and Gulielma married in 1672.

Again Penn was arrested and imprisoned for his disagreements with the Anglican Church. This time he went to the Tower of London for seven months. While in the Tower, he continued to write Quaker literature. See the picture below. In fact, Penn continued to write all his life as long as his health permitted. When his beliefs changed as he got older, he wrote to refute things he had written earlier. He was willing to see his errors rather than try to defend them.

William Penn, the Activist

When the British Parliament passed another law to keep people from expressing views different from those taught by the Anglican Church, many Quakers went to prison. Much of their property was taken, including the property of Gulielma Springett Penn's family. William Penn fought back through the English court system. He argued for freedom of religion. Penn became a famous speaker. Thousands went to hear him speak. He visited Germany and Holland to find out how Quakers were treated in those countries. He liked the Dutch policy of toleration. Many persecuted Jews and Protestants were moving to Holland because of this policy.

Writing in the Tower of London

William Penn Plans a "Holy Experiment"

Penn tried to get King Charles II and Charles' brother James to support religious freedom, but they refused. Penn decided that religious freedom was not going to be granted in his home country, so he looked to the New World. William Penn asked King Charles II for a charter so he could form a colony in America. The king granted this request and suggested the name Pennsylvania to honor William's father, Admiral Penn. Pennsylvania means "forests of Penn." To Penn, Pennsylvania was a "Holy Experiment."

William Penn made plans for a city he called Philadelphia, which means "brotherly love." Penn advertised for "adventurers" to settle his new colony. He wanted carpenters, day laborers, farmers, masons, merchants, smiths, tailors, tanners, shoemakers, shipwrights, and weavers. English families began going to Penn's colony in America. Penn wrote letters to the Dutch, Finnish, and Swedish settlers already living there, telling them not to worry about his new government. He told them they would live under laws they made themselves.

Penn Sails to Pennsylvania

First Trip to America

William Penn sailed to Pennsylvania on the *Welcome*, arriving in November, 1682. See the picture at left. His city of brotherly love was about a year old when he arrived. It had been laid out as he planned. Spruce, Broad, Pine and other streets in Philadelphia are still called by names Penn chose.

Penn wrote a constitution for the colony. It protected people's property, allowed them to conduct business freely, and granted those accused of violating the law the right of a trial by jury (a group of regular citizens who decide a person's guilt or innocence in court). Thomas Jefferson complimented William Penn as "the greatest law-giver the world has produced."

William Penn enjoyed good relationships with native tribes. They respected him for coming among them without weapons, for learning their languages, and for his physical strength. He could run faster than many native men. He won their affection with courtesy and fairness. His leadership began peaceful relationships with natives that lasted for many years, even after his death. At right is a wampum belt labeled "The Belt of

Copyright, 1905, by John D. Morris & Company

THE BELT OF WAMPUM DELIVERED BY THE INDIANS TO WILLIAM PENN AT THE "GREAT TREATY" UNDER THE ELM TREE AT SHACKAMAXON, IN 1682

Wampum Delivered by the Indians to William Penn at the 'Great Treaty' under the Elm Tree at Shackamaxon, in 1682." On page 101 is an illustration from the Library of Congress, labeled "Treaty between William Penn and the Indians."

Pennsylvania became a haven for people suffering religious persecution. Settlers came from England, Ireland, and Germany. Catholics and Jews came, as did Mennonites, French Huguenots, Lutherans, and others. Although it was the twelfth English colony to be founded, by the time of the American Revolution in 1776, Pennsylvania was the third largest.

Treaty Between Penn and Native Americans

Back in England

In August 1684, Penn returned to England where he continued to help English people who were being persecuted. He helped many Quakers to be released from prison, including Quaker founder George Fox. He also continued to write. In 1694 he published *A Brief Account of the Rise and Progress of the People Called Quakers*. Penn's wife Gulielma died that year. He married Quaker Hannah Callowhill two years later.

Second Trip to America

William Penn brought Hannah to Pennsylvania in 1699. While in America they lived in Pennsbury Manor, a home on the Delaware River. The only way to get to this elaborate wilderness retreat was by water. When the Penns ordered supplies, they came by flatboat. William Penn had children by both of his wives. One was born while he and Hannah were staying at a friend's home in Philadelphia. Penn named his only baby born in America John. John always had the nickname, "the American."

Perhaps the most important accomplishment made during Penn's second visit to Pennsylvania was the adoption of a new constitution for the colony in 1701. It was called the Charter of Privileges. See Penn at right.

A Final Trip Home to England

William and Hannah Penn returned to England later that year. During the next seventeen years, Penn did more writing. He also

Penn in His Later Years

faced more persecution during the reign of William III and experienced poor health beginning in 1712. Penn died in the nation of his birth in 1718 and was buried at Jordans, in the countryside near London. See the painting of Jordans at right.

Jordans, Burial Place of William Penn

Penn left behind a colony that became accustomed to freedom. His city of brotherly love would play a key role in a fight for freedom about one hundred years after its founding. In 1751 Pennsylvania celebrated the fiftieth anniversary of their Charter of Privileges that had been adopted just before its founder left the colony for the last time. As part of this celebration, the colony had a bell cast. The bell became a famous American symbol—the Liberty Bell. Engraved on the bell are these words from Leviticus:

> Proclaim liberty throughout all the land
> unto all the inhabitants thereof.
> Leviticus 25:10, KJV

Activities for Lesson 18

Thinking Biblically – William Penn used his time in prison to write about the Christian faith. The apostle Paul wrote some of his letters while he was in prison for his faith. Read 2 Timothy 1:1-12.

Map Study – Complete the assignments for Lesson 18 on Map 7 "The Thirteen Colonies" in *Maps of America the Beautiful*.

Timeline – In *Timeline of America the Beautiful* next to 1682, write: William Penn sails to Pennsylvania.

Literature – Read "Salvation from Sin by Christ Alone" in *We the People*, page 17, and chapters 6-8 in *The Sign of the Beaver*.

Student Workbook or Lesson Review – If you are using one of these optional books, complete the assignment for Lesson 18.

Printing Books in Colonial America

Printing Press

The first books published and printed in America reflected the faith of its first European settlers and their desire to share that faith with native peoples.

The Cambridge Press

In 1630 New Towne was established across the Charles River from Boston. It served as capital of Massachusetts Bay until 1634. In 1636 Harvard University was organized in New Towne. It was the first college in America, and its purpose was the training of ministers. In 1638 New Towne was renamed Cambridge, after Cambridge, England. That same year, minister Jesse (or Jose) Glover and his wife left England for the Massachusetts Bay Colony. Locksmith Stephen Daye came with them. Glover brought a printing press with him. He planned to use the press while sharing the gospel with Native Americans. Glover died on the way to America, but the next year Mrs. Glover began a printing business in Cambridge with Stephen Daye serving as manager. Their press probably looked something like the drawing above.

John Eliot

The Bay Psalm Book

In 1640 the Cambridge Press printed the *Bay Psalm Book*, the first book printed in America. The book, also called the *Whole Book of Psalmes Faithfully Translated into English Metre*, was compiled by two ministers, John Eliot, pictured at left, and Richard Mather, pictured on page 104. Both were born in England. Eliot immigrated to America in 1631 and Mather in 1635.

John Eliot and the Eliot Bible

John Eliot is known as the Apostle to the Indians. He was born in 1604 and was educated at the University of

Cambridge in England. Eliot was influenced by Puritan minister Thomas Hooker (mentioned in lesson 15). Eliot came to America at age twenty-seven and became a teacher in the Roxbury church. He wanted to share the gospel with local Algonquians. Eliot and his wife welcomed into their home an Algonquian youth. The youth taught Eliot how to speak his native language. Eliot was later able to preach to Native Americans without an interpreter. See the illustration at right.

The English Parliament established the Society for the Propagation of the Gospel among the Indians in 1649. The Society supported Eliot's efforts. In 1654 he

John Eliot Preaching to Natives

published *A Primer or Catechism in the Massachusetts Indian Language*. It was the first book printed in a Native American tongue. In 1663 Eliot published *The Holy Bible Containing the Old Testament and the New, Translated into the Indian Language*. It is known as the Eliot Bible and was the first Bible printed in America.

Richard Mather

The Mather Family

Richard Mather was a minister who came to the Massachusetts Bay colony in 1635. He served the Dorchester, Massachusetts, church from 1636 until his death in 1699.

Richard Mather's son Increase was born in Dorchester in 1639. Increase graduated from Harvard at age 17. He went to Ireland to study and later preached in England for a short time. See his picture at right.

In 1664 Increase Mather became the minister of North Church in Boston. In 1676 he published *A Brief History of the War with the Indians in New England*. The war was called King Philip's War, after the Wampanoag chief named Metacom who had taken the English name of Philip.

In 1682 Increase Mather helped Mary Rowlandson publish *The Sovereignty and Goodness of God . . . A Narrative of the Captivity and Restoration of Mary Rowlandson*. Rowlandson had been captured by the Narragansett tribe during King Philip's War.

Increase Mather

Increase Mather served at North Church until his death. For sixteen years, he also served as the president of Harvard.

Cotton Mather was the son of Increase and grandson of Richard Mather. His mother Maria was the daughter of John Cotton, who has been called the Patriarch of New England.

Cotton Mather was born in Boston. He went to school at Harvard and then served alongside his father at North Church in Boston. See the picture of North Church below.

Cotton Mather, pictured at right, wrote many books, including *Magnalia Christi Americana*, which means *The Great Works of Christ in America* (1702). This book is a detailed history of New England that praises the Puritan founders. In 1706 he published *The Negro Christianized*, which encouraged the education of Africans who were being brought to America as slaves. The book also proposed that African slaves be able to join the Congregational church.

Cotton Mather

John Cotton, The Patriarch of New England

While John Cotton, grandfather of Cotton Mather, was serving as a minister in England, he was called to appear before the archbishop of Canterbury because of his Puritan beliefs. Instead of going to Canterbury and possibly being reprimanded or punished, John Cotton fled from England to Boston in 1633. He served First Church in Boston until he died. He had a good reputation among many settlers and was admired for his piety. Cotton strongly supported punishing people for not conforming to Puritan laws. In 1645 he published *The Way of the Churches of Christ in New England*. See his bookplate below.

Bookplate Belonging to John Cotton

Boston's North Church built this building in 1723. It is the oldest standing building in Boston.

Roger Williams

Roger Williams, founder of Rhode Island, wrote *A Key into the Language of America* in 1643. In this book, he wrote about the Narragansett language and about customs of the natives of New England.

Puritan Poets

In the 1600s, many Puritans wrote journals and devotional poetry. The purpose of their writings was to examine their hearts and lives. Social gatherings sometimes included reading personal poems aloud. Anne Bradstreet was the first American to publish a book of poetry. Her book, *The Tenth Muse Lately Sprung Up in America*, was published in England in 1650. Pages from her book are pictured on page 106.

From Anne Bradstreet's Book, The Tenth Muse Lately Sprung Up in America

American Children's Literature of the 1600s

Benjamin Harris published *The New England Primer* in Boston in 1687. It included an alphabet in rhyme, the Lord's Prayer, the Ten Commandments, and other rhymes and stories. A well-known prayer in the *Primer* is "Now I Lay Me Down to Sleep." See some pages from the *Primer* below. In 1646 John Cotton published *Spiritual Milk for Boston Babes,* which was a thirteen-page book of questions and answers. Early editions of *The New England Primer* included John Cotton's book.

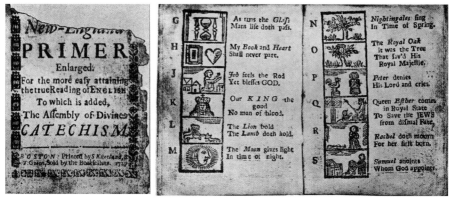

Pages from The New England Primer

A man is finding individual letters in printer trays kept on a rack.

Early American Printers

Cambridge Press was the main printing company in America for thirty-four years. It published only one book each year. Printing presses began operating in Boston in 1674, in Philadelphia in 1685, and in New York City in 1693. Early American printers served as publishers, printers, and booksellers. Often they had printing presses in the back of their businesses and a bookshop in the front. Notice the remaining illustrations on these two pages. At left a man is finding individual letters in printer trays kept on a rack. On the next page, at top left, a woman sews printed pages together to make a book. At right, a printer works at a printing press, while a younger man works with ink.

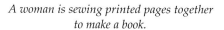
A woman is sewing printed pages together to make a book.

A printer is working at a printing press while a younger man works with ink.

In 1750 almost all men and about 90 percent of the women in New England could read. Parents in New England wanted their children to be able to read the Bible, so they taught them how to read when they were young. The parents understood their children's need to know the word of God. As taught in Psalms:

> How can a young man keep his way pure?
> By keeping it according to your word.
> Psalm 119:9

Activities for Lesson 19

Timeline – In *Timeline of America the Beautiful* next to 1640, write: The *Bay Psalm Book* is printed. It is the first book printed in America.

Literature – Read "New England Primer Rhyming Alphabet" in *We the People*, page 18, and chapters 9-10 in *The Sign of the Beaver*.

Creative Writing – In your notebook, write one or more paragraphs about how being able to read and having access to books help you.

Family Activity – Follow the instructions for the Colonial Printing activity on pages 421-422.

Student Workbook or Lesson Review – If you are using one of these optional books, complete the assignment for Lesson 19.

God Created Cape Cod, Martha's Vineyard, and Nantucket

Enjoying a Day on Cape Cod

When Europeans formed colonies in America, they began to establish new businesses. Businesses depend on the natural resources that God has created. Two important early business endeavors in America were fishing and whaling. Both used the natural resources God created near Cape Cod, Martha's Vineyard, and Nantucket. Commercial and recreational fishing are still important in this region. The beautiful area is also a popular tourist destination, as seen in the photo at left.

Hold up your arm like a strong man flexing his muscle. You have made the shape of Cape Cod. Cape Cod is the easternmost region of Massachusetts, extending into the Atlantic Ocean. Inside the crook of Cape Cod is Cape Cod Bay. North of Cape Cod Bay is Massachusetts Bay. The Plymouth settlement lies at the head of Cape Cod. The head of a cape is where it joins the mainland. South of Cape Cod are the islands of Nantucket and Martha's Vineyard. Nantucket Sound lies between the cape and these two large islands.

Cape Cod

In 1602 English explorer Bartholomew Gosnold saw many codfish in the waters around a cape on the eastern coast of America. He named it Cape Cod. The cape is sandy and hilly. It is dotted with lakes, ponds, and thick forests. Today the main crop on Cape Cod is cranberries. Fishing is still important, especially at the northern tip. Cape Cod is also a popular summer resort. Look at the photograph at right and imagine looking at the moon from the shore of Cape Cod.

Provincetown at the northern tip has a large, safe harbor. The Pilgrims dropped

Moonlight Ocean View from Cape Cod, Massachusetts, Winter, 1875

anchor there before they chose Plymouth as their place to settle. The first English child born in New England was born on the *Mayflower* while it was anchored in Cape Cod Bay. His name was Peregrine White.

In 1961 the U.S. government established the Cape Cod National Seashore to protect historic sites and natural habitats in northeast Cape Cod. It protects beaches, cliffs, dunes, freshwater ponds, marshes, and woodlands. Cape Cod is home to Marconi's Wireless Station, the first wireless station in the United States. Marconi was an Italian engineer and inventor who developed a way to send telegraph signals across the Atlantic Ocean without using wires. This led to the development of radio. The cape has

Nobska Lighthouse

eighteen lighthouses, including the Nobska Lighthouse, pictured above. The current Nobska Light was built in 1876.

Arctic Tern Drawn by John James Audubon

Arctic terns nest on Cape Cod. This bird, pictured at left, is an amazing traveler. The Arctic tern migrates farther than any other bird that God created. Some migrate 25,000 miles round trip, from the Arctic to the Antarctic and back!

The Cape Cod Canal crosses the neck of Cape Cod. Private businessmen built the eight-mile canal between 1909 and 1914. The U.S. government bought it in 1928. Since the canal opened, ships have been able to travel between New England and the mid-Atlantic states without having to travel the dangerous route around Cape Cod. The route through the canal is also much shorter.

Martha's Vineyard

Martha's Vineyard is an island that is part of Massachusetts. See the marsh pictured below. Before English settlers moved there, the Wampanoag tribe lived on the island. Bartholomew Gosnold, who named Cape Cod, also named Martha's Vineyard. English colonists settled there in 1642, just twenty-two years after the founding of Plymouth. Today the island is mainly a summer resort.

A Marsh on Martha's Vineyard

A sizable deaf population lived on Martha's Vineyard in the 1800s. Some of the island's early settlers carried a gene that caused some of their children to be born deaf. The island was isolated from the rest of the colonies, so residents often married others from the island. Over the years, several deaf children were born. Both deaf and hearing residents often used sign language. A special sign language developed called Martha's Vineyard Sign Language. As deaf schools were started on the mainland, children went away from the island and often married people from other places. The last descendant of these early deaf residents died in the 1950s.

The main town on the island is Edgartown on the east coast. It was called Nunnepog when it was settled in 1642. In 1671 it was renamed Edgartown to honor Edgar, son of King James II. It was a whaling port in the 1700s and 1800s.

A Home on Martha's Vineyard Decorated with Gingerbread

In 1835 Methodists began holding camp meetings at Wesleyan Grove on Martha's Vineyard. Camp meetings were common in the early 1800s. Many people gathered together to camp and to hear preaching. At the early camp meetings on Martha's Vineyard, churches from the mainland brought large tents to the campground. Men would sleep on one side of the tent and women would sleep on the other side with a canvas wall between. Later, families began to lease lots and bring their own tents. Then they began to build small wooden cottages. At one time there were about five hundred of these cottages. Today there are still three hundred. The cottages are painted bright colors and are decorated with fancy woodwork called gingerbread. Families pass the cottages down from generation to generation. Look closely at the picture above of a gingerbread cottage on Martha's Vineyard. The camp meetings still continue each summer. Today's preachers come from many denominations.

At Home in Nantucket

Nantucket Island

The Wampanoag Indians also lived on Nantucket Island. English colonists settled there in 1659. The sandy island is only fourteen miles long and three to six miles wide. It has good beaches and is a popular tourist attraction. Nantucket was once part of New York, but the island has been a part of Massachusetts since 1692.

God created the bright, colorful, deep-sea tilefish and placed it in the waters off the coast of New England. It was discovered near Nantucket Island in 1879. The tilefish can be as long as three feet and can weigh up to 50 pounds. It has a reddish head and a bluish-green back with yellow and rose speckles.

In 1745-46, Nathan Wilbur built Nantucket Windmill, illustrated at right. Wilbur had learned about windmill construction while visiting Holland as

Nantucket Windmill

110

a sailor. Back home in Nantucket, he built the octagonal-shaped windmill using wood from wrecked ships. The windmill stands fifty feet tall and has four arms that are thirty feet long and six feet wide! Since 1897, the mill has been owned by the Nantucket Historical Society. In summer, it still grinds corn into cornmeal. Notice the illustrations of Nantucket at right and on page 110.

A Beach on Nantucket Island

Whaling

God created whales to live in all of the world's oceans. People have found many uses for these mammals and have hunted them for centuries. Whales have provided people with meat, oil, baleen (also known as whalebone), and other products.

Nantucket Fisherman Returns Home, 1879

The Vikings hunted whales during the early Middle Ages. The Dutch, English, Japanese, Norwegians, Russians, and Basques have all been heavily involved in whaling at different times.

When Europeans first came to America, Native Americans were already hunting whales in the Pacific Ocean. However, the first people known to hunt whales along the Atlantic coast of America were Europeans. Whaling began in the American colonies in the 1600s. The original whaling centers of the colonies were Nantucket Island, Cape Cod, and the eastern end of Long Island. At that time, whales were caught near the shore. In the 1800s, American whalers (often called Yankee whalers) began hunting whales farther from shore. Then New Bedford, Massachusetts, became the center for American whaling. See the ocean-going whaling ships below.

Early American whalers hunted mostly baleen whales, including the gray whale. Whale oil and baleen became important American products. The toothless baleen whales trap krill in the hard, long, baleen plates that grow in their jaws. Gray whales can have has many 260 to 360 of these baleen plates. Baleen is flexible and was used for spokes in umbrellas, stays for corsets, and hoops for hoop skirts. It was also used for combs and to keep collars stiff. A good place to learn about American whaling is the New Bedford

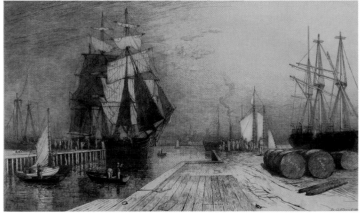

Return of a Whaler

Whaling Ship Near the Shore

Whaling National Historical Park in New Bedford, Massachusetts, just a few miles from Cape Cod.

Sailors of old as well as modern sailors are able to see wonders of God's creation that some people will never see in their lifetimes. Isaiah tells them:

Sing to the Lord a new song,
Sing His praise from the end of the earth!
You who go down to the sea and all that is in it,
You islands, and those who dwell on them.
Isaiah 42:10

Activities for Lesson 20

Map Study – Complete the assignments for Lesson 20 on Map 2 "God's Wonders" and Map 9 "Cape Cod, Martha's Vineyard, and Nantucket" in *Maps of America the Beautiful*.

Timeline – In *Timeline of America the Beautiful* next to 1835, write: Methodists begin holding camp meetings on Martha's Vineyard.

Vocabulary – In your notebook, write a paragraph using all of these words: attraction, engineer, isolated, migrate, whaling. Consult a dictionary if you need help with their definitions.

Literature – Read chapters 11-13 in *The Sign of the Beaver*.

Student Workbook or Lesson Review – If you are using one of these optional books, complete the assignment for Lesson 20. If you are using the Lesson Review, take the quiz for Unit 4.

Colonial Life in America During the 1700s

5

This week we learn about the founding of the last of America's thirteen English colonies. We also learn about the work of colonial craftsmen and merchants. We see how tensions increased between England and her American colonies. Our American Biography is about Benjamin Franklin. Born into a humble family, he worked hard and creatively, becoming one of the most important leaders in the colonies. We finish the week with a lesson about Colonial Williamsburg, where colonial leaders came together and began to talk about their problems with England.

This drawing of a May Day during colonial times was created in 1888.

Lessons in Unit 5

Lesson 21 – Our American Story: Thirteen American Colonies
Lesson 22 – Daily Life: Colonial Craftsmen and Merchants
Lesson 23 – Our American Story: Trouble Brews Between England and Her
        Thirteen American Colonies
Lesson 24 – An American Biography: Benjamin Franklin, Scientist and Statesman
Lesson 25 – An American Landmark: Colonial Williamsburg, Capital of Virginia

Books Used in Unit 5

- *Maps of America the Beautiful*

- *Timeline of America the Beautiful*

- *We the People*

- *The Sign of the Beaver* by Elizabeth George Speare

Thirteen American Colonies

General James Edward Oglethorpe

The last English colony founded in America was Georgia. The establishment of Georgia brought the total number of English colonies in America to thirteen.

The Founding of Georgia

The first European settlers in Georgia were the Spanish, who called the area Guale. In 1566 they established a mission and fort on Saint Catherine's Island. They built more missions and forts along the coast during the next century. Priests from the missions converted many Native Americans to Catholicism. England also claimed the area and enticed Native Americans to help them attack Spanish missions. The Spanish had left Guale by 1686.

In 1732 King George II of Great Britain asked Member of Parliament James Edward Oglethorpe, pictured above, and twenty others to form the colony of Georgia. These men became trustees. They planned for Georgia to be a sanctuary for the poor, those suffering religious persecution, and people who were in prison for debt. Oglethorpe became a champion for prison reform after a personal friend died in a debtors' prison. His friend had died of smallpox caught from his cell mate.

In 1733 Oglethorpe sailed to Yamacraw Bluff along the Savannah River. There he met Tomochichi, the elderly chief of the new Yamacraw tribe, which included about two hundred people from the Creek and Yamassee peoples. Chief Tomochichi gave his consent for Oglethorpe to build a settlement there. See the picture at right.

Oglethorpe Meets Tomochichi

114

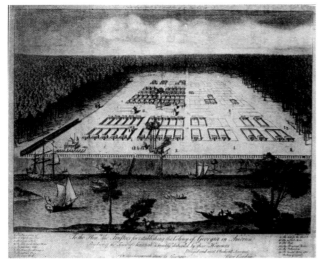
Early Map of Savannah

Soon 114 settlers founded the city of Savannah on the Yamacraw Bluff. Savannah was the first permanent European settlement in Georgia. Oglethorpe designed Savannah with twenty-four public squares surrounded by homes and other buildings. Twenty-one squares survive today as beautiful public parks. See an early map of Savannah at left and one of its public squares below.

In 1734 Chief Tomochichi went to England with Oglethorpe. The chief was a man of noble character who adapted graciously to English customs. He asked the English to give his people education and fair trade. When he returned home, he encouraged other natives to work peacefully with the settlers.

In 1736 English ministers John and Charles Wesley visited Georgia. They met Tomochichi. He asked them for Christian education for his people. That fall, the Wesleys' traveling companion, Benjamin Ingham, helped begin a school for the Yamacraw.

Just as God provided Squanto at the right time to help the Pilgrims of Plymouth, He provided Tomochichi to help the

Statue of Oglethorpe in One of Savannah's Squares

colonists in Georgia. The elderly chief died just six and a half years after meeting Oglethorpe and was given an English military funeral. He was probably in his nineties. His grave is an honored historic site in Georgia.

Over the next twenty years, German Lutherans and persecuted believers from central Europe emigrated to Georgia. People from Wales, Switzerland, northern Italy, and Scotland came, too. See Scottish settlers below.

Oglethorpe tried to create an ideal society where no one would be rich or poor. Trustees paid the way for some settlers to come to America. They gave them supplies and fifty acres of land. Others, who paid their own way across the Atlantic, received five hundred acres.

Oglethorpe Meets Scottish Settlers

The trustees outlawed strong drink and slavery, but not everyone agreed with the good intentions of the trustees. Many people wanted Georgia to become like the other colonies. By 1750 Georgians could make and sell liquor and own slaves.

Everyday People in the Thirteen Colonies

European settlers came to America from many nations. History books remind us of the few who were leaders. Most settlers, however, were regular men, women, and children. People who had never been on a ship before risked their lives to sail across a wide ocean. Most had a common purpose: to improve their lives and the lives of their families.

However, some of those who came to America were forced to come as slaves. In addition to its thirteen colonies in America, Great Britain also controlled some islands in the Caribbean. The Caribbean Islands were then called the West Indies. Englishmen set up tobacco plantations and later sugar plantations there. See the sugar plantation at left. Many laborers were needed to produce sugar. Caribbean colonists did not have enough indentured servants to produce sugar, so they bought slaves. To obtain slaves, English slave traders traveled to Africa, where powerful African leaders from one tribe

African slaves work on a sugar plantation in the West Indies.

captured members of other tribes and sold them to the traders. The traders brought the slaves to the Caribbean on terribly overcrowded ships. Many died before they reached the islands.

Thousands of Africans came to America because they were forced to come. Most came first to the Caribbean Islands. Later they or their descendants were brought to the colonies. Slavery was legal in America until the 1860s. See the former slave pictured at right.

New England, Mid-Atlantic, and Southern Colonies

While daily life in the thirteen colonies had many similarities, there were also differences. Connecticut, Massachusetts, Rhode Island, and New Hampshire made up New England. Most New Englanders (or Yankees) were descendants of

Former Slave Betty Simmons from Beaumont, Texas, 1937

the Puritans. They shared similar religious beliefs and customs. With its cold climate and rocky soils, New England farms could provide for the needs of its residents, but they did not produce much to sell to other colonies or to Europe.

Delaware, New Jersey, New York, and Pennsylvania were the mid-Atlantic colonies. They had a diverse population. The region had descendants of the Quakers from England and Wales, the Dutch of New Netherlands, French Huguenots, Irish Catholics, Germans, and others. Immigrants from Northern Ireland also moved to the mid-Atlantic region. They were called Scots-Irish because they had emigrated from Scotland to Northern Ireland before coming to America.

Virginia, Maryland, North Carolina, South Carolina, and Georgia were the southern colonies. Most southern colonists were English. They began large plantations that grew rice and tobacco in the mild southern climate. The plantation owners needed many laborers. At first, they used indentured servants; but later they imported African slaves. Rice farmers purchased many slaves from the rice-growing regions of Africa. These slaves were valuable to the plantation owners because they brought their techniques with them and helped make the plantations profitable.

Colonial Government

Americans today are accustomed to freedom, but Americans did not have as many freedoms in the 1700s. The colonies were part of the British Empire. Its king appointed royal governors in most colonies. Each colony also elected an assembly. The British thought of these assemblies as acting with the permission of the king, but the colonists began to think of them as acting with the permission of the colonists.

The Great Awakening

Many colonists became wealthier during the late 1600s and early 1700s. Look at the family in the picture at right. Though they continued to attend church, some of the colonists became like the thorny soil Jesus described in the parable of the sower.

Congregationalist minister Jonathan Edwards noticed this problem in his church in Northampton, Massachusetts. He changed his preaching style and started trying to convict people of sin. A revival began in Northampton. Traveling ministers in other places began to preach this way, too, as did English preacher George Whitefield (pronounced whit-field). Whitefield came to America and preached in 1739 and 1740. He preached to thousands in New England and Georgia. In Philadelphia, he

A family sits in its own box pew. Notice the preacher in the lofty pulpit.

preached to 10,000! Jonathan Edwards was deeply moved when he heard Whitefield. Revivals began in a few scattered places before spreading to all thirteen colonies. Many who came to believe in Jesus joined Baptist, Methodist, and Presbyterian churches; and these denominations grew. This time of revival is called the Great Awakening.

Like the psalmist, many Americans called on God to revive them:

Let Your hand be upon the man of Your right hand,
Upon the son of man whom You made strong for Yourself.
Then we shall not turn back from You;
Revive us, and we will call upon Your name.
O Lord God of hosts, restore us;
Cause Your face to shine upon us, and we will be saved.
Psalm 80:17-19

Activities for Lesson 21

Thinking Biblically – Read Romans 6:1-14, remembering the Great Awakening and the way it changed people's view of sin and their need for Jesus.

Map Study – Complete the assignments for Lesson 21 on Map 7 "The Thirteen Colonies" in *Maps of America the Beautiful*.

Timeline – In *Timeline of America the Beautiful* next to 1736, write: English ministers John and Charles Wesley visit Georgia.

Literature – Read "The Pharisee and the Publican" in *We the People* page 19, and chapters 14-16 in *The Sign of the Beaver*.

Student Workbook or Lesson Review – If you are using one of these optional books, complete the assignment for Lesson 21.

Colonial Craftsmen and Merchants

Blacksmith and Apprentice

"The Village Blacksmith," a poem by Henry Wadsworth Longfellow, describes the life of a craftsman. It tells of a man who worked hard with his own hands, owned his own business, was not in debt, went to church, and had a family whom he loved. It reveals values that were important in colonial America.

Apprenticeships

Colonial craftsmen taught their trade to apprentices, who were usually teenagers. Most apprentices were boys, but a few were girls. Often an apprenticeship lasted until the apprentice was twenty-one years old. The apprentice lived with his master. He often did not receive any wages; but he did receive room and board, training in the trade, and instruction in reading, writing, and arithmetic. Sometimes the craftsman gave the apprentice a set of tools or clothes when his apprenticeship was completed. A blacksmith and his apprentice are pictured above.

When an apprentice finished his training, he became a journeyman. A journeyman earned wages working for a craftsman. He saved money and looked forward to the time when he could begin his own business. Many craftsmen taught their own sons how to do their craft.

Blacksmiths

A blacksmith makes metal objects by hand. The main metal he uses is iron. Metal can be shaped by melting it and pouring it into a mold. This is called casting. A blacksmith uses a different method called forging. To forge metal, the blacksmith heats it until it is red hot and then uses a hammer and other tools to shape it as he wishes. See the forged candleholder at right. As America's slave population increased, many

Forged Candleholder

119

A blacksmith shoes a horse.

Silver Bowl Made by Paul Revere

Early American Silver Objects

African Americans worked as blacksmiths. Today people who specialize in making horseshoes and shoeing horses are called farriers. In colonial times, the village blacksmith also did the work of a farrier. See illustration at left.

One famous blacksmith who lived later in American history was John Deere. He produced the first steel plowshare in the 1830s. The John Deere Company eventually made other farm implements; it still does today.

A silversmith meets with a customer.

Silversmiths, Pewtersmiths, and Tinsmiths

Silversmiths, pewtersmiths, and tinsmiths made dinnerware and other household objects. Silversmiths made bowls, tankards, pitchers, and tea sets for the wealthy. See the silversmith with a client above. The most famous silversmith during the colonial period was Paul Revere. While still young, he became a highly-respected artisan. Look at the silver bowl by Paul Revere and other silver objects above.

Pewter Tableware

Pewtersmiths made pewter plates, porringers, pitchers, utensils, and other dinnerware like the pieces shown at right. Pewtersmiths often engraved their initials and the date on each piece. Very little of the oldest American pewter survives because it was usually returned to a pewtersmith when it was damaged so the metal could be used again. Antique pewterware is valuable.

Tin Lanterns

Pewter is an alloy. An alloy is a substance that contains two or more metals. Colonial pewter was made of tin and lead until the mid-1700s. Pewter made from tin, antimony, and copper became popular after the mid-1700s because lead was discovered to be toxic.

Tinsmiths like the one pictured below made inexpensive plates and cups, eating utensils, and household objects such as the lanterns at left.

Glassmakers

Colonial glassblowers (also called gaffers) made bottles and other glass objects. Glass is made mainly from silica, which is taken from sand, flint, or quartz rocks. Glassmakers heated silica until it was a thick liquid called molten glass. They added other ingredients like lead, soda, and lime, depending on the object they were making. Glassblowers used a blowpipe and simple tools like scissors, tongs, and a wooden paddle, to shape molten glass. The first American bottlemaking shop began in Virginia in 1608. Bottlemaking and glassmaking were important American industries during the colonial years. Notice the colonial bottle designs below.

Tinsmith

Colonial Bottles

Lumberjacks and Sawmill Workers

Much of the land east of the Mississippi River was forested when Europeans arrived. Some businessmen began logging operations in America's forests. Others began sawmills, which cut the logs into boards. Notice how the man in the picture at right is sawing by hand. The wood was used to build houses, businesses, and ships. Some of it was exported to Europe. New Hampshire forests yielded masts for English ships. Jamestown settlers began to export hand-sawed boards to England in 1607.

Cabinetmakers

Cabinetmakers in the colonies built furnishings needed for businesses, homes, and government offices. They also repaired furniture. Cabinetmakers had shops in cities like Boston, New York, Williamsburg, and Philadelphia, and in many towns and villages. Philadelphia became a center of

Sawing Lumber

Turning a Table Leg on a Lathe

Colonial Furniture

furniture making, where an elaborate and graceful style developed.

Quaker cabinetmakers built simpler designs. Germans decorated furniture with carvings and paintings similar to those used in Germany. The Dutch introduced a tall cabinet with elaborate doors that was called an armoire. Though European styles influenced cabinetmakers, an American Pilgrim style developed. Pilgrim-style furniture was built of oak and stained to look like walnut. American chairs were copies of styles popular in England, Germany, Holland, and Sweden. The Windsor chair was a common style in the colonies. It was an English style made of ash, hickory, or oak. In the drawing at left above, a colonial cabinetmaker uses a lathe to turn a table leg. Look at the examples of colonial furniture shown above.

Wheelwright

Wheelwrights

Colonial wheelwrights made wheels for wagons and coaches. They needed both carpentry and blacksmithing skills. Wheels were needed for horse-drawn wagons, which hauled goods on farms, from place to place in a village, between villages, and to markets along the coast.

People also rode in wagons. Wealthy people rode in a coach or a carriage. A coach is a wagon with walls, doors, windows, and a roof. People who wanted to travel long distances could also pay a fare and ride a stagecoach. Notice the wheelwright at left and the carriage makers on page 123. A carriage maker needed the skills of both carpenters and wheelwrights.

Shipwrights

New England had hundreds of shipwrights who built oceangoing ships, like the one below. They used the services of sawmills, sailmakers, and blacksmiths. British and American tradesmen bought ships made in America.

Carriage Makers

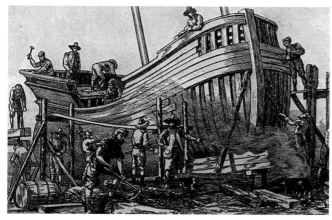

Shipwrights build a ship.

Bricklayers, Stonecutters, Masons, and Carpenters

Churches, homes, businesses, and public buildings were built of brick, stone, and wood. Bricklayers used brick made by colonial craftsmen. They often laid it in patterns that had been popular near their ancestors' homes in Europe. Look at the design above the door shown at right. Stonecutters quarried stone and masons laid stones and bricks for buildings, walls, and bridges. Carpenters built with wood. See carpenter tools below and a carpenter at right.

Colonial Design Above a Door

Colonial Woodworking Tools

Carpenter

Wigmakers and Hatters

In the late 1600s, King Louis XIII of France began to wear a large curled wig to cover his baldness. Louis XIV wore a tall wig so he would look taller. Other men followed the fashion. In the 1700s, men began to wear powdered wigs tied in a pony tail with a black ribbon. Wigmakers supplied these wigs for colonists, and hatters supplied hats. See illustrations at left and right.

Hatters

Wigmaker

Storekeepers and Peddlers

Businessmen built stores and stocked them with imports, like cloth and window glass from England and sugar and molasses from the West Indies. Farmers could receive a shopkeeper's goods in exchange for their farm crops. Farmers also supplied them with homemade shingles and barrel staves, as well as ashes which were used in glass making. Village shopkeepers could ship what they received from the farmers to larger towns and to coastal cities.

Peddlers supplied goods for people who lived far away from towns. They also visited towns where they sold goods not readily available locally. Look at the picture below of a peddler and his cart.

Peddler and His Cart

Teamsters

Teamsters began to carry goods from one place to another for pay. A teamster was a person who drove a wagon with a team of horses. Today many people who move goods in tractor-trailer trucks are members of a union called the Teamsters Union.

Innkeepers

Some farmers and businessmen began to provide places for travelers and teamsters to eat and sleep along the way. They built inns, called taverns, with sleeping quarters and stables for the travelers' horses.

Cooper at Work

Other Craftsmen

Brass founders used molds to fashion bells, shoe buckles, drawer pulls, and other objects from brass. Tanners prepared animal skins and supplied leather for shoes, saddles, and harnesses. Cobblers made shoes, sometimes traveling from house to house making custom shoes for individuals. Colonial coopers, like the one pictured at left, made barrels that were used by households, shopkeepers, and exporters.

Colonial craftsmen and merchants used the talents and the abundant natural resources God gave them. In the colonies, people could make a better life for themselves and their families than they could have in Europe. Some of these creative men and women were unwilling to be mistreated by England. Soon they showed a willingness to join together and make great sacrifices to keep their new way of life in America.

Paul told the Thessalonians to work with their hands. Craftsmen honor God when they do that:

. . . make it your ambition to lead a quiet life and attend to your own business
and work with your hands, just as we commanded you, so that you will
behave properly toward outsiders and not be in any need.
1 Thessalonians 4:11-12

Activities for Lesson 22

Thinking Biblically – Look up these Bible verses and make a list in your notebook of the people and their occupations: Matthew 4:18; Mark 6:2-4; Acts 9:43; Acts 16:14; Acts 18:1-3; Acts 19:24; 2 Timothy 4:14.

Timeline – In *Timeline of America the Beautiful* next to 1608, write: The first American bottlemaking shop begins in Virginia.

Literature – Read "The Village Blacksmith" in *We the People*, page 20, and chapters 17-18 in *The Sign of the Beaver*.

Creative Writing – In your notebook, write one or more paragraphs about which of the colonial trades you would like to learn and why.

Student Workbook or Lesson Review – If you are using one of these optional books, complete the assignment for Lesson 22.

Trouble Brews Between England and Her Thirteen American Colonies

The French and Indian War

France and England had been enemies since the Middle Ages. With both countries claiming land in the New World, their conflict spilled over into America. Both countries wanted the land between the Ohio River and the Great Lakes. Both recruited native tribes as allies. France built Fort Duquesne (pronounced doo-cane) where the Allegheny and Monongahela Rivers come together to form the Ohio River. Great Britain built Fort Necessity nearby on the Ohio.

Virginia's Governor sent troops to Fort Necessity. They were led by young George Washington. The Governor wanted the troops to push the French out. The French won a battle against Washington and his men on July 4, 1754. This was the first battle of the French and Indian War. Though the French had victories early in the war, England soon gained ground. After a British victory, the French abandoned Fort Duquesne in 1758. The British built Fort Pitt in its place. Fort Pitt was located in what is now the city of Pittsburgh, Pennsylvania.

While fighting continued in America, France and Great Britain also fought in Europe. In Europe the conflict was called the Seven Years War because it lasted from 1756 to 1763. This war ended when the two sides signed the Treaty of Paris in 1763. France lost all its colonies on the North American mainland. Though Great Britain won the war, it had been expensive. To get more revenue, Britain began to require the American colonies to pay high taxes. Colonial resentment about those taxes was eventually one of the causes of the American Revolution.

King George III

King George III Issues the Royal Proclamation of 1763

During the 1700s, most American settlers lived on or near the east coast. Just west of the coastal plain were foothills (called the Piedmont), and then plateaus, and west of those were the Appalachian Mountains. At this time Cherokee Indians lived in the southern Appalachians. Read about their villages in the box on page 127.

After the French and Indian War, Native Americans began new attacks on colonists who lived in the western parts of the colonies.

King George III, pictured on the previous page, issued the Royal Proclamation of 1763. He said that all land between the Appalachians and the Mississippi River belonged to natives and that settlers could not move there. The proclamation led to resentment among colonists who wanted to move farther west. They believed that they had helped fight in the French and Indian War so that they could move west.

Most people living in the thirteen colonies were English. Most of their parents or grandparents had been born in England. Most were loyal to Great Britain and thought of themselves as subjects of the king. Many in the upper classes sent their children to schools in England. However, life in America was different from life in Britain. The British people generally accepted the social class into which they were born. In America, people had opportunities to change their lives for the better. Their parents or grandparents had come to the new American frontier. Now, these American colonists looked toward the west and saw a new frontier they could enter.

A basic conflict was growing. Great Britain wanted even more control over its colonies, while colonists wanted more freedom. After the French and Indian War, the British sent troops into the colonies. They made the colonists keep soldiers in their homes. Britain said the troops were there to defend the colonies if an enemy attacked them. The colonists believed they were there to squash the colonists if the British government felt a need.

1762 Map of Cherokee Villages

Henry Timberlake (1730-1765) spent time with the Overhill Cherokee, who lived west of the Appalachians. In his journal, he wrote detailed descriptions of life among the Cherokee. He also made this map which showed their villages on the lower Little Tennessee River in what is now Tennessee. Shortly before his death, he took three Cherokee leaders to London. Imagine what it was like for Timberlake to meet the Cherokee, visit their villages, and learn about their customs.

The Stamp Act

Great Britain passed many laws for colonists to obey, including the Stamp Act of 1765. The Stamp Act required colonists to buy government stamps to put on newspapers and many business documents. Some colonists became angry about this Act.

While colonists agreed that Great Britain could regulate America's trade with Great Britain and other countries, they did not believe it should put a tax on business that took place within the colonies. The British people elected members to serve in Parliament who made Great Britain's laws. Colonists did not have members of Parliament to represent

This newspaper is protesting the Stamp Act.

them. They believed that the colonies should not be taxed because they did not have members to represent them.

Men in the colonies joined Sons of Liberty groups. These groups tried to stop people from using the stamps. Colonial representatives formed a Stamp Act Congress, which protested the law. Newspapers, like the one at left, criticized the Stamp Act.

The Boston Massacre and the Boston Tea Party

Parliament finally repealed the Stamp Act, but they passed a law saying that they had the right to tax the colonies. Conflict continued as Parliament passed more laws. American protesters pressured business owners and government officials. They convinced people to stop buying products from Britain. On March 5, 1770, a mob of protestors came in contact with British troops stationed in Boston. The two groups of men insulted one another. They threw rocks and snowballs. As seen in the drawing at right, the British troops also fired shots. When the fight was over, five American colonists were dead and eight were hurt. The first man to die was Crispus Attucks, an African American. Americans called the incident the Boston Massacre.

The Boston Massacre

The British soldiers were brought to trial. Future President John Adams was the defense attorney for the British soldiers. Adams helped make the trial fair. He blamed both sides. He called the Americans a "motley rabble," but he also condemned British policies that angered Americans.

Another act by the British Parliament made Americans angry. In 1773 Parliament passed the Tea Act, allowing the East India Company to sell cheap tea in the colonies. Americans were afraid the colonies would become dependent on this tea and that the East India Company would become too powerful. In many ports, Americans refused to let the tea be delivered or they locked up the tea so it could not be sold. On December 16, 1773, Americans dressed up like Indians boarded three British ships, as seen on page 129. Crowds on shore cheered as the men dumped tea into Boston harbor. This was called the Boston Tea Party.

Boston Tea Party

Parliament punished Massachusetts. They wanted the punishment to scare the other colonies. They passed the Coercive Acts in 1774. Colonists called them the Intolerable Acts. The Coercive Acts kept Boston merchants from exporting and importing products. This backfired on Great Britain. Instead of becoming afraid, people in other colonies got angry and supported Boston.

The First Continental Congress

In September of 1774, delegates from all of the colonies except Georgia met at Carpenter's Hall in Philadelphia. This meeting was called the Continental Congress. Delegates condemned the Coercive Acts. Some colonists began to collect weapons and ammunition. They wanted to be ready to defend themselves, their families, and their possessions if the British government tried to hurt them.

The population in the colonies was growing. In 1700 about 250,000 people lived there. By 1750 the population was one million. By 1775 it was 2.5 million. England itself had only five million people.

What Was Happening in Other Parts of America?

Pirate

We have learned in this lesson what was happening along the Atlantic coast of America. What was happening in other places?

1700 through 1774 — Some Native American tribes continued to live the way they had before Europeans began to move to America, while others began to trade with Europeans and to adopt their customs.

Early 1700s — Pirates, like the one pictured at left, robbed and committed acts of violence off the Atlantic coast.

1718 — The Spanish established San Antonio, which is now in Texas.

1728 — Russians had first begun looking for land in the North Pacific Ocean in the 900s. Danish navigator Vitus Bering, pictured at right, sailed toward Alaska while on an expedition for Russian Czar Peter the Great in 1728. Bering made further explorations in the region in 1741.

1744 — Spanish Franciscan missionaries built a church in San Antonio. It later became known as the Alamo.

1767 — Daniel Boone made his first trip through the Cumberland Gap of the Appalachian Mountains into the western wilderness.

Vitus Bering

1775 — The British forced French settlers in Acadia (now the Maritime Provinces of eastern Canada) to leave their homes. Many came to the area around New Orleans. The Cajuns of Louisiana are descendants of these Acadians. See the illustration below.

1776 — The Spanish built a mission and military post near San Francisco Bay. They named it for Saint Francis of Assisi.

The British government did not show respect for the Acadians, nor for the colonists. Soon the British would pay a price for that lack of respect. In any conflict each person should honor God's teachings in James:

The British forced Acadians from their homes.

This you know, my beloved brethren.
But everyone must be
quick to hear, slow to speak
and slow to anger;
for the anger of man
does not achieve the righteousness of God.
James 1:19-20

Activities for Lesson 23

Timeline – In *Timeline of America the Beautiful* next to 1732, write: Russian Mikhail Gvozdev and his crew explore Alaska.

Literature – Read "The Evening of the 5th of March" in *We the People*, page 21, and chapters 19-20 in *The Sign of the Beaver*.

Vocabulary – In your notebook, write your own definition for each of these words: resentment, regulate, backfire, rabble, represent. Look in the lesson for clues to the meaning of each word. When you are finished writing your definitions, look in a dictionary for comparison.

Family Activity – Have a peaceful Boston Tea Party. See the instructions on page 423.

Student Workbook or Lesson Review – If you are using one of these optional books, complete the assignment for Lesson 23.

Benjamin Franklin, Scientist and Statesman

Benjamin Franklin was a printer, author, inventor, scientist, and philosopher. He served America as a statesman and a diplomat. When Franklin died in Philadelphia in 1790, his funeral was attended by 20,000 people.

Benjamin Franklin has become one of America's most famous historic figures. In 1847 when the U.S. Post Office began to use its first adhesive stamps, Benjamin Franklin's face was on the five-cent stamp. From 1948 to 1963 Franklin was on U.S. half-dollar coins. His face is now on our one hundred dollar bills. America has many towns, counties, and schools named for him. Notice the portrait of Franklin at right and his statue below. What was the secret of the success of Benjamin Franklin?

Franklin Portrait by Antoine Maurin

Franklin's Youth

Benjamin Franklin was born in Boston, Massachusetts, in 1706. His father Josiah Franklin had seventeen children. His mother Abiah Folger Franklin was Josiah's second wife. Benjamin was his father's fifteenth child and his tenth son. Josiah was a candlemaker by trade.

Young Benjamin attended school in Boston from age eight to ten. Throughout his life he continued to study, investigate, and educate himself. His readings as a boy included *Pilgrim's Progress* by British preacher John Bunyan and *Essays to Do Good* by American preacher Cotton Mather. At age ten, Benjamin Franklin began to work for his father. When he was thirteen, his brother James brought a printing press from England. Benjamin became his apprentice.

In 1721 James began the *New England Courant* newspaper. Benjamin, at only fifteen years of age, wrote for it at night and delivered it in the daytime. Benjamin wrote a column in which he pretended to be the widow of a minister. He called himself Silence Dogood.

Franklin Statue in the United States Capitol

Benjamin soon had disagreements with his brother. At age seventeen, Benjamin left Boston and moved to Philadelphia. There he became friends with the colonial Governor of Pennsylvania, Sir William Keith. Governor Keith encouraged Benjamin to go to London to get more training as a printer and to open his own printing business. Benjamin decided to do so and arrived in London in December 1724. He was eighteen years old. In London Benjamin got employment at two printing houses.

Franklin in His Working Years

In 1726 when Benjamin Franklin was twenty years old, he returned to Philadelphia. Two years later he opened his own print shop. See the print shop illustration on page 133. When he was twenty-three, he bought the struggling *Pennsylvania Gazette* newspaper.

Franklin married Deborah Read two years later. Deborah ran a general store in the front of the print shop. Benjamin and Deborah were married for forty-four years. They had two children, Francis and Sarah.

In 1731, when Franklin was only twenty-six, he founded a library in Philadelphia. The next year Benjamin Franklin published the first edition of his *Poor Richard's Almanac.*

Franklin wrote funny and practical sayings in his *Almanac*, using the pen name Richard Saunders. It became popular in the colonies and was published for twenty-six years. Americans still quote from *Poor Richard's Almanac.*

In 1736, at age thirty, Franklin began to work as the clerk of the Pennsylvania General Assembly. He also founded a volunteer fire department called the Union Fire Company. In 1737 he became Postmaster of Philadelphia. In 1743 Franklin co-founded the American Philosophical Society. It promoted the pursuit of knowledge and community service.

In 1748 Franklin sold his successful printing business. At age forty-two, he retired a wealthy man and was able to pursue his intellectual, political, and scientific interests. See Franklin's portrait on page 133.

Franklin – Candlemaker, Author, Printer, Experimenter with Electricity, Reader, Investigator of Ocean Currents, Statesman, and Paris Socialite

Franklin in His Retirement Years

Franklin spent his retirement years avidly pursuing his chosen interests, while continuing to be a public servant. See the illustration on page 132. In 1752 in Philadelphia, he organized the first effective fire insurance company in the United States. It is still in operation.

Franklin began to experiment with electricity when he was forty-one years old. In 1752 he performed a very dangerous experiment to prove that lightning is a form of electricity. Many people have died trying to do the same experiment! His discoveries and writings about electricity brought him honors in Great Britain, including honorary degrees from Oxford and the University of St. Andrews.

In 1753 Franklin became the postmaster general for the thirteen colonies. In 1754 during the conflict leading up to the French and Indian War, Franklin wrote the Albany Plan of Union. This proposal suggested that all of the colonies be united under one government. The Albany Plan was never adopted, but it has similarities to the United States Constitution that was later adopted in 1787.

In 1757 Franklin went to Europe to represent the interests of the colonies. From then until 1764, he spent most of his time in England and France. As he traveled on ships, he studied ocean currents and made discoveries about the Gulf Stream. Franklin loved music and played the violin, harp, and guitar. While in Europe, he invented the Glass Armonica, a musical instrument that became very popular there. Mozart and Beethoven later wrote music for the instrument.

In England, Benjamin Franklin helped convince Parliament to repeal the Stamp Act and some of the Townshend Acts, but he was unable to reconcile the conflict between Great Britain and its American colonies. He came home to Philadelphia on May 5, 1775, at age 69.

Franklin had served his country, been successful in business, and invented several

Illustration of Franklin's Printshop in Philadelphia

In this portrait, Franklin was portrayed as a man who pursued knowledge. Notice the electrical storm visible through the window.

useful objects. Still, some of his most important work would be accomplished in the last fifteen years of his life. Franklin continued to serve America as its conflict with Great Britain worsened. In 1776 he returned to Europe, where he represented American interests over the next ten years. Franklin came back to America in 1785 at age seventy-nine. Look at the illustration below. In his eighties, he helped America create its present form of government when he worked on creating the U.S. Constitution.

Franklin, a Man of Faith

Benjamin Franklin believed in God, believed that God should be worshiped, and believed the soul to be immortal. He believed that the best way to serve God was to serve people. In 1787, when he helped write the U.S. Constitution at the Constitutional Convention, he formally asked that preachers come to the meetings and offer a prayer each morning. He evidently believed in miracles because he wrote:

> We hear of the conversion of water into wine at the marriage in Cana as of a miracle. But this conversion is, through the goodness of God, made every day before our eyes. Behold the rain which descends from heaven upon our vineyards; there it enters the roots of the vines, to be changed into wine; a constant proof that God loves us, and loves to see us happy. The miracle in question was only performed to hasten the operation, under circumstances of present necessity, which required it.

Benjamin Franklin returned to America in 1785. Find these things in the picture: Benjamin Franklin with cane, men in three-corned hats, women wearing bonnets, two African American servants, and a sedan chair. Benjamin Franklin sometimes rode in a sedan chair.

During Franklin's lifetime, he invented swim fins, bifocals, a lightning rod, an extension arm, a special library chair, and the Franklin stove. He did not patent any of his inventions. He simply wanted them to be helpful to his fellow man.

Franklin was a man of diligence, as illustrated by the pictures at right. In Proverbs, King Solomon teaches the importance of being diligent:

The plans of the diligent lead surely to advantage,
but everyone who is hasty
comes surely to poverty.
Proverbs 21:5

Editing and Writing

Founding a Library in Philadelphia

Activities for Lesson 24

Thinking Biblically – Read John 2:1-11, about Jesus' miracle of changing water into wine.

Timeline – In *Timeline of America the Beautiful* next to 1753, write: Benjamin Franklin becomes postmaster general for the thirteen colonies.

Literature – Read "Autobiography and Poor Richard's Almanack" in *We the People*, pages 22-23, and chapters 21-23 in *The Sign of the Beaver*.

Creative Writing – In your notebook, write one or more paragraphs about why Benjamin Franklin was able to accomplish so much in his life and what we can learn from him.

Experimenting with Electricity

Student Workbook or Lesson Review – If you are using one of these optional books, complete the assignment for Lesson 24.

Colonial Williamsburg, Capital of Virginia

In 1633 English colonists settled on a peninsula between the James and York Rivers in Virginia. They named their settlement Middle Plantation. It became the capital of Virginia in 1699 and was renamed Williamsburg to honor England's King William III. The town grew into a center of culture and social activity. During the controversy between Great Britain and its American colonies, great political debates were held in Williamsburg.

Colonial Williamsburg, Living History Museum

Today Williamsburg is home to the world's largest outdoor history museum, Colonial Williamsburg. Colonial Williamsburg has over 120 buildings. Many have been restored to the way they looked in the 1700s, while others have been reconstructed on their original sites.

The State Capitol Building

A main attraction in Colonial Williamsburg is the state capitol, pictured at right. It was rebuilt to look as it did in 1705 when it still served as the colonial capitol.

The first representative assembly in the American colonies was in Virginia. It was called the House of Burgesses. It met for the first time on July 30, 1619, in Jamestown. The people elected to serve as representatives were called burgesses. Each Virginia county had two burgesses; Williamsburg, Jamestown, Norfolk, and the

Reconstructed State Capitol

Inside the State Capitol

College of William and Mary had one burgess each. The other members of the House of Burgesses were the Virginia Governor, who was appointed by the King of England, and the Governor's council. The burgesses were given the right to make laws, but the Governor and his council could veto them. The House of Burgesses began meeting in Williamsburg after it became the capital of Virginia. (Richmond became the capital of Virginia in 1780.)

American patriots Patrick Henry, Thomas Jefferson, and George Washington all served in the House of Burgesses. Each of them became involved in the protest against Great Britain's treatment of the colonies. When Patrick Henry opposed the Stamp Act of 1765, he encouraged the House of Burgesses to pass several resolutions which condemned taxes that were not passed by colonists themselves. The House of Burgesses led the effort that resulted in the First Continental Congress. After Great Britain punished the city of Boston for the Boston Tea Party, the burgesses declared a day of prayer in support of the city.

The College of William and Mary

Williamsburg is home to America's second oldest college, the College of William and Mary, founded in 1693. Its charter was granted by King William III and Queen Mary II of England. Its original purpose was the training of Anglican priests. The kings of England supported the college until 1776. Future Presidents Thomas Jefferson, James Monroe, and John Tyler were educated there. Classes are still held in the college's most famous building, the Christopher Wren Building, which was built in 1695. See the photographs below.

Chapel Inside the Christopher Wren Building

Christopher Wren Building at the College of Wiliam and Mary

Peyton Randolph House

Visitors to Colonial Williamsburg can visit the home of Peyton Randolph. Randolph was born in Williamsburg in 1721 and later attended the College of William and Mary. He served in the House of Burgesses for twenty-seven years and was its Speaker from 1765 until his death in 1775. Randolph strongly opposed the way Great Britain treated colonists, and he worked to end British injustices. He served as president of the First Continental Congress.

Raleigh Tavern

Several members of the House of Burgesses joined together in 1769 to oppose the Townshend Acts passed by the British Parliament. These laws required colonists to pay duties on lead, paint, paper, and tea. The acts also changed some ways the colonies were governed. The House of Burgesses passed resolutions against the Townshend Acts. The colonial Governor at that time was Governor Botetourt. When he heard about the resolutions,

Governor's Palace

he dissolved the House of Burgesses. They began meeting at Raleigh Tavern. Look at the picture on page 139. While meeting at Raleigh Tavern, George Washington introduced a

Bruton Parish Church

resolution calling for a boycott of several imported products until the Townshend duties were taken away. Several of the burgesses, including Thomas Jefferson, signed a pledge of action, agreeing to Washington's resolution.

The last colonial Governor of Virginia was Lord John Murray Dunmore. Though he also dissolved the House of Burgesses in 1772, 1773, and 1774, they continued to meet. See the photo of the Governor's Palace above.

Daily Life in Colonial Williamsburg

Colonial residents of Williamsburg went to the theater. The first theater in America was built there in 1716. They read the *Virginia Gazette*, Virginia's first newspaper. It was established in Williamsburg in 1736. Villagers traveled in carriages on cobblestone streets. They strolled in the town's beautiful English-style gardens. They attended services at Bruton Parish Church, pictured above. The church was constructed in 1715. Members of the community could trade in small shops run by craftsmen such as boot-makers, silversmiths, blacksmiths, and jewelry-makers. They could buy remedies at the apothecary. See the picture on page 139.

Modern visitors to Colonial Williamsburg meet museum staff dressed in historic costumes. Tourists can watch demonstrations of colonial crafts and activities. Notice the man working in the woodshop at right.

Williamsburg Woodshop

Actors portray a scene at Raleigh Tavern.

Restoring Williamsburg

Work to restore Colonial Williamsburg began in 1926. American philanthropist John D. Rockefeller Jr. provided major funding for the project. A philanthropist is a wealthy person who gives large amounts of money to help people in need or to support educational or

Historic Actors at the Williamsburg Apothecary

cultural activities. John D. Rockefeller Sr. became wealthy in the petroleum business during the 1800s. He created the Rockefeller Foundation, which gave money to charities. His son, John D. Rockefeller Jr., continued the charitable work of his father. Williamsburg has been a popular tourist attraction since its restoration began.

The Rockefellers blessed future generations with their kind charity. Paul told Timothy:

Instruct those who are rich in this present world not to be conceited or to fix their hope on the uncertainty of riches, but on God who richly supplies us with all things to enjoy. Instruct them to do good, to be rich in good works, to be generous and ready to share.
1 Timothy 6:17-18

Activities for Lesson 25

Map Study – Complete the assignment for Lesson 25 on Map 3 "American Landmarks" in *Maps of America the Beautiful*.

Timeline – In *Timeline of America the Beautiful* next to 1926, write: Work begins to restore Colonial Williamsburg.

Vocabulary – In your notebook, write each sentence below, filling in each blank with one of these words: peninsula, controversy, charter, philanthropist, petroleum

1. The visitor from the oil refinery explained how _____ is collected.
2. Ponce de León and his crew thought Florida was an island and tried to sail around it, but they couldn't because it is a _____.
3. The original _____ was signed by the eight founders of the university.
4. After years of spending money on luxuries, the millionaire became a _____ later in life.
5. The teachers tried to work together, but their different teaching styles caused _____ between them.

Literature – Read "Advertisements in the *Virginia Gazette*" in *We the People*, page 24, and chapters 24-25 in *The Sign of the Beaver*.

Student Workbook or Lesson Review – If you are using one of these optional books, complete the assignment for Lesson 25. If you are using the Lesson Review, answer the questions on *The Sign of the Beaver* and take the quiz for Unit 5.

Actors demonstrate lawn bowling on the green at Colonial Williamsburg.

The American Revolution

In 1775 war erupted between the American colonies and England. The first two lessons this week are a timeline of the American Revolutionary War. The war ended near the shore of one of God's Wonders, Chesapeake Bay. Our American Landmark this week is historic Boston, where many revolutionary leaders lived and where important events occurred. The week ends with a lesson about early American crafts that women did at home.

Lessons in Unit 6

Lesson 26 – Our American Story: From Lexington to Yorktown,
　　　　　Timeline of the Revolution (Part 1)
Lesson 27 – Our American Story: From Lexington to Yorktown,
　　　　　Timeline of the Revolution (Part 2)
Lesson 28 – God's Wonders: God Created Chesapeake Bay
Lesson 29 – An American Landmark: Historic Boston
Lesson 30 – Daily Life: Early American Home Crafts

Books Used in Unit 6

- *Maps of America the Beautiful*

- *Timeline of America the Beautiful*

- *We the People*

- *Amos Fortune: Free Man* by Elizabeth Yates

*Lighthouses Along Chesapeake Bay
at Cape Henry, Virginia*

From Lexington to Yorktown, Timeline of the Revolution (Part 1)

After the First Continental Congress met in Philadelphia in September of 1774, the British Parliament declared Massachusetts to be in rebellion. Great Britain took away the colonies' right to trade with any country not in the British Empire and their right to fish in the North Atlantic. The colonists took action. Each colony formed a militia. They collected weapons and ammunition. Groups of Minute Men organized in some of the New England colonies, volunteering to fight at a minute's notice.

England's King George and Parliament refused to compromise with the colonies. They arrogantly believed that an American Army could be quickly defeated. Step by step the American colonies and their mother country headed toward war. Lessons 26 and 27 are a timeline of that war, which is called the American Revolutionary War. In these lessons, we find out about key people and events and when and where these events took place.

Patrick Henry

1775 – War Begins

March 23, Richmond, Virginia – Because Virginia's House of Burgesses supported Massachusetts, their royal Governor dismissed the body. At first they kept meeting in Raleigh Tavern in Williamsburg, but the burgesses were afraid they would be found guilty of treason against Great Britain. They found a place to meet a few miles away—St. John's Episcopal Church in tiny Richmond, Virginia. When they met on March 23, 1775, George Washington and Thomas Jefferson were among those in attendance. A young lawyer named Patrick Henry, shown at left, gave a moving speech. He encouraged the burgesses to stand up to England. During the speech, he declared, "Give me liberty or give me death!"

April 19, Lexington and Concord, Massachusetts – Thomas Gage, royal Governor of Massachusetts, told British troops to go to Lexington to arrest two American patriots, Samuel Adams and John Hancock, and to go to Concord to seize the American weapons stored there. During the evening of April 18, British troops left Boston by boat. Soon they came back to land and began to march into the country. Patriots found out and sent Paul Revere, pictured on page 143, and William Dawes to warn Adams, Hancock, and the local militias. Dr. Samuel Prescott and other riders also spread the word.

On the morning of April 19, British troops met the local patriot militia and killed several Americans at the Battle of Lexington.

Minute Man Statue in Concord, Massachusetts

Later that day, British troops and Massachusetts militia fought in the Battle of Concord. This time the militia triumphed and the British retreated to Boston. The militia continued to fight while the British retreated. What happened that day in Concord and Lexington is called "the shot heard 'round the world." Minute Men fought bravely and are honored today in Minute Man National Historical Park in Concord. See statue at left. These were the first battles of the war.

Paul Revere

May 10, Philadelphia, Pennsylvania – The angry colonists sent representatives to a Second Continental Congress which began meeting in Philadelphia on May 10. It acted as the colonies' legislature until 1789. During 1775 they elected John Hancock to serve as president of the congress, created a navy, began to seek foreign aid for their efforts, and chose George Washington to organize an army. In the 1800s, printmakers Currier and Ives created many prints depicting American scenes, including the illustration at right of Washington when he was appointed Commander-in-Chief.

June 17, Breed's Hill near Boston, Massachusetts – Breed's Hill and Bunker Hill were outside of Boston. The British had put Boston under martial law, so Americans built fortifications on Breed's Hill on June 16. The next morning, lines of British soldiers in their red coats marched up the hill. The

Washington is appointed Commander-in-Chief.

American officers told their troops to wait to fire on the British until they "saw the whites of their eyes." With great difficulty, the British finally took Breed's Hill. This battle is called the Battle of Bunker Hill, because both hills are part of an area called Bunker Hill.

August 23, London, England – King George III declared the colonies to be in a state of rebellion. By the time the king made this declaration, he was already arranging to pay German soldiers to fight with his British troops against the Americans. Since many of the paid German soldiers came from the Hesse-Kassel region, the German soldiers came to be called Hessians.

December 31, Quebec, Canada – Americans hoped that Canada would join their efforts against Britain, but they became enemies instead. Brigadier General Richard Montgomery led American troops north through the Lake Champlain area. They invaded Canada and captured Montreal. Meanwhile Major General Benedict Arnold led American troops through Maine. Both Montgomery and Arnold attacked Quebec but were unable to capture it.

1776 – Americans Declare Their Independence

January 10, Philadelphia – Thomas Paine published a pamphlet called "Common Sense." See pamphlet at right. It said that the colonies received no benefits from being part of the British Empire and called for a break with England. It sold 500,000 copies and convinced many Americans that they should fight for independence.

July 4, Philadelphia – While the Second Continental Congress was meeting during the summer, Richard Henry Lee of Virginia offered a resolution stating that

Title Page from Common Sense

"these united colonies are, and of right ought to be, free and independent states." The delegates selected Benjamin Franklin, Thomas Jefferson, John Adams, Robert Livingston, and Roger Sherman to draft a declaration of independence. See the picture at left. Jefferson did most of the writing. On July 4, 1776, the Continental Congress adopted the Declaration of Independence which they sent to King George.

Delegates Drafting the Declaration of Independence

August 27, New York City – British troops defeated American troops in the Battle of Long Island. After the battle, General Washington realized that his troops were in a vulnerable position and could easily be trapped. Some Massachusetts soldiers were familiar with boats through their work as Atlantic fishermen. Two nights later a Massachusetts regiment bravely ferried all of Washington's troops to safety on Manhattan Island. They used every kind of boat available, while the troops kept completely quiet. The British troops were surprised when they awoke the next morning and all of Washington's men had disappeared.

September 16, Manhattan Island, New York – American (also called Continental) soldiers won the Battle of Harlem Heights. The battle happened at what is now Broadway and 106th Street in Manhattan. This victory boosted American morale.

September 22, New York – Twenty-one year old Nathan Hale volunteered to serve as a spy for General Washington. After completing his assignment, Hale started back to the American Army. He was captured by the British. Before he was executed as a spy, Hale spoke eloquently about his desire to do his duty. According to some reports, one thing he said was, "I only regret that I have but one life to lose for my country."

Though successful at first, American troops soon had to leave Manhattan; and the British took control of New York City.

October 26, Philadelphia – The Second Continental Congress assigned Benjamin Franklin, Silas Deane, and Arthur Lee the job of getting European nations to help the Americans in their effort to win independence from Great Britain.

October 28, New York – British commander General William Howe and his British troops defeated General Washington and his Continentals in the Battle of White Plains. Howe's 13,000 troops could have pursued Washington and his 2,000 men, but Howe hesitated and Washington was able to cross the Hudson River and enter New Jersey. Howe lost a chance to defeat the Americans soundly and perhaps end the Revolutionary War.

December 23, Philadelphia – Thomas Paine began publishing a series of pamphlets called "The Crisis." The first pamphlet began with the words, "These are the times that try men's souls." The series encouraged revolutionaries to continue their struggle for independence. George Washington ordered that the first pamphlet of "The Crisis" be read to his troops.

Washington Crossing the Delaware, *an 1851 painting by Emanuel Leutze*

December 25-26, Delaware and New Jersey – The Massachusetts regiment again used their boating skills when Washington and his troops crossed the icy Delaware River on Christmas Day. See the painting above. The Americans surprised Britain's Hessian soldiers the next day, defeating them in the Battle of Trenton. In the illustration on page 146, Washington inspects the colors (flags) his Army captured in the battle.

Nathan Hale and others loved their country and were willing to die to help make it free. Jesus showed His love for the whole world when He died to make us spiritually free. In Romans, Paul wrote:

For while we were still helpless, at the
right time Christ died for the ungodly.
For one will hardly die for a righteous man;
though perhaps for the good man
someone would dare even to die.
But God demonstrates
his own love toward us,
in that while we were yet sinners,
Christ died for us.
Romans 5:6-8

Washington Inspects the Colors After the Battle of Trenton

Activities for Lesson 26

Map Study – Complete the assignments for Lesson 26 on Map 10 "Battles of the American Revolution" in *Maps of America the Beautiful*.

Timeline – In *Timeline of America the Beautiful* next to 1775, write: Patrick Henry declares, "Give me liberty or give me death!"

Literature – Read "The Declaration of Independence" in *We the People*, page 25, and the chapter titled "Africa 1725" in *Amos Fortune: Free Man*.

Student Workbook or Lesson Review – If you are using one of these optional books, complete the assignment for Lesson 26.

From Lexington to Yorktown, Timeline of the Revolution (Part 2)

1777 – Battles in the North and in the Mid-Atlantic

January 3, Princeton, New Jersey – British General Charles Cornwallis prepared to attack the Continentals in New Jersey, but Washington quickly and quietly led his troops to safety, leaving their campfires burning. When the Americans came upon a British regiment marching to help Cornwallis, they attacked them and won the Battle of Princeton.

June 14, Philadelphia – Congress adopted the Stars and Stripes. They declared that the American flag would have thirteen stripes of alternating red and white and thirteen stars on a field of blue. During 1777 Congress also commissioned twenty-year-old French volunteer Marquis de Lafayette as a major general. He became a close aide to General Washington and a member of his staff. See the illustration below.

July 6, Near Lake Champlain in New York – Ethan Allen and Colonel Benedict Arnold led the "Green Mountain Boys" from Vermont. In 1775 they had captured Fort Ticonderoga from the British. During the July 6, 1777, Battle of Ticonderoga, British General John Burgoyne recaptured the fort. Though Burgoyne and his men were victorious the next day in the Battle of Hubbardton, they met strong resistance from Vermont's Green Mountain Boys.

August 16, Bennington, Vermont – Burgoyne sent Hessian soldiers and Native Americans under German Colonel Friedrich Baum to capture American supplies at Bennington. Vermont and New Hampshire forces defeated them.

September 11 and October 4, Pennsylvania – Great Britain's General William Howe and General Charles Cornwallis

The First Meeting of Lafayette and Washington

defeated General Washington's Continentals in the Battle of Brandywine Creek. Afterwards, the British took control of Philadelphia. The Continental Congress had to flee the city. On October 4, Washington surprised British forces at nearby Germantown. Other American commanders involved were General Nathanael Greene and General "Mad" Anthony Wayne. Though they lost the battle, Americans were encouraged that Washington could attack again so soon after the defeat at Brandywine. Lafayette was wounded in the battle.

September-October, Saratoga, New York – British General John Burgoyne led an army from Canada into New York. The British wanted to take control of the Hudson River, cut off New England from the rest of the colonies, and force the Americans to stop fighting. Along the way, his forces had already fought the Americans at Ticonderoga, Hubbardton, and Bennington. As Burgoyne continued south on September 19, American General Horatio Gates and his 7,000 men fought him at Freeman's Farm. Neither side won this First Battle of Saratoga. Gates again fought Burgoyne, his British and Hessian soldiers, and their Native American allies on October 7. Americans won in this Second Battle of Saratoga. The British withdrew, but American troops surrounded their army. Burgoyne surrendered to Gates on October 17. This victory convinced France to support the

Americans in the war. The American victory at Saratoga is considered the turning point in the American Revolution. No longer did the British dominate the war.

Winter of 1777-1778, Valley Forge, Pennsylvania – American soldiers suffered from a lack of food and clothing during a cold winter at Valley Forge, Pennsylvania. The illustration at right of General Washington in prayer was created in 1853.

General Washington Praying at Valley Forge

1778 – British Fight in America and Europe

March 16, London – Three days after the French ambassador informed Great Britain that France would officially recognize the United States, the British formed a peace commission to send to the Continental Congress in Philadelphia. The British commission agreed to all American demands except independence. Congress rejected the offer.

April 22-23, Whitehaven, England – Commanding the American ship USS *Range*, American Admiral John Paul Jones carried the war to the island of Great Britain when he attacked a British port at Whitehaven in England. See the picture of Jones on page 149.

June 28, Monmouth, New Jersey – Washington and his troops fought the British at the Battle of Monmouth. Neither side won decisively, but the British withdrew.

July 2, Philadelphia – British forces withdrew from Philadelphia in June after learning that France had entered the war. The Continental Congress returned to the city on July 2. In 1776 Richard Henry Lee had proposed the formation of a union among the thirteen states. For well over a year Congress had been working on a written document to govern their union. The final copy of the Articles of Confederation was ready for delegates to sign on July 9, 1778.

John Paul Jones

July 4-6, Kaskaskia and Cahokia on the Mississippi River – Both American and British forces vied for control of former French territory along the Mississippi River. Frontiersman George Rogers Clark, who had recently founded a settlement at what would later become Louisville, Kentucky, led troops who captured the river settlements of Kaskaskia and Cahokia.

July 8, West Point, New York – General George Washington set up a headquarters for his Continental Army at West Point. Polish engineer Tadeusz Kościuszko helped significantly in building its fortifications.

December 29, Georgia – British Redcoats captured Savannah, Georgia.

1779 – American Successes

February 23-24, Vincennes on the Wabash River – George Rogers Clark captured the French town of Vincennes on the Wabash River. Today the Wabash forms part of the border between Indiana and Illinois.

July 8 and 11, Connecticut – British forces burned the Connecticut settlements of Fairfield and Norwalk.

July 15-16, King's Ferry, New York – With permission from General Washington, American General "Mad" Anthony Wayne carried out a careful plan to surprise British forces at King's Ferry, New York. He captured Fort Stony Point along with 543 prisoners.

August 19, Paulus Hook, New Jersey – "Lighthorse Harry" Lee , a Continental calvary commander (and distant relative of Richard Henry Lee), led a surprise attack on British forces in Paulus Hook, New Jersey. Paulus Hook is now Jersey City.

September 23, Coast of England – John Paul Jones and the crew of the *Bonhomme Richard* approached *Serapis,* a British man-of-war (a type of military ship). The British demanded that Jones surrender, but he replied, "I have not yet begun to fight." The Americans captured the vessel.

1780 – Battles in the South

May 12, Charleston, South Carolina – Continental forces in Charleston suffered the greatest loss of American troops during the war when they surrendered to the British.

July 11, Newport, Rhode Island – French troops landed at Newport, Rhode Island, to come to the aid of the Continental Army.

August 16, Near Camden, South Carolina – From May to August, both sides won minor battles, but the British won the major Battle of Camden in South Carolina.

September 25, West Point, New York – American General Benedict Arnold's treason was discovered. Arnold had been conspiring against the Americans since May of 1779. He was commander of West Point and had planned to give it into the hands of the British. His treason was revealed when Americans captured a British messenger. Arnold escaped capture by the Americans, and Great Britain made him a brigadier general. He continued to fight in the Revolution, but now he fought against America.

October 7, Kings Mountain, South Carolina – Despite King George's 1763 Proclamation, small settlements of colonists lived west of the Appalachian Mountains in what is now Tennessee. John Sevier and Isaac Shelby led Tennessee riflemen, called "Overmountain Boys," over the Appalachians to fight the British. In a sixty-five-minute battle, they defeated one-third of General Cornwallis' army.

1781 – Victory for the Colonies

January 17, Cowpens, South Carolina – Continental troops led by American General Daniel Morgan surprised British General Cornwallis at Cowpens in South Carolina. Cowpens was so named because it was once used for cattle roundups.

March 15, Guilford Courthouse, North Carolina – Though the British won the Battle of Guilford Courthouse, General Nathanael Greene began to wear down British forces. He used hit and run tactics and made the British fight where Greene decided.

August 1, Yorktown, Virginia – British General Charles Cornwallis established a base at Yorktown, Virginia.

September 5-8, Chesapeake Bay, Off the Coast of Yorktown, Virginia – The French Navy ousted the British Navy when twenty-nine French warships defeated thirty-three British warships. The British warships retreated, leaving Cornwallis and his troops trapped in Yorktown.

September 28 - October 19, Yorktown, Virginia – After confrontations lasting almost a month, General Cornwallis surrendered to General Washington on October 19, 1781. The British soldiers laid down their weapons, and their army band played an old Scottish song called "The World Turned Upside Down." See the Currier and Ives illustration on page 151 entitled "Surrender of Cornwallis."

After six years of war, the British finally conceded that they could not defeat the Americans. In 1782 peace negotiations began in Paris, France. On November 30 of that year, Benjamin Franklin and John Adams signed a preliminary agreement with Great Britain stating that the American colonies were now independent from Great Britain. The final peace agreement was called the Treaty of Paris. The United States Congress ratified the treaty on April 15, 1783.

Americans were thankful for their victory at the end of the American Revolution. The apostle John wrote about the most important victory:

For this is the love of God, that we keep His commandments;
and His commandments are not burdensome.
For whatever is born of God overcomes the world;
and this is the victory that has overcome the world–our faith.
1 John 5:3-4

Activities for Lesson 27

Map Study – Complete the assignments for Lesson 27 on Map 10 "Battles of the American Revolution" in *Maps of America the Beautiful*.

Timeline – In *Timeline of America the Beautiful* next to 1777, write: Congress adopts the Stars and Stripes flag.

Literature – Read "Letter from Valley Forge" in *We the People*, page 26, and the chapter titled "The Middle Passage" in *Amos Fortune: Free Man*.

Creative Writing – After reading the letter from Nathanael Greene in *We the People*, write an imaginary reply from Joseph Webb to Nathanael Greene in your notebook.

Student Workbook or Lesson Review – If you are using one of these optional books, complete the assignment for Lesson 27.

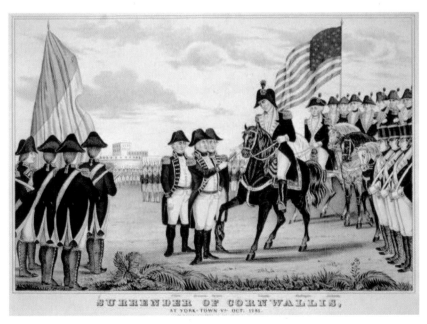

Currier and Ives Illustration of the Surrender of Cornwallis

God Created Chesapeake Bay

Along the coast of Maryland and Virginia, God created a large inlet called Chesapeake Bay. Chesapeake Bay is an estuary. An estuary is a coastal area where saltwater from an

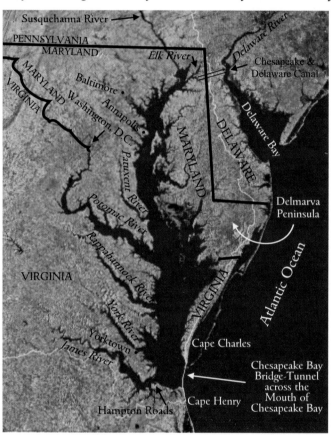

Satellite Image of Chesapeake Bay, United States Geological Survey

ocean mixes with freshwater from rivers. Half of the world's ocean life lives in estuaries. Chesapeake Bay is the largest estuary in the United States and one of the largest in the world. Examine the satellite image of it at left.

God created the world so that all plants and animals depend on one another. He created the perfect habitat for each living being. As in other areas where water and land meet, God brings many habitats together in and around Chesapeake Bay.

Riding a Boat Up Chesapeake Bay

This lesson will take you on an imaginary boat ride northward from the mouth of Chesapeake Bay to the head of the bay in Maryland. First, you will pass between Virginia's Cape Henry and Cape Charles. A cape is a piece of land that juts into a lake, sea, or ocean. Cape Charles is at the tip of the Delmarva Peninsula. A peninsula is similar to a cape, only much larger. Delmarva is named for Delaware, Maryland, and Virginia, since a portion of each state is on this peninsula.

When you first enter Chesapeake Bay, you see a highway that goes over a bridge and then disappears into a tunnel beneath the bay. The road rises again onto another bridge, and then enters a tunnel again! This is the twenty-three-mile-long Chesapeake Bay Bridge-Tunnel. The bridge-tunnel allows cars to cross between the capes while still allowing ships to enter the bay.

Your boat is floating on a bay containing fifteen trillion gallons of water. About half is saltwater from the Atlantic. The other half is freshwater from underground streams and from about 150 above-ground rivers and streams that empty into the bay. During a winter cruise, your first wildlife sighting could be a migrating whale. In summer, you may see a bottle-nosed dolphin. Chesapeake Bay is shallow. The average depth of the water is twenty-one feet. Much of the bay is only a few feet deep, but the bay also has troughs as deep as 174 feet!

Raking in the Shallows, 1890

Aquatic Reefs in the Bay

Aquatic reefs lie at the bottom of parts of Chesapeake Bay. These form when eastern oysters pile on top of one another. The bottom of most of the bay is soft. Oyster reefs provide a hard surface where oyster larvae and other creatures can attach. Large fish visit these reefs, as do diamondback terrapins. Aquatic reefs provide habitat for hundreds of species, like sea squirts, boring sponges, redbeard sponges, and whip coral. Oysters and a redbeard sponge are pictured below.

Oysters filter bay water by pumping it through their gills. One oyster can filter 50 gallons a day. They ingest food as they do so. Anemones, sea nettles, blue crabs, oystercatchers (a shorebird), and other animals eat oysters. People do, too. Since the 1800s, bay residents have caught, shucked, packed, and shipped eastern oysters. Shucking is the the process of opening the oyster shell and removing the flesh from inside. The oyster industry is a rich part of the culture of the bay area. Look at the illustration of men raking for oysters above and the photograph of women shucking them at left.

Shucking Oysters in a Baltimore, Maryland, Oyster House, 1905

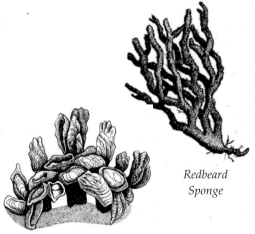

Redbeard Sponge

Oysters

153

The Open Waters of Chesapeake Bay

Sea Cucumber

While traveling over the deepest parts of the bay, you are in the open waters habitat. Aquatic reefs lie at the bottom. Tiny zooplankton and phytoplankton float on top, providing food for some bay creatures. Many kinds of fish live in the open waters. Hundreds of thousands of ducks hunt for fish here during the winter. Residents of the open waters include the brief squid, comb jellies, jellyfish, northern puffers, sea robins, and sea cucumbers. See the drawing above. Bufflehead ducks, pictured on page 157, spend winters on the open waters of the Chesapeake. They are the smallest diving ducks in North America.

The men at right have caught one open water resident, a striped bass. Since Colonial times, sportsmen have enjoyed catching this tasty, hard-fighting fish. Most striped bass living along the Atlantic coast began their long, ten- to thirty-year lives in one of the Chesapeake's streams or rivers. Young striped bass live two years in their nursery area before going to the open waters of the Chesapeake or to the Atlantic Ocean. Striped bass females lay more and more eggs as they get older. During the spawning season, a fifteen-year-old can lay three million eggs!

Fishermen with Striped Bass

Rivers and Streams of the Chesapeake Bay

While still in Virginia, your boat will pass the mouth of the James River. This region, including the last ten miles of the James River and the land around it, is known as Hampton Roads. The ports of Norfolk, Portsmouth, Newport News, and Hampton are along this Hampton Roads section.

Continuing northward, you will pass the mouths of the York, Rappahannock, and Potomac Rivers. As you pass the Potomac, you enter Maryland, since the Potomac River forms part of the Virginia-Maryland border. You could take a detour up the Potomac and pass Washington, D.C., and Mount Vernon, the home of George Washington. See the photo at left.

Aerial View of the Potomac and Mount Vernon

Chesapeake Bay depends on the rivers and streams that flow into it. These provide places for fish such as catfish and sunfish to live and places for migratory fish to lay their eggs. Rivers and streams also provide a habitat for creatures like snapping turtles, river otters, black-crowned night herons, and pumpkinseed fish, as well as a variety of worms, aquatic insects, salamanders, and frogs.

You may see fishermen as you ride up the Chesapeake. Some fish for American shad, a migratory fish. It is anadromous, which means that it migrates from the ocean to fresh water to lay its eggs. The American shad's scientific name means "most delicious." Native Americans taught

American Shad

Europeans how to catch these fish. In the American Revolutionary War, the shad was called the "savior fish" because it helped Washington's troops keep from starving at Valley Forge. During the Revolution, shad were nailed to boards, smoked, and salted to be eaten in winter. Local residents know when the shad are migrating through the Chesapeake Bay because the shadbush blooms at the same time. Area gardeners use shad for fertilizer. The American shad is illustrated above.

If your imaginary trip was in October, American eels would swim past your boat as they migrate south to spawn. Most American eels live in streams, ponds, or in fresh or brackish rivers of Chesapeake Bay (brackish water is a combination of saltwater and fresh). American eels are catadromous, meaning that they travel from fresh water to saltwater to lay their eggs. In October mature eels swim through the bay and into the Atlantic Ocean. They continue southward thousands of miles until they reach the Sargasso Sea, west of the Bahamas. There the females lay eggs, males fertilize them, and the eels die.

After the eggs hatch, the transparent eel larvae drift through the ocean for nine to twelve months. By the time they reach the mouth of Chesapeake Bay they have turned brown and the 2.4-inch eel babies have become elvers. Some stay in the bay, but most continue northward and enter a river or stream, swimming until they come to fresh water. American eels will slide over dams, rocks, and even wet grass to get to their destination. After they reach their habitat, they will grow into adults. Most return to the Bahamas when they are about five years old. Here they reproduce and then die, but some wait until they are fifteen to twenty years old before they return to the Bahamas. Eels are a delicacy in Asia and Europe. Few Americans eat eels, so most eels caught in Chesapeake Bay are exported. Look at the drawing at right.

American Eel

Forests of the Bay Area

A watershed is an area where rain and melted snow from higher elevations flow into rivers and streams. The Chesapeake Bay watershed encompasses portions of six states and all of the District of Columbia. Fifty-eight percent of the bay watershed is forested. Forests clean water before it enters rivers, streams, and groundwater. Forests also make rivers and streams cooler, so fish can have the right temperature to lay eggs. Bay area forests are home to bobcats, Delmarva fox squirrels, eastern screech-owls, northern red salamanders, copperheads, red foxes, and wild turkeys.

The Shallows of Chesapeake Bay

As you travel up the Chesapeake, you will notice its jagged shores. If you walked along the whole shoreline from Cape Henry to Cape Charles, you would walk over 11,500 miles!

Because of its twists and turns, Chesapeake Bay's coastline is longer than the whole west coast of the United States!

The waters near the shorelines with depths of ten feet or less are called shallows. The shallows are warm in summer and sometimes covered with ice in winter. Clams, crabs, fish, muskrats, waterfowl, worms, and microscopic plants and animals live in the shallows. Birds of prey, shorebirds, wading birds, and migrating birds find food in and around them.

Sixteen species of underwater bay grasses live in the Chesapeake Bay shallows. Where each grows depends on the saltiness of the water. Species of these grasses include coontail, curly pondweed, eelgrass,

Picking Crabs for Market on the Shores of the Chesapeake, 1909

redhead grass, water chestnut, and wild celery. Minnows eat the tiny organisms that live on the grasses. Some fish use underwater grassy areas as a place to lay their eggs.

The blue crab is one of the best known Chesapeake shellfish. Colors vary from olive to bluish green, but their claws are bright blue. Though found throughout the area, great

Blue Crab

numbers live in the shallows during summer and in deeper waters during winter. Fish, birds, and people like to eat blue crabs. The Chesapeake Bay yields millions of dollars worth of food each year. The blue crab harvest provides many of those dollars. Notice the blue crab at left and people picking crabs above. To "pick" a crab means to separate the usable parts from the parts that will be thrown away.

Unusual residents of the shallows include the Atlantic needlefish, hogchokers, the lined seahorse, and the cownose ray. Muted swans and tundra swans also live on the shallows. Diamondback terrapins do, too. Terrapin is an Algonquin Indian word referring to edible turtles that live in brackish waters. On rare occasions, bay visitors may spot a manatee feeding in the shallows of the Chesapeake.

Chesapeake Bay Wetlands

Duck Hunter with Chesapeake Bay Retriever

Chesapeake Bay has non-tidal wetlands with freshwater and tidal wetlands with saltwater and brackish water. Some wetlands are marshes that grow grasses, some are bogs that grow shrubs, and others are wooded swamps. Plants of bay wetlands include bald cypress, cattails, marsh hibiscus, saltmeadow cordgrass, and the shadbush. Waterfowl that live in Chesapeake Bay wetlands include American black ducks, snow geese, wood ducks, willets, and hooded mergansers. Look at the illustrations of birds on pages 157 and 158.

Bufflehead Ducks

American Black Ducks

Snow Geese

If you travel close to the shore, you may see a hunter with a Chesapeake Bay Retriever (or Chessie), hunting in a wetland. In 1807 residents of Maryland rescued two Newfoundland puppies from an English boat that wrecked along its coast. They were bred to local retrievers. The resulting breed is the Chesapeake Bay Retriever. Chessies are strong hunting dogs that can break through ice to retrieve a bird. Some can retrieve several hundred birds in a single day. See the Chesapeake Bay Retriever on page 156.

Traveling to the Head of the Bay

As you continue north, you will pass the mouth of the Patuxent River before reaching Annapolis on your port side (port means left). Annapolis is the state capital of Maryland. It is the home of the U.S. Naval Academy. Past Annapolis is Baltimore with its deepwater port.

Throughout your trip, you will enjoy the birds of the Chesapeake. Bald eagles live in many places. Bald eagles in the bay area tend to stay all their lives, and other eagles migrate there to spend the winter. Chesapeake Bay has the largest osprey population in the world. Two thousand pairs nest there each spring and stay for the summer. See the illustration below. Ducks, geese, swans, and songbirds visit the Chesapeake Bay while migrating.

Chesapeake Bay is narrow in some places and wide in others. It varies from four to 30 miles across. When you complete your 190-mile trip from the mouth of the Chesapeake to its head or top, you will see the mouth of the Susquehanna River. It is the longest river on America's Atlantic coast. When your boat reaches the head, you can turn east and enter the 19-mile-long Chesapeake and Delaware Canal. Americans built the canal (first opened in 1829) to cross the Delmarva Peninsula and connect the bay with the Delaware River. This canal allows boats to travel from the Chesapeake to Wilmington, Delaware, and on to Philadelphia, Pennsylvania.

The American Revolution In and Around Chesapeake Bay

Chesapeake Bay played an important role in two battles of the American Revolution. In June of 1777, an English fleet with 256 boats sailed south from Sandy Hook, New Jersey. When the fleet reached the Delmarva Peninsula, they sailed through the mouth of Chesapeake Bay and continued

Osprey in Foreground with Bald Eagle in Upper Right Corner

157

Wood Ducks

Willets

Hooded Mergansers

northward until they entered the Elk River in Maryland. After a 34-day voyage, they reached the Head of the Elk. There British General Howe and his 17,000 troops disembarked and marched toward Philadelphia. On September 11, 1777, American and British forces fought in the Battle of Brandywine, a creek twenty-five miles from Philadelphia. British forces won the battle and captured Philadelphia.

Four years later, French Admiral François Joseph Paul de Grasse brought twenty-nine French warboats into the bay. General George Washington commanded French and American troops near Yorktown, Virginia. Between the American troops and the French fleet were British Lieutenant General Charles Cornwallis and his British troops. The French warboats kept Cornwallis from retreating and prevented British warships from coming to his aid. As you learned in lesson 28, this was the last major battle of the American Revolution.

Chesapeake Bay is a beautiful place to see what God created on the fifth day, described by Moses in Genesis:

Then God said, "Let the waters teem with swarms of living creatures, and let birds fly above the earth in the open expanse of the heavens."
Genesis 1:20

Activities for Lesson 28

Map Study – Complete the assignments for Lesson 28 on Map 2 "God's Wonders" and Map 11 "Chesapeake Bay" in *Maps of America the Beautiful*.

Timeline – In *Timeline of America the Beautiful* next to 1829, write: The Chesapeake and Delaware Canal opens.

Vocabulary – Copy these words in your notebook, each on a separate line: satellite, aquatic, ingest, delicacy, watershed. Look up each in the dictionary. Next to each word, write what part or parts of speech it is.

Literature – Read the chapter titled "Boston 1725-1740" in *Amos Fortune: Free Man*.

Student Workbook or Lesson Review – If you are using one of these optional books, complete the assignment for Lesson 28.

Historic Boston

Cambridge, Massachusetts, and the Charles River in 1768 with Boston in the Distance

Modern Boston

Boston was the capital of the Massachusetts colony, and today it is the capital of the Commonwealth of Massachusetts. It was one of the largest cities in the colonies. Boston remained one of the top ten cities in America in each U.S. census taken from 1790 to 1950. In 1960, it was 13th and in 2000, it ranked 20th with a population of over 580,000 people. Compare the 1768 illustration of Boston above with the modern photograph.

Modern Tourists in Boston

A Walk on the Freedom Trail

Boston residents were some of the strongest protesters against Great Britain's colonial policies. The first battles of the Revolution were fought nearby. Today visitors to Boston can see many historic sites from Colonial and Revolutionary times. In 1958 Boston citizens organized a two-and-a-half mile Freedom Trail to preserve their city's history. The trail is marked by a red line of brick or paint. It leads visitors to important sites in historic Boston. The tourists at left are using a Freedom Trail map. Keep reading to find out what to see on the Freedom Trail.

1. The Freedom Trail begins at **Boston Common**. Dating from 1634, it is America's oldest city park. In Boston's early history, the area was designated as a place for cattle to graze. Look at the photograph of Boston Common on page 160.

2. Adjacent to the park is the **Massachusetts State House**. Shortly after the American Revolution, state leaders decided to build this grand new capitol for Massachusetts. It was completed in 1798.

Boston Common with Brewer Fountain and the Massachusetts State House in the distance on Beacon Hill

3. In 1804 Christians, including several from Old South Church, were concerned about how some New England churches were drifting away from faith in Jesus Christ. A small group began to hold weekly prayer meetings and lectures. In 1809 they formed a church with twenty-six founding members. That year the cornerstone was laid for the **Park Street Church**, pictured below. It began one of America's first Sunday schools in 1816. In 1819 the church sent the first Protestant missionaries to Hawaii. For several years the church hosted anti-slavery lectures on July 4. On July 4, 1829, William Lloyd Garrison spoke, giving his first anti-slavery address. He became a famous abolitionist. The church's first organist, Lowell Mason, composed the music to "Nearer My God to Thee," "Joy to the World," and many other hymns. America's first prison ministry began there in the 1820s. The church was the site of the first public performance of "America" ("My Country 'Tis of Thee"), written by Samuel Francis Smith. The Park Street children's choir sang it on the church steps on July 4, 1831. In 1923 America's oldest radio ministry began there. Evangelist Billy Graham held his first Boston crusade at Park Street in 1949.

Park Street Church

4. Beside Park Street church is the **Granary Burying Ground**, established in 1660. Among those buried there are three signers of the Declaration of Independence—Samuel Adams, John Hancock, and Robert Treat Paine; patriot and silversmith Paul Revere; five victims of the Boston Massacre; and Benjamin Franklin's parents.

5. Nearby is **King's Chapel** and the adjacent **Burying Ground**, the oldest cemetery in Boston proper. John Winthrop and John Cotton (see pages 82 and 105) are buried there, as is Mary Chilton, the first woman to step off the *Mayflower*. The first King's Chapel was a wooden structure built in 1689. The current stone building was built in 1754. King's Chapel Church was the first Anglican Church in New England. King James II ordered its construction, but no one would sell land suitable for building. Authorities seized part of the burying ground and built the church there.

6. A **statue of Benjamin Franklin** sits on the site of the **Boston Latin School**. Franklin, Samuel Adams, and John Hancock all attended the school, which is still in operation in a different location.

7. Next is the **Old Corner Bookstore** where famous authors visited. The building, pictured in the circle below, was constructed in 1712 and became a bookstore in 1829. Like other bookstores in the Colonial era, it was also a publishing house. Nathaniel Hawthorne's *The Scarlet Letter* was published here. Famous visitors have included American authors Ralph Waldo Emerson, Nathaniel Hawthorne, Oliver Wendell Holmes Sr., and Henry Wadsworth Longfellow, as well as English author Charles Dickens.

8. The **Old South Meeting House,** pictured at right, was built in 1729 and was the largest building in colonial Boston. It housed a Puritan congregation. The Boston Tea Party began at this church. Samuel Adams and Benjamin Franklin were members of the congregation.

Old South Meeting House

9. The **Old State House**, built in 1713, is the oldest public building in Boston. Look at the two pictures below. The Declaration of Independence was read from the balcony of the Old State House on July 8, 1776.

10. In front of the Old State House is the site of the **Boston Massacre**.

11. Patriots Samuel Adams and James Otis gave speeches at **Faneuil Hall**, a marketplace and meeting hall built in 1742 by wealthy merchant Peter Faneuil. It continues to be used for the same purposes.

12. **Paul Revere's Home** was built around 1680. His family occupied the home from 1770 to 1800. During the 1800s, Jewish, Irish, and Italian immigrants lived there.

Above: Historic View of the Old State House; Right: Modern View

13. On the night before the Battles of Lexington and Concord, patriots looked to the belfry of the **Old North Church** to see whether one or two lanterns were hung there. The number of lanterns told patriots about how the British were coming, "One if by land, and two if

Old Corner Bookstore

by sea." Old North is also called "Christ Church in the City of Boston." It was built in 1723. Inside are original high box pews, brass chandeliers, the church's first clock, and the first church bells brought to America. Paul Revere was one of the church's bell ringers.

Historic and Modern Views of the USS Constitution

14. **Copp's Hill Burying Ground** was founded in 1659. Among the thousands of graves are those of colonial leaders Increase Mather and Cotton Mather (see pages 104-105); Robert Newman, who placed the signal lanterns in the steeple of the Old North Church; and hundreds of African Americans.

15. While George Washington was President of the United States, he ordered that six ships be built. One was the **USS *Constitution***, which was launched in 1797. The ship is the oldest commissioned naval vessel afloat in the world. Look at the pictures above.

16. The last site on the Freedom Trail is the **Bunker Hill Monument** on Breed's Hill. It commemorates the first major battle of the American War for Independence.

Fun Facts about Boston

Robert McCloskey published *Make Way for Ducklings* in 1941. It is the story of a pair of mallard ducks who raise their ducklings on an island in the Boston Public Garden lagoon. It has sold over two million copies. Boston Public Garden, pictured below, has a statue of the mother and her eight ducklings. It is the official children's book of Massachusetts. McCloskey studied at Boston's Vesper George Art School.

Boston Terrier

The Boston Terrier breed developed in Boston stables after the Civil War. It is a cross between an English bulldog and a white English terrier. Almost all modern Boston Terriers are descendants of "Hooper's Judge," who was owned by a Bostonian in 1870. In 1891 they became known as Boston Terriers. The breed was recognized by the American Kennel Club in 1893. See the photo of a Boston Terrier at left.

Transportation in Boston has always been challenging since it is built on a peninsula and is therefore surrounded on three sides by water. With the Charles River to the west and Boston Harbor to the east, Boston's first mass transportation was a ferry service that began in 1631. After the American Revolution, bridges were built to cross the river and the harbor. In the early 1800s,

Boston Public Garden

residents began to travel to nearby towns on stagecoaches. In the 1820s a Bostonian could travel within his city on a long, enclosed, horsedrawn carriage called an omnibus. In 1830 Boston citizens began traveling by steam locomotive on the new rail line to Lowell, Massachusetts. In 1856 the first horsecar line opened in Boston. A horsecar was a long, enclosed vehicle that ran on rails and was pulled by horses. On January 1, 1889, an electric streetcar line began in Boston. Soon Boston had too many streetcars. Some of them needed to go underground. Boston opened America's first subway system in 1897. Four years later, a system of elevated trains began there. Today, over one million passenger trips are made each day on some type of Massachusetts Bay Transit Authority vehicle, which includes buses, the subway, commuter rails, and ferries. If you ever experience Boston traffic, as illustrated in the picture on page 159, you can understand why Bostonians use their public transportation, which they call the "T."

Whether walking on the Freedom Trail or traveling on the "T," we should walk in God's ways:

> Give me understanding, that I may observe Your law and keep it with all my heart.
> Make me walk in the path of Your commandments, for I delight in it.
> Psalm 119:34-35

Activities for Lesson 29

Thinking Biblically – Read about transportation in the Bible in these verses: Genesis 18:16; Genesis 46:29; Exodus 4:20; 1 Samuel 30:17; 1 Kings 10:22; Esther 6:11; Matthew 9:1. Make a list of these Biblical transportation methods in your notebook.

Map Study – Complete the assignment for Lesson 29 on Map 3 "American Landmarks" in *Maps of America the Beautiful*.

Timeline – In *Timeline of America the Beautiful* next to 1634, write: Boston Common is created. It is America's oldest city park.

Literature – Read "The Liberty Song" in *We the People*, page 27, and the chapter titled "Woburn 1740-1779" in *Amos Fortune: Free Man*.

Student Workbook or Lesson Review – If you are using one of these optional books, complete the assignment for Lesson 29.

Early American Home Crafts

While their husbands were away fighting for independence, most American women continued to spend their days doing what they had done before the war, plus managing the family farm or business. If they had enough money to buy them, women living in towns and cities could buy some items they needed for their households. However, farm women were busy in their homes or on their farms, making most of the things their families needed. Even wealthy women had the responsibility of overseeing servants who produced what the family needed.

Early American Homes

The typical early American home was made of wood from the land's abundant forests. A large stone fireplace provided heat and a place to cook. Home styles varied depending on where a family's ancestors had lived in Europe. Swedes in Delaware built log homes as they had in Sweden. When Germans and Scots-Irish moved to America, they copied the Swedish style and also built log cabins. French settlers built houses with porches across the front or porches that went all around the house. In New England houses were usually one and a half stories tall and covered with clapboard siding. The Dutch built brick houses.

This drawing from 1876 is entitled "A New England Kitchen A Hundred Years Ago."

Since America had few architects, a wealthy man who wanted to build a magnificent home might study books from England to learn how to design his own. George Washington's home, Mount Vernon, has details found in architectural books popular in the 1700s.

In this lesson we explore what American women were doing in these homes. Look at the women cooking, baking, spinning, and churning butter in the illustration on page 164.

Spinning Wheel

Spinning

Early American women used spinning wheels to spin flax and wool fibers into thread and yarn. See spinning wheels at right. They used the yarn and thread for weaving, knitting, crocheting, and sewing.

Before the Revolution, even women who could afford to buy fabric made in England, stopped buying it just to protest British policies. "Daughters of Liberty" met in Providence, Rhode Island, to spin yarn. Other women of New England also participated in these spinning bees. This was their way to protest. Sometimes they gave the yarn they made to ministers or to needy families.

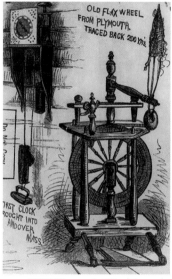

1876 Harper's Weekly
Illustration

Weaving

Weaving creates fabric out of yarn. A weaver attaches her warp threads to her loom and then passes her weft (or filling) thread over and under the warp threads to create fabric. A common fabric woven in early America was linsey-woolsey, a combination of flax and wool. See loom at right.

Loom

Knitting

Colonial Mother and Daughter

Before Europeans came to America, knitting was popular in England and Scotland. Immigrants brought the skill to America. Tools for knitting are simple. All that is needed is yarn and two needles, which can easily be whittled from wood. Look at the picture at left. A mother is knitting while she teaches her daughter her letters.

Sewing

In the 1700s, women had to make sheets, pillowcases, tablecloths, curtains, and towels. They sewed clothing for their husbands, children, and themselves. They used their homespun cloth for work clothes, but some purchased fine English fabrics for dress clothes. Wealthy women purchased buttons of brass, mother-of-pearl, ivory, painted porcelain, tortoise shell inlay, and engraved gems.

General Washington, Robert Morris, and Colonel George Ross Visit Betsy Ross

The most famous seamstress from this period is Betsy Ross of Philadelphia. Betsy had been a good seamstress since her youth. Her husband was an upholsterer, who also served in the militia. He died in 1776 in a gunpowder accident. After his death, Betsy ran his upholstery business.

In 1870 William Canby published a story about his grandmother, Betsy Ross. He told about General George Washington, Colonel George Ross, and businessman Robert Morris visiting his grandmother in 1776 and asking her to sew a flag for America. Betsy Ross agreed and made the first American flag, the Stars and Stripes. See illustration above.

Betsy Ross married Captain John Ashburn in 1777. They had two children. Ashburn was captured by the British and died in a British prison in 1782. The next year, Betsy married John Claypoole, Ashburn's fellow prisoner. They had five more children.

Quilting

Dutch and English colonists brought the first quilts to America. They were appliqued, like the bedspreads and canopies in the picture at right. Patchwork quilts became popular in America because they could be made from scraps of leftover fabrics and from pieces of clothing that could no longer be worn. Patchwork quilts are made by sewing different pieces of fabric together, while an applique quilt is made by cutting shapes from fabric and stitching them on top of a larger piece of fabric. American women enjoyed expressing themselves artistically by making their own patchwork quilt designs. They also liked to get together at quilting bees like the one pictured on page 167.

Embroidering

Embroidery involves using thread and a needle to make designs on fabric. European girls learned the art of embroidery and continued to do the craft as adults. They brought their supplies and skills to the New World, where embroidery remained a popular craft. In America, as well as Europe, embroiderers made samplers. A sampler is an embroidery piece that includes different kinds of stitches. Early American samplers

Applique Quilting

A Quilting Bee

often had an alphabet and the numerals 1 through 10. Many also had a Bible verse or a saying. Samplers were often framed and hung on the wall. Some school teachers taught girls to make samplers while other girls made them at home. See the embroidered sampler at right.

Rug Making

Innovative American women used scraps and pieces of clothing to braid rugs. The process involves cutting strips of fabric, braiding them, and then sewing the braids together into the desired shape. Another common homemade floor covering was the floor cloth. To make these, women stenciled a design onto canvas and then covered the cloth with several coats of varnish. Other rugs were woven, like the one below. These were nailed to the floor. Narrow versions of these were sometimes nailed to stairways.

Early American Embroidered Sampler

Candle Dipping

Woven Colonial Rug

To make a dipped candle, early American homemakers needed two things: tallow, produced from sheep or beef fat, and flax or cotton wicks. The first step was to cut wick string into equal lengths. The second step was to fold these wicks in half and hang them over an iron bar. The third step was to dip the hanging wicks into melted tallow. The fourth step was to hang the wicks to let them dry and cool. The third and fourth steps

167

Colonial Woman Dips Candles

were repeated until the candles were the desired size. The illustration at left shows a woman dipping candles. Other candles were made using candle molds.

Many women of Colonial times were like the woman in the last chapter of Proverbs:

> She stretches out her hands to the distaff,
> and her hands grasp the spindle.
> She extends her hand to the poor,
> and she stretches out her hands to the needy.
> Proverbs 31:19-20

Activities for Lesson 30

Thinking Biblically – In the illustration on page 165, you see a young girl holding a horn book, which was a common learning tool in Colonial times. Many horn books had the text of the Lord's Prayer. Copy the Lord's Prayer from Matthew 6:9-13 in your notebook.

Timeline – In *Timeline of America the Beautiful* next to 1870, write: William Canby publishes the story of his grandmother Betsy Ross making the first American flag.

Literature – Read "Chester" in *We the People*, page 28, and the chapter titled "Journey to Keene 1779" in *Amos Fortune: Free Man*.

Creative Writing – In your notebook, write a one-page story about a colonial woman trying to manage her farm and household while her husband is away serving in the Revolutionary War.

Family Activity – Create your own set of colonial marbles and bag. The instructions are on pages 424-425.

Student Workbook or Lesson Review – If you are using one of these optional books, complete the assignment for Lesson 30. If you are using the Lesson Review, take the quiz for Unit 6.

7

A New Nation and a New Frontier

After America won its independence, the country needed a new government. At first Americans tried to live under a government founded on the Articles of Confederation. When that did not work well, our founding fathers wrote the United States Constitution. In this unit, our American Biography is about George Washington, our first President and the man who is called the father of his country. This week's American Landmark is historic Philadelphia, which served as the United States capital before Washington, D.C., was built. During the presidency of George Washington, more people began to cross over one of God's Wonders, the Appalachian Mountains. This week we learn about these mountains and the daily lives of the trappers, longhunters, and pioneers who climbed through the Appalachians to lands in the West.

Longhunter and Pioneer Daniel Boone has been a popular American hero since before his death. The above display from 1941 advertises Daniel Boone clothing for boys.

Lessons in Unit 7

Lesson 31 – Our American Story: A New Government for a New Nation
Lesson 32 – An American Biography: George Washington, Father of His Country
Lesson 33 – An American Landmark: Historic Philadelphia
Lesson 34 – God's Wonders: God Created the Appalachian Mountains
Lesson 35 – Daily Life: Trappers, Longhunters, and Pioneers

Books Used in Unit 7

- *Maps of America the Beautiful*

- *Timeline of America the Beautiful*

- *We the People*

- *Amos Fortune: Free Man* by Elizabeth Yates

A New Government
for a New Nation

Thirteen little colonies on the coast of North America had defeated the world's most powerful nation. They had won their independence, but could they keep it? The Articles of Confederation, ratified during the Revolution, had established a weak government that was unable to handle the problems of the new nation.

The Revolutionary War left the American government in debt. The new nation also had problems on its frontier. When the Treaty of Paris was negotiated, Britain recognized that American territory extended westward to the Mississippi River (though the Florida region still belonged to Spain). This meant that the homelands of many Native Americans that lay south of the Great Lakes were part of America. Before and during the Revolution, small numbers of pioneers had moved into the frontier. Now more Americans wanted to move there. Native Americans resented this and attacked them. Settlers wanted the American government to protect them.

The Northwest Ordinance of 1787

One major accomplishment during these early years was the Northwest Ordinance. Congress made rules for the portion of the American frontier west of Pennsylvania and north of the Ohio River called the Northwest Territory. Look at the map at right.

Map of the Northwest Territory

The Northwest Ordinance described how parts of the Northwest Territory could become states. It declared that new states would be completely equal with the original thirteen. The ordinance gave religious freedom and legal rights to individuals, stated that Indian tribes would be treated fairly, and outlawed slavery there. Congress also passed a law that allowed people to buy land from the Federal government in the Northwest Territory. These sales gave the new nation much-needed money.

The Constitutional Convention of 1787

Several state legislatures expressed the desire to make the Articles of Confederation more effective. In May of 1787, fifty-five delegates from all states except Rhode Island began meeting in Philadelphia. Soon, a majority decided that mere changes would not be

*James Madison,
Father of the Constitution*

sufficient. They decided to write a completely new constitution. George Washington agreed to serve as the President of the Constitutional Convention. Afraid that rumors about what they were doing would cause uneasiness among citizens, the delegates agreed to keep everything secret. They even kept the windows closed throughout the hot summer.

Delegates decided to create a strong government that could act when needed, while protecting the rights of states and citizens. They decided to have three branches of government: a legislative branch that would make laws; an executive branch headed by a President to carry out the laws; and a judicial branch to apply the laws through a system of courts. The delegates wrestled with these three main problems:

1. The Legislature. Large states wanted the legislature to be based on population. Smaller states thought that was unfair. The delegates compromised and created two houses with different numbers of Representatives. Each state would have two members in the Senate. The number of members each state would have in the House of Representatives would be based on population.

2. The President. Some delegates wanted the President to be selected by the legislature. Others wanted the people to vote for him. They compromised by creating the electoral college. Each state could decide how it wanted to select its electors. The electoral college would then choose the President.

3. Slavery. Northern and southern states were divided over slavery. Northern states questioned it. Southern states defended it. The delegates compromised and agreed to count three-fifths of a state's slaves when deciding how many Representatives the state would have in the House of Representatives. If a state had to pay taxes based on population, only three-fifths of the slaves would be counted when determining a state's share. Delegates also agreed to allow slaves to be imported until 1808.

James Madison was a young, five-foot-tall delegate from Virginia. See his picture above. He came to the convention with strong ideas, provided good leadership, and came to be called the "Father of the Constitution." Madison kept the only written record of the convention. Each day he took shorthand notes and transcribed them at night. He decided not to allow his notes to be published until the last delegate died. As it turned out, the last one to die was Madison himself.

Thirty-nine of the fifty-five delegates signed the Constitution. They agreed that it would go into effect when nine states ratified it. Delaware became the first state to ratify the Constitution. The ninth was New Hampshire. Look at the chart at right.

The First Thirteen States
Ratify the Constitution

1787
Delaware – December 7
Pennsylvania – December 12
New Jersey – December 18

1788
Georgia – January 2
Connecticut – January 9
Massachusetts – February 6
Maryland – April 28
South Carolina – May 23
New Hampshire – June 21
Virginia – June 24
New York – July 26

1789
North Carolina – November 21

1790
Rhode Island – May 29

George Washington, America's First President

The electors in the first electoral college each cast two votes to select a President. Each elector cast one of their votes for George Washington. John Adams received the second highest number. Washington became the first President and Adams the first Vice President. Electors from only eleven states elected these men because North Carolina and Rhode Island had not yet ratified the Constitution.

Washington took his oath of office in America's first capital, New York City, on April 30, 1789. At the end of the oath, he added the words "so help me God." Every President since then has added the same words. Washington did not want people to give him a fancy title like "Your Highness." Instead he wanted to be called simply "Mr. President." That is still the way people address the President. Washington was aware that what he did as President would likely be repeated by future Presidents. In other words, he knew that he was setting precedents.

Martha Washington became America's first First Lady. With their two grandchildren, she joined her husband in New York in 1789 and then in Philadelphia when the capital moved there in 1790. She was a gracious hostess who gave elaborate parties.

When Washington completed his first term, he wanted to go home to Mount Vernon; but he agreed to serve for four more years. He was once more elected by a unanimous vote. Again Adams received the second highest number and continued as Vice President. At the end of two terms (1789-1797), Washington decided not to serve any longer.

The First Congress and the First Supreme Court

The first United States Congress also began in 1789. It created departments to help President Washington. Washington appointed heads for each of those departments. He named Thomas Jefferson (of Virginia) to serve as Secretary of State, Henry Knox (of Boston) to serve as Secretary of War, and Alexander Hamilton (of Philadelphia) to serve as Secretary of the Treasury. President Washington appointed John Jay (of New York) to serve as the first Chief Justice of the Supreme Court. Look at the pictures of these men at right.

Many Americans were concerned about the rights of individual citizens, so the first Congress passed twelve amendments to the Constitution guaranteeing personal freedoms. These amendments also limited the power of the national government. States voted on the amendments individually. Ten of the amendments passed. These first amendments to the Constitution became known as the Bill of Rights.

Top: John Jay, Alexander Hamilton
Bottom: Henry Knox, Thomas Jefferson

John Adams, America's Second President

Washington was strongly opposed to political parties, but two had developed by the time he left office: Federalists, who believed in a strong central government, and Republicans, who supported the rights of individuals. The electoral college selected Federalist John Adams as the second President and Republican Thomas Jefferson as Vice President. During Adams' presidency, France caused problems for America and some Americans wanted to go to war. Adams wisely helped restore peace.

A New Capital, a New Presidential Home, and New Stars in the Flag

Since 1777, residents of eastern New York had wanted to be independent. At first they called their area New Connecticut and later Vermont. New York gave up its claim to the area and, in 1791, Vermont joined the U.S. as the fourteenth state. Kentucky followed in 1792, and Tennessee in 1796.

In 1800 Federal City in the District of Columbia became the permanent U.S. capital. Federal City was later renamed Washington. John Adams became the first President to reside in the White House.

John Adams ran for a second term as President, losing after a bitter campaign to his own Vice President, Thomas Jefferson. Read more about John Adams in the box below.

New States

1791 Vermont
1792 Kentucky
1796 Tennessee

John Adams
America's Second President
March 4, 1797 - March 4, 1801

John Adams was a brilliant man with deep Christian faith. When the Revolution began, his family had lived in Massachusetts for four generations. He served sacrificially, both in the Continental Congress and as America's representative in France and Great Britain. Adams and his wife, Abigail, had a beautiful, loving relationship. They had five children, including John Quincy, who later became President. Adams' service in the Revolution kept him away from home for most of ten years. Letters the couple wrote to each other reveal the sincere faith they both had. They also provide detailed accounts of the times. At right are Abigail Adams, John Adams in his later years, and his birthplace in Quincy, Massachusetts.

America had a new government, frontier territories had government guidelines, and new state governments were beginning. America was slowly becoming a nation with law and order. As the new country grew, most Americans agreed with Paul's teaching:

Every person is to be in subjection to the governing authorities,
for there is no authority except from God,
and those which exist are established by God.
Romans 13:1

Activities for Lesson 31

Thinking Biblically – Read Paul's instructions about submitting to the government in Romans 13:1-7.

Map Study – Complete the assignments for Lesson 31 on Map 7 "The Thirteen Colonies" and on Map 20 "The Lower 48" in *Maps of America the Beautiful*.

Timeline – In *Timeline of America the Beautiful* next to 1800, write: John Adams is the first President to live in the White House.

Literature – Read the "Preamble to the Constitution" and "Letter to Abigail Adams" on pages 29-30 in *We the People* and the chapter titled "The Arrival at Jaffrey" in *Amos Fortune: Free Man*.

Student Workbook or Lesson Review – If you are using one of these optional books, complete the assignment for Lesson 31.

George Washington, Father of His Country

On February 22, 1732, a boy was born to Augustine and Mary Ball Washington at Wakefield Farm in Westmoreland County, Virginia. Augustine had two older sons, Lawrence and Augustine, from his first marriage. The Washingtons named Mary's first son George. The family Bible shows no middle name. Augustine and Mary had three more boys and two girls. Samuel, John Augustine, Charles, and Betty grew to be adults; but the other sister died while still a child.

George Washington grew up near Fredericksburg, Virginia. He was homeschooled, studying arithmetic, astronomy, geography, spelling, and surveying. Like other children, he learned handwriting by copying into a copybook 110 guidelines from a book called *Rules of Civility & Decent Behavior in Company and Conversation*. The artist who created the illustrations below of Washington's boyhood portrays young George doing things that were important to him when he grew up: writing letters and keeping detailed records, managing his farm, and serving as a military leader.

George's mother lived to be 82 years old, but his father died when George was only eleven. After his father's death, George's older half-brother Lawrence guided him. Lawrence lived in a small house his father had built on a plantation he owned beside the Potomac River. The property had been in the Washington family since 1674 when it was owned by George and Lawrence's great-grandfather. Lawrence named this farm Mount Vernon.

Lawrence Washington had a friend, George William Fairfax, who was a surveyor. When George Washington was 16 years old, Fairfax allowed George to accompany him on a surveying trip to the frontier. Before leaving, young George reviewed his studies and practiced surveying Lawrence's turnip field. While on the surveying trip, Fairfax and Washington traveled on horseback and slept in the open. George Washington kept journals. He wrote about conversations with Indians and about eating with them. He described watching the Indians dancing in the firelight.

Mount Vernon

Washington, the Gentleman Farmer

George grew to be about six feet tall. He was a good wrestler and impressed people with his physical abilities, especially his skill at throwing objects long distances. Thomas Jefferson described him as "the most graceful figure that could be seen on horseback."

When George was 20, his half-brother Lawrence died. Lawrence's widow allowed George to lease Mount Vernon. He began to improve and enlarge the plantation from 2,000 acres to almost 8,000. Over the years he turned the four-room house into a mansion. See the photo above. Washington made the home look like stone by replacing the wooden siding with pine blocks coated with sand and paint. He made the home two and a half stories tall and built a two-story porch. He added the cupola on the roof which brought in river breezes in warm weather. After the Revolution, Washington added a dove of peace weathervane to its top. See interior rooms on page 177.

Washington enjoyed his life as a gentleman farmer. He oversaw his farm operations and the creation of beautiful landscaping. Look at the picture at right.

Washington, the Soldier

Washington went to the Ohio River Valley in 1753 on a mission given to him by the Governor of

Washington Directing Slaves on His Plantation

Virginia. Soon George was fighting on the side of the British and colonists in the first battles of the French and Indian War. In a terrible battle in 1754, four bullets went through Washington's coat and two horses were shot out from under him. Washington later became a colonel and continued to serve as a soldier in the Shenandoah Valley of Virginia.

Family Life at Mount Vernon

George married a young widow, Martha Dandridge Custis, in 1759. Martha came to live at Mount Vernon, along with her children, John ("Jacky") and Martha ("Patsy"). Washington became a devoted step-father. In 1761 Lawrence Washington's widow died and George inherited Mount Vernon. George and his family enjoyed plantation life, as illustrated below. The Washingtons hosted friends and relatives at fox hunts and parties.

Washington's Library

Washington's Bedroom

The Washington Family

Washington, the Public Servant

Washington began to serve Virginia as a member of the House of Burgesses in 1765. When other colonists became angry with England in the early 1770s, George joined in their protests. He was tired of paying high taxes, paying high prices for poorly made English products, and receiving low prices for his goods.

George Washington

Martha Washington

Martha's daughter Patsy died in 1773 at age seventeen. The following year George went to Philadelphia to serve in the First Continental Congress. In 1775 he represented Virginia in the Second Continental Congress.

General Washington, Commander-in-Chief

At age forty-three, Washington became commander of the Continental Army. He required hard work and discipline from his soldiers. He paid attention to details and was a good organizer. Congress was not able to provide the troops with enough food or supplies. On one occasion, Washington wrote a letter to the residents of New Jersey, Pennsylvania, Maryland, and Virginia asking them to give cattle to feed his Army.

At the beginning of the war, Washington's Army was no match for the British; so he chose his battles carefully. He refused to let the British draw him into battles that he did not believe his soldiers should fight. He led

George and Martha Washington with Their Adopted Grandchildren, George and Nelly, and a Servant

his 10,000 men well and stayed with them. He only visited his home ten days during the war. Martha often traveled to be with Washington when the Army was not fighting. She was even with him during the hard winter at Valley Forge.

After the American Revolution

The end of the war was bittersweet for George and Martha, when Cornwallis surrendered at Yorktown. Martha's son Jacky died there of camp fever. He and his twenty-three-year-old wife had four children. When Jacky died, his two youngest children came to live with their grandparents. Eleanor ("Nelly") Parke Custis was two and a half years old and George Washington Parke Custis was six months old.

When the Treaty of Paris was signed in 1783, Washington resigned from the Army. He went home to Mount Vernon where he hoped to live the remainder of his life as a farmer and citizen. However, George Washington was always a servant of his country. When its citizens needed him again, he served first as president of the Constitutional Convention and then as President of the United States. At left is an illustration of George and Martha while he was serving as President.

George and Martha at Church on Easter Sunday, 1795

When he and his family were finally able to move back home, thousands of people visited them each year. Still, Washington was able to enjoy quiet evenings, often listening to his granddaughter play music. George, Martha, and their grandchildren are pictured above.

In December of 1799, George Washington got a sore throat after riding horseback in a storm. Because he was elderly, his sickness worsened. He died at home less than three years after he left the presidency.

After Washington's Death

About 340 people were living on the Mount Vernon plantation when Washington died, including his granddaughter Nelly, her husband, and their new baby. George and Martha had 316 slaves and several employees, including a farm manager, five overseers for their slaves, a housekeeper, two gardeners, a miller, a distiller, and a weaver. In his will, George Washington freed his slaves.

After Washington's death, the country went into mourning for their beloved hero. One of his generals, Henry Lee, wrote a eulogy and read it to the United States Congress. Lee said that Washington was "first in war, first in peace, and first in the hearts of his countrymen."

The Washingtons at Mount Vernon

Like King David in the Bible, George Washington understood:

Both riches and honor come from You, and You rule over all,
and in Your hand is power and might;
and it lies in Your hand to make great and to strengthen everyone.
1 Chronicles 29:12

Activities for Lesson 32

Thinking Biblically – George Washington used his gifts to serve other people and his country. Copy 1 Peter 4:10 into your notebook.

Timeline – In *Timeline of America the Beautiful* next to 1674, write: The property now known as Mount Vernon is purchased by George Washington's great-grandfather.

Literature – Read "George Washington and the Cherry Tree" and "Rules of Civility & Decent Behavior in Company & Conversation" in *We the People*, pages 31-32, and the chapter titled "Hard Work Fills the Iron Kettle 1781-1789" in *Amos Fortune: Free Man*.

Creative Writing – In your notebook, write one or more paragraphs about why George Washington was so well-respected.

Student Workbook or Lesson Review – If you are using one of these optional books, complete the assignment for Lesson 32.

Historic Philadelphia

In the early 1900s, thousands of soldiers at Fort Dix, New Jersey, formed this human Liberty Bell. The real Liberty Bell is in Philadelphia.

Philadelphia, Pennsylvania, is called "The Birthplace of the Nation," because of its role in the fight for American independence. It is also called "The City of Brotherly Love." The city was founded by Quaker William Penn in 1682. It served as the United States capital from 1790 to 1800. Philadelphia has a high concentration of America's most treasured symbols.

The Old City and Society Hill

At the center of the original plan for Philadelphia is Penn Square. It is home to Philadelphia's City Hall, built between 1871 and 1901. At the top of City Hall is a statue of William Penn.

Within one square mile of Penn Square are the Old City and Society Hill neighborhoods. The Old City is where the first Pennsylvania Quakers settled. Society Hill has more homes built in the 1700s and early 1800s than any neighborhood in America. Federal and Georgian rowhouses line Society Hill's cobblestone streets. The terms Federal and Georgian refer to architectural styles. Georgian buildings were built from 1715 to 1820 during the reigns of England's Kings George I, II, III, and IV. Buildings in the Federal style were popular from 1780 to 1820. Federal architecture was an American style, designed to break away from English influences. Rowhouses are homes with two or more stories that are built touching one another with no land in between. Look at the rowhouses in the photo at right.

Portions of the Old City and Society Hill have been set aside to

Philadelphians stand on roofs of rowhouses to watch a World Series baseball game on October 19, 1914.

180

form the forty-five-acre Independence National Historical Park. The park, established in 1956, is home to sites important during the American struggle for independence and the founding of America.

Independence Hall

Independence Hall was constructed between 1732 and 1753 to be the State House of the Province of Pennsylvania. Scottish immigrant Andrew Hamilton chose the site and designed the building. Look at the picture at right. Hamilton had immigrated to America in 1700. He became a lawyer in Philadelphia and an amateur architect.

In Independence Hall are the desk and chair where members of the Second Continental Congress sat to sign the Declaration of Independence in 1776. Members of the Constitutional Convention worked out the details of the United States Constitution here in 1787.

Andrew Hamilton is accompanied by two ladies while he and a foreman discuss the construction of the Pennsylvania State House in this Jean Leone Gerome Ferris painting, titled "Building the Cradle of Liberty."

The chair George Washington used when he presided over the Constitutional Convention still sits in Independence Hall. It is called the Rising Sun Chair. During the convention, Benjamin Franklin said that he wondered if the sun carving on the chair's back was a rising sun or a setting sun. When the Constitution was completed, he said he believed it was a rising sun.

Throughout the history of America, Independence Hall has continued to be the scene of public gatherings. Notice the 1876 celebration at left.

The Liberty Bell

Around the crown of the Liberty Bell is a quote from Leviticus: "Proclaim LIBERTY throughout the Land unto all the inhabitants thereof." Originally the bell honored William Penn's work to assure freedom in the Pennsylvania colony. In the early 1800s,

On January 1, 1876, a celebration was held in front of Independence Hall marking the beginning of the year America turned one hundred years old. Frank Leslie's Illustrated Newspaper *published this illustration.*

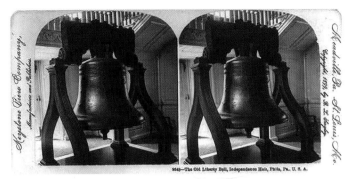
1899 Stereoscopic Photo of the Liberty Bell

abolitionists used it as a symbol of the need to end slavery in America. They began to call it the Liberty Bell.

The history of the Liberty Bell began in 1751 when the Pennsylvania assembly ordered a bell from England to celebrate the fiftieth anniversary of the Charter of Privileges, written by William Penn in 1701 (see Lesson 18).

When the bell arrived, it was defective. A local Philadelphia business, Pass and Stowe, melted and recast it twice before it was finally hung in the tower of the Philadelphia State House (now Independence Hall) in 1753. The bronze bell weighs over 2,000 pounds. The distance around its lip is twelve feet. When rung, its peal is an E-flat.

According to tradition, the bell, pictured above, was rung on July 8, 1776, after the first public reading of the Declaration of Independence. When the British captured Philadelphia in 1777, the Liberty Bell was hidden in nearby Allentown. Philadelphians hid other bells, too, so that the British would not melt them down to make ammunition. The Liberty Bell was returned to the Independence Hall tower in 1778. It was rung every Fourth of July and on other national occasions until 1835. According to tradition, the bell cracked while it rang to honor the death of Chief Justice John Marshall. The Liberty Bell now resides in Liberty Bell Center. Look at the human Liberty Bell on page 180.

Independence Hall and the Liberty Bell are the main attractions in Independence National Historical Park. Other historic sites in the park include:

Carpenter's Hall — In 1724 Philadelphia carpenters founded a guild to help each other develop skills in architecture and to help one another's families when they were in need. They built Carpenter's Hall in 1770. The First Continental Congress met here in 1774. During the American Revolution, the Hall was used as a hospital and an arsenal.

Christ Church — Christ Church was built between 1727 and 1754. It is a beautiful example of colonial craftsmanship. See the picture below.

Congress Hall —The United States Congress met here from 1790 to 1800. The House of Representatives met on the lower floor and the Senate met on the upper floor. Though Congress now meets in the U.S. Capitol in Washington, D.C., the House of Representatives is still called the "Lower House" and the Senate is called the "Upper House." Congress Hall was the scene of Washington's second inauguration, the adoption of the Bill of Rights, and the inauguration of John Adams. The building was originally a county court house.

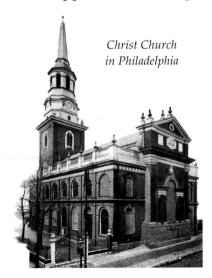
Christ Church in Philadelphia

First and Second Banks of the United States — The First Bank is the oldest bank building in the United States. The Second Bank now houses a collection of paintings of explorers, military officers, political leaders, and scientists from the Colonial and Revolutionary periods and from the early years of the United States. Several paintings are by Charles Willson Peale, who lived from 1741 to 1827. Peale settled in Philadelphia in 1775. He served as a colonel in Philadelphia's militia and fought in the American Revolution. He painted many military portraits, including fourteen of the commander of the Continental Army, George Washington.

Franklin Court — A monument to Benjamin Franklin now stands on the site of his home. Underneath Franklin Court is a museum. Nearby are three of his rental properties.

Free Quaker Meeting House — Quakers who laid aside the pacifist views of their fellow Quakers and supported the fight for American Independence met here. Among them was Betsy Ross. Free Quakers were sometimes called "Fighting Quakers."

Old City Hall — Old City Hall was completed in 1791 to house Philadelphia's city government. The United States Supreme Court also met here from 1791 to 1800.

The Betsy Ross House

Near Independence National Historical Park is the home Betsy Ross rented from 1773 to 1786. It was built around 1740. The home is two and a half stories tall and has nine rooms. It was in this house that John and Betsy Ross ran their upholstery business (see page 166) and where General Washington visited Betsy Ross to discuss her sewing the Stars and Stripes. The Betsy Ross Memorial Association acquired the house in the late 1800s. Beginning in 1898, two million Americans donated dimes so that the house could be made into a memorial for Betsy Ross. Since 1937 the home has been owned by the city of Philadelphia. It is one of the most popular tourist destinations in the city. See picture at right.

Betsy Ross' Home

American Philosophical Society Library

The library of the American Philosophical Society is near Independence Hall. Benjamin Franklin founded the society in 1743. Its purpose is to promote scientific knowledge and technology. Science and technology were once called natural philosophy. The American Philosophical Society still meets today. Over a dozen U.S. Presidents, more than two hundred Nobel prize winners, scientists Madam Curie and Albert Einstein, naturalist and artist John James Audubon, cellist Yo-Yo Ma, Supreme Court Justice Sandra Day O'Connor, South African political activist Nelson Mandela, and many others have been members.

Independence Hall and the American Philosophical Society Library

The Society's historic meeting place and library was constructed in 1789 with generous donations from Franklin and others. The picture on page 183 includes a third floor which was added in 1890. In 1949 the third floor was removed to return the structure to its original design. At one time the University of Pennsylvania met in the building. Students were called to class with the ringing of the nearby Liberty Bell.

The society's library has more than seven million manuscripts, including an original manuscript of William Penn's 1701 Charter of Privileges. It also has maps, prints, periodicals, and paintings, including an original Gilbert Stuart portrait of George Washington and a Thomas Sully portrait of Thomas Jefferson. The Society's collection also includes an armchair that Thomas Jefferson used while writing the Declaration of Independence.

In Philadelphia tourists can visit America's symbols of liberty. Jesus offers real liberty to all the people of the world.

Jesus was saying to those Jews who had believed Him,
"If you continue in My word, then you are truly disciples of Mine;
and you will know the truth, and the truth will make you free."
John 8:31-32

Activities for Lesson 33

Map Study – Complete the assignment for Lesson 33 on Map 3 "American Landmarks" in *Maps of America the Beautiful*.

Timeline – In *Timeline of America the Beautiful* next to 1753, write: The Liberty Bell is hung in the tower of the Philadelphia State House (now Independence Hall).

Literature – Read "O Sing a Song of Bethlehem" in *We the People*, page 33, and the chapter titled "Amos on the Mountain" in *Amos Fortune: Free Man*.

Vocabulary – Look up each of these words in a dictionary: concentration, architecture, abolitionist, peal, pacifist. Copy each word and its definition in your notebook.

Family Activity – Create a Liberty Bell Mosaic. See the instructions on page 426.

Student Workbook or Lesson Review – If you are using one of these optional books, complete the assignment for Lesson 33.

God Created the Appalachian Mountains

God created the beautiful Appalachian Mountains. They begin in Canada and continue southward 1,500 miles to northern Georgia and Alabama. Twisting and turning for 2,158 miles through the mountain range is the Appalachian National Scenic Trail. Construction on the trail began in 1928. Hikers begin near Mount Katahdin in Maine and hike through New Hampshire, Vermont, Massachusetts, Connecticut, New York, New Jersey, Pennsylvania, Maryland, West Virginia, Virginia, Tennessee, and North Carolina, before reaching Mount Oglethorpe in Georgia. Walking the entire trail takes an adult about 5,000,000 steps!

God placed asbestos, coal, emery, granite, iron, limestone, mica, slate, and zinc inside the Appalachians. He covered the mountains with forests. Americans have found many ways to use these resources.

Appalachian Animals

Mammals in the Appalachians include bats, bears, beavers, bobcats, chipmunks, coyotes, deer, elk, fishers, flying squirrels, gray foxes, groundhogs, lemmings, martens, mice, minks, moose, muskrats,

The Great Smoky Mountains are part of the Appalachians.

Clockwise from top left: Porcupine, Marten, Wild Boar, Weasel, Fisher

185

Veery   *Red-Eyed Vireo*   *Ovenbird*   *Scarlet Tanager and His Mate*

opossums, porcupines, rabbits, raccoons, red foxes, shrews, skunks, snowshoe hares, squirrels, voles, weasels, wild boars, and woodchucks. See the pictures on page 185.

Forty species of salamanders live in the Appalachians, as do bullfrogs, green frogs, tree frogs, lizards, box turtles, wood turtles, garter snakes, and black rat snakes.

Water is abundant in the Appalachians in the form of bogs, lakes, ponds, streams, and waterfalls. Bass, bream, catfish, crayfish, sunfish, and trout live in the streams. Rare creatures living near the water are zig-zag salamanders, northern cricket frogs, triangle floater mussels, broadhead skinks, Shenandoah salamanders, and squawfoot mussels.

Appalachian residents and visitors hear bluebirds, scarlet tanagers, black-billed cuckoos, and varieties of thrushes, warblers, wrens, and nuthatches in these mountains. They spot bald eagles, falcons, hawks, ravens, and vultures soaring overhead and see quail, ruffed grouse, spruce grouse, and wild turkeys on the forest floor. At night horned owls and barred owls call. Along the Appalachian Trail you might catch a glimpse of whippoorwills, flycatchers, and swallows. Deep in the Appalachian woods, the kinglet, ovenbird, pewee, red-eyed vireo, and veery sing. Pileated woodpeckers live in the Appalachians, too, along with ducks and other water birds. Look at different types of Appalachian birds in the pictures above.

Appalachian Wildflowers, Trees, and Shrubs

In spring and summer, beautiful wildflowers like those pictured at right grow in the mountains. The lady's slipper is a kind of orchid. In the Great Smoky Mountains, they are called moccasin flowers. Appalachian hikers may

Clockwise from top left: Lady's Slipper, Solomon's Seal, Trillium, Bluets, Dutchman's Britches, Columbine, Jack-in-the-Pulpit

see a Jack-in-the-Pulpit near a trail. The plant grows a cluster of red berries in late summer. Solomon's Seal blooms in summer and has long black berries in late summer and early fall. When the stem dies in the fall, it is thought to resemble King Solomon's official seal.

Native insects and hummingbirds pollinate Appalachian wildflowers. Carrion flies pollinate trillium, which have three petals, three sepals, and three leaves. Only bumblebees have tongues long enough to pollinate the Dutchman's britches. Hummingbirds and long-tongued insects pollinate the columbines with their red and yellow flowers. The columbine gets its name from the Latin word for dove because its petals look like doves.

From New England to northern Georgia and Alabama, the Appalachians are known for beautiful fall colors. First, the red maple and sugar maple leaves turn red. Next, the birch and hickory leaves turn yellow. Finally, beech leaves turn golden bronze and oak leaves turn deep red or brown. Acorns from oak trees provide food for Appalachian wildlife. Fir trees are in these mountains, too, with balsam firs in New England and Fraser firs in the South. Eastern hemlock, red spruce, silver bell, yellow buckeye, and mountain ash are also found in the South. In spring the southern Appalachians are adorned with the beautiful white blossoms of both dogwood trees and the small shadbush (also called a serviceberry tree), like those found near Chesapeake Bay.

Spring is also the time to see flowering shrubs like Catawba rhododendrons with their pink flowers; azaleas in pink, red, orange, and yellow varieties; and mountain laurel with honeycomb-shaped white and pink flowers.

The Northern Appalachians

Many smaller mountain ranges make up the Appalachian Mountains. We'll discuss these by regions: northern, central, and southern. The Blue Ridge Mountains are in both the central and southern regions, so this lesson has a separate section on them. See the chart at right.

The northern section of America's Appalachians begins in Maine and extends south to the Hudson River in New York. Mountain ranges in the northern Appalachian region include the Maine Highlands, the White Mountains, and the Green Mountains.

The highest mountain in the Maine Highlands is Mount Katahdin. Residents of the Maine Highlands enjoy picking blueberries, raspberries, blackberries, and fern fiddleheads, a delicacy Native Americans enjoyed.

While hiking there in 1939, twelve-year-old Donn Fendland got separated from his father, two brothers, and a friend. He wandered alone for nine days before being

---

Smaller Mountain Ranges Within the Appalachian Mountains

Northern

Maine Highlands
White Mountains, including the Franconia Mountains and the Presidentials
Green Mountains

Central

Taconic Mountains
Berkshire Mountains
Catskill Mountains
Kittatinny Mountains
Pocono Mountains
Allegheny Mountains
Blue Ridge Mountains

Southern

Blue Ridge Mountains, including the Black Mountains and the Unaka Mountains (The Great Smoky Mountains are part of the Unaka Mountains.)
Cumberland Plateau
Cumberland Mountains

rescued. The story of his faith and God's faithfulness during this ordeal is told in the book *Lost on a Mountain in Maine*. Mount Katahdin is at right.

Mt. Katahdin in Maine

The White Mountains include the Franconia Mountains and the Presidentials. The "Old Man of the Mountain" geological feature on the side of Profile Mountain was once a famous tourist destination in the Fraconias. See the photo at right. Novelist Nathaniel Hawthorne made the "Old Man of the Mountain" famous with his 1850 story of "The Great Stone Face." Rocks making up the man's profile fell off in 2003. The "Old Man of the Mountain" is featured on New Hampshire's commemorative U.S. quarter.

The best-known mountain in the Presidentials is windy Mount Washington, the highest mountain in the northeastern U.S. In 1934 a wind speed of 231 miles per hour was recorded at its top. Look at the photo below. Below 3,200 feet it is forested, but from there to its peak at 6,288 feet, it is rocky and treeless. Mount Washington has beautiful gorges, pools, streams, and waterfalls. It is famous as a skiing destination.

"Old Man of the Mountain" in New Hampshire

Adventurous settlers began climbing Mount Washington in the mid-1600s. Today visitors can reach the weather station and information center at the top by trail, cog railway, or car. Other mountains in the Presidentials include Mounts Adams, Jefferson, Monroe, Madison, and Eisenhower.

God put slate, granite, and high-quality marble inside the Green Mountains. Tourists and locals enjoy fishing in their lakes and streams, viewing the fall colors, and skiing their slopes. See the photo below at right. Sugar maples from the Green Mountains provide sap for Vermont's famous maple syrup. Vermont's "Green Mountain Boys" helped America win its war for independence from Great Britain.

Mt. Washington in New Hampshire

Skiing in the Green Mountains in Vermont

Central Appalachian Mountain Ranges

The central Appalachians run from New York's Hudson River Valley to the New River in Virginia and West Virginia. The region includes the Allegheny, Berkshire, Catskill, Kittatinny, Pocono, and Taconic Mountains, plus part of the Blue Ridge Mountains.

The Catskills lie near the Hudson River in New York. They were a favorite subject of painters of the Hudson River School, a group of American artists who shared a similar style and painted from around 1820 to 1900. Washington Irving's story of Rip Van Winkle took place in the Catskill Mountains. Tourists enjoy the cool summers and good fishing of the area. See a Catskills waterfall at left.

Waterfall in the Catskills of New York

God placed rich coal deposits in the Allegheny Mountains. Presidents Martin Van Buren, John Tyler, and Millard Fillmore visited the Alleghenies during summer months. They used President's Cottage in the resort city of White Sulphur Springs, West Virginia, as a summer home.

The Pocono Mountains are in northeastern Pennsylvania. See a Pocono Mountain waterfall at right.

Waterfall in the Pocono Mountains

The Blue Ridge Mountains

As already mentioned, the Blue Ridge Mountains are considered part of both the central and southern Appalachians. Many peaks of the Blue Ridge Mountains are over 6,500 feet high, making them the highest mountains of the Appalachians. Mists on their forested peaks make them appear blue. Tourists enjoy Blue Ridge vistas when they travel the 470-mile Blue Ridge Parkway.

The Black Mountains of North Carolina and the Unaka Mountains of Tennessee and North Carolina are part of the Blue Ridge range. Mount Mitchell is the tallest peak in the Black Mountains. At 6,684-feet-high, Mount Mitchell is the highest point east of South Dakota's Black Hills. See the photo at left.

The most famous section of the Unaka Mountains is the Great Smoky Mountain range. See the picture on page 185. Great Smoky Mountain National Park was established in 1930. It is the most visited national park in the United States. A haze, created when the region's lush vegetation

Mount Mitchell in North Carolina,
Highest Point in the Appalachian Mountains

Stereoscopic Photo of Umbrella Rock on Lookout Mountain around 1905

releases water vapor and natural oils, makes the mountains look smoky. The Smokies still contain large areas of virgin timber. One hundred species of native trees have been identified there.

Southern Appalachian Mountains

The southern Appalachians extend from the New River in Virginia and West Virginia into northern Georgia and Alabama. The southern Appalachians are split into two branches, the Blue Ridge Mountains to the east and the Cumberland Plateau and Cumberland Mountains to the west.

Much of the Cumberland Plateau has a rocky surface with thin soil. Coal lies under much of the limestone, sandstone, and slate surface. The mountains of the Cumberland Plateau are not very tall.

Oddly-shaped rock formations atop the Plateau's Lookout Mountain, near Chattanooga, Tennessee, have been attracting the curious since the early 1800s. Look at the photo above. Some of these first visitors called the formations "Rock City." In the middle of the 1900s, Rock City was advertised on nine hundred barn roofs from Michigan to Texas. Sign painters painted the words "See Rock City" on the roofs. Lookout Mountain was also the site of the Civil War Battle of Lookout Mountain, also called the Battle Above the Clouds.

Highest Peaks in the Appalachians By State			
State	**Mountain**	**Elevation**	**Mountain Range**
North Carolina	Mount Mitchell	6,684	Black Mountains
Tennessee	Clingman's Dome	6,643	Great Smoky Mountains
New Hampshire	Mount Washington	6,288	Presidential Mountains
Virginia	Mount Rogers	5,729	Blue Ridge Mountains
Maine	Mount Katahdin	5,267	Maine Highlands
West Virginia	Spruce Knob	4,862	Allegheny Mountains
Georgia	Brasstown Bald	4,784	Blue Ridge Mountains
Vermont	Mount Mansfield	4,393	Green Mountains
New York*	Slide Mountain	4,180	Catskill Mountains
Kentucky	Big Black Mountain	4,145	Cumberland Mountains
Massachusetts	Mount Greylock	3,492	Taconic Mountains
Maryland	Backbone Mountain	3,360	Allegheny Mountains
Pennsylvania	Mount Davis	3,213	Allegheny Mountains
Connecticut	Mount Frissell	2,454	Taconic Mountains
Alabama	Mount Cheaha	2,413	Blue Ridge Mountains
New Jersey	High Point	1,803	Kittatinny Mountains
* Note: The highest point in New York is Mount Marcy; but it is in the Adirondack Mountains, which are not part of the Appalachians.			

The Cumberland Mountains lie between the northern portions of the Cumberland Plateau and the Blue Ridge Mountains. Cumberland Gap is a narrow mountain pass near the point where Kentucky, Tennessee, and Virginia come together in the Cumberland Mountains. The first European to discover it was Thomas Walker in 1750. As seen in Lesson 35, many early settlers of Kentucky and Tennessee passed through Cumberland Gap.

The chart on page 190 lists each state that is home to a portion of the Appalachian Mountains. The chart tells the tallest Appalachian peak in each of those states and how tall that peak is. It also gives the name of the Appalachian Mountain range that contains that peak.

God created the Appalachian Mountains and the streams that run through them. He cares for the creatures that live there. As is beautifully described in Psalm 104:

> He sends forth springs in the valleys;
> They flow between the mountains;
> They give drink to every beast of the field.
> Psalm 104:10-11a

Activities for Lesson 34

Thinking Biblically – Read these Bible verses about mountains: Joshua 11:16, 1 Samuel 25:20, Psalm 95:4, Matthew 14:23, and Mark 11:1. Choose one of them to copy in your notebook.

Map Study – Complete the assignments for Lesson 34 on Map 2 "God's Wonders" and Map 12 "Appalachian Mountains" in *Maps of America the Beautiful*.

Timeline – In *Timeline of America the Beautiful* next to 1928, write: Constuction begins on the Appalachian Trail.

Literature – Read the chapter titled "Auctioned for Freedom" in *Amos Fortune: Free Man.*

Creative Writing – In your notebook, make a list of supplies you would need if you were hiking the Appalachian Trail.

Student Workbook or Lesson Review – If you are using one of these optional books, complete the assignment for Lesson 34.

Trappers, Longhunters, and Pioneers

Kentucky and Tennessee were the first states west of the Appalachian Mountains. Kentucky and Tennessee were rich with game, which was hunted first by Native Americans. Before and during the American Revolution, French adventurers entered this region to trap animals and to trade for furs with the Indians. Americans of English descent came from the east as longhunters, so called because they spent a long time hunting in the forests of Kentucky and Tennessee. See the picture at right. The most famous longhunter was Daniel Boone.

A Longhunter

The Boone Family in Pennsylvania and North Carolina

English Quaker George Boone, a weaver by trade, sent three of his children to Pennsylvania in 1713 to explore the possibility of the family emigrating from England. Boone brought his family to Pennsylvania in 1717. In 1720 his son Squire Boone married Sarah Morgan, also a Quaker. Her parents had been born in Wales, but Sarah was born in Pennsylvania. A family friend of the Boones was John Lincoln, grandfather of Abraham Lincoln.

Sarah gave birth in 1734 to her sixth child, Daniel, in their log cabin in Berks County, Pennsylvania. As a child, Boone walked his mother to church, carrying a gun. On one side of the gun, Daniel carved this: "D. Boon. 1746. My Mother Chirch Gun." On the other side, he carved: "D. Boon. Cilled. Big Panther. this gun. I was 13 year Old in Bucks Ca. Pa."

When Daniel was 16 years old, the family settled in North Carolina. Daniel became a hunter. At age 21, he fought in the French and Indian War. The following year, he married fellow Quaker Rebecca Bryan. In 1757 she gave birth to the first of their ten children.

While on a long hunt in the winter of 1760, Boone crossed over the Blue Ridge Mountains. In the winter of 1767 and 1768, he went into the Cumberland region. The next year, he went through the Cumberland Gap. On June 7, 1769, he saw what is now Kentucky for the first time. Today the Kentucky Historical Society celebrates June 7 as Boone Day.

After passing through Cumberland Gap, Boone continued following a Native American trail called Warrior's Path. Six years later, in 1775, Daniel Boone led about thirty men through Cumberland Gap. By cutting down trees, they expanded Warrior's Path, turning it into the Wilderness Road. The Wilderness Road was over two hundred miles long. For the next fifty years, this road was the main route for people moving into Kentucky and Tennessee. The Wilderness Road was also called Boone's Trace.

The Wilderness Road was completed the same year that the first shots of the American Revolution were fired at Lexington and Concord. That year Daniel Boone moved his family to Kentucky where he founded Boonesborough. His wife and daughters were the first Anglo-American women to live in Kentucky. An Anglo-American is an American with British ancestors. The Continental Congress adopted the Declaration of Independence in July 1776. In August a copy reached Boonesborough.

On Christmas Day in 1779, Boone established another Kentucky settlement named Boone's Station, during one of the coldest winters the pioneers had ever known. Today tourists can visit Fort Boonesborough State Park near Richmond, Kentucky, and Boone Station State Historic Site near Lexington.

Most men who settled in Kentucky in the late 1700s served in the Kentucky militia. Boone served as a militia colonel. Before, during, and after the Revolution, the British helped Native Americans fight Kentucky settlers. The British supplied the Native Americans with weapons and at times fought alongside them. While Boone lived at Boone's Station, about fifty British soldiers and about three hundred Native Americans attacked 182 Kentucky militiamen. This battle, called the Battle of Blue Licks, occurred on August 8, 1782, ten months after Cornwallis surrendered at Yorktown.

Daniel moved back across the Appalachians and lived near Point Pleasant, Virginia, (now in West Virginia) from 1788 to 1798. In 1799 he moved into Spanish territory in Missouri. This area became U.S. territory in 1803. Boone lived in Defiance, near St. Louis, until his death on September 26, 1820, at almost 86 years of age. Artist Chester Harding painted the portrait at right in the year Boone died.

Daniel Boone

Daniel Boone, the Legend

Daniel Boone went on his last hunt in 1817 at age 83. He lived a colorful life, but the legends about him are even more colorful. A legend is a story that may be based in fact, but parts of the story are imagined or exaggerated. People began writing stories about Boone while he was still alive. Kentucky pioneer John Filson wrote *Discovery, Settlement, and Present State of Kentucke* in 1784. He included an appendix that was written as if it had been written by Boone himself. It was called "The Adventures of Col. Daniel Boon, Formerly a

honor of Lafayette, Timothy was toasted as "the grand old man of Tennessee and the first white man to settle the Cumberland country." He and Lafayette conversed in French.

Demonbreun died in 1826. In 1996 descendants of Demonbreun erected a statue in his honor near the Cumberland River in Nashville.

Moses Winters and the Founding of Nashville

James Robertson,
"Father of Tennessee"

In 1779 Moses Winters and his family were living in the Watauga settlement in what later became eastern Tennessee. James Robertson was preparing to leave the Watauga area to lead a large group of settlers into Middle Tennessee. There they planned to build a settlement at the French Salt Lick on land purchased from the Cherokee. The Winters family joined Robertson's group. James Robertson is pictured at right. He is called the Father of Tennessee.

Believing that an overland route would be difficult for women and children, the settlers decided that only the men and older boys would travel across the Cumberland Mountains. In the fall, the overland group left for the French Salt Lick, driving cattle before them.

According to their plan, some of the men stayed in Watauga to build thirty flatboats which would bring the women, children, and slaves by way of the Tennessee River. John Donelson stayed behind to lead this group. None of the men had ever traveled to Middle Tennessee by boat. They were only guessing that it could be done. Due to delays in building the boats, it was December before they left on their journey. Among the boat travelers were Moses' wife Elizabeth and their seven daughters. Another girl on the flatboats was John Donelson's daughter Rachel, who later married Andrew Jackson (see Lesson 46).

Map with Tennessee, Ohio, and Cumberland Rivers
(The dot marks Watauga and the star marks Nashville.)

The men reached the salt lick in December. This was the same cold winter that Daniel Boone established Boone's Station. The Middle Tennessee settlers reached their destination on the same day Boone reached Boone's Station, Christmas Day of 1779. Robertson knew that he wanted to build their first fort on the southern side of the Cumberland River, but their route brought them to the north side. Robertson wondered how they would cross the river. This problem was solved by the cold winter. The river was frozen solid, so they simply drove their cattle across the ice. Soon they began to build Fort Nashborough. See a photo of the reconstructed fort on page 197. Gradually men began to venture beyond the fort to build cabins for their wives and children whom they expected to arrive in January. These men were in constant danger of attack from Native Americans who lived in the area. The lands of Middle Tennessee were hunting grounds for Native Americans. Other tribes probably did not recognize the sale made by the Cherokee.

Fort Nashborough has been reconstructed in downtown Nashville.

The boat travelers were having tremendous difficulties. During their voyage, they were attacked by Native Americans. Some contracted smallpox. They were surprised by the treacherous waters of the Muscle Shoals in what is now northern Alabama. The settlers thought that the Tennessee River would come close to the French Salt Lick, but they were badly mistaken. The boat travelers had to travel all the way to the Ohio River and then paddle against its current to the Cumberland River. They then had to paddle against its current all the way to Fort Nashborough. See the illustration of a flat boat at left.

Traveling by Flatboat

It was late April before the boat travelers arrived. They had traveled 1,000 miles. On the map on page 196, trace the overland route through southern Kentucky and the boat route.

Moses Winters received a Revolutionary War land grant in 1784. On this land, about twenty miles from Nashville, he cleared an area and planted an apple orchard.

Moses and Elizabeth Winters became members of the Baptist Church of Christ in 1791. Their son Caleb was an active church member and preached on occasion. Moses and Caleb began to serve on juries in the county court. Moses and Elizabeth spent the rest of their lives in Middle Tennessee and were buried under an ash tree in Robertson County (named for James Robertson).

A Personal Note

I grew up in a small town in Middle Tennessee during the 1950s and 1960s with my father, mother, and younger brother. We were a simple, average family. My mother was a seamstress and my father worked in his father's grocery store. Like your family and every other American family, there was an historic reason why I grew up where I did. My own ancestors moved into Middle Tennessee during the late 1700s. I am a descendant of Timothy Demonbreun on my father's side of the family. I remember my grandfather telling me about our ancestor Timothy Demonbreun who lived in a cave by the Cumberland River. On my mother's side, I am a descendant of Moses Winters, his son Caleb, and Caleb's daughter Sally. When I was a girl, my family often crossed the bridge over Caleb's Creek when we traveled between the homes of my two sets of grandparents. I am thankful for my pioneer ancestors and for my grandparents and parents who taught me the "faith of their fathers." Ask your parents and grandparents how your family came to live where you do.

Charlene Notgrass

Daniel Boone's mother taught him faith in God. When he was 72 years old, he wrote a letter to his sister-in-law. With his poor spelling and grammar, he expressed a real faith:

I am as ignerant as a Child all the Religan I have to Love and fear God believe in Jesus Christ. Dowall the good to my Neighbors and my Self that I can and Do as Little harm as I can help and trust in God's mercy for Rest.

Let us trust God the way Daniel Boone did. As the apostle John wrote:

Grace and mercy and peace will be with us, from God the Father and from Jesus Christ, the Son of the Father, in truth and love.
2 John 3

Activities for Lesson 35

Timeline – In *Timeline of America the Beautiful* next to 1774, write: Timothy Demonbreun is a fur trader at the French Salt Lick.

Literature – Read "The Adventures of Colonel Daniel Boone" in *We the People*, page 34, and the chapter titled "Evergreen Years 1794-1801" in *Amos Fortune: Free Man*.

Vocabulary – Write five sentences in your notebook, using one of these words in each: emigrate, militia, appendix, interpreter, treacherous. Check in a dictionary if you need help with their definitions.

Creative Writing – Ask one of your parents the following questions: How did you decide that we would live here in ____? How did you choose this house (or apartment, etc.)? Do you want to stay here, or do you think about moving to a new place? Write a few paragraphs about what you learned from the interview.

Student Workbook or Lesson Review – If you are using one of these optional books, complete the assignment for Lesson 35. If you are using the Lesson Review, answer the questions on *Amos Fortune: Free Man* and take the quiz for Unit 7.

Americans Explore West of the Mississippi River

8

After America purchased millions of acres from France in 1803, President Thomas Jefferson sent Meriwether Lewis and William Clark on an expedition to find out about the nation's new lands. The first two lessons this week tell this American story while also exploring the wonders of God's creation which Lewis, Clark, and their Corps of Discovery found along the way. As Lewis and Clark explored the Louisiana Purchase, they met many Indians of the Great Plains; our Daily Life lesson is about the tribes who lived there. This week our American Landmark is the Gateway Arch in St. Louis, which honors Jefferson's role in America's expansion into the West. Our American Biography is about Noah Webster, who published his first dictionary the same year that Lewis and Clark returned from their expedition.

*Great Plains Native
from the Wichita Tribe, 1927*

Lessons in Unit 8

Lesson 36 – God's Wonders and Our American Story: Thomas Jefferson Sends Lewis and Clark on a Voyage of Discovery

Lesson 37 – God's Wonders and Our American Story: The Corps of Discovery Completes Its Mission and Returns Home

Lesson 38 – Daily Life: Natives of the Great Plains

Lesson 39 – An American Landmark: The Gateway Arch in St. Louis, Missouri

Lesson 40 – An American Biography: Noah Webster, Father of the American Dictionary

Books Used in Unit 8

* *Maps of America the Beautiful*

* *Timeline of America the Beautiful*

* *We the People*

Thomas Jefferson Sends Lewis and Clark on a Voyage of Discovery

In 1800 Thomas Jefferson was serving as Vice President under John Adams. The two men had worked together during the American Revolution and had become close friends. When Adams sought re-election, Jefferson ran against him. The presidential campaign was bitter and mean. It cost Adams and Jefferson their friendship. Jefferson is the only Vice President in American history who has run for the presidency against the President with whom he served. Thomas Jefferson was victorious over Adams.

Thomas Jefferson Becomes the Third American President

Thomas Jefferson became the third President of the United States in 1801. Adams did not even attend Jefferson's inauguration. The former friends never saw each other again, though they eventually made peace with one another and kept in contact through letters.

Thomas Jefferson tried to be a spokesman for everyday people and called his election the "Revolution of 1800." Jefferson believed that states should govern themselves without interference from the national government. He believed in individual rights, though he did not extend those rights to African American slaves. Jefferson himself was a slave holder, and slavery remained legal throughout his presidency. The national government did pass a law making it illegal to import slaves into the country after January 1, 1808. While he was President, Jefferson was able to reduce the cost of the national government and lower America's debt. America gained its 17th state in 1803 when Ohio joined the Union.

Trouble with Great Britain

New State

1803 Ohio

While Napoleon Bonaparte was emperor of France in the early 1800s, France and Great Britain fought against each other in the Napoleonic Wars. Though the United States remained neutral, Great Britain began to stop some American ships heading for France. Sometimes the British Navy captured Americans and required them to work on British ships, a practice called impressment. In 1807 a British ship fired on an American warship. Britain later apologized, but relations between America and Great Britain suffered. Jefferson tried to help the situation by asking Congress to pass the Embargo Act of 1807. Congress passed this law, which made it illegal for an American ship to carry goods to Great Britain. Jefferson hoped the law would keep the British from harassing

American ships. Instead, it hurt American businesses. The Embargo Act was repealed three days before Jefferson left office in 1809.

A Surprising Opportunity

When Thomas Jefferson was elected in 1800, the country's western boundary was the Mississippi River. France had control of a large area west of the Mississippi called the Louisiana Territory. It extended from Louisiana to Montana. Look at the map below. Napoleon decided in 1803 to sell the Louisiana Territory to the United States to raise money for his wars. France sold the 828,000-square-mile territory for fifteen million dollars, which is only three cents an acre. The Louisiana Purchase was announced on July 4, 1803.

Lewis and Clark Prepare to Explore the Louisiana Territory

Rumors abounded about this new territory. Were there volcanoes there? Were there woolly mammoths? Was there a mountain of salt? Was there a water route all the way to the Pacific Ocean? President Jefferson decided to send explorers into the territory to observe the geography, plants, and animals; to visit the Native American tribes of the region; and to look

THE LOUISIANA PURCHASE (1803)

It is not possible to create an exact map of the boundaries of the Louisiana Purchase. The boundaries were vague when America and France made their agreement since neither knew exactly what lay beyond the Mississippi.

for a water passage to the Pacific. The President chose Meriwether Lewis, his personal secretary and an Army veteran, as the leader of the expedition, which Jefferson called the Corps of Discovery. See illustration of Lewis at right below.

Jefferson sent Lewis to learn from leading scientists to prepare for the expedition. Lewis studied astronomy, biology, botany, medicine, and navigation. Lewis chose William Clark as his assistant. See Clark at left below. William Clark was the younger brother of Revolutionary War hero George Rogers Clark (see page 149).

With money allocated by Congress, Lewis gathered the best supplies available at the time. To help with scientific observations, he purchased a compass, telescope, and other mathematical instruments. He also purchased books about botany, minerals, astronomy, and other subjects. He bought paper, ink, and drawing crayons to record what they discovered. Lewis gathered fish hooks, fishing lines, guns, and ammunition so the Corps

could obtain food. He bought clothes, blankets, and knapsacks for his men. He purchased tent fabric, mosquito curtains, and other camping supplies. He also obtained medicines, syringes, tourniquets, and other medical supplies. Lewis acquired hand saws, hatchets, chisels, and other tools. He bought gifts for Native Americans, including pocket mirrors,

William Clark

Meriwether Lewis

sewing needles, scissors, sewing thread, silk ribbons, brightly-colored fabric, face paint, beads, and more.

Lewis traveled to Pittsburgh, where he oversaw the construction of a fifty-five-foot keelboat, which is a sort of barge which could could be sailed, rowed, poled, or towed. When the keelboat was completed, Lewis traveled down the Ohio River. Along the way, he picked up Clark and some of the men recruited for the expedition. In the fall of 1803, Lewis and Clark established Camp Dubois in Illinois territory on the eastern bank of the Mississippi River. There they recruited and trained more men.

The Corps of Discovery had thirty-three permanent members. Lewis and Clark called one another captain, though Clark was actually a lieutenant. The Corps had four sergeants, twenty-three privates, and six non-military members, including Clark's slave York. Each man was chosen because he had certain skills such as hunting, woodcutting, craftsmanship, or interpreting. In addition to those of English ancestry, three were Irish, one German, one French-Canadian, and one part French and part Omaha Indian. Recruits from Kentucky and Tennessee had developed frontier skills useful to the expedition. Other men and one woman, the now-famous Sacajawea, would later travel with them for portions of the expedition.

1804 – Lewis and Clark Begin a Voyage of Discovery

As Lewis completed business in St. Louis, Clark and several members of the Corps of Discovery set out from Camp Dubois on May 14, 1804. They sailed a few miles up the Mississippi River before Lewis and more Corps members joined them at the small French settlement of St. Charles. They stayed for a few days, gathering more supplies, attending church services, and socializing with the townspeople.

On May 23, the Corps began their long voyage up the Missouri River. See the drawing at right. The Corps had the keelboat and two small wooden boats called pirogues, one red and one white. The

The Corps of Discovery sailed up the Missouri .

Missouri River is 2,540 miles long, the longest river in the United States. French explorers Marquette and Joliet had been the first Europeans to see the river. The Corps would eventually travel all the way to the Missouri's source high in the Rocky Mountains. They had to work hard all the way to travel upstream against the current. The Missouri picks up great quantities of silt as it meanders toward the Mississippi River, thus it is known as the "Big Muddy." Because it is so wide, it is also called the "Wide Missouri."

The expedition quickly passed all of the small French settlements along the river. They passed the mouth of the Femme Osage River near where Daniel Boone was living at the time. They then entered the Great Plains region. Because of rumors they had heard, Corps members feared they would soon meet natives who were warlike, cruel, and of gigantic

Left to Right: Coyote, Bull Snake (or Gopher Snake) with Least Tern, Black-Billed Magpie, and Black-Tailed Prairie Dog

stature. As a precaution, they sometimes camped on river islands. The Corps did not actually see any Indians until August 2 when members of the Oto and Missouri tribes came to their camp. The next day the Corps held a council with Oto and Missouri chiefs. The Corps handed out gifts and American flags, showed the natives their scientific instruments, and held a military parade to show their strength. Lewis told the natives about Thomas Jefferson, their new "great father" in the east. He gave them a peace medal with a picture of Jefferson on one side and two hands shaking on the other. The Corps repeated these ceremonies as they met other tribes during the expedition.

The Corps had problems with only a few tribes. Often natives gave them invaluable help. Many natives were fascinated by the visitors, especially by York because of his black skin. The Corps eventually encountered over fifty tribes of the Great Plains, Great Basin, Plateau, and Northwest Coast regions.

Day by day, as the Corps traveled northward, they experienced many wonders of God's creation. They saw bluffs like the one on page 204. Some were decorated with Indian paintings. While in Missouri, they saw Missouri beavers, northern raccoons, plains horned toads, and plains gray wolves. While traveling on the Missouri River between Nebraska and Iowa, they saw bull snakes, black-billed magpies, and black-tailed prairie dogs like the ones above. On one occasion, while hunting for elk in this area, William Clark became so fascinated by the beauty of the vast prairies that he forgot about the elk he was chasing.

By late October, the Corps of Discovery reached a group of Mandan and Hidatsa villages on the eastern bank of the Missouri River in North Dakota. Captains Lewis and

Toussaint Charbonneau with his wife Sacajawea and their son Jean Baptiste

Clark decided to spend the winter there, so they built Fort Mandan across the river from the Mandan village of Mitutanka. While there, they studied the culture of the Mandan and Hidatsa people and described them in their journals. The Hidatsas gave them valuable information about the Missouri River and its great waterfall. Notice the Mandan man in the picture on page 204. He is wearing a buffalo robe.

Toussaint Charbonneau was a French-Canadian fur trader living in one of the villages. He is pictured at left with Sacajawea, one of his two wives. Sacajawea was a Shoshone girl the Hidatsas had captured five years before from the

Great Basin region. Lewis and Clark hired Charbonneau as an interpreter. Sacajawea became an important member of the expedition, serving as an interpreter and guide.

While the Corps waited for the weather to allow the expedition to continue, privates Pierre Cruzatte and George Gibson entertained other Corps members with their fiddle-playing. The men celebrated Christmas and the New Year with music, singing, dancing, and special foods. During the winter, Corps members went on a buffalo hunt with the Mandans. Sacajawea gave birth to a baby boy named Jean Baptiste.

The Americans and the natives alike experienced a frigid winter. Temperatures that year reached as low as 45 degrees below zero! God is the One who makes winter weather:

A Mandan man, wearing a buffalo robe, stands on a bluff beside the Missouri River in this 1908 photograph.

> He gives snow like wool;
> He scatters the frost like ashes.
> He casts forth His ice as fragments:
> Who can stand before His cold?
> Psalm 147:16-17

Activities for Lesson 36

Thinking Biblically – Read Numbers 13:1-14:9 about an exploring trip taken by a group of Israelites.

Map Study – Complete the assignments for Lesson 36 on Map 13 "Lewis and Clark's Voyage of Discovery" and on Map 20 "The Lower 48" in *Maps of America the Beautiful*.

Timeline – In *Timeline of America the Beautiful* next to 1804, write: Sacajawea joins the Lewis and Clark expedition.

Literature – Read "Letter to Thomas Jefferson Smith" in *We the People*, pages 35-36.

Vocabulary – Look up these words in a dictionary: spokesman, astronomy, botany, tourniquet, invaluable. Write each word with its definition in your notebook.

Family Activity – Make the "Supplies for the Voyage of Discovery" game and play it. See the instructions on page 427.

Student Workbook or Lesson Review – If you are using one of these optional books, complete the assignment for Lesson 36.

The Corps of Discovery Completes Its Mission and Returns Home

After the cold winter of 1804-1805, the Corps of Discovery prepared to leave Fort Mandan to continue exploring the Louisiana Territory. In March, Lewis wrote a letter to his mother. While describing the immense Missouri River and the broad prairies they had traveled through thus far, he called it one of the fairest places on earth.

1805 – From Fort Mandan to the Rocky Mountains

In April of 1805, Lewis and Clark sent some of the party back down the Missouri River on the keelboat. They carried reports and maps to President Jefferson. They also took animal skeletons and skins, mineral samples, Native American artifacts, and live animals including a prairie dog, a magpie, and a long-tailed weasel to Jefferson. The men carried letters members of the Corps had written to loved ones.

The remaining Corps members, along with Charbonneau, Sacajawea, and little Jean Baptiste, boarded the two pirogues and six dugout canoes. They left Fort Mandan and headed west on the Missouri River. In North Dakota, the explorers found birds such as horned owls, cedar waxwings, western meadowlarks, killdeer, Nutall's poorwills, and northern flickers. They saw water birds like geese, pelicans, ducks, and cranes. They encountered small mammals like ground squirrels, jackrabbits, muskrats, swift foxes, ermine, otters, badgers, and Dakota pocket gophers. Look at the pictures on page 206 of other creatures the Corps saw and read their names aloud. Native Americans had told Meriwether Lewis about how fierce grizzlies are, but he didn't believe them until he tried to kill one himself.

From North Dakota, the Corps of Discovery headed into what is now Montana. They continued on the Missouri River, passing magnificent geological formations as well as barren deserts. In Montana they found more grizzly bears, a mountain lion, and gigantic herds of bison. See a bison and its calf at left. They saw small mammals like the North American porcupine and

Bison with Calf

Bighorn Sheep

Mule Deer

Red Fox

Grizzly Bear

Striped Skunk

the bushy-tailed woodrat. Birds that were sighted included the Brewer's blackbird, Pacific nighthawk, pinion jay, and Lewis' woodpecker. See the picture on page 207.

On May 31, the Corps members were awed by the beautiful White Cliffs of the Missouri. Today canoeing enthusiasts paddle through the White Cliffs, seeing scenery that has changed little since Lewis and Clark saw it. Though realizing that they were not made by human hands, Lewis thought they looked like the ruins of grand buildings with statues.

On June 2, 1805, the Corps came to a fork in the Missouri. Lewis and Clark chose to follow the south fork, though all their men believed that the north fork was actually the Missouri River. Soon they found the Great Falls of the Missouri. The Hidatsas had told them about the falls, so they knew they had chosen the right way. The Great Falls were beautiful. A mist rising above them made a rainbow. Lewis was sorry he had not brought along an artist to record their beauty. Still, these falls and those that followed made it impossible for them to continue by boat. The Corps had to make

Prairie Sharp-Tailed Grouse

Long-Billed Curlew

Pronghorn

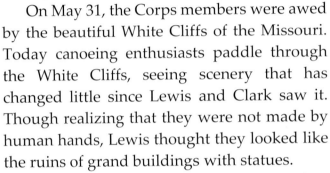

Mountain Lion

North American Porcupine

wooden carts to haul their canoes and supplies past the falls. The tiresome job took almost a month. Finally, they were able to travel again on the Missouri. Soon they went through a dark and gloomy canyon that Lewis named the Gates of the Mountains.

In late July 1805, the explorers came to the Three Forks of the Missouri (now in Montana's Missouri Headwaters State Park). They named these three rivers the Jefferson (after President Jefferson), the Gallatin (after Albert Gallatin, Secretary of the Treasury), and the Madison (after James Madison, Secretary of State). The Corps traveled slowly upstream on the Jefferson River. As they traveled along, Sacajawea saw places familiar to her. Soon they came upon the place where she had been captured by the Hidatsas. She assured the Corps that they would soon be in the land of the Shoshones (see Lesson 3). Lewis and Clark hoped that they could obtain horses.

Clark's Nutcracker

Many birds help plants spread. First, a bird eats a seed. After the seed passes through the bird's digestive tract, the bird "plants" the seed in its droppings.

God created the Clark's nutcracker so that it has a vital role in the spread of whitebark pine trees. Whitebark pinecones do not open naturally, so God gave Clark's nutcrackers the ability to crack them open.

The Clark's nutcracker uses its bill to hammer into the cones. After plucking its seeds, the bird stores them in a pouch under its tongue. When it has collected about eighty seeds, it finds a storage site. The bird digs a trench, coughs up one seed at a time, and buries three to five in the trench before covering it with soil. It then proceeds to dig another trench. One Clark's nutcracker has been known to bury 35,000 seeds in 9,500 trenches in one season. For the next nine months, they remember the sites where they have buried their seeds.

Clark's nutcracker is named for William Clark.

1805 – Over the Rocky Mountains and On to the Pacific Ocean

In August Lewis left the river and headed out with three scouts to search for the Shoshones. On August 12, they reached the Continental Divide of the Rocky Mountains. All streams west of the Divide flow to the Pacific Ocean, and all streams to the east flow to the Atlantic. Lewis and the scouts then climbed up to Lemhi Pass. Lewis had believed that from there he would see the Missouri River flowing into the Pacific Ocean. Actually, he was in the midst of the Rocky Mountains and a long way from the Pacific. In this area, the Corps saw mountain goats, the yellow-bellied marmot, and the Clark's nutcracker. Read about Clark's nutcracker at left.

Lewis' Woodpecker, Named for Meriwether Lewis

On August 17, Lewis and his scouts came to a Shoshone village. Clark and the other men reached the village that same day. Surprisingly, the chief of the village was Cameahwait, brother of Sacajawea!

On August 31, 1805, the Corps of Discovery left the village with a mule, twenty-nine horses, and a Shoshone guide named Old Toby. First, they went over a mountain pass and into a valley. They camped near present-day Missoula, Montana, at a place they called Traveler's Rest. They then entered the Bitterroot Mountains, some of the most rugged mountains in the Rockies. Food was scarce and early fall snows began. Old Toby led them on the ancient trail the Nez Perce tribe used each year to cross the mountains to hunt buffalo on the plains. It took eleven days to get through the Bitterroots. Along the trail, the Corps saw the Franklin's spruce grouse and the ruffed grouse. The ruffed grouse is pictured above.

Ruffed Grouse

Bobcat

When they finally crossed the Bitterroots, they left the Louisiana Territory and entered lands claimed by the British. Soon they found the Nez Perce tribe of the Plateau region (see Lesson 3 for a reminder about this tribe.) Chief Twisted Hair taught them how to make pine canoes. On October 7, they launched five new canoes on the Clearwater River. This was the first time in the entire voyage that they were able to float downstream. Soon they entered the Snake River. Finally, they came to the Columbia River, which forms most of the border between present-day Washington and Oregon.

Roosevelt Elk

While on the Columbia, the Corps spotted the Roosevelt elk and harbor seal. They are pictured at left and below. They passed Beacon Rock on the Washington side of the river. This 848-foot-high rock is pictured on page 209. The British had explored and mapped these areas. On October 18, William Clark spotted Mount Hood in the distance, so they knew that they were nearing the Pacific Ocean. They went through the falls of the Columbia and entered the beautiful Columbia River Gorge, a deep 80-mile-long canyon that cuts through the Cascade Mountains. The Corps encountered bad storms; but they finally got a clear view of the Pacific on November 16, 1805, over 4,000 miles from where they began their expedition.

The Corps had to hurry to build shelter for the winter. Everyone voted on where to build the fort. Slaves and women could not vote in the rest of the United States, but York and Sacajawea voted in this situation. The Corps chose the south side of the

Harbor Seal

Beacon Rock, on the banks of the Columbia River in Washington, is one of the world's largest rocks.

Columbia River as the site of Fort Clatsop. There they celebrated the second Christmas of the expedition. Captains Lewis and Clark gave out handkerchiefs as presents. They met many tribes of the Northwest Coast while at Fort Clatsop. The Corps observed much wildlife, including the mountain beaver, pictured above, and the bobcat, pictured on page 208.

Mountain Beaver

1806 – From Fort Clatsop to St. Louis

After a long, uneventful winter, Lewis and Clark gave Fort Clatsop to the nearby Clatsop tribe of the Northwest Coast. On March 23 they headed east. The Corps tried to travel upstream on the Columbia but decided instead to travel on horses they purchased from the Walla Walla Indians (a Plateau tribe).

In early May, the Corps returned to the Nez Perce and waited for the snows to melt on the Bitterroot Mountains. While there, Lewis studied more of God's creation, while Clark took care of sick members of the Nez Perce tribe. When they left the Nez Perce on June 10, each man of the Corps rode one horse and led another one. They tried to cross the Bitterroots, but found it too difficult because there was still ten feet of snow. Therefore, they returned to the Nez Perce. This time Lewis and Clark hired guides from the tribe. With the help of the guides, the Corps crossed the mountains and finally reached Traveler's Rest on June 30.

The Corps split into two exploring parties on July 3. They reunited on August 12. Two days later, they reached the Mandans. There they said farewell to Charbonneau, Sacajawea, and their little boy Jean Baptiste whom Corps members called Pomp. The Corps hurried to St. Louis, arriving on September 23, 1806. One thousand people greeted them from the bank of the Mississippi River. The Corps had been gone for over two years, and many people thought the members of the Corps of Discovery had died.

Mandan Woman in a Bull Boat

Results of the Heroic Expedition

Captains Lewis and Clark returned to Washington, D.C., and received a heroes' welcome. During the expedition, Lewis, Clark, and other Corps members wrote journals, drew pictures, and made maps. In these they recorded native lifestyles and the geology and geography of the region. They described 178 plants and 122 animals that had never before been recorded by scientists. Information from these diaries has been published often in the last two centuries. The illustration at right, entitled "Captain Lewis Holding a Council with the Indians," was published in 1810 in the journal of Private Patrick Gass.

"Captain Lewis Holding a Council with the Indians," an Illustration from the Journal of Patrick Gass

The Lewis and Clark expedition created great excitement in America. Many people decided to go into the Louisiana territory as fur trappers, traders, or pioneers. Those who traveled on the Missouri often sang river songs like "Oh, Shenandoah," in which each verse ends with the words, "across the wide Missouri."

Members of the Corps of Discovery traveled on five of the longest rivers in the United States. First, Lewis brought the keelboat down the Ohio. Then Clark and others traveled briefly on the Mississippi before entering the Missouri River and traveling all the way to its source. In the far West, they traveled on the Snake and Columbia Rivers. Find these rivers on the chart on page 211.

Thomas Jefferson chose wisely when he picked Meriwether Lewis to lead the Corps of Discovery. Lewis wisely chose Clark as his assistant. Read about Jefferson's life below.

Thomas Jefferson
America's Third President
March 4, 1801 - March 4, 1809

Thomas Jefferson was born into a wealthy Virginia family in 1743. His father, Peter Jefferson, died when Thomas was only 14. Thomas inherited over 5,000 acres and many slaves from his father. In 1760 Jefferson graduated from William and Mary College in Williamsburg, Virginia (see lesson 25). He began to study law in 1762 and became a lawyer five years later. In 1772 he married a widow, Martha Wayles Skelton. She died in 1782, after the birth of their sixth child. Thomas never remarried.

Jefferson soon retired from law. He managed his estate and oversaw the continuing construction of his beautiful home, Monticello. Look at the picture on page 211. Jefferson got up each morning with the sunrise and made note of the temperature, wind speed, wind direction, and amount of precipitation. He also kept records of bird migrations and when flowers first appeared. Jefferson was an avid gardener. Over the years he tried 250 varieties of vegetables in his garden. He said that "those who labor in the earth are the chosen people of God." He enjoyed touring his farm on horseback. His home was filled with his inventions, like his letter copier and his Great Clock, which his laborers could hear three miles away.

Before the Revolution, Thomas Jefferson served in Virginia's House of Burgesses and in the Second Continental Congress. He was the primary author of the Declaration of Independence. Before becoming President, Jefferson served in Congress under the Articles of Confederation, as American Ambassador to France, as President Washington's Secretary of State, and as John Adams' Vice President.

After his presidency, Jefferson entertained, managed his estate, enjoyed his many interests, and kept up his correspondence. In his lifetime, he wrote almost 20,000 letters. He was a devoted grandfather.

Books were important to Jefferson. In 1815 he sold his library of 6,487 volumes to the Library of Congress and afterwards began to collect books for himself again. He founded the University of Virginia, which opened in 1825. Thomas Jefferson and John Adams both died on the Fourth of July in 1826, exactly fifty years after the approval of the Declaration of Independence.

Monticello, Home of Thomas Jefferson

Members of the Corps of Discovery were blessed to be able to see amazing wonders that God created. We are blessed that they recorded their observations and discoveries.

By awesome deeds You answer us in righteousness,
O God of our salvation, You who are the trust
of all the ends of the earth and of the farthest sea;
Who establishes the mountains by his strength,
Being girded with might.
Psalm 65:5-6

Activities for Lesson 37

Map Study – Complete the assignments for Lesson 37 on Map 13 "Lewis and Clark's Voyage of Discovery" in *Maps of America the Beautiful*.

Timeline – In *Timeline of America the Beautiful* next to 1805, write: Lewis and Clark reach the Pacific Ocean.

Literature – Read "Journals of Lewis and Clark" in *We the People*, pages 37-38.

Creative Writing – Imagine that your family hosted some members of the Corps of Discovery when they returned to St. Louis, Missouri. In your notebook, write a letter to your cousin in Washington, D.C., telling about your dinner with the explorers.

Student Workbook or Lesson Review – If you are using one of these optional books, complete the assignment for Lesson 37.

20 Longest Rivers in America	
Missouri	2,540 miles
Mississippi	2,340 miles
Yukon	1,980 miles
Rio Grande	1,900 miles
St. Lawrence	1,900 miles
Arkansas	1,460 miles
Colorado	1,450 miles
Atchafalaya	1,420 miles
Ohio	1,310 miles
Red	1,290 miles
Brazos	1,280 miles
Columbia	1,240 miles
Snake	1,040 miles
Platte	990 miles
Pecos	926 miles
Canadian	906 miles
Tennessee	886 miles
Colorado (of Texas)	862 miles
North Canadian	800 miles
Mobile	774 miles

Natives of the Great Plains

People often think of Native Americans as people who wore feathered warbonnets, slept in tepees, and went on buffalo hunts. While these images are not accurate for all American Indians, they were a part of the culture of many living in the Great Plains. The Great Plains region stretches across most of the area between the Mississippi River and the Rocky Mountains. In old movies about Indians, cowboy actors sometimes say, "How," when greeting an Indian. Actually "How" does sound similar to the greeting, "Hau," used by some of the Sioux tribe of the Great Plains. Indians in those movies sometimes used sign language. Though tribes of the Great Plains spoke many different languages, they did sometimes use a form of sign language to communicate between tribes. It is called Plains Sign Language.

Yankton Sioux

Tribes of the Great Plains

The Corps of Discovery encountered several Great Plains tribes on their expedition. Meriwether Lewis met members of the Osage tribe from southern Missouri and Oklahoma while he was in St. Louis before the expedition began. Other tribes of the southern Great Plains include the Lipan Apache, Tonkawa, Comanche, and Wichita who lived in Texas; the Kiowa of Kansas and Oklahoma; and the Quapaw of Arkansas. In this lesson we will concentrate on the tribes Lewis and Clark saw or came near during their expedition.

Kanza (or Kaw) – The Corps of Discovery camped on the site of a Kanza village but did not meet anyone from this tribe, since they were away from home on a hunting trip.

Oto and Missouri Tribes – At the time the Corps of Discovery met them in 1804, the Oto and Missouri were living together. The main Oto chief then was Little Thief and the main Missouri chief was Big Horse. An Oto warrior and a Missouri warrior are pictured at right.

German Prince Maximilian zu Wied-Neuwied explored the Missouri River from 1832 through 1834. He hired Swiss Painter Karl Bodmer to draw pictures of natives they met, such as this picture of a Missouri warrior, an Oto warrier, and a Ponca chief.

Yankton Sioux – Captain William Clark was impressed with the neatly-arranged Yankton Sioux tepee camp he saw in late August of 1804. The tepees were decorated with different colors of paint. The Corps camped nearby. Yankton Sioux musicians led about seventy tribesmen to the Corps' camp. When Clark went to the Yankton Sioux village, six braves carried him on a fancy painted buffalo robe. They did not let him touch the ground until they placed him on a white robe in their grand council house. While the Corps visited the Yankton Sioux, Chief Weuche's braves displayed their skills with the bow and arrow and showed the Corps several ceremonial dances. The tribe has an oral tradition that Meriwether Lewis wrapped a newborn Sioux baby in a United States flag and proclaimed that he was an American. See a picture of a Yankton Sioux on page 212.

In 1820 President James Monroe sent Major Stephen Long to explore the central regions of the Great Plains. Soldiers, hunters, scientists, and an artist accompanied Long. This illustration of Long meeting with a Pawnee council was published in 1823.

Pawnee – When the Corps of Discovery first entered the lands of the Pawnee, the tribe was away on their summer buffalo hunt. In the fall when they returned to harvest the crops they had planted in April, they met the Corps. In October the Pawnee left again for their winter buffalo hunt. Look at the illustration of the Pawnee council above.

Teton Sioux – When the Corps of Discovery passed close to what is now Pierre, the state capital of South Dakota, the Teton Sioux were living in two nearby villages. The tribe depended on the neighboring Arikaras for food and horses. They provided the Arikaras with supplies, such as clothing and guns. The Teton Sioux were powerful and ready to fight to get what they wanted. They required large gifts from people passing by on the Missouri River. They asked the Corps of Discovery for one of their boats. The Corps'

Lakota Man, Four Women, and Three Babies

three-day visit with the Teton Sioux was tense. Chief Black Buffalo helped keep the two sides from fighting. The Corps witnessed several Teton Sioux celebrations while staying with them. The Teton Sioux were also called Lakota. See the photo above.

Omaha – In August of 1804, the Corps passed an empty Omaha village. Its residents were away on a buffalo hunt. The only Omaha that they saw on their expedition were forty-eight Omaha imprisoned by the Teton Sioux. See the picture of an Omaha woman at left.

Omaha Woman

Ponca – The Corps of Discovery tried to meet with Ponca Indians. William Clark sent members of the Corps to one of their villages. The men found a village of earth lodges, but the villagers were on a hunting trip. See a drawing of a Ponca chief on page 212.

Karl Bodmer drew this Mandan village atop a bluff.

Arikara – On October 8, 1804, the Corps of Discovery found three Arikara villages on a three-mile-long island. About 2,000 Arikaras lived there. They were good farmers. In addition to beans, corn, and squash, they grew pumpkins, tobacco, and watermelons. Women did the farming using tools made from buffalo or deer bones. In years when their crops had low yields, they also hunted buffalo. The Corps stayed with them five days. See the picture below of an Arikara girl.

Mandan – The Mandans lived in two villages, Mitutanka and Nuptadi, along the Missouri River. The Corps of Discovery built their first winter camp nearby. A core belief of Mandan culture was that each village should work together for the benefit of the village and for each family and clan that lived there. At the center of the village was a central plaza. A cedar post they thought to be sacred stood in the middle of the plaza and a medicine lodge stood at the northern end. Each village had forty or fifty earth lodges that housed about ten people each. The location of a family's lodge indicated the family's importance. In the winter the Mandans moved away from

A Hidatsa Man Named Long Time Dog

their villages temporarily. They built lodges in lower, forested areas beside the Missouri where they found protection from winter storms. Look at the pictures of a Mandan village above and a Mandan man at lower left.

Fields surrounded the Mandan villages. In the fall, the Mandans hosted other Plains tribes at a trade gathering with an attendance of about 1500. French and British traders also came to exchange goods with the Mandans. The Corps of Discovery arrived at the Mandan-Hidatsa villages in November of 1804, just after they had their fall trade gathering. During the winter of 1804-1805, the Mandans supplied food for the Corps of Discovery in exchange for goods the Corps had brought on their expedition.

Hidatsa – Hidatsa Indians had villages near the Mandans. Hidatsa villages had a central plaza surrounded by earth lodges. Encircling the village was a log wall. The smallest Hidatsa village the

Arikara Girl

Mandan Man

214

Cheyenne Woman, 1910

Crow Child, 1905

Horse Capture,
an Atsina Man, 1908

Agichida, an
Assiniboine Man, 1927

Corps of Discovery saw had about fifty lodges and the largest had 130. The traditional way for young Hidatsa warriors to become leaders was to prove their bravery by attacking Shoshone and Blackfeet tribes. It was during one of those attacks that Sacajawea came to live among the Hidatsas. A Hidatsa man is pictured on page 214.

Cheyenne, Plains Cree, and Assiniboine – The Corps met members of the Cheyenne, Cree, and Assiniboine tribes while in the Mandan villages during the winter of 1804-1805. The Cheyenne were nomadic, so they traded horses and their beautiful quillwork clothing for the corn grown by others. During the Corps' visit with the Mandan on the return trip in 1806, a Cheyenne chief invited William Clark and others to his tepee. The tepee impressed Clark because it was new and made of twenty buffalo skins.

The Plains Cree were a nomadic people who lived in tepees and hunted buffalo. They used controlled fire to herd buffalo where they wanted the buffalo to go. Assiniboine is an Ojibwe word meaning stone water people. The Assiniboine used hot stones to boil water for cooking. They lived in tepees and were also nomads. The Assiniboine hunted buffalo, elk, deer, bighorn sheep, and rabbits. They were suspicious of Americans. Members of the Corps of Discovery were afraid of the Assiniboine. Though they saw evidence that the tribe had been there, the Corps never encountered the Assiniboine in their own lands. See the pictures of a Cheyenne woman and an Assiniboine man above and a Cree woman below.

Blackfeet – Members of this tribe wore dark moccasins, so they were called Blackfeet. See the Blackfeet man at right. By the time Lewis and Clark explored their lands, they were already trading with British traders from Canada. The Blackfeet supplied wolf and beaver pelts, while the British supplied guns and ammunition. These natives lived in tepees. They hunted buffalo. They also ate berries, nuts, steamed camas roots, and small animals like ground squirrels.

Atsina – The Atsina were a nomadic tribe that followed buffalo herds. See the Atsina man above. When Lewis and

Left: Cree Woman Carrying Moss, 1927; Right: Blackfeet Man

Clark met the Shoshones, the Shoshones had recently been raided by the Atsina, but the Corps did not meet the Atsina tribe on their journey.

Crow – The Corps of Discovery did not encounter the Crow until July of 1806. While the Corps was divided into smaller exploring parties, tribesmen sneaked into Clark's camp and stole half of their horses. Look at the Crow girl on page 215 and the Crow man at right.

Other tribes who lived in the northern Great Plains were the Arapaho (see picture at left), Gros Ventre, Iowa, and two other Sioux tribes, the Yanktonai and the Santee.

Elderly Arapaho Man, 1910

Crow Man in Halo Warbonnet

Warbonnets and Face Paint

Men in some Great Plains tribes, including the Blackfeet, Cheyenne, Cree, Crow, and Sioux, wore ceremonial warbonnets made from golden eagle feathers. They had to earn each feather by acts of bravery. The Crow man in the top photograph is wearing a halo warbonnet, with feathers fanning out around his face. Below him is a Blackfeet man in a straight-up headdress. At bottom right is a Dakota Sioux wearing a trailer warbonnet, which had a long tail of one or two rows of feathers. Assiniboine men sometimes wore feathered warbonnets, but they also wore buffalo skin hats that had horns on the sides and a tail hanging down the back. Missouri, Oto, and Kiowa Indians wore turbans made from otter skin.

Blackfeet Man in Straight-Up Warbonnet

Great Plains warriors often wore buckskin war shirts, decorated with ermine tails, quillwork, and beads. The Cheyenne and Blackfeet created beautiful quill embroidery. Some warriors wore buffalo horn armor over their chests. The Assiniboine decorated their clothing with fringe, porcupine quills, beads, elk's teeth, and painted designs. In some tribes, men and women wore tattoos. Assiniboine men wore them on their arms and chests, while women tattooed their faces. Men in some tribes painted their faces. Colors and designs depended upon whether the purpose was for war or for religious ceremonies.

Tepees and Earth Lodges

Many tribes of the Great Plains supplemented their diet by hunting buffalo. To follow the buffalo, they needed a shelter that could be assembled quickly. Therefore, they constructed tepees (also spelled tipis or teepees) from tanned buffalo skin. Natives set up lodge pole pines in a cone shape. They sewed together the skins of fourteen to twenty buffalo. With these skins, they covered the poles. They left an opening in the top so that smoke could escape. In the center of the

Dakota Sioux in Trailer Warbonnet

Horses carry members of the Atsina tribe in 1908, while pulling travois. Notice the tepees in the background.

Dakota Sioux Woman Returns to Tepee After Gathering Wood, 1908

tepee, they dug a fire pit. They laid buffalo rugs on the floor and placed beds beside the walls.

A tepee lasted about ten years. When natives built a new one, they kept the old one to make other things or to patch other tepees. When it was time to move to another place, native women took the tepees down and placed the hides and poles on a travois. Dogs or horses pulled the travois. A whole village could be ready to move in about an hour. Some Great Plains Indians, like the Kiowa and Cheyenne, lived in tepees all the time, while others lived in them only while on buffalo hunts. Look at the pictures at left.

Many Great Plains Indians lived in circular earth lodges for most of the year. In the Hidatsa tribe, women built these homes. They could complete one in seven to ten days. The lodges were about ten to fifteen feet high and between thirty and sixty feet long. One woman served as the construction supervisor. She laid out a circular floor plan and marked the place for each post. Hidatsa women used stone tools to cut down cottonwood trees to use for posts and beams. They carefully dug holes for the posts so that each one would rise to the same height. Men helped the women put up the main posts and crossbeams. After this step, the women gave a feast to thank the men for their help.

The women completed the frame for the circular wall and the roof. Then they added split logs and willow branches. Over this they placed a layer of dry prairie grass and then a layer of sod. Sod is a section of grass-covered dirt including the grass roots. They left a hole in the center of the roof to let out smoke. When a lodge was completed, another feast was held to thank all those who helped. The female supervisor was paid with a soft buffalo skin and other items. Look at the earth lodge diagram and floor plan below. See smoke coming through the roofs. Notice the dogs and travois in front of the lodges.

Earth lodges lasted about ten years. By then, the posts that were in the ground had begun to rot. Hidatsa women carefully took the earth lodge apart, saved what could be reused, and burned the rotten pieces.

In the Hidatsa tribe each earth lodge was home to between ten

Floor Plan

Illustrations of Earth Lodges

217

and twenty people. Usually sisters and their families lived together. Raised beds lined the outer wall. The beds had buffalo blankets and skin pillows stuffed with grass or animal hair. Beds for adults had curtains made from old tepees. They were decorated with marks of honor won by the husband. The tribe's best horses shared the homes at night, staying in indoor corrals.

In the center of the home was the firepit. When rains or snows were heavy, they placed a bull boat over the roof hole and propped it up so the smoke could still escape. See the bull boat at right and the one on page 209.

Hidatsa Bull Boat

Hunting Buffalo

Many Plains tribes lived along rivers and streams. There they grew beans, corn, and squash. Many tribes supplemented their diet with buffalo meat. The tribes living in the higher, drier northern plains were more dependent on the buffalo for food because crops did not grow as well there. Before the Spanish brought horses to North America, men of the Great Plains hunted buffalo on foot using bows and arrows. Some tribes herded buffalo into a corral or off a cliff. Sometimes they wore disguises to do so, as illustrated in the painting at left. It was painted by George Catlin, who traveled the Great Plains in 1832-1833. After obtaining horses, the Great Plains tribesmen hunted on horseback, as pictured below.

Buffalo Hunt Under the Wolf-Skin Mask by Catlin

Great Plains natives found over fifty ways to use the buffalo, including boiling the hooves to make glue, making shields from buffalo humps, and making clothing and rugs from their skin and fur. The Kanza (or Kaw) tribe used buffalo killed in summer for leather and those killed in winter for fur because the winter fur was thicker. The Hidatsas tied buffalo ribs together to make sleds, which their children enjoyed in winter. The Blackfeet strung buffalo teeth to make necklaces. The Sioux wove thick ropes from buffalo tail fur and made spoons from their horns. They also made rattles from buffalo hooves. They tied the rattles to doorways so they would know when someone entered, and they also used them in ceremonies. Members of most Great Plains tribes wore buffalo skin moccasins. Some tribes, like the Crow, left the fur on when they made warm winter moccasins.

As white Americans moved onto the Great Plains, they had more and more contact with Native Americans. Read the box on page 219, which shows that Native Americans also traveled east to meet with American leaders.

Hunting Buffalo on Horseback

Native Americans Visit Washington, D.C.

When Thomas Jefferson sent Meriwether Lewis on his great expedition, the President told Lewis to invite tribal chiefs to visit him in Washington, D.C. In 1804 leaders of the Osage tribe visited Jefferson. In March of 1805, he welcomed a Missouri chief and the Oto Chief Little Thief. On New Year's Day in 1806 Thomas Jefferson entertained chiefs from the Arikara, Missouri, Oto, and Yankton Sioux tribes.

American artist George Catlin described the Osage as the tallest men in America. Most of their men were at least six feet tall, many were six and a half, and some were seven feet tall. Perhaps these are the natives of "gigantic stature" the Corps of Discovery feared. The Osage men who met President Coolidge in 1925 were of average height, as seen below.

Natives of the Great Plains were created in the image of God. Therefore they were able to create beauty and to use the abundant resources that God gave them.

Bless the Lord, O my soul,
And all that is within me,
bless His holy name. . . .
Who satisfies your years with good things,
So that your youth is renewed
like the eagle.
Psalm 103:1,5

Activities for Lesson 38

Map Study – Complete the assignment for Lesson 38 on Map 4 "Native Peoples of North America" in *Maps of America the Beautiful*.

Timeline – In *Timeline of America the Beautiful* next to 1805, write: Native American chiefs visit President Thomas Jefferson in Washington.

Vocabulary – In your notebook, copy each sentence below. Fill in each blank with the right word from this list: oral, tense, yield, plaza, encounter.

1. The dinner was _____ because the guests arrived two hours early.
2. While walking through the _____, we saw street performers and vendors selling produce.
3. Sometimes my mother gives me _____ instructions and sometimes she writes them down.
4. The tomato plant did not have the high _____ that the catalog had promised.
5. My second grade math book was my first time to _____ the multiplication table.

Literature – Read "Myths and Legends of the Sioux" in *We the People*, pages 39-40.

Student Workbook or Lesson Review – If you are using one of these optional books, complete the assignment for Lesson Lesson 38.

The Gateway Arch in St. Louis, Missouri

The tallest monument in America stands alongside the Mississippi River in St. Louis, Missouri. The Gateway Arch symbolizes the role St. Louis played in opening up the West to American exploration and settlement. The Arch is located in the Jefferson National Expansion Memorial Historic Site, a 193-acre park honoring Thomas Jefferson's role in American expansion. The park is administered by the National Park Service. Beneath the Arch is the Museum of Westward Expansion.

The Basilica of Saint Louis, pictured on page 221, is also in the Jefferson National Expansion Memorial Historic Site. The Catholic Church began building the Basilica in 1831, but church services have been held on the site since French fur traders founded St. Louis in 1764. It is named in honor of King Louis IX who became king of France in 1226 when he was twelve years old. In 1248 Louis IX went to fight Muslims in Egypt on the seventh Crusade. He was defeated and captured. After his release, he spent time in Palestine before returning to France. He died in 1270 during another Crusade. The Catholic Church proclaimed Louis a saint in 1297.

The Louisiana Purchase Exposition of 1904

St. Louis citizens are proud of the city's role in America's expansion to the west. The official transfer of the Louisiana Purchase from France to America was made in St. Louis in 1804, while it was still a town of less than 1,000 residents. In 1904 a mass was held in the Basilica of St. Louis to commemorate the 100th anniversary of the transfer. That same year the Louisiana Purchase Exposition was held in St. Louis. See the postcard picture below. The Liberty Bell was brought to St. Louis for the exposition. See the picture at the top right on page 221.

Postcard with a Panoramic View of the Entire Louisiana Purchase Exposition

At left: Sioux Family in the "Primitive" Exhibition of the Exposition
Right: The Liberty Bell is moved from a truck to a train after being displayed at the 1904 Louisiana Purchase Exposition

One of its largest exhibitions was called the "primitive" exhibition. Native Americans and other people that organizers viewed as primitive were on display at the fair. See the picture of a Sioux family above. They wore traditional clothing and erected traditional homes. Today's Museum of Westward Expansion is more respectful of native peoples.

The Design and Designer of the Gateway Arch

In the early 1940s, land was cleared to build the Jefferson National Expansion Memorial. In 1947 and 1948, architects submitted design ideas. Eero Saarinen submitted the winning design.

Saarinen was born in Finland in 1910. His father was Eliel Saarinen, a famous architect. When Eero was thirteen, the family immigrated to America. At age 24, he graduated from Yale School of Architecture and became a partner with his father.

Saarinen's designs vary greatly. His other major works include the Kresge Auditorium at the Massachusetts Institute of Technology with its triangular-shaped roof; the TWA terminal at Kennedy International Airport in New York with its wing-like shapes; and the Dulles International Airport in Washington, D.C., with a roof of concrete hung by cables. Saarinen died in 1961, before construction on the Arch began.

Mass at the Basilica of St. Louis in 1904 to Commemorate the 100th Anniversary of the Transfer of the Louisiana Territory to America

For the Jefferson National Expansion Memorial, Saarinen designed a stainless steel arch. He chose a catenary curve shape because this design makes an arch strong. To visualize the curve of the Gateway Arch, hold the ends of a chain or rope in both hands and let it hang. The curve you create is called a catenary, or elliptical, curve. Strength is

important for such a large outdoor structure. The Arch can sway 9 inches in each direction in a 150-mile-per-hour wind. It usually sways about one half inch.

The design of the Arch creates an illusion. As seen in the photograph at left, the arch appears to be taller than it is wide; but actually the Arch is 630 feet high and 630 feet wide at the base. People normally view the Arch from the ground. Because the Arch is so large, and because things appear smaller when they are far away from us, it is difficult for the human eye or the camera to show accurately the real dimensions of the Arch.

The Arch is hollow and has a triangular shape. Look at the photographs on page 223. In the top picture, the photographer stood on the ground under the arch, near one of its legs. This picture shows two sides of the triangle. The line in the center of the photograph is the place where those two sides meet. In the bottom picture, the photographer stood outside the Arch, showing the third side. At the base of the Arch, each leg is fifty-four feet wide. The Arch tapers to a 17-foot width at the top of the curve. To get an idea of the size of the Arch, look at the people standing near the arch in the bottom photo.

The outside of the Arch is made of stainless steel. Underneath the stainless steel is reinforced concrete. Crews began constructing the Arch in February of 1963. They put in the last piece on October 28, 1965. Crews used nine hundred tons of stainless steel. The total weight of the Arch is 17,246 tons. The cost of construction was thirteen million dollars.

Visitors can go underground below the Gateway Arch and board a tram car, which will take them upward inside the Arch. Getting to the top takes four minutes. There visitors can look out observation windows and see the Mississippi River and the flat lands of Illinois to the east and the city of St. Louis to the west.

The Museum of Westward Expansion

The Museum of Westward Expansion is in an underground museum beneath the Arch. In the museum visitors learn about native tribes and American pioneers who lived in the West. It has a life-size tepee and a life-size covered wagon.

The Indian Peace Medal exhibit educates visitors about relations between the American government and native tribes. It teaches about Indian agents, native chiefs, and American military personnel who served in the American West.

The museum displays artifacts explaining the life of a Western cowboy and life in a pioneer sod house. It teaches about the importance of the Appaloosa horse, the longhorn steer, the bison, the beaver, and the grizzly bear in the history of the American West.

The Gateway Arch is made of stainless steel. The main component of steel is iron. God created iron as part of the dry ground He tells us about in the first chapter of Genesis. People have been using iron since the earliest days of the history of the world.

> As for Zillah, she also gave birth to Tubal-cain,
> the forger of all implements of bronze and iron.
> Genesis 4:22

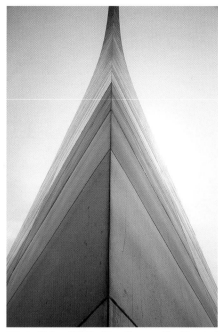
Photo Taken While Standing on the Ground Beneath the Arch

Activities for Lesson 39

Thinking Biblically – Jesus talked about a gate (or door) as an image of Himself. Copy John 10:9 in your notebook.

Map Study – Complete the assignment for Lesson 39 on Map 3 "American Landmarks" in *Maps of America the Beautiful*.

Timeline – In *Timeline of America the Beautiful* next to 1965, write: The Gateway Arch is completed in St. Louis.

Vocabulary – Look up each of these words in a dictionary: expansion, administered, transfer, primitive, illusion. Write each word and its definition in your notebook.

Creative Writing – In your notebook, write an imaginary newspaper article for a St. Louis newspaper as if the arch was just completed and open for visitors.

Photo Taken While Standing Outside the Arch

Student Workbook or Lesson Review – If you are using one of these optional books, complete the assignment for Lesson 39.

Noah Webster,
Father of the American Dictionary

Noah Webster

In 1806, the same year that Lewis and Clark returned from their great Western adventure, Noah Webster published his first dictionary, *A Compendious Dictionary of the English Language*. Webster had an extraordinary influence on American English. See his picture at left.

Noah Webster was born in 1758 in West Hartford, Connecticut. His ancestors had come to New England in the 1600s. His was the sixth generation of Websters to live in America. The famous politician and speaker, Daniel Webster, was Noah Webster's cousin. Noah was the fourth child born to Noah Webster Sr. and his wife Mercy Steele Webster. Mercy was a descendant of Governor William Bradford, a leader of Plymouth Plantation (see page 77).

Noah Webster Jr. was born in a four-room house with a chimney in the center. Two rooms were downstairs and two were upstairs. After the birth of Noah's youngest brother, the house was often home to eight people: Noah, his parents, his four siblings, and his grandmother Steele. Like other New England children, Noah probably began elementary school when he was seven. When he was 14, Noah asked the local minister of the Congregational Church to help him prepare for college at Yale. Webster began to love learning and books and continued to love them throughout his life. He studied with the minister for two years. In 1774 Noah Webster entered Yale University in New Haven, Connecticut.

The following year, General George Washington passed through New Haven while serving as Commander-in-Chief of the Continental Army. Noah played a flute while other students sang to the General. Noah Webster served in the Connecticut militia but did not actively participate in the American Revolutionary War as a soldier. Before the Battle of Saratoga in 1777 (see page 148), Noah, his father, and his two brothers headed toward Saratoga to help; but the battle was over before they arrived.

School Teacher and Lawyer

After graduating from Yale in 1778, Webster became an elementary school teacher and also began to study law. He became convinced that Americans should have their own textbooks. He didn't want students to be dependent on English ones. This patriotic American thought books in American schools should contain American words (like skunk, hickory, and chowder) and also American geography. He wanted to promote a truly American form of English. Though he passed the bar and became a lawyer in 1781, Noah Webster continued teaching and began to write a spelling book. He published it in 1783. It became known as *The Blue-Backed Speller*. The speller was part of Webster's three-volume *Institute*, which also included a grammar book (1784) and a reader (1785). Webster wrote his *Institute* to show the differences between American and British grammar, pronunciation, and spelling. In 1785-1786, Webster traveled from one state to another to get people interested in his books.

The Blue-Backed Speller was the best-seller of his *Institute* series. It sold all over America. The book became so popular that an advertisement in an 1848 edition states that it sold over a million copies each year. In the late 1840s, it was printed using the fastest steam press in the country. The press made 5,250 copies a day. It was built especially for printing Webster's speller. By 1889 sixty-two million copies had been sold. Though the book was called a speller, it was also used to teach children to read. Since children from many places grew up learning from the same book, children in different parts of the country began to pronounce and spell words the same way.

In 1787 Noah began to court Rebecca Greenleaf from Boston. Rebecca refused his first proposal of marriage. Afterwards, Webster wrote her a love letter and sent her a lock of his hair. Webster finally succeeded in wooing Rebecca, and they were married in 1789. He and his beloved Becca had six daughters and two sons. One of their granddaughters described Rebecca as a small, pretty woman.

Noah Webster at Work

Dictionary Writer

Webster realized that America needed a dictionary. He wanted it to include words Americans used as well as new scientific and technical words. Look at the picture of Webster at work at right. He published a short version in 1806 that defined 40,000 words. About one-eighth of those words were new words used by American authors. The country was enthusiastic about this new reference book. Americans felt patriotic about Webster's truly American dictionary.

Webster continued to publish new editions. He reviewed the Greek, Latin, and Hebrew he had learned in college. He also studied Anglo-Saxon, Danish, French, German, Old Irish, Persian, Welsh, and other languages to better understand origins of English words. He did research in America, England, and France. After years of dedicated effort, Webster reached the end of his task. As he recalled:

When I had come to the last word, I was seized with a trembling which made it somewhat difficult to hold my pen steady for writing. The cause seems to have been the thought that I might not then live to finish the work, or the thought that I was so near the end of my labors. But I summoned strength to finish the last word, and then walking about the room a few minutes I recovered.

Webster published the final version of the *American Dictionary of the English Language* in two volumes in 1828, at age seventy. Webster's dictionary defined 70,000 words, and he had written it by hand with no typewriter or computer—just paper and quill.

Webster's definitions were excellent. After its publication, many people thought it was the best English dictionary in either America or England. State legislatures, courts, and the United States Congress adopted it as their official dictionary.

While Noah Webster was writing and publishing his books, he also worked on copyright laws. Today when a person writes a book, poem, or song or takes a photograph, he can copyright what he created. A copyright keeps someone else from using that person's work without paying the author for it. When Webster first published his *Blue-Backed Speller*, there was no national copyright law. Anyone could make copies of a book, and the author would not earn any money from those copies. In 1790 the United States Congress passed the first national copyright law. In 1831 Webster went to Washington, D.C., and proposed a better law. His cousin, Senator Daniel Webster, sponsored the bill in the U.S. Senate. His proposal was passed by both Houses of Congress. President Andrew Jackson signed it into law.

Webster lived in New York City; Philadelphia; Amherst, Massachusetts; and several towns in Connecticut. He founded a magazine and a newspaper. Webster wrote several essays. In 1790 twenty-eight of his popular essays were published in a book called *The Prompter*. This book was also popular. During a sixty-year period, one hundred editions of *The Prompter* were published. See pages from *The Prompter* below.

Webster became acquainted with many famous people. When American Revolutionary War hero Marquis de Lafayette visited Hartford, Connecticut, in 1784, Webster dined with him. As a young man, Webster socialized with Benjamin Franklin. In 1786 Franklin wrote Webster telling him that he would support Webster's *Institute*. Webster visited with George Washington at Mount Vernon. Washington once asked Webster to come to his home to tutor his grandchildren. Webster told Washington that he could not tutor his grandchildren because he must write instead. He said that writing was a happiness he could not sacrifice. James Madison, Father of the Constitution and fourth U.S. President, admired Webster's writings about government. Some historians believe Webster's writings may have influenced the writing of the Constitution. In 1831 President Andrew Jackson invited Noah Webster to dine with him at the White House.

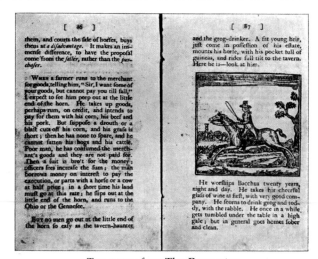

Two pages from The Prompter

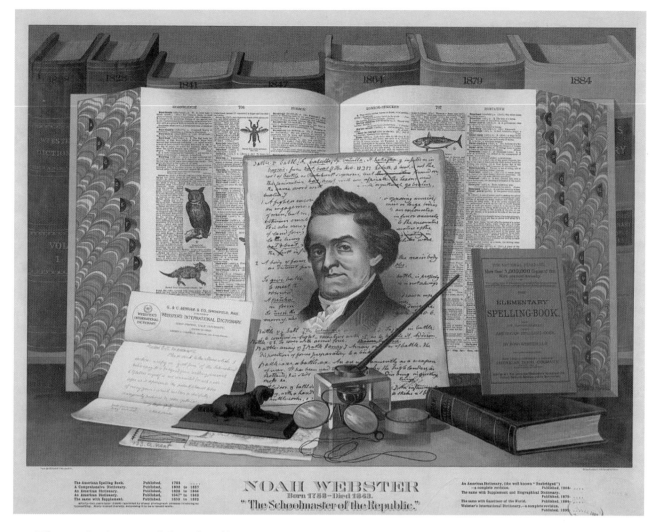

NOAH WEBSTER
Born 1758—Died 1843.
"The Schoolmaster of the Republic."

The printing and bookselling company G. & C. Merriam bought unsold copies of Webster's dictionary during the 1840s. They also obtained the rights to publish revised editions. The company hired Webster's son-in-law, Chauncey Goodrich, to edit the 1848 edition of Webster's dictionary. The Merriam-Webster company continues to publish revised editions of Webster's dictionary.

The print above, "Noah Webster: The Schoolmaster of the Republic," was published in 1891. The books standing in the back are the two volumes of his 1828 dictionary, plus the 1841, 1847, 1864, 1879, and 1884 editions. The book lying on the table is his 1806 dictionary. Standing on top of it is *The Blue-Backed Speller*.

Working for the Cause of Christ

From the 1790s to the 1840s, Americans experienced a second revival of interest in following Jesus. Historians call this period the Second Great Awakening (the Second Great Awakening is discussed in Lesson 41). Noah Webster's wife and children invited him to an evangelistic meeting in 1808, where he experienced a religious conversion.

Webster moved to Amherst, Massachusetts, four years later. He worked to raise money for a school there that would educate both boys and girls. Webster opened Amherst Academy in 1815 with a student body of ninety girls and over one hundred boys. He served as the chairman of the board of trustees. Students paid no tuition. Their food cost one dollar per week. A major purpose of the school was to educate young men who were talented and pious yet poor, so that they could become ministers. Noah Webster donated several books to the Amherst library. Subjects of these books included arctic zoology, botany, philosophy, theology, sermons, speeches, and the histories of Greece, Rome, and the American Indians.

Webster's Legacy

Noah Webster died in 1843 at age 86. He and his wife are buried in the city of his birth. His influence on language and education has continued throughout America's history. The McGuffey Readers, published in 1836, replaced Webster's reader in many American schools, but students continued to use Webster's speller for many years.

The U.S. Postal Service issued a 4-cent stamp in 1958 commemorating the 200th anniversary of Noah Webster's birth. The Amherst College Library hosted an exhibit in 2008 commemorating the 250th anniversary of his birth. The library displayed books from their archives which were written by Webster.

Webster's 1828 dictionary is filled with quotations from the Bible. Often when he defined a word, he used a Bible quotation or a Biblical teaching to explain the word's meaning. It is said of Noah Webster: "He taught millions to read and not one to sin." Everyone should be careful not to cause others to sin. As Jesus said:

And whoever receives one such child in My name receives Me; but whoever
causes one of these little ones who believe in Me to stumble, it would be better for him
to have a heavy millstone hung around his neck, and to be drowned in the depth of the sea.
Woe to the world because of its stumbling blocks! For it is inevitable that stumbling
blocks come; but woe to that man through whom the stumbling block comes!
Matthew 18:5-7

Activities for Lesson 40

Thinking Biblically – Read these verses to learn more about God's view of learning and knowledge: Proverbs 1:7, 2:6, 8:10-11, and 20:15.

Timeline – In *Timeline of America the Beautiful* next to 1828, write: Noah Webster publishes his complete dictionary.

Literature – Read "Domestic Economy, or the History of Thrifty and Unthrifty" in *We the People*, page 41.

Creative Writing – In your notebook, write one or more paragraphs about a textbook you would enjoy writing and how it could help people and bring glory to God.

Student Workbook or Lesson Review – If you are using one of these optional books, complete the assignment for Lesson 40. If you are using the Lesson Review, take the quiz for Unit 8.

New Ways of Life in the Early 1800s

This week Our American Story will tell about the presidencies of James Madison, James Monroe, and John Quincy Adams and about the War of 1812. In the God's Wonders lesson, we learn about Mammoth Cave, the world's longest known cave. Slaves mined saltpetre there to make ammunition for the War of 1812. The American Landmark is the Erie Canal, an engineering wonder completed in 1825. In our American Biography lesson, we learn about Sequoyah. After fighting in the War of 1812, he invented a writing system that made it possible for the Cherokee people to become a literate nation. We finish the week learning about the fur trapping mountain men of the West.

Modern Visitors at Mammoth Cave

Lessons in Unit 9

Lesson 41 – Our American Story: The War of 1812 and
Presidents Madison, Monroe, and Adams
Lesson 42 – God's Wonders: God Created Mammoth Cave
Lesson 43 – An American Landmark: The Erie Canal
Lesson 44 – An American Biography: Sequoyah, Creator of the Cherokee Syllabary
Lesson 45 – Daily Life: Mountain Men of the West

Books Used in Unit 9

- *Maps of America the Beautiful*

- *Timeline of America the Beautiful*

- *We the People*

- *Brady* by Jean Fritz

The War of 1812 and Presidents Madison, Monroe, and Adams

After serving two terms as President, Thomas Jefferson was ready to go home to Monticello. In the 1808 presidential election, he supported his Secretary of State James Madison. Madison was elected and became the fourth President in 1809. While Madison was President, part of the new Louisiana Territory became a state when Louisiana joined the Union in 1812. Indiana became the 19th state in 1816.

The New Madrid Earthquakes

In December 1811 and January 1812, America experienced several earthquakes centered in New Madrid, Missouri. The strongest of these quakes was one of the most powerful earthquakes in the history of the world. The force of one quake awakened President Madison far away in Washington, D.C., and caused church bells to ring in Charleston, South Carolina! These quakes made a crevice in northwest Tennessee. The Mississippi River ran backwards and filled the crevice, creating Reelfoot Lake. That winter, people on the first steamboats that ever traveled on the Mississippi River saw the destruction caused by the earthquakes. Not many people died as a result of the earthquakes because so few people lived in the area.

Battle of Tippecanoe in Indiana

The War of 1812

Great Britain continued to cause problems for America. Its navy continued to harass American ships. When Native Americans in the Northwest Territory attacked frontier settlers, Americans suspected that the British were helping them. Shawnee warrior Tecumseh tried to unite native tribes against American settlers. His followers led an attack on General William Henry Harrison's forces in Indiana. In November 1811, the Americans defeated Tecumseh and his warriors at the Battle of Tippecanoe, as pictured above. After the battle, Americans found British-made rifles on the battlefield, so they knew the British had supplied Tecumseh's warriors with guns.

Finally, President Madison asked Congress to declare war against Great Britain. Congress was divided over the issue, with about two-thirds in favor of war and one-third against it. Many southerners and westerners wanted to fight the British. Most of those who opposed the war lived in the Mid-Atlantic states and in New England. Though divided, Congress declared war on June 18, 1812. James Madison was re-elected later that year.

Much of the fighting in the War of 1812 involved the British and American navies. America started the war with only about

Admiral Oliver H. Perry during the Battle of Lake Erie

20 military ships, while the British had almost one hundred ships in American waters alone. When an American ship fought one-on-one against a British ship, the Americans usually won. The United States relied on privateers, civilian ships authorized to capture enemy ships. In the box below is a list of bodies of water important during the war.

Strategic Bodies of Water in the War of 1812

Great Lakes – During the war, Great Britain captured Detroit and controlled most of the Great Lakes area.

Lake Erie – Admiral Oliver Perry led American forces to victory in the Battle of Lake Erie. He sent a message to General William Henry Harrison, saying, "We have met the enemy and they are ours." See illustration above.

Lake Champlain – American forces defeated the British on Lake Champlain.

Atlantic Ocean – The USS *Chesapeake* and the HMS *Shannon* fought a few miles from Boston Harbor. The American Captain James Lawrence was mortally wounded. As Lawrence was dying, he told his men, "Don't give up the ship," but the British captured the *Chesapeake*.

Chesapeake Bay – British forces entered Chesapeake Bay and sailed up the Potomac to attack first Washington, D.C., and then Baltimore.

Gulf of Mexico – British forces in the Gulf of Mexico attacked American forces at New Orleans.

In August of 1814, British forces invaded Washington, D.C. Soldiers entered the presidential home and ate the meal prepared for President Madison's family. When the

Ruins of the United States Capitol After It Was Burned by the British

family fled, First Lady Dolley Madison rescued a portrait of President George Washington painted by Gilbert Stuart. The British burned the White House and the United States Capitol. See the illustration at left and the photo in the middle of page 232.

The Battle of New Orleans

Many people living in Tennessee supported the war. When its Governor asked for men to fight, thousands volunteered. This led to Tennessee's state nickname, "The Volunteer State." Nashville lawyer Andrew Jackson went through the state calling for volunteers. Jackson's devotion to his men reminded them of the strength of a hickory tree, thus he came to be called "Old Hickory."

During the war, Jackson led attacks against the Creek Indians in Alabama.

The Battle of New Orleans

He invaded Spanish territory in Florida and defeated British forces at Pensacola. Finally, Jackson entered New Orleans. By this time, his troops included members of the U.S. Army; volunteers from Louisiana, Tennessee, Kentucky, and Mississippi Territory; free blacks;

A White House secretary holds a medicine cabinet. A British sailor took it from the White House in 1812 and his descendants returned it in 1939.

Native Americans; and a band of pirates. When the British attacked on January 8, 1815, Jackson and his men won an overwhelming victory. See the picture above. Those who fought in the Battle of New Orleans had not received the news that the war was already officially over. American and British diplomats had signed the Treaty of Ghent in Belgium on December 24, 1814. Still, Americans were thrilled with the victory. Andrew Jackson became a national hero.

Treasured American Symbols

The War of 1812 gave America two of its most treasured symbols. After the British attacked Washington, D.C., they sailed further up Chesapeake Bay. The British attacked Fort McHenry at Baltimore but were unable to capture it. During this battle, Francis Scott Key wrote the poem, "The Star-Spangled Banner." It was later set to music and became our national anthem.

New York businessman Samuel Wilson shipped supplies to the Army. The crates were stamped "U.S." Soldiers said, "Here's another shipment from Uncle Sam." Later cartoonists took this idea and drew an old man wearing patriotic clothing, calling him Uncle Sam. He became a symbol of America. See a man dressed as Uncle Sam in the 1898 photo at right.

Read about James Madison's life on page 233.

Man Dressed as Uncle Sam

James Madison
America's Fourth President
March 4, 1809 - March 4, 1817

James Madison was born in Virginia in 1751, the first of twelve children. He began school at age eleven and later studied at home under a tutor. In 1769 he entered the College of New Jersey (now Princeton). He graduated in 1771.

During the American Revolution, Madison served in the Continental Congress. Other men who worked to write the U.S. Constitution called Madison the "Father of the Constitution." Along with other leaders, he helped write *The Federalist Papers* to encourage states to adopt the Constitution. Madison was respected as a man of integrity.

After a brief courtship in 1794, Madison married widow Dolley Payne Todd. They were married for 41 years. Though they had no children, Madison raised her son as his own.

Madison served as Secretary of State under President Jefferson. He worked to secure the Louisiana Purchase and was responsible for signing the checks for Lewis and Clark and for reimbursing the expenses of their expedition. Dolley and other women in Washington society gave items to the Corps of Discovery to use on the expedition.

After Madison served two terms as President, he and Dolley retired to their Virginia home, Montpelier. In 1819 Madison founded the American Colonization Society, which sought to free slaves and return them to Africa. He died in 1836 at age eighty-five.

President James Monroe and the Missouri Compromise

President Monroe

President James Madison used his influence to have his Secretary of State James Monroe elected as America's fifth President. Monroe served two terms, from 1817 to 1825.

Mississippi became a state in 1817, Illinois in 1818, and Alabama in 1819. When Alabama became a state, the total number of states allowing slavery was eleven. There were also eleven non-slave states. Missouri, which allowed slavery, applied to become the twenty-third state. Members of Congress from northern non-slave states worried that people living in other parts of the Louisiana Territory would also want to form slave states. Congress worked out the "Missouri Compromise," which allowed Maine to enter the Union as a non-slave state in 1820 and Missouri to enter as a slave state in 1821. Congress also banned slavery in any part of the Louisiana Territory north of Missouri's southern border. Read about Monroe's life on page 234.

New States Admitted

1812 Louisiana
1816 Indiana
1817 Mississippi
1818 Illinois
1819 Alabama
1820 Maine
1821 Missouri

James Monroe
America's Fifth President
March 4, 1817 - March 4, 1825

James Monroe was born in 1758 in Virginia. While at the College of William and Mary in 1776, he enlisted in the Army. He was with George Washington when he crossed the Delaware, was wounded at the Battle of Trenton, and spent the winter of 1777-1778 at Valley Forge (see Lessons 26-27). After the Revolutionary War, he became a lawyer. In 1786 Monroe married Elizabeth Kortright from New York City. They had three children. The family lived at Highland, their plantation next to Jefferson's Monticello.

Before becoming President, Monroe served in the Confederation Congress and in the United States Senate. He also served as Minister to France, Britain, and Spain, and as Governor of Virginia. He was Secretary of War during the War of 1812.

Monroe helped America gain territory. In 1803 President Thomas Jefferson sent Monroe to Paris, France, to help negotiate the Louisiana Purchase. While Monroe was President, America acquired Florida from Spain. James Monroe is remembered for the Monroe Doctrine which defined American policy concerning relations between Europe and North and South America. Monroe declared that Europe should form no new colonies in the Western Hemisphere and that America would not interfere with European colonies that were already formed.

Like President Madison, Monroe supported returning slaves to Africa. When the African country of Liberia formed as a home for former slaves, the capital was named Monrovia. Monroe died in New York on Independence Day, July 4, 1831.

President John Quincy Adams

John Quincy Adams, son of President John Adams, served as James Monroe's Secretary of State. Many thought he was the logical choice for America's sixth President. However, others wanted Henry Clay from Kentucky, Andrew Jackson from Tennessee, or William Crawford from Georgia. Jackson won the most votes but did not receive a majority, as required by the Constitution to be elected. Speaker of the House Henry Clay used his influence to get John Quincy Adams elected. Adams then appointed Clay to be Secretary of State. Jackson believed that the presidency was stolen from him in a "corrupt bargain." Like his father, Adams served only one term. Read about Adams' life below.

John Quincy Adams
America's Sixth President
March 4, 1825 - March 4, 1829

In 1767 John Quincy Adams was born in Braintree, Massachusetts to two of America's greatest heroes, John and Abigail Adams. According to tradition, the cradle pictured at right was used by five generations of the Adams family, including President John Adams and President John Quincy Adams. John Quincy grew up during the American Revolution. He traveled with his father on diplomatic missions to Europe twice during the war. At age fourteen, he traveled with the Continental Congress'

Minister to Russia, serving as his personal secretary and translator. After the war, Adams attended Harvard and became a lawyer. In 1797 he married Louisa Catherine Johnson, daughter of an American diplomat serving in England.

Adams served as Ambassador to the Netherlands under Washington, Ambassador to Prussia under his father, Senator from Massachusetts, professor at Harvard College, and Ambassador to Russia and Ambassador to England under Madison. He served as Secretary of State under President Monroe. He helped establish peaceful relations with Great Britain.

After leaving the presidency, Adams was elected to the U.S. House of Representatives from his home state of Massachusetts. He is the only person who has ever served in the House after leaving the presidency. He died in 1848 while still serving in the House of Representatives.

Second Great Awakening

The Second Great Awakening, which had begun around 1801, continued during the presidencies of Madison, Monroe, and Adams. In 1801 thousands of people traveled to Cane Ridge, Kentucky, just outside of Lexington. They gathered in a large field for a camp meeting. For six days they experienced spiritual revival. Preachers delivered fervent sermons. Many confessed faith in Jesus Christ. A spiritual revival had begun. When attendees returned home, they continued to seek God. New groups formed that wanted to discard religious traditions and return to the Christianity found in the Bible.

Hundreds of other camp meetings and evangelistic meetings were held. In 1808 Noah Webster committed his life to Christ after attending an evangelistic meeting; in 1835 camp meetings began on Martha's Vineyard (see pages 110 and 227). This time of spiritual renewal is called the Second Great Awakening (the first Great Awakening had begun in the mid-1700s; see pages 117-118). Modern revivals and gospel meetings had their beginnings in the Second Great Awakening.

Boy Scouts decorate the graves of soldiers from the War of 1812 at Arlington Cemetery in May, 1925.

> For I am not ashamed of the gospel,
> for it is the power of God for salvation
> to everyone who believes,
> to the Jew first and also to the Greek.
> Romans 1:16

Activities for Lesson 41

Map Study – Complete the assignments for Lesson 41 on Map 20 "The Lower 48" in *Maps of America the Beautiful*.

Timeline – In *Timeline of America the Beautiful* next to 1801, write: The Cane Ridge camp meeting is held.

Literature – Read "The Star-Spangled Banner" in *We the People*, page 42, and chapters 1-2 in *Brady*.

Creative Writing – In your notebook, write a paragraph about why you think the British burned the White House during the War of 1812.

Student Workbook or Lesson Review – If you are using one of these optional books, complete the assignment for Lesson 41.

God Created Mammoth Cave

God placed limestone under the Green River valley of south central Kentucky. Into that limestone, He carved beautiful, majestic, and mysterious Mammoth Cave, the longest known cave system in the world. Some people have thought that Mammoth Cave was named for woolly mammoths, an extinct animal that was like a fur-covered elephant; but actually it is called mammoth because of its great size. The second longest cave in the world is Optimisticeskay Cave in the Ukraine, and the third longest is Jewel Cave, beneath the Black Hills of South Dakota. If the Optimisticeskay and Jewel Caves were joined, Mammoth Cave would still be almost one hundred miles longer!

Mammoth Cave has been a World Heritage Site since 1981 and an International Biosphere Reserve since 1990. It has five levels. The deepest is 379 feet below ground. Several underground streams flow through the cave, including the Echo River, which flows at the lowest level. Another underground stream is the Styx River. Both are pictured at right.

Tourists on the Echo River in 1891

Tourists on the Styx River in 1877

Stalactites, Stalagmites, and Cave Bacon

In Mammoth Cave, God has created giant chambers, miles and miles of passages, and beautiful geological formations. The cave has chambers so large that people have called them ballrooms and once held banquets in them. Cave explorers have charted over 360 miles of passages so far. One especially narrow section is called Fat Man's Misery. Some

Stalactites hang from a ceiling in Mammoth Cave. Notice the pillar on the right side of the photograph.

formations have been given names like Martha Washington's Statue and Bridal Altar, pictured on page 238.

God continues to reveal His artistic creativity in the cave's ever-changing geology. When water seeps through the ground above a cave, it picks up minerals (a mineral is a non-living substance found in the earth). When water enters the cave's roof, it forms a drop. When it evaporates, minerals are left behind. As more drops seep in, the mineral deposits get larger, creating cave formations. Many of these grow into an icicle shape and are called stalactites. See stalactites at left. Sometimes water seepage forms thick, hollow tubes. The common name for these is soda straws.

When drops of water enter the cave quickly, they fall to the floor. When those drops evaporate, they create stalagmites. An easy way to remember the difference between stalactites and stalagmites is to think of stalactites as hanging *tight* to the ceiling and stalagmites as formations that *might* reach the ceiling. A stalagmite often forms directly beneath a stalactite. When the two build up to the point that they meet, they are called pillars (or columns). See stalactites and pillar above.

Flowstone forms after water has flowed over walls, floors, or older cave formations. See flowstone below. Rimstone forms around pools of water. Cave bacon (or drapery) forms when minerals are left behind by water that has flowed on an angled cave ceiling.

The main mineral in Mammoth Cave's formations is calcium carbonate. It is white. Colored crystals of calcite, gypsum, and other minerals give some cave formations pretty hues. Some gypsum deposits in Mammoth Cave look like flowers.

Mammoth Cave and the War of 1812

Saltpetre is a mineral used to make gunpowder. Early American settlers had to mine a great deal of saltpetre to make gunpowder for hunting. During the War of 1812, America needed large quantities of gunpowder to fight the British. Mammoth Cave was a major source of saltpetre during the war.

The people who owned Mammoth Cave sent about seventy African American slaves into the cave to mine saltpetre. They dug dirt from the cave and put it onto oxcarts. The oxen pulled the carts to leaching vats in

Flowstone in Mammoth Cave

two of the cave's large chambers, the Rotunda and Booth's Amphitheater. Once the vats were filled, workers flooded the dirt with water brought into the cave through wooden pipes from the cave entrance. This water absorbed calcium nitrate from the cave soil. When this was completed, the soil/water solution was pumped by hand through other wooden pipes until it reached the cave entrance. There slaves poured it through wood ashes and then boiled it until saltpetre crystals formed. The slaves' masters shipped the crystals to gunpowder manufacturers in the East.

God placed other useful substances inside Mammoth Cave. Epsomite is used for a medicine known as Epsom salts. Pioneers used flint (or chert) to make tools and to start fires. Gypsum is useful for medicine and can be used to make plaster and cement.

A couple sits beneath Bridal Altar in 1891.

Mammoth Cave Tourism

In the late 1790s, pioneer John Houchins became the first white American known to enter Mammoth Cave. According to tradition, he wounded a bear and followed it into the cave. Historians do not believe that Native Americans were using the cave at that time. Though saltpetre miners found Native American artifacts in the cave, archaeologists believe that those artifacts were from before the time of Christ.

News of archaeological discoveries and reports about the gigantic size of Mammoth Cave made people curious. By 1816 guides were leading visitors through the cave. Mammoth Cave is one of the oldest tourist attractions in America. See the illustration below.

Dr. John Croghan, a medical doctor from Louisville, Kentucky, bought Mammoth Cave in 1839. He improved trails through the cave. He also purchased a nearby hotel. Croghan bought the services of three slaves who worked for him as guides. One of these guides was Stephen Bishop. His master brought him to Mammoth Cave in 1838 while he was still in his late teens. Other guides taught him how to give tours, and he began to explore on his own. He went into many unknown places, including a deep cave shaft called the Bottomless Pit. Beyond the Bottomless Pit are places now popular on cave tours. Two of the best-known places he opened up for tourists are Fat Man's Misery and Mammoth Dome. Tourists were captivated by Bishop's manner of speech and his singing voice. Bishop gained his freedom in 1856; but he died not long afterwards, leaving a wife and one son.

In 1859, the Illustrated London News *published this illustration of a Mammoth Cave trail.*

Tourists in Mammoth Cave

Slave guide Nick Bransford took tourists on cave tours for over fifty years. He married Stephen Bishop's widow. Bransford was generous and spiritually-minded, giving land for a school and serving as a deacon in the local Pleasant Union Baptist Church. According to tradition, he bought his freedom by selling the cave's eyeless fish to tourists.

In the early 1900s, Nick Bransford's grandson Matt Bransford promoted Mammoth Cave to African Americans. He traveled to large cities to encourage them to visit the cave. Much of American life was segregated then, which meant that in many places black and white Americans did not stay at the same hotels or eat in the same restaurants. Matt led special cave tours for African Americans. He and his wife Zemmie operated a hotel out of their home to give these tourists a place to stay. In all, four generations of Bransfords guided tours of Mammoth Cave. In the photo above, tourists climb a ladder inside Mammoth Cave.

Dr. Croghan and His Mammoth Cave Hospital

Dr. Croghan believed that the climate of Mammoth Cave might be beneficial to patients suffering from consumption, now known as tuberculosis. In 1842 patients began living in huts along the main trails of the cave. See photo at right. The experiment ended in 1843 because many patients got worse or died. Though the cave climate did not prove to be a cure, the experiment added to medical knowledge about the disease. Two stone huts remain in the cave today.

In 1912 tourists visit one of the huts Dr. Croghan used to treat people with tuberculosis.

Music in Mammoth Cave

Dr. Croghan himself died of tuberculosis in 1849. His nieces and nephews served as trustees of Mammoth Cave after his death. In the early 1900s, while the cave was being managed by the trustees, Mammoth Cave Hotel owners sponsored musical entertainment inside the cave. See the hotel and grounds on page 240. From the mid-1800s to the early 1900s, several songs were published about Mammoth Cave, including the "Mammoth Cave Waltz" by J. C. Cook in 1850, "Come to Mammoth Cave in Old Kentucky" by Ray Hibbeler in 1921, and "In the Grand Old Mammoth Cave" by J. Herschell Hoffman in 1924.

Mammoth Cave Hotel and Grounds in 1915

Mammoth Cave National Park

The last trustee chosen by Dr. Croghan died in 1926. That year, Congress authorized Mammoth Cave as a national park, but it did not actually become a park until 1941. Today the park covers 52,830 acres. It includes the cave, a portion of the Green River valley, and historic structures people built there before 1941. The park has seventy churches and many cemeteries, including one called Old Guides Cemetery, where Stephen Bishop is buried.

Animals of Mammoth Cave

One hundred and thirty species of animals live in Mammoth Cave. Some, including one species of shrimp, have been found nowhere else in the world. Cave crickets have the largest population of any animal in Mammoth Cave. Second are the cave beetles. Both live in the twilight zone. This is the area near an entrance to a cave where there is some light but no direct sunlight.

About one-third of the animal species in Mammoth Cave live there during their entire life cycle. These are called troglobites. They live only on the dark, lowest level of Mammoth Cave. Examples are blind fish, eyeless fish, blind shrimp, and blind crayfish.

One-third of the animal species in Mammoth Cave could live either outside or inside the cave. Scientists call them troglophiles. Salamanders, springtails, and spiders are troglophiles. See the long-tailed salamander below.

The other species in Mammoth Cave live there for parts of their lives, but they must go outside the cave to obtain food. These are called trogloxenes. Bats are trogloxenes. Bat species in Mammoth Cave include the brown bat pictured on page 241, eastern small-footed bat, evening bat, gray bat, Indiana bat, Rafinesque's big-eared bat, and the southeastern bat. Another important trogloxene animal in Mammoth Cave is the woodrat. Many trogloxene live in the twilight zone. The animals that go outside the cave to find food bring in substances that nourish the animals that stay inside all their lives.

Long-Tailed Salamander

Mammoth Cave National Park is a complex ecosystem. In fact, the park has many different kinds of habitats in addition to the cave habitat. It has woodlands, springs, ponds, ridges, valleys, river bottoms, sinkholes, forest swamps, and more. The diverse habitats of the park are home to over 1,300 species of flowering plants.

God created the world so that each part of creation depends on other parts. He designed each living creature so that it could live in a particular ecosystem. "For the Lord is a great God and a great King above all gods, in whose hand are the depths of the earth . . . ." (Psalm 95:3-4).

When Jesus was on earth, He performed one of His most amazing miracles at a cave:

Brown Bat

> So Jesus, again being deeply moved within,
> came to the tomb.
> Now it was a cave,
> and a stone was lying against it. . . .
> He cried out with a loud voice,
> "Lazarus, come forth."
> The man who had died came forth . . . .
> John 11:38, 43b-44a

Activities for Lesson 42

Thinking Biblically – Read about caves in these Bible passages: Genesis 23:7-9, 1 Samuel 24:1-22, 1 Kings 19:9-18

Map Study – Complete the assignment for Lesson 42 on Map 2 "God's Wonders" in *Maps of America the Beautiful.*

Timeline – In *Timeline of America the Beautiful* next to 1816, write: Guides lead tourists through Mammoth Cave in Kentucky.

Vocabulary – Write four sentences in your notebook, using one of these words in each: stalactites, stalagmites, leaching, ecosystem. Check in a dictionary if you need help with their definitions.

Literature – Read chapters 3-4 in *Brady.*

Student Workbook or Lesson Review – If you are using one of these optional books, complete the assignment for Lesson 42.

The Erie Canal

During the presidencies of James Madison, James Monroe, and John Quincy Adams, Americans continued to move beyond the Appalachian Mountains. A few even moved west of the Mississippi River. As more Europeans emigrated to America, many of them moved into the West, too.

People began to develop better ways to travel and to move goods. The Federal government paid for the construction of a National Road from Cumberland, Maryland, to Wheeling, Virginia (now in West Virginia). It was also called the Cumberland Road. It was later extended to Vandalia, Illinois. See its route below. Today U.S. Route 40 generally follows the route of the original Cumberland Road. States and counties built roads, too. Some were called turnpikes. When travelers paid the required toll, an attendant turned a "pike" (or stake) which allowed the traveler to continue down the road.

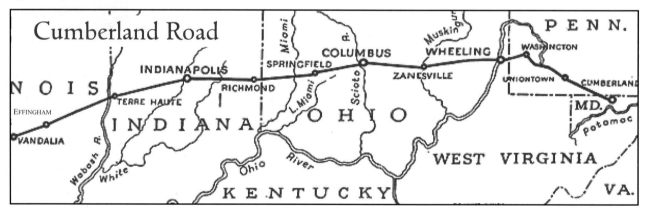

Americans began to use steam energy to travel by water. The first steamboat in America traveled up the Hudson River in 1807. Over two hundred steamboats were traveling on American rivers by 1829. Americans also began building canals. America had over 3,000 miles of canals by 1837. The best known canal was the Erie Canal, which connected Lake Erie and the Hudson River. Look at the map at right.

"Clinton's Ditch"

New Yorkers had long wanted a canal through the forests and swamps of upstate New York. They had tried to get the Federal government to help pay for it. Presidents Thomas Jefferson and James Madison rejected the proposal.

Route of the Erie Canal

242

DeWitt Clinton served as mayor of New York City before becoming Governor of New York State in 1817. He believed that New York City would someday become a center of business, manufacturing, banking, and shipping. To help that happen, he proposed that the state build a canal. Shortly before Clinton was sworn in as Governor, the New York legislature agreed to fund the construction of a canal from Buffalo on the eastern shore of Lake Erie (one of the Great Lakes) to Albany, New York, a town on the upper Hudson River.

Though many agreed with the plan, others made fun of it and called it Clinton's Ditch, Clinton's Folly, or Governor's Gutter. Opposition was so strong that Clinton was voted out of office in 1822. He was then re-elected in time to dedicate the new canal in 1825. He sailed from Buffalo to Albany on the canal and then on the Hudson River to New York City. Townspeople along the way cheered the Governor as he sailed on the *Seneca Chief*. When he arrived in New York City, he emptied two containers of water from Lake Erie into the Atlantic Ocean as seen at right. He called this the "Marriage of the Waters."

"Marriage of the Waters"

Building the Erie Canal

The commission in charge of building the Erie Canal chose four New Yorkers to lead the project. None were engineers. One was a school teacher, while the other three were judges who knew how to survey land. Judges sometimes learned how to survey because it helped them make decisions in property disputes. The schoolteacher taught himself how to survey, too. All four learned about engineering as they worked on the canal.

Construction began in Utica, New York, in 1817, where crews began digging in both directions, east and west. Workers used their own muscles, horsepower, and machines they invented for the project. In a few places, they used an explosive substance called black powder to blast through rock. At a place called Deep Cut, workers hauled away almost one and a half million cubic yards of rock. The commission hired residents who lived along the canal route to work on sections near their homes. They also hired Irish immigrants.

Since the land of New York has mountains and valleys, construction crews had to build locks. Locks help boats travel safely as the elevation of a canal or river changes. At first, canal designers planned to build the locks out of wood. Since the wood would have rotted and required frequent replacement, they decided instead to use a natural cement rock they found along the way. Look at the Erie Canal lock pictured at left.

When they finished in 1825, crews had completed a canal four feet deep, forty feet wide, and 364 miles long.

Erie Canal Lock near Niagara, New York

How the Erie Canal Helped New York

In 1825 a trip from Albany to Buffalo took two weeks by stagecoach or wagon. A ride on the canal took only five days. When the Erie Canal opened, the price of shipping goods by road was $100 per ton. Shipping the same amount on the canal cost $10. People shipped more and more goods on the canal. Between 1829 and 1841, the amount of wheat shipped on the canal rose each year. It went from 3,640 bushels per year to 1,000,000!

In the early years, mules walked alongside the canal, pulling barges loaded with goods, as in the drawing below. Canal workers often sang canal songs. Songwriter Thomas Allen wrote "Low Bridge, Everybody Down" in 1905. It told about life on the Erie Canal in the 1800s and is often called "Fifteen Miles on the Erie Canal."

Businesses paid a toll to use the canal. In just nine years after the canal opened, New York had earned back all of the money spent in constructing the waterway. Soon New York City became the busiest port in the United States. More goods were shipped through the Port of New York than through Baltimore, Boston, and New Orleans combined.

The canal also carried passengers. Settlers could travel faster to western New York, western Pennsylvania, and the Northwest Territory, which became Illinois, Indiana, Michigan, Ohio, and Wisconsin. Farmers in those regions could ship their produce, miners their minerals, loggers their lumber, and manufacturers their goods to the growing Port of New York. The major New York cities of Albany, Schenectady, Utica, Syracuse, Rochester, and Buffalo all grew because of the Erie Canal. Today nearly 80% of the upstate New York population lives near the canal.

Along the Erie Canal

The Erie Canal Today

The state of New York continued to build and improve canals during the 1800s. See the illustration at right. However, the amount of goods shipped on these canals eventually declined because of competition from railroads, highways, and the construction of the St. Lawrence Seaway in the 1950s. Today, New York residents and tourists use the Erie Canal and other waterways of the New York State Canal System for recreation and for learning about an historic way of life.

New York City has honored Governor Clinton's service to the state of New York in many ways. Statues of Clinton stand at the Museum of the City of New York, at his grave in Green-Wood Cemetery in the Bronx, and in front of the New York County Courthouse. The city has a DeWitt Clinton Park and DeWitt Clinton High School. See the mural on page 245.

Mules pull barges along the Erie Canal.

In 1905, this illustration, "First Boat on the Erie Canal," decorated the DeWitt Clinton High School.

DeWitt Clinton Park opened in 1905. It has an Erie Canal Playground. Until 1932 the park featured a children's farm garden with 356 four-by-eight-foot garden plots for children to use. Frances Griscom Parsons was the first female park administrator in New York City. She taught little farmers about plants and nutrition at the park.

The Erie Canal used one of God's most amazing creations—water. At home, we drink it, clean with it, and cook with it. At play, we splash in it and swim in it, float on it in boats, and glide across it on water skiis. Farmers depend on water for their crops, both from rain and from irrigation. Miners depend on water when they extract minerals. Manufacturers use water to make paper, steel, petroleum, and more. Many of God's creatures live in water. The list of uses for water seems endless. God has provided for our every need:

The One who builds His upper chambers in the heavens
And has founded His vaulted dome over the earth,
He who calls for the waters of the sea and pours them out on the face of the earth,
The Lord is His name.
Amos 9:6

Activities for Lesson 43

Map Study – Complete the assignments for Lesson 43 on Map 3 "American Landmarks" and Map 14 "The Erie Canal" in *Maps of America the Beautiful*.

Timeline – In *Timeline of America the Beautiful* next to 1825, write: The Erie Canal in New York opens for traffic.

Literature – Read "Low Bridge, Everybody Down" in *We the People*, page 43, and chapter 5 in *Brady*.

Family Activity – Create models representing New York before and after the Erie Canal. See instructions on page 428.

Student Workbook or Lesson Review – If you are using one of these optional books, complete the assignment for Lesson 43.

Sequoyah, Creator of the Cherokee Syllabary

About six years before Americans declared their independence from Great Britain in 1776, Wut-teh, daughter of a Cherokee chief, gave birth to a baby boy at the Cherokee village of Tuskeegee on the Little Tennessee River in Tennessee. The baby's father was Nathaniel Gist, a Virginia fur trader. The baby boy was named Sequoyah. Today tourists can visit the Sequoyah Birthplace Museum at Vonora in eastern Tennessee. Sequoyah grew up among his mother's people, but at times was called by his English name, George Gist.

Sequoyah became a talented silversmith. Like other men in his tribe, he also worked as a farmer, fur trader, hunter, and warrior. Sequoyah married a Cherokee woman and they had children. One of them was a little girl named Ayoka.

Cherokee Alphabet.

Sounds represented by Vowels.

Consonant Sounds

Sequoyah Becomes Interested in "Talking Leaves"

As a boy, Sequoyah knew that people wrote down words with letters, but he never learned the English alphabet himself. In middle age, he would become the first person in the history of the world to invent a completely new system of writing single-handedly.

The Cherokee language was only a spoken language; no one had ever written it down. Native Americans called the writing of their English neighbors "talking leaves." According to traditional stories told by the Cherokee people, Sequoyah became interested in writing in 1809, while he was recovering from a hunting accident. He realized that the written communication of Europeans was a powerful tool and that the Cherokee people needed to have that ability.

During the War of 1812, Sequoyah and other Cherokee joined the militia led by

Sequoyah

General Andrew Jackson. They fought alongside Americans against the British and the Creek Indians. While serving under General Jackson, Sequoyah noticed that the Cherokee could not read orders given to them by their officers nor could they keep journals. He was sad that they could not write letters home to their families.

Sequoyah Creates a Syllabary

After the war, Sequoyah began working diligently to create writing for his people's language. He tried to design symbols. Some of his own people ridiculed him and accused him of being insane. According to one story, his wife believed he was practicing witchcraft and once threw his work into the fire.

For twelve years, Sequoyah kept trying. He found that every word in the Cherokee language contained one or more of eighty-five different syllables. He created a symbol for each one. Because the symbols stand for syllables, Sequoyah's system is a syllabary rather than an alphabet. English, on the other hand, has twenty-six letters that stand for individual sounds within syllables. These twenty-six letters make up our alphabet. Sequoyah's system made the Cherokee writing system very easy to learn. Once someone memorized the eighty-five sounds and symbols, they could read or write anything. Look at the picture of Sequoyah above and the chart on page 246.

The Cherokee Nation Adopts Sequoyah's Syllabary

Sequoyah designed a game using the symbols. He taught his daughter Ayoka how to write the symbols. In 1821 the father and the daughter showed Cherokee leaders the invention. The leaders were convinced that Sequoyah's idea was good and adopted the system for the Cherokee Nation.

Thousands of Cherokee learned how to read and write in their native tongue. The tribe soon had a higher literacy rate than the American citizens who lived around them. Notice the *Cherokee Primer* at right.

Masthead of the Cherokee Phoenix, *Published on Wednesday, June 4, 1828*

Printing in Cherokee

In 1825-1826, Samuel Austin Worcester was living near Chattanooga, Tennessee, where he served as a missionary to the Cherokee. He helped get the new syllabary ready for printing. He convinced a missionary board to provide a hand printing press and to create type for the Cherokee syllabary. In 1828 Cherokee tribal leaders began to use the press to publish a newspaper they called the *Cherokee Phoenix*. It was the first national bilingual newspaper in the United States, containing columns in both English and Cherokee. See the masthead of the June 4, 1828, edition of the *Cherokee Phoenix* at the bottom of page 247.

The Cherokee nation and missionaries published the Bible, hymn books, and tracts in Cherokee. They also printed almanacs and government publications. By the time of Sequoyah's death in 1843, over four million pages had been printed in the Cherokee language. These publications record Cherokee history and culture.

Bronze Sequoyah Door at the Library of Congress

Honoring Sequoyah

When Thomas L. McKenney and James Hall published *History of the Indian Tribes of North America* from 1836 to 1844, the set of books included biographical sketches and stories about the men they considered the principal chiefs of native tribes. They also featured 120 portraits of Native Americans, including the portrait of Sequoyah on page 247. In that portrait, Sequoyah is wearing a silver medal designed in his honor and given by the Cherokee people. For his service to their nation, they also gave him a lifetime pension.

German immigrant Lee Lawrie created sculptures in 1939 for the bronze entrance doors of the John Adams Building, which is part of the Library of Congress complex in Washington. Relief sculptures illustrating the history of writing adorn these doors. Most figures are mythical, but one of the characters on the bronze doors at the east entrance is Sequoyah. Notice the photo of that door above. The giant Sequoia tree, which is native to California, was named in honor of Sequoyah. See the photo at left.

Sequoia Tree

In 1917 the state of Oklahoma donated the statue of Sequoyah pictured at right as one of its two statues in the National Statuary Hall in the United States Capitol.

Sequoyah's syllabary helped spread the gospel among the Cherokee. Many became believers in Jesus Christ:

For it is written,
"As I live, says the Lord,
every knee shall bow to me,
and every tongue shall give praise to God."
Romans 14:11

Activities for Lesson 44

Thinking Biblically – God used Sequoyah to help Cherokee people be able to learn about God's love and truth. Copy Psalm 67:1-2 into your notebook.

Timeline – In *Timeline of America the Beautiful* next to 1821, write: Sequoyah completes the Cherokee syllabary.

Sequoyah Statue in National Statuary Hall

Vocabulary – In your notebook, copy each of the following sentences. Fill in each blank with one of the following words: ridicule, syllabary, bilingual, tracts, pension.

1. A person who speaks two languages is _____.
2. The evangelist handed out _____ at the ballgame.
3. Sometimes people experience _____ for being different or for standing up for what is right.
4. My grandfather receives a _____ from the factory where he used to work.
5. A set of written characters that each represent a syllable of speech is a _____.

Literature – Read "Come, Holy Spirit, Dove Divine" in *We the People*, page 44, and chapters 6-7 in *Brady*.

Creative Writing – Imagine that you just learned how to write. What is the first thing that you would want to write down? A letter to someone? A description of yourself or your family? A prayer? Using a half-page in your notebook, write as if this is the first thing you have been able to write for yourself.

Student Workbook or Lesson Review – If you are using one of these optional books, complete the assignment for Lesson 44.

Mountain Men of the West

In 1822, trader William Ashley placed this advertisement in the *St. Louis Gazette and Public Advertiser*:

> To Enterprising Young Men:
> the Subscriber wishes to engage
> One Hundred men
> to ascend the river Missouri to its source
> to be employed for one, two, or three years . . .

Ashley was looking for men to become fur trappers in the Rocky Mountains. About one hundred men wanting excitement and a way to earn money answered the ad. Ashley's partner, Andrew Henry, led them west. They built a fort before groups of two or three men headed out to trap animals for their fur.

For two hundred years, English, French, and Spanish fur traders had been working along the Missouri and Columbia Rivers. There they traded with Native Americans, exchanging blankets, beads, knives, and guns for a variety of furs. See the illustration at right. The Louisiana Purchase of 1803 and the discoveries of Lewis and Clark and their Corps of Discovery in 1804-1806 caused Americans to expand their own fur trade. The Missouri Fur Company, the St. Louis Fur Company, and the American Fur Company each had headquarters in St. Louis by 1809. The work by Ashley and Henry led to the formation of another fur business, the Rocky Mountain Fur Company.

At this time felted hats made from beaver fur were fashionable in America and Europe. Therefore, the main interest of American trappers was beaver pelts. Demand for pelts was high, with hatters purchasing 100,000 each year at $6 to $9 each. Perfumers also purchased castoreum, an oil found in two glands in a beaver's abdomen.

The fur traders who pursued beavers became great explorers. After beaver hats went out of fashion, many traders stayed in the West and continued to explore. Some became wagon train guides or scouts for the United States Army. Mountain men of the West helped Americans in the East know more about the great Western frontier. Soon Americans seeking permanent homes, farms, and ranches followed the mountain men into that frontier.

Today mountain men clubs reenact lifestyles of the Western mountain men of the early 1800s. They enjoy shooting historic guns like flintlocks and caplocks, developing and demonstrating skills necessary for mountain life, and preserving the natural environments that the mountain men explored.

Beaver Pelt

The Life of a Mountain Man

The Western mountain man let his hair grow long and his beard get scraggly. He wore clothes made of buckskin. A few mountain men traveled alone, some took Native American wives along, and others traveled in small groups. For most of the year, mountain men worked in the Rockies, trapping beavers and preparing their fur for sale. It was a lonely life. Freezing weather, rugged landscapes, attacks from Indians, fierce grizzly bears, and food shortages made it a dangerous existence, too.

The best times to trap beavers were in fall and spring. In summer, their fur was too thin; in winter, temperatures were too cold. When a trapper found a stream or pond where he believed beavers were living, he set one of his five-pound traps in the water near the bank, and attached its chain to a dead branch. He put castoreum from a beaver he had already killed on the branch to attract another beaver. Once the animal was trapped, the trapper pulled it out of the water by the chain. He then skinned it and prepared the pelt for sale before adding it to his growing bundle. See the pelt above.

Once each year, traders from St. Louis came to a designated place to buy pelts. There the buyers and the trappers had a rendezvous. Trappers obtained supplies, like salt and sugar and new traps; traders purchased furs. These gatherings lasted about two weeks. Though the rendezvous attracted Native Americans wanting to trade, mountain men supplied most of the beaver fur. At the end of the rendezvous, the mountain men headed back into the Rockies; and the traders and their mule trains carried the pelts to St. Louis and other cities.

John Jacob Astor owned the American Fur Company. The fur trade made him one of the richest men in America. In 1828 the company established Fort Union Trading Post, pictured on page 252, and continued using it until 1867. Today tourists can visit the Fort Union Trading Post National Historical Site near Williston, North Dakota. Artists George Catlin, Karl Bodmer, and John James Audubon all visited Fort Union, as did the German Prince Maximilian (see pages 212, 214, and 218, and lesson 60).

The American Fur Company's Fort Union Trading Post with Nearby Tepees

Jedediah Smith, Christian Mountain Man

One famous mountain man, Jedediah Smith, was a Christian. Smith was one of the hundred men who responded to William Ashley's advertisement in 1822. Smith led groups of mountain men from 1823 to 1830. Smith quickly showed leadership ability and was known for his bravery. On his first excursion into the West, a grizzly bear attacked him. Men traveling with him had to sew his ear and part of his scalp back on afterwards.

Smith was on the first expedition that reached California by land. He explored the Rocky Mountains and the Southwest United States. Smith crossed the dry Mojave Desert and the Great Basin, becoming perhaps the first native or white man to cross both of those areas *and* go all the way to the Great Salt Lake. Smith also traveled through the area that became Yellowstone National Park.

While exploring, Jedediah Smith prepared records and maps. He died on the Santa Fe Trail in 1831. When trader William Ashley became a United States Congressman that same year, he shared with Congress the information Smith had gathered before he died.

More Famous Mountain Men

Etienne Provost and Jim Bridger also went west to trap furs for William Ashley. Provost explored in present-day Utah. Provo, Utah is named in his honor.

Jim Bridger was seventeen years old when he joined William Ashley. He became a well-respected trapper who was known for his tall tales. As illustrated at right, Bridger was the first white man to see the Great Salt Lake. He also discovered a pass through the

Jim Bridger Discovers the Great Salt Lake in Utah

Jim Bridger

Rockies that came to be called Bridger's Pass. One day the Union Pacific Railroad would use this pass through the Rockies. Today Interstate 80 goes through it. At left is an illustration of Bridger in his later years.

Mountain man John Colter was a member of the Corps of Discovery that Lewis and Clark led west in 1804. On the Corp's return trip in 1806, Colter met two trappers at Fort Mandan. He obtained a discharge from the Corps and headed back into the West with the trappers. He later left the mountain man way of life. Using money he earned as a trapper, he bought land and settled in Missouri where he married and had a son.

One of the most famous mountain men was Kit Carson. Many fur operations were based in St. Louis; but Carson was based in Taos, New Mexico. Carson was known for his clean living. One man who knew him called him "clean as a hound's tooth." See his picture at right.

Like Davy Crockett and Daniel Boone, Kit Carson became a legend while he was still living. In 1842 Carson met John C. Fremont and began to work as his guide. Fremont wrote reports of their expeditions. Many people read Fremont's stories, and Kit Carson became an American hero. Like the legends told about Paul Bunyan, legends grew up about Kit Carson and his supposed superhuman abilities. Fremont became the first presidential candidate of the new Republican Party in 1856.

Kit Carson

Mountain man Seth Kinman, pictured below, was a California hunter of elk and grizzly bears. For a time, he supplied meat for the U.S. military serving in the West. Kinman once killed fifty elk in one

Mountain Man Seth Kinman

month. By age seventy, he claimed to have killed more than eight hundred grizzly bears. In 1856-1857, he made a chair from elk horns. He gave it to President James Buchanan, who was pleased with the present. Kinman also presented chairs made from animal hides, bones, and fur to Presidents Abraham Lincoln, Andrew Johnson, and Rutherford B. Hayes. Hayes' chair was made of the hide and bones of a grizzly bear.

Throughout the history of the world, people have made clothing from animal skins and fur. God made the very first clothing that was made from animals:

The Lord God made garments of skin
for Adam and his wife,
and clothed them.
Genesis 3:21

Activities for Lesson 45

Thinking Biblically – Jedediah Smith and Kit Carson honored God by their choices not to follow the crowd in doing wrong. Think of a person in the Bible who honored God while others were living sinfully. Write a paragraph in your notebook about how he or she honored God.

Map Study – Complete the assignments for Lesson 45 on Map 18 "The West" in *Maps of America the Beautiful*.

Timeline – In *Timeline of America the Beautiful* next to 1857, write: Seth Kinman gives a chair made out of elk horns to President James Buchanan.

Mountain Man Seth Kinman

Vocabulary – In your notebook, write a paragraph using all of these words: reenact, scraggly, rendezvous, superhuman. Consult a dictionary if you need help with their definitions.

Literature – Read "The Legend of Paul Bunyan" in *We the People*, page 45, and chapters 8-9 in *Brady*.

Student Workbook or Lesson Review – If you are using one of these optional books, complete the assignment for Lesson 45. If you are using the Lesson Review, take the quiz for Unit 9.

America in the Jacksonian Era

This week Our American Story will tell about the presidencies of Andrew Jackson and Martin Van Buren. In the God's Wonders lesson we learn about America's islands and what was happening on some of them at that time. The American Landmark for this unit is the Alamo in San Antonio, Texas. The Battle of the Alamo was fought while Jackson served as President. John Jay, one of America's founding fathers, died the same year that Jackson began his first term. In our American Biography lesson we learn about Chief Justice Jay and his service as president of the American Bible Society. We wrap up this week with a Daily Life lesson about the Cherokee Indians and their hardships on the Trail of Tears.

Wild Pony on Assateague Island

Lessons in Unit 10

Lesson 46 – Our American Story: Old Hickory, First President from
  West of the Appalachians
Lesson 47 – God's Wonders: God Created America's Islands
Lesson 48 – An American Landmark: "Remember the Alamo!"
Lesson 49 – An American Biography: John Jay, President of the
  American Bible Society
Lesson 50 – Daily Life: The Trail of Tears

Books Used in Unit 10

- *Maps of America the Beautiful*

- *Timeline of America the Beautiful*

- *We the People*

- *Brady* by Jean Fritz

Old Hickory, First President from West of the Appalachians

President Jackson

Though America was expanding into the west, until 1829 all of its Presidents had been from only two states. Presidents George Washington, Thomas Jefferson, James Madison, and James Monroe were from Virginia; Presidents John Adams and John Quincy Adams were from Massachusetts. When Tennessee's Andrew Jackson defeated John Quincy Adams in the election of 1828, he and his supporters believed that they had taken power away from privileged men in the East and returned it to the common people. See Jackson's portrait at left.

Jackson Faces Difficult Issues

President Jackson led America through several difficult problems. Some people from South Carolina, including Jackson's Vice President John Calhoun, believed that if a state disagreed with a law passed by the Federal government, that state could refuse to enforce it. In 1828 Congress passed high tariffs on goods imported into the United States. When Congress passed more high tariffs in 1832, South Carolinians met in a special convention and declared that the tariffs would not be enforced in South Carolina. They also declared that a state could secede from the United States. (In Lesson 66, we will see that they did exactly that in 1860.) President Jackson strongly disagreed with Vice President Calhoun and those who met in South Carolina. Senator Henry Clay of Kentucky helped work out a compromise. Tariff rates were gradually lowered over the next ten years.

When Jackson became President, the United States had a national bank. Jackson opposed a national bank because he did not believe the Constitution authorized one. He also believed that its actions had been harmful to America.

When Jackson ran for a second term as President in 1832, Henry Clay opposed him. Clay made the bank a major campaign issue. When Congress passed a bill renewing the national bank's charter, Jackson vetoed the bill. Congress did not have enough votes to override his veto, so the national bank went out of existence in 1836.

America Builds Railroads

America's railroads expanded while Jackson was President. Americans had used railways since 1809 to haul rocks from quarries. Just as mules pulled boats on canals, horses pulled containers of rock on America's first quarry railways. John Stevens built a circular track in 1826 on his land in Hoboken, New Jersey. There he demonstrated travel by rail, using a steam-powered vehicle. The first commercial railroad company in America was the Baltimore and Ohio (or B & O) which opened fourteen miles of track in 1830. At first, it used horsepower; but it began using an American-made steam-powered locomotive in 1831. By 1833 America had the longest steam railroad in the world, the 136-mile-long line between Charleston and Hamburg, South Carolina, owned by the South Carolina Canal and Rail Road Company. Railroads began to influence American travel and business, but they had stiff competition from canal companies during their early years.

Two new states joined the Union during the Jackson presidency, Arkansas in 1836 and Michigan in 1837. Read about President Jackson's life below.

Brady Studio Daguerrotype of Jackson

New States Admitted

1836 Arkansas
1837 Michigan

Andrew Jackson
America's Seventh President
March 4, 1829 - March 4, 1837

In 1765 Andrew and Elizabeth Jackson and their sons Hugh and Robert emigrated to America from Northern Ireland. They settled in the Waxhaw settlement near Camden, South Carolina. Andrew died in 1767, shortly before the birth of his third son. Elizabeth named him after his father.

Andrew Jackson grew up with his mother, brothers, and a large extended family of aunts, uncles, and cousins who had also emigrated. The Revolutionary War caused many hardships for young Andrew. He and two of his brothers took part in the war. One brother died of heat stroke after a battle. Andrew and his other brother were both captured by the British. While in captivity they both contracted small pox. Andrew survived but his brother died. Later his mother nursed sick and injured American soldiers in Charleston. She caught cholera there and died.

The American Revolution left Andrew an orphan. He lived briefly with his mother's family before going to school in Charleston and later studying law in North Carolina. Jackson received his law license at age twenty. He had grown into a tall, thin man. His eyes were blue and his hair red. He was known for his hot temper, daring personality, and wild living.

In 1788 Jackon traveled the Wilderness Road through the Appalachian Mountains and settled in Jonesborough, the oldest town in Tennessee. There he practiced law and trained racehorses. That fall he began to practice law in Nashville also. For two years he traveled between the two towns. He stayed in frontier forts, which were often called stations. At John Donelson's Station he met Donelson's daughter Rachel. The Donelson family was a founding family of Nashville (see page 196). Rachel had married Lewis Robards, but they had a troubled marriage. Rachel's mother sent her away on more than one occasion to visit friends near Natchez, Mississippi. On one of these visits, Rachel heard that Robards had divorced her. Andrew Jackson and Rachel were married in Natchez. When they came back to Nashville, they found out that the report of the divorce was not true. After this, Robards did divorce Rachel and in 1794 Andrew and Rachel married again in Nashville. This kind of communication breakdown was common on the sparsely-populated frontier. These events would become a major problem for the Jacksons during Jackson's 1828 campaign for the presidency. Andrew and Rachel never had any children by birth, but they took in two of her nephews, one of whom they named Andrew Jackson Jr., and also a Native American boy.

Jackson worked to make Tennessee America's 16th state in 1796. He helped draft the state constitution. He became Tennessee's first member of the U.S. House of Representatives and one of its first Senators. However, in 1799 he left Washington and returned to Nashville to manage his business affairs. Over the years, his businesses included plantations, boat-building operations, thoroughbred horseracing tracks, and general stores. He traveled to Baltimore, New Orleans, Philadelphia, and Washington, D.C., to buy the latest fashions for his stores.

Jackson was elected Major General of the Tennessee militia in 1802. In 1804 he purchased a neighbor's farm and named it The Hermitage. The home he built there in 1820-21 is one of America's most visited homes.

In 1806 Jackson killed a man in a duel. His own wounds took months to heal. Jackson's youthful reputation for having a hot temper continued for many years into his adult life.

Jackson's service during the War of 1812 (see Lesson 41) made him a national hero. After losing the presidential election of 1824, he won in 1828. However, during the bitter campaign, opponents sharply criticized his marriage to Rachel and greatly defamed the character of this fragile, devoutly religious woman. Rachel had been unwell for some time, and the strain of the harsh campaign caused her health to deteriorate further. Rachel died on December 22, 1828. She was buried in the garden at The Hermitage on Christmas Eve. Rachel's tomb is pictured below. A sad Andrew Jackson soon traveled to Washington, D.C., to become the seventh U.S. President.

After serving for eight years in the White House, Jackson returned to his beloved Hermitage in 1837. There he often visited Rachel's grave. Jackson kept up his interest in politics. He wrote letters to people in Washington, D.C., and subscribed to twenty newspapers. Jackson joined the Presbyterian Church in 1838. In the evenings, a milder Andrew Jackson gathered with his children and grandchildren to have evening devotions. Notice the daguerrotype image of Jackson on page 257. It was taken in 1844 by the Brady Studio, one of America's earliest portrait studios. Jackson died on July 8, 1845, surrounded by his family and his slaves. On July 10, ten thousand people attended his burial at The Hermitage.

Rachel's Garden Tomb

The Van Buren Presidency

During his first term in office, Andrew Jackson chose Martin Van Buren to be his Secretary of State. When Jackson ran for a second term, he chose Van Buren as his Vice President. See his portrait at left.

In 1836 Martin Van Buren was elected America's eighth President. Just three months after his inauguration, the country suffered severe economic problems. His opponents began to call him Martin Van Ruin. Van Buren inspired other nicknames. Some called the five-foot-six politician Little Magician because he was good at making political deals. Another Van Buren nickname was Old Kinderhook, because he was from Kinderhook, New York. Old Kinderhook was often shortened to "OK."

President Van Buren

During Van Buren's presidency, Texans wanted to become part of the United States. Van Buren opposed this because he did not want to see slavery expand. He was also afraid that the issue would lead to war with Mexico. When Van Buren ran for a second term in 1840, he was defeated. Read about Van Buren's life below.

Martin Van Buren
America's Eighth President
March 4, 1837 - March 4, 1841

Martin Van Buren was born in 1782 into a large family in Kinderhook, New York. Like many New Yorkers, his parents were descendants of Dutch immigrants. His father kept a tavern and farmed. Van Buren was the first President born after America declared its independence from Great Britain.

Though his parents were unable to send him to college, Van Buren became a law clerk and studied law on his own. In 1807 he married his cousin Hannah Hoes, with whom he had grown up in Kinderhook. Martin and Hannah were married for twelve years and had five sons. One died in infancy. Hannah Van Buren died of tuberculosis at age 35. Martin never married again. Hannah was remembered as a Christian woman who was loving and gentle.

Van Buren became involved in New York politics and was elected as one of its U.S. Senators in 1821. In 1837 Van Buren moved into the White House with his four bachelor sons. Dolley Madison, wife of former President James Madison, brought her young relative Angelica Singleton to the White House to call on the President. Van Buren's oldest son Abraham came to care about the young beauty and married her. Abraham served as his father's private secretary and Angelica Van Buren served as his First Lady.

Martin Van Buren purchased Lindenwald, an estate near Kinderhook, around 1840. He remained active in politics. He even ran for President again in 1848 but was defeated. During the 1850s, he wrote his memoirs, traveled, and visited with his children and grandchildren. Van Buren died at Lindenwald in 1862 during the Civil War. He was seventy-nine years old.

The Jacksonian Era

Andrew Jackson had a great impact on the American presidency by showing strong leadership and not just going along with what Congress decided. Historians call the time of the Jackson and Van Buren presidencies the Jacksonian Era.

Andrew Jackson respected Martin Van Buren and called him "a true man with no guile." To be without guile means to be true and without deceit. May the same be said of each of us. In the first chapter of John, Jesus complimented Nathanael when the two met for the first time. Jesus said:

> Behold an Israelite indeed,
> in whom is no guile.
> John 1:47 KJV

Activities for Lesson 46

Map Study – Complete the assignments for Lesson 46 on Map 20 "The Lower 48" in *Maps of America the Beautiful*.

Timeline – In *Timeline of America the Beautiful* next to 1830, write: The Baltimore and Ohio opens the first commercial rail line in the United States.

Vocabulary – Look up each of these words in a dictionary: compromise, existence, circular, expand, sparse. Write each word and its definition in your notebook.

Literature – Read chapters 10-11 in *Brady*.

Creative Writing – In your notebook, write one or two paragraphs about why you think Andrew Jackson is one of America's most famous Presidents.

Student Workbook or Lesson Review – If you are using one of these optional books, complete the assignment for Lesson 46.

God Created America's Islands

When thinking about islands, do you think of beaches, palm trees, and warm ocean breezes? It is true that you can find those things on many islands around the world, but God created other kinds of islands, too. He created thousands of islands in America, placing them in lakes, in rivers, and along the coasts. Some do have beaches, palm trees, and warm ocean breezes, but others are covered in snow in the winter!

The "Sphinx" in the Apostle Island Chain in Wisconsin

We have already learned about a few of America's islands, like Roanoke Island in Lesson 11, a few Great Lakes islands in Lesson 13, Manhattan Island in Lesson 17, Martha's Vineyard and Nantucket in Lesson 20, and Long Island in Lesson 26. Most of America's largest islands are in Hawaii and Alaska; we will learn more about them in Units 23 and 25. Today we will explore some of America's many other islands and learn about some island activities during the Jacksonian Era.

Lake Islands in America

The American Woodcock lives in the Apostle Islands.

All of the Great Lakes contain islands. In Lake Superior is the Apostle Island chain with twenty-two islands. See the photo above. All except Madeline Island are in the Apostle Islands National Seashore. The oldest settlement in Wisconsin is La Pointe on Madeline Island. The Apostle Islands have eight lighthouses. The American Woodcock, pictured at left, is a resident of the Apostle Islands.

For all of America's history, fishing has been important to its economy. Michigan's Mackinac (Mack-a-naw) Island in Lake Huron was a fur trading center until the 1830s, when John Jacob Astor's American Fur Trading Company switched to fishing instead of trapping. Its former fur warehouses became fish warehouses.

Later in the 1800s, people began enjoying beautiful Mackinac Island, pictured below, as a summer resort. In 1875 it became the home of America's second national park. After

Mackinac Island, Michigan

twenty years, the U.S. government gave the park to the state of Michigan. Michigan made it the state's first state park. The island is still a resort. Visitors can tour a British fort built in 1780 and a house used by employees of the American Fur Company. They can also enjoy carriage and bicycle rides on an island where no cars are allowed.

The largest island in the Great Lakes is Michigan's Isle Royale, a 209-square-mile island in Lake Superior. In the 1840s, Americans began to mine copper there. They were not the first copper miners on the island; Isle Royale is dotted with ruins of ancient Native American copper mines. Isle Royale and the four hundred smaller islands that surround it are now protected in Isle Royale National Park. Descendants of Scandinavian immigrants still live on the island for part of the year and continue commercial fishing like their ancestors.

The tiny state of Vermont has seventy-eight islands. Vermont's largest island, South Hero Island, is in Lake Champlain. The largest New Hampshire island is one of many islands in America that is called Long Island; it is in Lake Winnepesaukee. The Great Salt Lake in Utah has eleven islands, the largest of which is Antelope Island. America's largest free-roaming bison herd lives there. Pine Island in Vermillion Lake is the largest island in Minnesota. Wild Horse Island in Flathead Lake is the largest in Montana. North of Grand Teton National Park is Jackson Lake, home to Elk Island, the largest island in Wyoming.

River Islands in America

Many of America's rivers contain islands. The islands of the Sheets Island Archipelago in the Susquehanna River in Pennsylvania cover 3,675 acres. The most famous river island in Pennsylvania is Three Mile Island, pictured at right. America experienced a nuclear power accident there in 1979. Pennsylvania also has a Six Mile Island and a Nine Mile Island.

Nuclear Plant on Three Mile Island

The Thousand Islands chain is in the St. Lawrence River. It actually has over 1500 islands. Some are part of New York and the rest are Canadian. Thousand Island salad dressing is named for these islands.

The largest island in the District of Columbia is East Potomac Park in the Potomac River. Another island in the Potomac River is Theodore Roosevelt Island, with its seventeen-foot-tall bronze statue of the President. Tennessee's largest island is Sunrise Towhead in the Mississippi River. Blennerhasset Island, in the Ohio River, is the largest island in West Virginia. Notice the drawing of a mansion on Blennerhasset Island at right. Saint Croix Island in Maine is in the St. Croix River along the Canadian-American border. Samuel de Champlain settled there in 1604. The National Park Service operates the Saint Croix International Historic Site there.

Blennerhasset Mansion on Blennerhasset Island in West Virginia

Lewis and Clark landed on Oregon's largest island in 1805. Around 1836 the Hudson Bay Company began dairy operations there. The island is named Sauvie Island for French Canadian Laurent Sauvé, who managed the dairies. Though Oregon is a coastal state with over 1800 islands, this largest island is not in the Pacific Ocean but in the Columbia River. Sauvie Island is so large that it is dotted with its own lakes that have their own islands!

Now that we have explored lake and river islands, we will look at a few of America's thousands of coastal islands, first in the Atlantic Ocean, then the Gulf of Mexico, and then in the Pacific Ocean.

American Islands Along the Atlantic Coast

From Maine to Mexico, barrier islands protect much of America's eastern and southern coastline. A barrier island is a long and sandy island that shields a coast from wind, waves, and storms. Only fifteen percent of the world's coastlines have such barrier islands. A bay, sound, or lagoon lies between a barrier island and the coastline. These provide habitat for many plants and animals, as do the beach, dune, barrier flat, and salt marsh habitats on the islands themselves. Some barrier islands also have small forests with magnolia, myrtle oak, sand live oak, and slash pine trees.

Piping Plovers

Over 360 species of birds either live on the barrier islands along America's eastern coastline or visit there during their annual migrations along the Atlantic flyway. One species is the endangered piping plover, pictured above.

Mount Desert Island. Maine's largest island is Mount Desert Island. At 1,530 feet, the island's Cadillac Mountain is the highest point along America's east coast. Mount Desert Island is home to Acadia National Park and the tourist town of Bar Harbor. Parts of it are rocky, while other areas have beautiful forests. French explorer Samuel de Champlain came to the island in 1604. He named it Monts Deserts, which means wilderness

Mount Desert Island, Maine

mountains. Atlantic puffins, like the one below, swim nearby. See a rocky portion of Mount Desert Island at left.

Aquidneck Island in Rhode Island. Most of Rhode Island is actually on the American mainland, but the state has islands, too. The largest is Aquidneck in Narragansett Bay. It is home to the popular summer resort of Newport. Newport is a yachting center that hosted the America's Cup Race for over fifty years. Touro Synagogue, America's oldest synagogue, was built there in 1763. In the 1800s and early 1900s, some of America's wealthiest families built summer homes in Newport. Though called cottages, they are actually large and elaborate mansions.

Long Island in New York — The Longest and Largest Island in the Continental United States. Long Island in New York is 118 miles long and covers 1,401 square miles, making it both the longest and the largest of the islands of the continental United States. In winter some parts of Long Island can have as much as seventy-five inches of snow. Long Island has its own barrier islands. One is Fire Island, home of the Fire Island National Seashore. During the Jacksonian Era, Long Island had a small rural population,

Atlantic Puffin

many of whom were farmers. The population began to grow after a railroad was built there in 1836. Today Long Island has more people than any other island in the United States. The nearby New York City borough of Manhattan encompasses Manhattan, Ellis, Governor's, Randall's, Ward's, Roosevelt, and Liberty Islands. The Statue of Liberty is on Liberty Island.

Absecon Island in New Jersey. One of New Jersey's barrier islands is Absecon Island, home to Atlantic City with its famous boardwalk.

Assateague Island of Maryland and Virgina. Assateague Island is a barrier island that lies offshore from Maryland and Virginia. The northern section of the island is in Maryland and the southern section is in Virginia. It is in the Assateague Island National Seashore. Wild ponies live on Assateague. Many people believe that the ponies' ancestors swam to the island from a Spanish ship that sank nearby during the 1500s. See photo on page 255.

For many years, people living near Assateague have captured some of the ponies to use for work and for pleasure riding. This practice is called pony penning. The first written record of pony penning was published in 1836

Leatherback, Loggerhead, Hawk's Bill, and Green Sea Turtles

while Andrew Jackson was President, though it probably began much earlier.

In the 1940s, the volunteer fire department from nearby Chincoteague Island in Virginia began using Assateague ponies to raise funds. Thousands of tourists come to Chincoteague each July for the annual pony penning celebration. Volunteers from Chincoteague Island capture ponies on Assateague. They herd them toward the beach and the ponies then swim over to Chincoteague Island where some are sold.

The Outer Banks of North Carolina. The Outer Banks of North Carolina is one of many barrier island chains on the Atlantic coast. North Carolina has three barrier island areas protected by the National Park Service: Cape Hatteras National Seashore, Cape Lookout National Seashore, and Fort Raleigh National Historic Site on Roanoke Island.

Sullivan's Island in South Carolina. The Civil War (1861 to 1865) began at Fort Sumter. Today visitors can tour Fort Sumter National Monument on Sullivan's Island.

The Sea Islands of South Carolina and Georgia. During the Jacksonian Era, slaves worked in rice plantations on the Sea Islands. Over the years these slaves developed a unique culture and language known as Gullah. Some African Americans from the region still speak Gullah and follow Gullah customs.

Canaveral Island and the Florida Keys in Florida. Sea turtles, including the four species

West Indian Manatee

United States Geological Survey Researcher Don Hickey installs testing equipment at the Sombrero Reef.

Notice the Great White Heron sitting atop exposed roots of mangrove trees growing on Florida's Boggy Key.

on page 264, make their home on Canaveral Island, a barrier island which is part of the Canaveral National Seashore in Florida. Cape Canaveral has been the site of many spacecraft launches conducted by America's space program.

The Florida Keys extend southwest from the tip of the Florida peninsula. The Florida Keys are made of limestone and coral. These 1700 islands are home to the world's third largest coral reef, the world's largest bed of sea grass, and over 5,500 marine species, like the West Indian manatee at top right. In the center photograph, a diver swims in Sombrero Reef. In the bottom photo, a Great White Heron sits on mangrove roots in the Florida Keys.

American Islands Along the Gulf of Mexico

River Otter

The Gulf Islands of Mississippi, Alabama, and Florida. The United States government has often chosen barrier islands as places to build forts for defense. Fort Pickens was begun in 1829 on Florida's Santa Rosa Island off the coast of the Florida panhandle. Fort McRee was begun in 1834 on nearby Perdido Key. Santa Rosa Island and Perdido Key are two of the Gulf Islands. Alabama's Dauphin Island is another of the Gulf Islands. It is home to Fort Gaines, completed in 1834. Today some Gulf Islands are part of the Gulf Islands National Seashore. There you might see a river otter like the one pictured above.

Marsh Island in Louisiana. Sometimes marsh islands lie between barrier islands and the mainland. One such island is named Marsh Island, the largest island in the state of Louisiana.

Padre and Galveston Islands of Texas. During the Jacksonian Era, ranchers began to raise cattle on Padre Island, the largest island along the coast of what is now Texas. In 1804 Spanish priest Padre Nicolas Balli established a settlement on the island, which was later named Padre in his honor.

Black Skimmer

In 1962 a channel was constructed across Padre Island, dividing it into North Padre and South Padre. On the north island is Padre Island National Seashore, with the longest stretch of undeveloped barrier island seashore in the world. Companies that owned mineral rights before the National Seashore was established still retrieve oil and natural gas from North Padre Island. Padre Island is a great place to go bird watching. You might see a black skimmer like the one at right.

Galveston Island lies two miles off the Texas coast in the Gulf of Mexico. In 1830, while Galveston was still a part of Mexico, the Mexican government established a small customs house on the island.

American Islands Along the Pacific Coast

The California Channel Islands and the Farallon Islands of California. Many islands lie along the Pacific coastline. See the picture at right. Near Los Angeles are the California Channel Islands: Santa Cruz, San Clemente, Anacapa, Santa Rosa, San Miguel, Santa Barbara, San Nicholas, and

Santa Catalina Island, a California Channel Island

Orca

Snowy Egret

Santa Catalina. Anacapa, Santa Cruz, Santa Rosa, San Miguel, and Santa Barbara Islands are part of Channel Islands National Park. During the Jacksonian Era, both sheep and cattle were raised on Santa Rosa and Santa Cruz Islands. On Santa Cruz is Painted Cave, a sea cave almost one-quarter-mile long. Among the birds that nest on the Channel Islands is the brown pelican, pictured below.

The Farallon Islands chain is near San Francisco. During the Jacksonian Era, Russians hunted seals there. Nearby in San Francisco Bay is Alcatraz Island. See the picture at lower right. It was home to an infamous maximum security Federal prison from 1934 to 1963. The first American-built lighthouse on the West Coast was constructed on Alcatraz in 1854. The first American fort on the West Coast was built there in 1859. The island is in the Golden Gate National Recreation Area. At left is a snowy egret, one of the many birds that come to Alcatraz.

Oregon Islands National Wildlife Refuge in Oregon. Along 320 miles of the Oregon Coast is Oregon Islands National Wildlife Refuge, which includes 1,853 islands, reefs, and coastal rocks. All of the refuge is off-limits to people, except for the one-acre section called Tillamook Rock, which has a lighthouse.

Whidbey Island and the San Juan Islands of Washington. The largest island in Washington is Whidbey Island in Puget Sound. The San Juan Islands lie between Washington and Vancouver Island in British Columbia, Canada. These islands were used by both Americans and the British during the Jacksonian Era. They did not become a part of America until 1872. One animal living around the San Juan Islands is the orca, also known as the killer whale. See the photograph above.

Brown Pelican

Alcatraz Island

All the islands of America belong to God. He made islands beautiful for the people who live there and for those who come to visit. Each morning He paints island sunrises and each night He paints their beautiful sunsets.

Behold, the nations are like a drop from a bucket,
And are regarded as a speck of dust on the scales;
Behold, He lifts up the islands like fine dust.
Isaiah 40:15

Activities for Lesson 47

Thinking Biblically – Copy Isaiah 40:15 in your notebook.

Map Study – Complete the assignments for Lesson 47 on Map 15 "America's Islands" in *Maps of America the Beautiful*.

Timeline – In *Timeline of America the Beautiful* next to 1836, write: First written record of pony penning on Assateague Island.

Literature – Read chapters 12-13 in *Brady*.

Student Workbook or Lesson Review – If you are using one of these optional books, complete the assignment for Lesson 47.

"Remember the Alamo!"

San Antonio de Valero, Later Known as the Alamo

We learned about Christopher Columbus and his explorations in the New World in Unit 2. We read about Spanish conquistadors like Hernando de Soto and Francisco Vásquez de Coronado, and about the Spanish founding St. Augustine. In the years before the Jacksonian Era, while Americans fought for independence from Great Britain, establishing a new national government in Washington, D.C., and moving westward, Spain continued to spread its influence in South America and Mexico, including the area that is now the states of Arizona, California, New Mexico, and Texas. For many years Spain controlled Florida, too, but finally Spain agreed to give it to the United States. Florida formally became a part of America in 1821 during the presidency of James Monroe.

Throughout their area of influence, the Spanish built Catholic missions to convert native peoples and to educate them. They founded San Antonio de Valero in 1718 on the site of what is now San Antonio, Texas. Missionaries began to build a chapel there in 1744. They abandoned the mission in 1793. See photos of the mission above and below.

In 1803 soldiers from Alamo de Parras, Mexico, began to use the mission for barracks. This is probably why the buildings there became known as the Alamo, though some historians believe the name refers to cottonwood trees that grew nearby. Álamo is Spanish for cottonwood. From 1803 to December 1835, first Spanish and then Mexican forces occupied the Alamo. One of the most famous battles in American history took place at the former Catholic mission in 1836.

Mexican Independence

Just as English and other European settlers had immigrated to the colonies of North America, Spanish colonists settled in South America and Mexico. Great Britain had ruled their thirteen colonies; likewise Spain ruled many parts of Central and South America. The Spanish took

Inside the Alamo

complete control of Mexico in 1521. By the early 1800s, the people of Mexico included native tribes who had lived there before the Spanish conquest, Spanish colonists and their descendants, and mestizos, people who had both Spanish and native ancestors.

Santa Anna

Many Mexicans wanted independence from Spain. After years of conflict and rebellion, Mexico declared itself a republic in 1823. This new republic included what would become the states of Arizona, California, New Mexico, and Texas. Guadalupe Victoria became the first president of Mexico. The Mexican people struggled to establish a new government and had several weak presidents. In 1833 Antonio López de Santa Anna became president and later dictator of Mexico. See the drawing at right.

Americans Migrate to Texas

In 1819, during Mexico's struggle for independence, American Moses Austin developed a plan to form an American colony in Mexico. The Mexican government agreed to the plan. Austin died two years later, but his son Stephen Austin continued his father's dream. Many Americans moved into what is now Texas, which was then one of the states of Mexico. Though only one Mexican state, the area was called Coahuila and Texas. The American settlers were called Texians. The Texian Governor was Henry Smith.

Texians wanted their new home to become part of the United States. The government of Mexico did not want to lose this large tract of land. Mexico sent soldiers into its state of Coahuila and Texas. Texians began to build forts. They organized an "Army of the People." Texians tried to gain their independence by talking with the Mexican government, but their army fought battles with Mexican soldiers, too. Former Tennessee Governor Sam Houston served as a general in the Army of the People.

The Battle of the Alamo

Bowie Knife

In December 1835, Mexican forces surrendered the Alamo to Texian forces. The Texians feared that the Mexicans would try to retake the Alamo because of its important location on the Old San Antonio Road. Colonel James Clinton Neill became commander at the Alamo. He worked to make it a strong fortress. General Sam Houston, who was in the settlement of Gonzales working to

Davy Crockett

organize the Texas army, worried about whether the Alamo could withstand a Mexican attack. He sent volunteers to gather information at the Alamo. Among them was explorer and adventurer Jim Bowie, who invented the Bowie knife, pictured above. Governor Smith sent young Lieutenant Colonel William B. Travis and his thirty-man cavalry unit to the Alamo. They arrived on February 3. Five days later a former U.S. Congressman from Tennessee, Davy Crockett, came to the Alamo with a few American volunteers. See Crockett's picture at left.

Colonel Neill had to leave the Alamo on February 14, after receiving word that his family was ill. While away, he tried to raise money to help the men there. With their commander away, the men at the Alamo decided that Colonel Travis would lead the members of the army and Jim Bowie would lead the volunteers. When Bowie became ill, Travis took full command.

The Alamo is now a tourist site.

The men at the Alamo heard that Santa Anna and many Mexican troops were on their way. On February 23, the Mexicans arrived. Santa Anna sent word that the Texians should surrender. Lieutenant Colonel Travis responded by firing a cannonball. Mexican troops attacked the Alamo that day and then kept it under siege day after day. Travis sent out an appeal to Texians and Americans, asking that they come to their aid. On March 1, a mere thirty-two reinforcements joined them. The men began to run out of food. It was just a matter of time before those inside the Alamo would die from hunger. The siege continued. Finally, on March 6, Santa Anna surprised his men by ordering another attack. Though they had no hope of final victory, those inside the Alamo fought back. About six hundred of Santa Anna's men were killed or wounded. Travis and all of his soldiers died. The only ones left alive in the Alamo were women, children, and slaves. Santa Anna gave each of them a blanket and two dollars and let them leave in safety. Two of these survivors were the wife of one of the slain soldiers and their infant daughter. This widow took the news of the Alamo to General Sam Houston. See the drawing below of the Alamo.

An Illustration of the Alamo from the London Illustrated News *in 1844*

On March 2, while the Alamo was under siege, Texians declared their independence from Mexico. When fellow Texians heard about the brave soldiers of the Alamo, they decided to continue the fight. General Sam Houston defeated Santa Anna in April at the Battle of San Jacinto River. The battle cry of Houston's army was "Remember the Alamo!" Houston, pictured on page 272, captured Santa Anna in the San Jacinto battle.

Sam Houston at the Battle of San Jacinto River

The Republic of Texas

Texians formed a new government as the Republic of Texas, an independent country. They chose Sam Houston as their president. The Republic of Texas asked to be a new state in the United States of America. Many Americans feared that doing so would cause a war with Mexico. Some Americans did not want to bring in Texas because many of its residents were slave holders. President Andrew Jackson did not agree to annex (or take in) Texas, but on his last day in office, he recognized the Republic of Texas as an independent nation. What to do about Texas continued to be a problem for the next ten years.

The Alamo in San Antonio is a Texas state monument. Since March 6, 1836, it has been a symbol of bravery, determination, and the desire for independence.

> The wicked flee when no one is pursuing,
> But the righteous are bold as a lion.
> Proverbs 28:1

Activities for Lesson 48

Map Study – Complete the assignment for Lesson 48 on Map 3 "America's Landmarks" in *Maps of America the Beautiful*.

Timeline – In *Timeline of America the Beautiful* next to 1744, write: The first stone chapel is constructed at the Alamo.

Vocabulary – In your notebook, write each of the following sentents. Fill in each blank with one of these words: convert, barracks, dictator, tract, cavalry

1. My family lives on the same _____ of land my great-grandfather bought in 1925.
2. The _____ unit had to arrange a place to stable their horses.
3. Many American missionaries worked to _____ Native Americans to Christianity.
4. The newspaper reported rumors of a revolution to remove the _____ from office.
5. When they were off-duty, the soldiers relaxed in their _____.

Literature – Read "Letter from the Alamo" in *We the People*, page 46, and chapters 14-15 of *Brady*.

Student Workbook or Lesson Review – If you are using one of these optional books, complete the assignment for Lesson 48.

John Jay, President of the American Bible Society

John Jay was one of America's founding fathers. Look at his picture below. Jay's ancestors were Huguenots, Protestant believers persecuted by the government in France. The French government abolished the rights of Protestants in 1685, so John Jay's great-grandfather Pierre Jay fled to England.

John Jay

Pierre's son Augustus emigrated from England to America. He went first to South Carolina and later to New York. Augustus Jay settled at Esopus, New York, among other French Protestants. From Esopus, he moved to New York City. In 1697 Augustus married a Miss Bayard, whose ancestors were also French Huguenots. Her family had emigrated first to Holland and then to America. Augustus Jay became a successful merchant.

One of Augustus' sons was Peter, who also became a merchant. Peter married Mary Van Cortlandt, who was Dutch. Peter and Mary had ten children, seven of whom lived into adulthood. John Jay was their sixth child. He was born in December of 1745. Shortly after John was born, the family moved from Manhattan to Rye, New York. Peter believed Rye would be a more suitable setting for his children, of whom two were blind and two had mental handicaps.

John's mother Mary taught him literature at home. When he was eight years old, he entered a school taught by a Huguenot minister. At age fourteen, John Jay entered an Anglican school in New York City called King's College. It is now Columbia University. He graduated in 1764 and became a law clerk. At age twenty-three, Jay became a lawyer. In April of 1774, John Jay married Sarah Van Brugh Livingston, daughter of New Jersey Governor William Livingston. John was twenty-nine years old.

John Jay and the American Revolution

The same year that John married Sarah, he was chosen to represent New York in the First Continental Congress. The next year, he wrote the first draft of the Constitution of

New York. During the American Revolution, he served as the first Chief Justice of the State of New York and President of the Second Continental Congress. Jay worked for the cause of American independence by serving as an Ambassador to Spain, where he sought Spanish aid to help America defeat the British. At the end of the war, he went to France where he, along with Benjamin Franklin, John Adams, and Henry Laurens, worked with the British to complete the Treaty of Paris.

The Federalist Papers

John Jay served as Secretary of Foreign Affairs while America was under the Articles of Confederation. He believed America needed a new constitution. Though he was not chosen to be part of the Constitutional Convention in 1787, he helped convince Americans to adopt it. During 1787 and 1788, Alexander Hamilton, James Madison, and John Jay wrote essays that are usually referred to today as the *Federalist Papers*. In these essays that were published in newspapers, Hamilton, Madison, and Jay encouraged the new American states to form a strong national government by adopting the new Constitution. Many people in Jay's home state of New York opposed the Constitution. Jay worked hard to encourage ratification there, and New York became the eleventh state to ratify the Constitution in July of 1788.

Chief Justice of the Supreme Court

When George Washington became the first President of the United States, he chose John Jay as the first Chief Justice of the Supreme Court. See his picture below. Jay filled the position from 1789 to 1795. While Jay was Chief Justice, President Washington sent him to

Chief Justice John Jay

Great Britain to negotiate a treaty to settle continuing differences between the two countries. The treaty he negotiated was controversial. It has become known as the Jay Treaty.

Governor of New York

When John Jay came home from England, he found that the state of New York had elected him as its Governor. He served two terms and then retired from public life in 1801.

Serving Christ During His Retirement

Upon retirement, Jay, along with his wife, two sons, and two daughters, retired to his family homestead in Katonah, New York. Jay had inherited a farm which had belonged to his mother's father, Jacobus Van Cortlandt. Jacobus had purchased the land in 1703 from Katonah, a Native American chief. John Jay had purchased additional land so that by the time he retired, his farm in Katonah had 750 acres. The family home, pictured below, is now a New York State Historic Site.

The Jay family honored God. Each morning they came together to worship Him and every evening at nine o'clock, John Jay read his family a chapter from the Bible. Sarah died in 1802, shortly after their move to Katonah.

Jay was interested in agriculture, and he maintained his interest in American and New York government. When his sons, Peter Augustus and William, grew up, he corresponded with them about politics. Jay also corresponded with other founding fathers.

While in retirement, he continued to try to help his fellow man. John Jay was active in the Episcopal Church. He was a founding member and first president of the New York Manumission Society, which worked to end slavery. He maintained a friendship with William Wilberforce, who was working to end slavery in Great Britain. Jay's son William was also an abolitionist, as was William's son John Jay II.

John Jay Homestead in Katonah, New York

John Jay and the American Bible Society

The American Bible Society (ABS) was founded in New York in 1816. Elias Boudinot was its first president and John Jay was its first vice president. In 1821 John Jay became the second president of the American Bible Society after the death of Boudinot. He served until 1828. The founding purpose of the American Bible Society was to provide people with Bibles. John Jay believed the ABS should distribute Bibles without note or comment.

One of the first efforts of the American Bible Society was to distribute Bibles to the crew of an American ship, the USS *John Adams.* The ABS continues to provide Bibles for the U.S. military today. The Society published the books of 1, 2, and 3 John with translations in English and Delaware Indian language side by side in 1818. Five years later the American Bible Society sent a donation to British missionary William Carey to support his efforts to translate the Bible in India. The group printed and gave away Bibles in China. In addition, the Society helped the New England Institution for the Blind provide the first Bibles for people who were visually impaired.

John Jay was not the only government official to serve as president of the American Bible Society. Following Jay as president was Richard Varick, former mayor of New York City. Two other ABS presidents in the 1800s were former members of the United States

Senate: Theodore Frelinghuysen served as ABS president from 1845 until his death in 1862. His nephew Frederick Theodore Frelinghuysen served from 1884 until his death in 1885.

John Jay remained a widower for twenty-seven years until his death in 1829 at age 83. He died the same year that Andrew Jackson became President.

John Jay was a man who honored the Word of God:

> For "all flesh is like grass, and all its glory like the flower of grass.
> The grass withers, and the flower falls off,
> but the word of the Lord endures forever"
> And this is the word which was preached to you.
> 1 Peter 1:24-25

Activities for Lesson 49

Thinking Biblically – In your notebook, copy 2 Timothy 2:15, which gives instructions about being a workman for God.

Timeline – In *Timeline of America the Beautiful* next to 1821, write: John Jay becomes president of the American Bible Society.

Literature – Read "Letter to Papa" in *We the People*, page 47, and chapters 16-17 of *Brady*.

Creative Writing – In your notebook, write three or four paragraphs about the good influence John Jay had in his life and the kind of influence you want to have throughout your life.

Family Activity – Your family can be a part of sharing God's Word with others. See page 429 for a way to do this.

Student Workbook or Lesson Review – If you are using one of these optional books, complete the assignment for Lesson 49.

The Trail of Tears

One of the saddest events in American history happened in 1838 and 1839 when thousands of Cherokee Indians died as they were forced to travel to Oklahoma from their homelands in North Carolina, Georgia, and Tennessee. In English the event is called the Trail of Tears; in Cherokee it is Nunna-da-ul-tsun-yi, meaning "the place where they cried." See the Cherokee home from Georgia pictured at right.

Home of Cherokee Leader John Ross at the Time of the Removal

Though some Americans, like William Penn and John Jay's grandfather, purchased land from Native Americans, others simply took it. During the presidencies of Madison, Monroe, John Quincy Adams, Jackson, and Van Buren, Native Americans from several eastern tribes, including the Cherokee, Chickasaw, Choctaw, Creek, and Seminole, signed many treaties with the United States government. In these treaties, they sold portions of their lands to the United States. However, the U.S. government did not keep all of its agreements with Native Americans.

The situation for Native Americans became worse in 1830 when Congress passed the Indian Removal Act, which stated that Native Americans living in the East must move west of the Mississippi River, mainly to Arkansas, Kansas, and Oklahoma. During the next twenty years, about 100,000 Native Americans moved west. Like the Cherokee, other tribes suffered many deaths along the way, including 3,500 Creek from Alabama.

Before becoming President, Andrew Jackson had fought alongside Native Americans in the War of 1812. In 1813 he adopted Lyncoya, a two-year-old Creek boy. Lyncoya grew up at the Hermitage and received a good education. He died from tuberculosis at age seventeen.

Despite his close contact with Native Americans, Jackson believed that Indians and whites could not exist peacefully as neighbors. In his inaugural address, Jackson stated that he wanted all Native Americans to move west of the Mississippi River. Even though he thought that separating the two peoples would be the best way for Native Americans to survive, forcing them to move to the West was not fair and caused much pain and suffering.

Cherokee and the Treaty of New Echota

When Europeans first began to explore and later to move into Cherokee lands, the Cherokee traded with them. Cherokee and Europeans often married one another. More and more the Cherokee began to live like white Americans. Some farmed plantations; some even purchased African American slaves. After Sequoyah created their written language, the Cherokee adopted even more American customs. Notice the clothing styles of the Cherokee men pictured in this lesson. Soon the Cherokee wrote their own constitution and established their government at New Echota, Georgia.

Major Ridge

The same year that the Indian Removal Act was passed, gold was found on Cherokee lands in Georgia. Whites began wanting Cherokee land even more. The State of Georgia gave whites the right to mine gold on Cherokee land and forbade the Cherokee from mining it themselves. Georgia even held lotteries to give whites Cherokee land. Georgia limited the kinds of business that the Cherokee could conduct. The Cherokee moved their capital to Red Clay, Tennessee. They took their grievances all the way to the U.S. Supreme Court and won, but President Jackson refused to enforce the court's decision.

The Cherokee tribe's Principal Chief was John Ross, pictured on page 279. He and other leaders struggled with what to do. Most of the Cherokee people wanted to hold onto their rights. A few Cherokee thought they must obey the Indian Removal Act and move to Oklahoma, believing it was the only way they could survive as a people.

David Vann

Representatives of the United States met with about four hundred Cherokee in the old capital of New Echota. Major Ridge and David Vann were two of the leaders of this group. See their pictures above. About twenty Cherokee signed the Treaty of New Echota, which gave the U.S. all of the Cherokee territory. U.S. representatives agreed to give the Cherokee $5 million and new lands in Oklahoma, then part of an area called Indian Territory. Over 15,000 Cherokee protested, believing the treaty to be illegal. On May 23, 1836, the United States Senate ratified the Treaty of New Echota. It passed the Senate by just one vote.

Waiting in Stockades

Principal Chief John Ross

John Ross did not believe that the United States would actually force them to move. However, President Martin Van Buren ordered the removal to begin in 1838. In May of that year, seven thousand soldiers began to force Cherokee into fenced areas called stockades. Though the soldiers were told to treat the Cherokee with kindness, the ordeal was a horrible experience for the people. Family members got separated from one another. Soldiers pointed guns at sick and elderly people to make them leave their homes. The Cherokee had to hurry to gather some of their cherished belongings. A few whites rushed into Cherokee homes and carried off their possessions while the Cherokee were being whisked away from their farms. A large number of Cherokee were Christians. Many sang hymns in the stockades as they waited for soldiers to lead them to Oklahoma.

About one thousand Cherokee from Tennessee and North Carolina escaped into the Great Smoky Mountains. They are now known as the Eastern Band of Cherokee Indians. Two members of the Eastern Band stand beside their cabin in the photo below. Today the story of the Eastern Band is told in the play "Unto These Hills," performed each summer in Cherokee, North Carolina.

The Trail of Tears Begins

Three groups of Cherokee left in the summer of 1838 from near Chattanooga, Tennessee. They traveled on boats, trains, and wagons. Fifteen thousand others waited to make the trip. They suffered in crowded conditions through a summer drought. They asked permission to wait until fall to travel to Oklahoma, saying they would go willingly. Their request was granted.

By the time the Cherokee left in the fall of 1838, many had died. Thirteen groups of about 1,000 each began the eight-hundred-mile trek to Oklahoma. Chief Ross was in the last group to leave. Some traveled across Tennessee to Memphis and then along the Arkansas River. Some went first through Nashville, Tennessee, and then through Kentucky, Illinois, Missouri, and Arkansas. Others began in Alabama and went through West Tennessee and Missouri. The travelers had little food. Their clothing was not warm enough. Many more died along the way.

Members of the Eastern Band of Cherokee

Remembering the Trail of Tears

By March 1839, the last of the travelers reached Oklahoma. One survivor of the Trail of Tears told of the people feeling bad about leaving their homes. He said that women, children, and men cried. He said the men said nothing, but just put their heads down and kept going. Another told of people getting sick along the way. He said that he lost one family member each day until they were all gone. Elizur Butler, a missionary doctor among the Cherokee, traveled with them. He estimated that more than 4,000 died. Today visitors can remember the Cherokee experience as they drive along the Trail of Tears National Historic Trail.

The Cherokee Nation in Oklahoma

In August of 1839 the Cherokee again elected John Ross as their Principal Chief. Ross served at their new capital, Tahlequah, Oklahoma, which remains the Cherokee capital today. The Cherokee established a new government, a new constitution, and a school system in both Cherokee and English. Sequoyah lived for a time among the Cherokee in Oklahoma.

Greed causes people to think more highly of things than of people. Greed played a major role in the horrible Trail of Tears. Jesus taught against greed when He said:

Beware, and be on your guard against every form of greed;
For not even when one has an abundance does his life consist of his possessions.
Luke 12:15

Activities for Lesson 50

Thinking Biblically – In your notebook, copy Mark 12:29-31, in which Jesus teaches about how we conduct ourselves toward God and other people.

Map Study – Complete the assignments for Lesson 50 on Map 16 "The Trail of Tears" in *Maps of America the Beautiful*.

Timeline – In *Timeline of America the Beautiful* next to 1838, write: The Trail of Tears begins.

Vocabulary – Look up each of these words in a dictionary: inaugural, ratified, stockade, cherished, greed. Write each word and its definition in your notebook.

Literature – Read "A Soldier Remembers the Trail of Tears" in *We the People*, page 48, and chapter 18 in *Brady*.

Student Workbook or Lesson Review – If you are using one of these optional books, complete the assignment for Lesson 50. If you are using the Lesson Review, answer the questions on *Brady* and take the quiz for Unit 10.

New Ways to Travel and to Communicate

11

During the presidencies of William Henry Harrison and John Tyler, Americans learned about new ways to travel and new ways to communicate. They took advantage of the mighty Mississippi River that God created. Wealthy southerners and their slaves were living on large plantations that had grown up on the river like the ones in Natchez, Mississippi. Steamboats began carrying people and goods on the Mississippi and on other rivers of America. Painter Samuel Morse invented the Morse code, which made it practical to send messages by telegraph.

Steamboat Captain

Lessons in Unit 11

Lesson 51 – Our American Story: Tippecanoe and Tyler, Too
Lesson 52 – God's Wonders: God Created the Mississippi River
Lesson 53 – An American Landmark: Natchez, Mississippi
Lesson 54 – Daily Life: Traveling and Working on a Steamboat
Lesson 55 – An American Biography: Samuel Morse, Artist and Inventor

Books Used in Unit 11

- *Maps of America the Beautiful*

- *Timeline of America the Beautiful*

- *We the People*

Tippecanoe and Tyler, Too

After his victory over Native Americans in the Battle of Tippecanoe Creek in 1811, William Henry Harrison became known as Old Tippecanoe. The Whigs chose him as their presidential candidate in 1840 and selected John Tyler, a slave-owner from Virginia, as their vice-presidential nominee. The Whigs' campaign slogan was "Tippecanoe and Tyler, Too!" They portrayed Harrison as a frontiersman who lived in a log cabin. They produced the campaign poster at right. It has twelve scenes from his life and is entitled "Log Cabin Anecdotes."

Democrats nominated President Martin Van Buren. In the election, Harrison received 234 electoral votes; Van Buren won only sixty.

By inauguration day on March 4, 1841, William Henry Harrison was

Campaign Poster for William Henry Harrison

sixty-eight years old. He stood in the cold and rainy weather and gave a long speech, caught pneumonia, and died just one month after becoming President. Read about William Henry Harrison's life on page 283.

William Henry Harrison
America's Ninth President
March 4, 1841 - April 4, 1841

William Henry Harrison was born in Virginia in 1773. His father was Benjamin Harrison, a signer of the Declaration of Independence. Harrison was born, not in a log cabin, but at Berkeley, a mansion on the James River. At age 18 he joined the U.S. Army and began to serve in the Northwest Territory (see Lesson 31).

In 1795 Harrison secretly married Anna Tuthill Symmes. Anna had been educated at a New York City boarding school before moving to Ohio with her father Judge John Cleves Symmes when she was 19. Judge Symmes did not want his daughter to suffer the hardships of life in frontier forts, but eventually he accepted his son-in-law.

After leaving the military, Harrison served as Secretary of the Northwest Territory and represented it in Congress. He served as the first territorial Governor of Indiana. In Vincennes, the territorial capital, Harrison built a seventeen-room mansion on a three-hundred-acre tract of land. He named it Grouseland because of the grouse game birds on the property. He negotiated many treaties to obtain land from Native Americans, often meeting with tribal leaders at his home. Once the Shawnee leader Tecumseh met with Governor Harrison at Grouseland, warning him that his people would fight. William Henry Harrison defeated Tecumseh and his braves in the 1811 Battle of Tippecanoe Creek.

During the War of 1812, Harrison led forces against the British and Native Americans at the Battle of the Thames in Canada. Tecumseh died in the battle.

Harrison and his family moved to North Bend, Ohio. There Anna gave birth to their ninth and tenth children. In Ohio, Harrison farmed and held various state and national political offices until being nominated as the Whig presidential candidate in 1840.

Anna Harrison was ill when her husband left Ohio to become America's ninth President, but she intended to join him in Washington, D.C. in May. Her husband died before she arrived. Anna Harrison lived until 1864 when she died at age eighty-eight. William and Anna's grandson Benjamin became the 23rd President of the United States in 1889.

A Vice President Takes Over as President

For the first time, an American President had died in office. Harrison's Vice President, John Tyler, was sworn in as the new President. He was only fifty-one years old, the youngest man to become President until that time. Political enemies called him "His Accidency," saying he had accidentally become President. Tyler insisted that he was fully President. He had formerly been a Democrat and did not really agree with what the Whigs wanted to do. He often vetoed laws passed by Congress. He was the first President to have a presidential veto overridden by Congress. All of his Cabinet resigned. The Whigs cast him out of their political party. Though they tried to impeach him, they did not succeed.

In 1842, after years of controversy, America and Canada agreed on a northern boundary for the state of Maine. Americans dedicated a monument commemorating the

Revolutionary War Battle of Bunker Hill in 1843. Florida became the 27th state in 1845. Tyler served only one term and then retired to his recently-purchased plantation in Virginia. Read about John Tyler's life below.

John Tyler
America's Tenth President
April 4, 1841 - March 4, 1845

Tyler was born in 1790 on a Virginia plantation. He studied law and began serving in the Virginia legislature when he was 21 years old. He married Lettia Christian on his 23rd birthday. They had eight children. Lettia is pictured at left above.

John Tyler served in many political offices. During his career, he served in the U.S. House of Representatives, as Governor of Virginia, and in the U.S. Senate.

By the time Tyler became President, his wife Lettia was an invalid. She was kind, gentle, and soft-spoken. She enjoyed knitting and reading her Bible and prayer book. Though ill, she still quietly managed the affairs of her household. During her years as First Lady, she made only one public appearance, when their daughter Elizabeth was married at the White House. Lettia died at the White House in 1842.

In 1844 John Tyler married Julia Gardiner. Tyler was the first President to marry while serving as President. Though thirty years younger than her husband, Julia became a devoted wife. She is pictured at right above.

While serving in the White House, President Tyler purchased a 1,200-acre plantation just three miles from his birthplace in Virginia. Tyler added on to the original house which was built in 1780, making it the longest private home in Virginia. Though it was 300 feet long, it was only one room deep! One of the additions was a ballroom. Some believe it was added so they could dance the Virginia Reel. Tyler named his retirement home Sherwood Forest because he thought of himself as a political Robin Hood. Below is a photograph of Sherwood Forest.

Sherwood Forest

John and Julia Tyler had seven children. With a total of fifteen children, John Tyler holds the record as the President with the most children.

When America divided over slavery, former President John Tyler sided with the Confederacy and was elected to its Congress. However, he died on January 18, 1862, before the Congress convened.

Girls should aspire to be kind and gentle like Lettia Tyler. Boys should decide that they will only choose to marry a girl with those traits. As Peter taught Christian women:

> Your adornment must not be merely external—
> braiding the hair, wearing gold jewelry, or putting on dresses;
> but let it be the hidden person of the heart,
> with the imperishable quality of a gentle and quiet spirit,
> which is precious in the sight of God.
> 1 Peter 3:3-4

Activities for Lesson 51

Thinking Biblically – John Tyler and the rest of the government had many conflicts during his term in office. Copy Romans 12:18 into your notebook.

Map Study – Complete the assignment for Lesson 51 on Map 20 "The Lower 48" in *Maps of America the Beautiful*.

Timeline – In *Timeline of America the Beautiful* next to 1842 write: America and Canada agree on a northern boundary for the state of Maine.

Literature – Read "To the People of the United States" in *We the People*, page 49.

Creative Writing – Think of someone you know who would make a good President. It could be your father or mother, a grandparent, or a friend. Imagine that person is campaigning for President and has asked you to give a speech at a campaign rally. Write a speech of 1-2 pages in your notebook introducing and endorsing him or her.

Student Workbook or Lesson Review – If you are using one of these optional books, complete the assignment for Lesson 51.

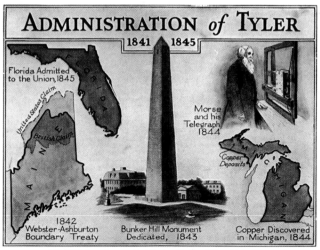

Highlights from the Years Tyler Was President

God Created the Mississippi River

When God created the Mississippi River, He made the largest river in North America. The Missouri is longer, but the Mississippi is bigger overall and has more water. *Mississippi* comes from an Ojibwe word meaning big water.

Lake Itasca, Source of the Mississippi River

The Mississippi River flows from Lake Itasca.

The Mighty Mississippi

The Mississippi River, also known as "Old Man River," begins at Lake Itasca in Minnesota and flows about 2,300 miles southward until it empties into the Gulf of Mexico about 95 miles south of New Orleans. Lake Itasca is pictured at left. The part of the Mississippi River north of Cairo, Illinois, is called the Upper Mississippi; the part below Cairo is the Lower Mississippi.

When Hernando de Soto and his men first saw the Mississippi River in 1541, Native American tribes were living along its banks. They used the river to transport both people and goods. Native Americans grew food in the fertile soil along the river. The river is still important in transporting goods. Farmers still grow crops on the farmland along the river.

Jesuit missionaries Louis Joliet and Jacques Marquette explored the river in 1673. In 1682 Rene-Robert Cavalier, Sieur de La Salle, claimed much of the area around the Mississippi for France. The French founded many towns along the Mississippi River including New Orleans, Louisiana, and St. Louis, Missouri.

A Trip Down the Mississippi River

Let's take an imaginary journey down the length of this great waterway.

Lake Itasca. In some places the Mississippi River is up to one mile wide, but in places at Lake

Itasca State Park you can wade across it. See lower photos on page 286. Itasca means "true head." Explorer and historian Henry Rowe Schoolcraft created the word after an Ojibwe guide named Ozawindib led him to the source of the Mississippi River in 1832. *Itasca* is formed from two Latin words. It contains the last two syllables of *veritas*, meaning truth, and the first syllable of *caput*, meaning head.

Sandhill Cranes

From Lake Itasca to the Falls of Saint Anthony. As the Mississippi River flows from its source, it passes first northward and then back south through the center of Minnesota. At first, the river flows through miles of wilderness. Imagine that you get into a canoe at Lake Itasca and head toward the Falls of Saint Anthony in Minneapolis. You would see varied landscapes along the way: swamp forests, marsh lands with thousands of cattails, hilly regions, farmland, high banks, and fields of wild rice. You would go through many lakes that are formed by the river. The largest is Lake Winnebigoshish, which is seven miles wide!

Fisherman with Northern Pike

Along the way, you might see beaver dams. You might spot a timber wolf, a black bear, a mink, or a sandhill crane. See sandhill cranes above. You might even see a bald eagle. In fact, you might see any one of over two hundred kinds of birds, twenty-three species of reptiles and amphibians, or fifty-seven species of mammals.

After you pass the city of Grand Rapids, Minnesota, the river becomes wide and shallow. If you cast a fishing line into the water, you could catch a walleye, a smallmouth bass, or a northern pike. See photo above. In this section of the river you will see different plant varieties, such as willows, bog birch, ferns, tall asters, wildflowers, and pussy willows, pictured at left. You might see a muskrat building a home; and you might see

Pussy Willow in Snow

turtles, too. The river will become enormous, and you will understand why it has been called the Father of Waters. Soon you enter areas with more towns and cities, but you will still pass through areas of wilderness like the more than thirty Beaver Islands at St. Cloud, Minnesota.

From St. Paul to the Missouri River. When you reach the twin cities of Minneapolis-St. Paul, Minnesota, you should have someone take care of your canoe while you begin to travel by barge. This is a much safer way to make the rest of the trip down river. Between St. Paul and the mouth of the Missouri River, most parts of the Mississippi River are between one thousand and two thousand feet wide. As you go southeast from Minneapolis and

St. Paul (the capital of Minnesota), your barge will travel between Minnesota and Wisconsin, then between Iowa and Wisconsin, then between Iowa and Illinois, and finally, between Missouri and Illinois. The Mississippi River forms the border between these states. In Wisconsin, you will pass by Maiden Rock, pictured at left below. Then you will pass Pepin, which is near the home Laura Ingalls Wilder described in the book *Little House in the Big Woods*. In Missouri, you will pass Hannibal, the hometown of author Mark Twain. Not long before you reach the Missouri River, the Illinois River will empty into the Mississippi near Alton, Illinois.

Maiden Rock in Wisconsin

*1874 Currier and Ives Print
Entitled "The Great St. Louis Bridge"*

Bridge Over the Mississippi River at New Orleans

The Mississippi River at Natchez, Mississippi

From the Missouri River to Cairo, Illinois. The Missouri River adds large amounts of water and dirt to the Mississippi, making it fast-flowing and muddy. As you travel the two hundred miles between the mouth of the Missouri River and Cairo, you will pass by St. Louis. Notice the 1874 print of a St. Louis bridge at left above. You will then pass Cape Girardeau, Missouri, where the river enters the six-hundred-mile-long Mississippi River Valley.

From Cairo to the Atchafalaya River. Almost half of the Mississippi River's water comes from the Ohio River, which flows into the Mississippi at Cairo, Illinois. The river's width from Cairo to New Orleans is usually between three thousand feet and one mile wide. If you look east and west as you continue south, you will see that the Mississippi River Valley varies from twenty-five to 125 miles wide. Traveling south, your barge will travel along the border between Missouri and Illinois, then between Missouri and Kentucky, and Missouri and Tennessee. In Tennessee you will pass by Memphis, a large city built on Mississippi River bluffs.

You will then pass along the border between Arkansas and Tennessee, and Arkansas and Mississippi. While still in Arkansas, you will see where the Arkansas River empties into the Mississippi from the west.

Soon you will come to the border between northern Louisiana and Mississippi. You will pass Natchez, which is discussed in Lesson 53. See the picture at the bottom of page 288. Then the river enters the state of Louisiana. You will pass Louisiana's capital city of Baton Rouge. Like New Orleans, Baton Rouge is a seaport. It would be fun to get off your barge at Baton Rouge and board an ocean-going vessel.

From the Atchafalaya to the Gulf of Mexico. About 110 miles north of the Gulf of Mexico, you will pass the Atchafalaya River. About one-fourth of the Mississippi's water flows into the Atchafalaya. As your barge continues past New Orleans (see large photo on page 288), the river will divide into distributaries, which are smaller branches. The captain of your ship will know which one of these to take to bring your vessel all the way south to the Gulf of Mexico. As you enter the Gulf of Mexico, you will have made it all the way down the Mississippi River! The ocean-going vessel will continue to travel through the Mississippi River's fresh waters for many miles before the river water begins to mix with the salt water of the Gulf.

The Mississippi Watershed

When rain falls on the earth, it runs down into streams and rivers. Those streams and rivers eventually carry the water to the sea. Water that falls on the land between the Rocky Mountains and the Appalachian Mountains eventually flows into the Mississippi River, which takes the water to the Gulf of Mexico. That is a lot of water!

When rainfall is heavy, the Mississippi sometimes overflows its banks. Many embankments, called levees, have been built beside the river to help prevent flood waters from harming people, homes, and businesses. Notice the levees at right. At top, men move barrels on a St. Louis levee in 1903. At bottom, cows graze on a levee near Lake Providence, Louisiana.

Levee in St. Louis, 1903

Levee Near Lake Providence, Louisiana, 1940

Levee at Tiptonville, Tennessee, During 1937 Flood

At left is a levee which lies between the Mississippi River and Reelfoot Lake at Tiptonville, Tennessee. Notice that sandbags have been placed behind that levee to make it stronger. Sometimes levees help and other times they make the flooding problems worse.

River flooding can be a blessing, too. Centuries of floods have deposited rich soil along the banks of the Mississippi. These rich farmlands produce soybeans and feed grains in the North and cotton and rice in the South.

People have built towns and cities along the banks of the Mississippi, like St. Paul, Minnesota, pictured at right. Many activities in the cities are related to the river. Grain elevators in river cities store commodities grown on surrounding farms. See St. Paul elevators below. In these river cities are roads and railroads which help transport products to and from the river. At bottom, notice the railroad beside the Mississippi River in Keokuk, Iowa, in 1907.

St. Paul, Minnesota

Moving Freight on the Mighty Mississippi

The first time Europeans floated cargo down the Mississippi was in 1705, when a load of 15,000 bear and deer hides bound for France were taken down the Mississippi. When people

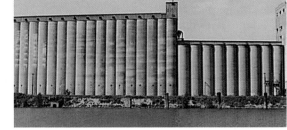

Grain Elevators at St. Paul, Minnesota, in 1939

moved into the area west of the Appalachians, they carried goods down the Mississippi River to New Orleans on flatboats. The first steamboat traveled down the Mississippi in 1811. By the 1830s, many steamboats were transporting freight on the river.

A barge is a large flat container that holds goods. See photo of barges on page 291. A barge has no power of its own but must be pushed or pulled. The first barges were pulled by people or by horses, mules, or oxen walking on the bank of a river. In the 1840s, steamboats began to push barges so they could transport more goods down river. Soon people using water transportation began to see the need for boats designed especially for moving barges. By the 1860s, people were building steam-powered towboats to move them. Around 1910, people began to build boats powered by diesel fuel. Diesel-powered vessels of all kinds began to replace those powered by steam.

Railroad Beside the Mississippi River in Keokuk, Iowa, 1907

Barges on the Mississippi at Minneapolis in 1939

The Falls of St. Anthony, 1909

Today people still use barges to transport goods on the Mississippi River. Almost three hundred million tons of freight were carried on the river in 2008. About sixty-three percent went down river, while the rest went up. Moving goods by river is much less expensive than by either trains or trucks. Today's typical barge can carry 1,500 tons of cargo. That is three million pounds! Though small in size, modern towboats have powerful engines. They can pull several barges that are tied together, called a barge tow. An average tow of fifteen barges carries as much freight as 225 railroad cars or 870 trucks. Some barge tows measure one-quarter of a mile long!

The Mississippi drops 1,425 feet from its highest point at Lake Itasca before it reaches sea level south of New Orleans. To make it easier for large barges to carry cargo up and down the Mississippi River, people have built many locks and a total of 43 dams.

The only waterfall on the river is the Falls of St. Anthony. Two dams and several locks make it possible for barges to travel around the falls. See the photo above. That picture shows the dam and lock structures that were there in 1909. Two new dams were completed in 1963.

Crossing the Mississippi River

Boat Captain on the Mississippi River, 1938

Native Americans as well as early explorers and settlers who wanted to cross the Mississippi had to ford the river where it is shallow or cross over on a ferry. First Bridge Park in Minneapolis, Minnesota, is the site of the first bridge built across the river in 1854. A few ferries still operate on the Mississippi River, but most people cross it on the many bridges that have been built over it. Notice the ferry, bridge, and toll booth in the photos at right and the boat captain above.

Mississippi River Ferry at Vicksburg, Mississippi, 1936

Bridge Across the Mississippi River at Memphis, Tennessee, 1942

Toll Booth for Mississippi River Bridge at St. Louis, 1939

Ice Skating Near Lake City, Minnesota, 1942

Mississippi River Baptisms

Enjoying the Mississippi River

The governors of the ten states that touch the Mississippi agreed in 1938 to create a Great River Road using existing roads near the river. Traveling the Great River Road is a fun way to enjoy the river's beauty and history. Read the story about a river cruise hero at right.

People have used the Mississippi River for more than economic purposes. Notice the people ice skating near Lake City, Minnesota, in the photo above. At right above, people are using the waters of the Mississippi to baptize people, the same thing that Philip and the Ethiopian eunuch did:

> As they went along the road they came to some water, and the eunuch said, "Look! Water! What prevents me from being baptized?" . . . and they both went down into the water, Philip as well as the eunuch, and he baptized him.
> Acts 8:36-38

Heroism on the Mississippi

In 1925 fifty-five people were on a scenic cruise near Memphis when their boat capsized in a strong current. Thomas Lee was alone on a nearby boat. Though he could not swim, he managed to rescue thirty-two of them. In the picture below, he is honored by President Calvin Coolidge.

Activities for Lesson 52

Thinking Biblically – Read Psalm 98. Look for the part that mentions how rivers praise the Lord.

Map Study – Complete the assignments for Lesson 52 on Map 2 "God's Wonders" and Map 17 "The Mississippi River" in *Maps of America the Beautiful*.

Timeline – In *Timeline of America the Beautiful* next to 1832, write: Henry Rowe Schoolcraft, led by an Ojibwe guide, reaches the source of the Mississippi River.

Literature – Read "Life on the Mississippi" in *We the People*, pages 50-51.

Student Workbook or Lesson Review – If you are using one of these optional books, complete the assignment for Lesson 52.

Natchez, Mississippi

Linden Mansion in Natchez

The Natchez Trace Parkway winds through beautiful countryside between Nashville, Tennessee, and Natchez, Mississippi. The route commemorates an old Native American trail. Granite markers along the way indicate actual locations of the original trail. Early frontier settlers floated goods down the Cumberland River to the Ohio River, down the Ohio to the Mississippi River, and down the Mississippi to New Orleans. They walked home on the Natchez Trace. Andrew Jackson and his men returned from the Battle of New Orleans along the Trace.

Natchez, Mississippi, sits atop bluffs on the eastern side of the Mississippi River. Here the summers are long and hot. Spanish moss hangs from trees, especially the live oak trees, pictured below. Many cultures important to America's history have been present in Natchez: Native American, French, Spanish, English, and African. Today portions of Old South cotton plantations have been preserved in Natchez. See the mansion above.

Natchez Indians

From around 1650 to 1750, the capital of the Natchez tribe was alongside the Mississippi River near what is now Natchez. Here they had a ceremonial ground and three mounds. Their main chief, whom they called the Great Sun, lived in this village. The site of the village has been preserved as the Grand Village of the Natchez.

Explorers from France entered the area. In 1716 they built Fort Rosalie nearby. Fort

Spanish Moss in Natchez

Spanish moss hangs in long gray strands from the limbs and trunks of trees. The plant has no roots to receive water and nutrients from the soil, but instead it takes in nutrients from dust that floats in the air. It also gets moisture from the air. People use Spanish moss as a packing material. They also use its fibers in upholstered furniture.

293

Rosalie had a stone house, officers' quarters, barracks for soldiers, and a magazine to store supplies and ammunition. The fort was surrounded by a moat. Though the Natchez welcomed the French at first, peace between the two peoples did not last. The Natchez destroyed the fort in 1729. The French soon built another one. At right is a proposed map of Fort Rosalie. Below is an illustration of an early fort at Natchez.

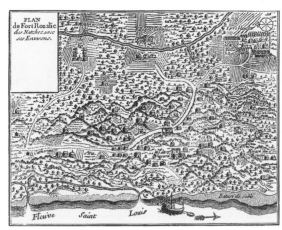
Plan for Fort Rosalie

The French left detailed records of how the Natchez lived. They eventually conquered the Natchez. They sold three hundred of them into slavery in the West Indies. The rest escaped or were taken in by other tribes. Today some people of Natchez descent live among the Creek and the Cherokee.

An Early Fort at Natchez

Origins of the City of Natchez

The British took control of the region when the French and Indian War ended in 1763. During the American Revolution, the Spanish captured the area. For a while, Spain controlled the southern part of what became the state of Mississippi and America controlled the north. During Spanish rule, Natchez citizens began to build beautiful mansions. Streets in the oldest parts of Natchez are those that were surveyed when the Spanish had control of the town.

Spain ceded Mississippi to America in 1797. When Mississippi was organized as an American territory in 1798, Natchez served as the first capital of the territory. When Mississippi became a state in 1817, it served as its first state capital. For many years it was the largest and wealthiest city in Mississippi. Below is a drawing of Natchez during the steamboat era.

The Natchez Trace

The United States government negotiated a treaty in 1801 with the Chickasaw and Choctaw tribes. The agreement allowed the United States government to make improvements on the old Natchez Trace so that it could be used as a mail route. It became an important route between the frontier of Tennessee and Kentucky and New Orleans.

Natchez During the Steamboat Era

The Federal government began improvements in 1934 to create the Natchez Trace Parkway. Travelers on the parkway can visit a Chickasaw Village in Mississippi. Here the

Chickasaw once defeated the French. In Tennessee is the Meriwether Lewis National Monument, placed near the site where Lewis died in 1809. At right is a photo of the modern Natchez Trace Parkway.

Natchez Trace Parkway

The Old South

The city of Natchez was home to many large cotton plantations. Plantation owners and their families lived in grand mansions. Their lives of luxury were similar to the English aristocracy. Slaves waited on them and farmed their fields. The slaves lived in small, simple cabins. Some slave owners treated their slaves harshly, while others treated them with love and kindness and made sure that they learned about God. However, even owners who treated slaves kindly did not treat them as equals. They saw themselves as superior and saw the slaves as their property.

Plantation owners thought of themselves as gentlemen. They enjoyed literature, politics, and socializing. Their wives were ladies who oversaw their homes and entertained many guests. The most important social season was Christmastime when families and friends gathered. During Christmas, men hunted wild birds and deer and played whist. In their grand ballrooms, people enjoyed dancing the Virginia Reel, the minuet, and other period dances.

Children of the southern aristocracy were trained at home. Girls had a governess and boys had a tutor. Later, the girls went to a girls' finishing school and the boys to preparatory school. Afterwards the young men went to college, often to the University of Mississippi, the University of Virginia, or Yale.

Life in the Old South

In Natchez today, tourists can learn about the lifestyles of the rich planters and of their slaves. Many antebellum homes have been preserved. The word antebellum refers to the period before the Civil War. A scene from life in the Old South is portrayed in the illustration at left.

Natchez National Historical Park

The National Park Service maintains Natchez National Historical Park. Sites in the park include Melrose Plantation, home of a prominent plantation owner, and the home of William Johnson, a free black who worked as a barber.

John T. McMurran, a northern lawyer, moved to Natchez in 1825. In 1831 he married the daughter of a prominent Mississippi family. The McMurrans began in 1841 to build a

Richmond Mansion, Built in 1784

grand home in the Greek Revival architectural style. They and their children moved into the home they called Melrose in 1849. It is one of the grandest mansions in Natchez. By the middle of the 1850s, Mr. McMurran was full- or part-owner of five cotton plantations. These plantations covered 9,600 acres and were worked by 325 slaves. McMurran died in a steamboat accident shortly after the Civil War.

William Johnson was born into slavery but was freed at age eleven. His brother-in-law taught him how to be a barber. In 1830 Johnson bought his brother-in-law's barber shop in Natchez. Johnson began to train black boys to become barbers. Johnson prospered and became well-known among the free blacks of Natchez. In 1835 he married Ann Battles, another free black. That year he began to keep a diary. Over the next sixteen years, Johnson filled fourteen leather journals. The diary is a rich source of information about the lifestyle of free blacks in the antebellum South. William and Ann had eleven children. Johnson enjoyed dressing well and hunting and fishing with his friends. He owned sixteen slaves. Johnson died in 1851. The Johnson family continued to own his home on State Street until 1976 when they sold it to a preservation society. It has been a National Park Service museum since 2005.

Visitors to Natchez can take tours of several other mansions that are open to the public. They can tour even more during the annual Natchez Pilgrimages. On this page are photographs of three Natchez mansions. They were taken in the 1930s and 1940s.

Scenes from everyday life in Natchez are pictured on page 297. These photos were also taken during the 1930s and 1940s. Notice that two pictures on page 297 show African American women carrying loads the way their ancestors carried them in Africa.

While Americans of European descent owned most of the African slaves in America, some Native Americans and free blacks owned slaves, too. Today it is hard to imagine that anyone would want to own another human being. We should take into our hearts what God said in Galatians:

Gloucester, Built c. 1803

The Rosalie Plantation, built in 1820, is on the site of Fort Rosalie.

For all of you who were baptized into Christ have clothed yourselves with Christ. There is neither Jew nor Greek, there is neither slave nor free man, there is neither male nor female; for you are all one in Christ Jesus.
Galatians 3:27-28

Activities for Lesson 53

Map Study – Complete the assignment for Lesson 53 on Map 3 "American Landmarks" in *Maps of America the Beautiful*.

Timeline – In *Timeline of America the Beautiful* next to 1835 write: William Johnson begins to keep a diary of his life in Natchez, Mississippi.

Vocabulary – Write five sentences in your notebook, using one of these words in each: ceremonial, nutrients, aristocracy, antebellum, lifestyle. Check in a dictionary if you need help with their definitions.

Family Activity – Have a plantation dinner. A suggested menu is on pages 430-431.

Student Workbook or Lesson Review – If you are using one of these optional books, complete the assignment for Lesson 53.

Natchez Pedestrians, 1940

Natchez Pedestrians, 1935

Natchez Business, 1935

Men Loading Cotton in Natchez, 1935

Both of these African American women carry bundles in an African way in 1940.

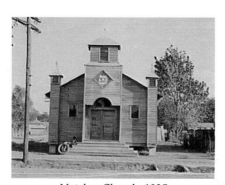

Natchez Church, 1935

African American Woman Carrying a Load in Natchez, 1940

Traveling and Working
on a Steamboat

In 1807 Robert Fulton piloted a steamboat up the Hudson River from New York City to Albany. The *Clermont* made the 150-mile trip upstream in thirty-two hours, an amazing speed of almost 4.7 miles per hour! The drawing below was in a book entitled *The Steam Engine and Its Inventors*, published in London in 1881. See Fulton's portrait at right.

Portrait of Robert Fulton

Fulton's invention demonstrated that rivers could become highways to transport Americans and their products. Other inventors had been experimenting with boats powered by steam; but the efforts of Robert Fulton and his business partner, Robert Livingston, finally made the idea practical. For twenty years, Fulton and Livingston operated a steamboat shipping business on the Hudson River. The statue of Fulton at left is in the main reading room in the Thomas Jefferson Building at the Library of Congress.

Fulton Statue

The *New Orleans*, First Steamboat on the Mississippi

The first steamboat to travel on the Mississippi River was built in Pittsburgh. One of Fulton's business associates, Nicholas Roosevelt, oversaw its construction. The *New Orleans* was launched on the Ohio River in October of 1811, bound for New Orleans. Nicholas Roosevelt, his wife Lydia, and their toddler daughter were among the passengers. This 1811 trip was not the first voyage Nicholas and Lydia made to New Orleans. Two years before they had traveled from Pittsburgh to New Orleans on a flatboat. As they set out this time, Lydia was expecting their second child. Also on board were the captain, the pilot, the engineer, a crew of six, a waiter, a cook, two servants for Mrs. Roosevelt, and the Roosevelts' dog, Tiger.

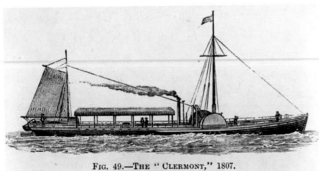

FIG. 49.—THE "CLERMONT," 1807.

Though a few towns were scattered along the Ohio and Mississippi Rivers, most of the trip was through wilderness. The *New Orleans* encountered several dangers on its twelve-week voyage. The rivers west of the Appalachian Mountains are shallow and have sandbars. The *New Orleans* sat low in the water. In Louisville, it began to scrape the bottom of the river. It was in Louisville that Lydia Roosevelt gave birth to a son. The *New Orleans* stayed in Louisville for five weeks while they waited for winter rains to raise the water high enough for the boat to go over the Falls of the Ohio.

In late December and early January, the travelers experienced the New Madrid earthquakes mentioned on page 230. In January the boat finally arrived in New Orleans.

When the crew of the *New Orleans* tried to make the return voyage, they found that the Mississippi River currents were too strong for the steamboat to continue past Natchez. The boat made trips between New Orleans and Natchez for two more years. It ran aground and sank in 1813.

Many years later in 1907, President Theodore Roosevelt made a trip down the Mississippi River. When the *New York Times* reported the President's voyage, it told about the voyage of the *New Orleans*, made by another Roosevelt almost one hundred years before. Nicholas Roosevelt was the great-uncle of President Roosevelt.

The Catherine Davis *on the Ohio River, 1943*

The Wenonah *on the Mississippi River at St. Louis, 1939*

Steamboat Improvements

Henry Miller Shreve and others began to design steamboats that would work better in rivers west of the Appalachians. Shreve's boat *Enterprise* left Pittsburgh in

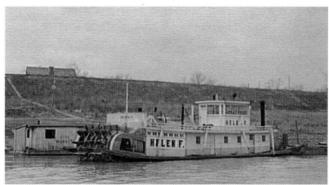

The Helen F. *on the Ohio River at Shawneetown, Illinois, 1939*

1814, taking supplies to General Andrew Jackson's men in New Orleans. In 1816 Shreve built the *Washington* in Wheeling, Virginia (now West Virginia). It had a flat, shallow hull and a high-pressure engine. In 1817 it went from Louisville to New Orleans and back again in 41 days.

People constructed shipyards along the Ohio River. More and more steamboats were built. Inventors and builders figured out how to make steamboats travel faster. Steamboat transportation increased. Steamboat trade helped the economy of Western lands. The trade brought new towns, jobs, and businesses. By 1833 cargo from 1,200 steamboat runs per year was being unloaded in New Orleans. Many steamboats were also running between St. Louis and the Falls of St. Anthony by 1840.

Accidents were common in the earliest years of steamboating. The average steamboat stayed in service for only three years. Boats caught fire; they hit snags; they blew up. Still, entrepreneurs continued using them because they made enough profit to replace boats when needed.

Traveling by Steamboat

Steamboats provided passengers with a faster means of travel. Before steamboats, the trip from Louisville to New Orleans took four months. Steamboats reduced travel time to twenty days by 1820 and to six days by 1838. Steamboats not only carried cargo; they provided pleasure trips for tourists. Builders furnished steamboats with elaborate decor. They added ornate woodwork, cut-glass chandeliers, thick carpets, and oil paintings. See photos of steamboat interiors at right. Dining rooms offered hot meals served by attentive waiters. Cabins featured comfortable furniture. A few boats offered entertainment. Though many people assume gambling was popular on steamboats, it was actually done on very few.

Steamboats needed a way to send loud signals to other boats and to

Interior staircase on left and purser's office in the background on the right.

Passenger Cabin

people on shore. At first, they had bells. Later, some steamboats had a steam whistle and others had a steam calliope, a loud musical instrument powered by steam. Look at the steamboats on pages 299 and 301.

Jobs on a Steamboat

- The **captain** was in charge of the entire crew.
- The **mate** was the officer below the captain.
- The **pilot** guided the steamboat through the water. He was responsible for navigation. In his book *Life on the Mississippi*, Mark Twain described the pilot house as high above the water. He called it a glass temple with red and gold window

curtains, a sofa, leather cushions, and a big stove to keep people warm in the winter. He said that a black man in a white apron brought up tarts, ices, and coffee.

- The **engineer** kept the engine running. He had to keep the boat going fast enough to be profitable while keeping the cargo and people safe.
- The **purser** took care of financial matters and also made sure that passengers received good service. Notice the purser's office in top photo on page 300.
- A **stoker** or **fireman** kept the fire going to make the steam that powered the boat. At first, wood was used as fuel. It was later replaced with coal.
- **Deckhands** were laborers who loaded and unloaded cargo.
- **Cooks** made meals and **waiters** served them.
- A **mud clerk** was a boy about ten to fourteen years old. He carried messages and made deliveries for other crew members. The mud clerk often got the dirtiest jobs on the ship.

Steamboat on the Ocklawaha River in Florida, 1902

Show Boats

Americans of the 1800s enjoyed being entertained on show boats. They were especially popular on the Mississippi and Ohio Rivers. The first show boat was called the *Floating Theater*. British actor William Chapman Sr. and his family sang, danced, and performed plays on their *Floating Theater*. They began in Pittsburgh and performed at various locations on their way to New Orleans.

The Broadway play *Show Boat* has given Americans the mistaken impression that a show boat is a steamboat, but a show boat was actually a barge pushed by a tugboat.

Vacationers on the Lake Steamer Twilight *at Moosehead Lake, Maine, c. 1884-1891*

A Steamboat Race

People like to race one another. When someone invents a new way to travel, others soon find a way to use that invention in races. Two steamboats had a race on the Mississippi River in 1870.

Steamboat in New York's Thousand Islands, 1902

They raced 1,278 river miles from New Orleans to St. Louis. The *Robert E. Lee* beat the *Natchez*, making the trip in three days, eighteen hours, and fourteen minutes. See the illustration of this race at left.

Jesus often spent time in boats. One time He used a boat so He could get away by Himself. When He came ashore again, he did what He always did. He served people.

The Great Race Between the Natchez *and the* Robert E. Lee

Now when Jesus heard about John [the Baptist] He withdrew from there in a boat
to a secluded place by Himself; and when the people heard of this,
they followed Him on foot from the cities. When He went ashore, He saw a large crowd,
and felt compassion for them and healed their sick.
Matthew 14:13-14

Activities for Lesson 54

Timeline – In *Timeline of America the Beautiful* next to 1807, write: Robert Fulton pilots a steamboat up the Hudson River.

Vocabulary – In your notebook, write these words: associate, decor, hull, chandelier, cargo. Beside each word, write the definition below that matches that word.

    a. an elaborate light fixture
    b. a partner or colleague
    c. goods transported by any method
    d. the frame or body of a ship
    e. the way the interior of a room or building is decorated

Literature – Read "Steamboat Songs" in *We the People*, pages 52-53.

Creative Writing – Imagine you are living in the mid-1800s, and you just took your first ride on a steamboat. In your notebook, write a letter to an imagined relative about your steamboat trip. Include some of the details about steamboats you learned in this lesson.

Student Workbook or Lesson Review – If you are using one of these optional books, complete the assignment for Lesson 54.

Samuel Morse, Artist and Inventor

Samuel Finely Breese Morse was born in Charlestown, Massachusetts, near Boston, in 1791. Look at the picture below. His father, Jedidiah Morse, was a Congregational minister and a famous geographer. Noah Webster was a family friend.

This photograph of Samuel Morse's birthplace was taken about 100 years after he was born.

Morse had two brothers who survived infancy, Sidney and Richard. Jedidiah called Samuel the hare and Sidney the tortoise. Their father said that Samuel was too quick and Sidney was too stubborn. When Samuel grew up, he often added a drawing of a hare to his letters to Sidney, while Sidney often drew a tortoise when writing Samuel.

The journal that Samuel kept when he was thirteen is in the Library of Congress. In it he wrote about his lessons and about local news. He described the books he was reading and told about the weather. The journal ends on the day he received the news that he had been admitted to Yale. The Library of Congress also has a letter Samuel wrote to his brothers that year. In the letter he tells of a death in the family and speaks of other family members who had died. He said that he hoped they would all meet them in heaven when they died. Samuel and his brothers all had deep Christian faith.

Samuel Morse, Artist

At age thirteen Samuel F. B. Morse entered Yale. Two special interests he enjoyed while studying there were painting miniature portraits and learning about electricity. After college, he went to England where he studied painting under Benjamin West.

Morse returned to America in 1815 and began to paint, first in Boston, and later in New Hampshire. There he met Lucretia Walker. They soon were engaged, and in 1818 they were married.

Morse became a much sought-after portrait painter. He painted portraits of President James Monroe, Noah Webster, and others. He and his brother Sidney also tried inventing, but they did not have financial success. Morse was commissioned in 1825 to paint a portrait

This portrait of the Marquis de Lafayette by Samuel F. B. Morse hangs in the City Hall of New York City.

of the Marquis de Lafayette who was visiting in America. While Morse worked on his commission in Washington, D.C., Lucretia died suddenly after the birth of their third child. Samuel's father sent him the news, but by the time Morse received it and was able to get home, Lucretia had already been buried. The Library of Congress has a letter Samuel wrote to Lucretia after she had already died, but before he received the news. In the letter, he told her of the election of President John Quincy Adams.

Morse left his children in the care of relatives in 1829 and went back to Europe. He visited London, Switzerland, Italy, and Paris. In Paris he visited Lafayette. The two remained friends for the rest of their lives. At left is Morse's portrait of Lafayette. The Library of Congress has a note Lafayette sent to Morse. In it, he calls Samuel his dear friend. While in Europe, Morse kept diaries, in which he described his travels. He drew many sketches of landscapes, historic buildings, and people he saw. He also copied the paintings of famous European artists. See his painting of his daughter below.

Samuel Morse, Inventor

Samuel F. B. Morse came back to America in 1832. On the trip home, he heard a conversation about a newly-invented electrical device called an electromagnet. Afterwards, Morse came up with an idea for improving the electric telegraph. A telegraph is a system that sends a message by sending electrical impulses over a wire. The earliest telegraph had 26 wires, one for each letter of the alphabet. Morse wanted to build one that used only one wire. While teaching art in New York City, he worked on a model telegraph.

In 1837 he found partners to help him. One of his earliest machines made a line on a tickertape. Morse developed a dictionary to decipher what the line was communicating. By 1838 he had developed the Morse code, a system of dots and dashes which represented letters. That year in New York, he demonstrated that his telegraph machine could send a message at a rate of ten words per minute. He also demonstrated the telegraph at the Franklin Institute in Philadelphia, before a commerce committee of the U.S. House of Representatives, and before President Martin Van Buren and his cabinet.

Morse needed financial backing to set up the first telegraph line in the United States. He received funds from the United States Congress in

Susan Morse, Painted by Her Father

Senate Chamber in U.S. Capitol From Which Morse Sent His Message: "What Hath God Wrought!"

1843. By May of 1844, telegraph poles and wires were set up between Baltimore, Maryland, and Washington, D.C., the first city-to-city electromagnetic telegraph line in the world.

From the Senate Chamber in the U.S. Capitol building, pictured at left, Samuel Morse sent the first formal message on the new Baltimore to Washington telegraph line. The message was "What Hath God Wrought!"

Morse became a national hero. Now people could receive messages quickly.

Private companies began to put up more telegraph lines. By 1847, Morse had earned enough money to bring his family back together. He bought a country home with one hundred acres near Poughkeepsie, New York. He named it Locust Grove. The following year, Morse married Sarah Elizabeth Griswold. She was his second cousin and twenty-six years younger than he. They had four more children.

Telegraph lines spread across America. The lines often followed railroads. By 1854, there were 23,000 miles of telegraph wire in use in the United States. Other countries were busy setting up telegraph systems also.

An undersea cable was successfully laid across the Atlantic Ocean in 1866. Now telegraph messages could be sent between America and Europe. Notice the illustration at right showing the Morse code and the telegraph apparatus in use in 1877.

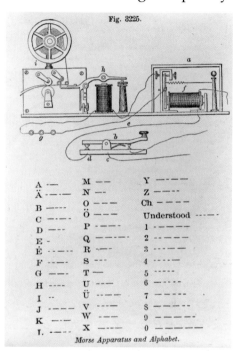

Illustration in Knight's Mechanical Dictionary, Volume 2, Published in 1877

Matthew Brady Studio Portrait of Samuel Morse

Samuel Morse, Photographer and Politician

Morse's interest in technology was not limited to the telegraph. In 1840 he opened a portrait studio in New York City. Here he taught others how to make daguerreotype pictures, an early form of photography. Among his students was Matthew Brady, who became a famous photographer. Brady is known especially for the Civil War photographs taken by him and his assistants. At left is a daguerreotype portrait of Samuel Morse, taken by the Matthew Brady Studio.

Samuel Morse cared deeply about political issues and twice ran for office. In 1841 he ran for mayor of New York City and in 1854 for a seat in the U.S. House of Representatives. He was not elected either time.

Morse became famous in America and in Europe. He received medals from many countries, as seen in the photo at right. In his later years, Morse donated money to colleges, churches, and missionary societies. In June of 1871, the statue below was unveiled in Central Park in New York City. When the statue was unveiled, Morse sent a telegraph message of farewell around the world. He died in New York City the next year at the age of 81.

Morse With Medals

Morse used his wealth to bless other people. We should remember to do what Paul told the Christians in Ephesus to do:

> In everything I showed you that by working hard in this manner
> you must help the weak and remember
> the words of the Lord Jesus, that He Himself said,
> "It is more blessed to give than to receive."
> Acts 20:35

Activities for Lesson 55

Thinking Biblically – Before the invention of the telegraph, every message one person wanted to deliver to another had to be delivered by hand. Read Acts 15:22-31 for a Biblical example of how messages were delivered for centuries before the telegraph changed communication.

Morse Statue in Central Park

Timeline – In *Timeline of America the Beautiful* next to 1838, write: Samuel F. B. Morse develops an improved telegraph and the Morse code.

Vocabulary – Write your own definition for each of these words: infancy, miniature, commission, formal, apparatus. Look in the lesson for clues to the meaning of the words. When you are finished, look in a dictionary to check your definitions.

Literature – Read "What Hath God Wrought!" in *We the People*, page 54.

Student Workbook or Lesson Review – If you are using one of these optional books, complete the assignment for Lesson 55. If you are using the Lesson Review, take the quiz for Unit 11.

A Belief in Manifest Destiny

James K. Polk served as America's eleventh President from 1845 to 1849. Polk and many other Americans at the time believed that America had a Manifest Destiny to extend from the Atlantic Ocean to the Pacific. This belief influenced Polk's decision to go to war with Mexico. Thousands of Americans acted upon the concept of Manifest Destiny when they moved west on the Oregon Trail.

Setting Out on the Oregon Trail

While Polk was President, the Smithsonian Institution began in Washington, D.C. People began taking tours of the Cave of the Wind at beautiful Niagara Falls and riding the *Maid of the Mist* steamboat across the Niagara River. John James Audubon had completed his *Birds of America* and was working on his mammal paintings for a new book.

Lessons in Unit 12

Lesson 56 – Our American Story: James K. Polk and the Mexican War
Lesson 57 – Daily Life: Moving West on the Oregon Trail
Lesson 58 – An American Landmark: The Smithsonian Institution
Lesson 59 – God's Wonders: God Created Niagara Falls
Lesson 60 – An American Biography: John James Audubon, Artist and Naturalist

Books Used in Unit 12

- *Maps of America the Beautiful*

- *Timeline of America the Beautiful*

- *We the People*

- *Bound for Oregon* by Jean Van Leeuwen

James K. Polk and the Mexican War

James K. Polk, Governor of Tennessee

When George Washington became the first President of the United States in 1789, he led just thirteen states huddled along the Atlantic coast, plus a territory that spread between those colonies and the Mississippi River. In 1803 America gained over 800,000 square miles with the Louisiana Purchase. Florida became part of the U.S. in 1821.

Manifest Destiny

Many Americans dreamed of a time when America could expand all the way to the Pacific Ocean. Some even believed that God wanted this to happen. In 1845 a newspaper editor wrote: "Our manifest destiny is to overspread the continent allotted by Providence for the free development of our yearly multiplying millions." People began to use the phrase Manifest Destiny to express this belief. It is sad that many Americans did not honor the Native Americans when they pursued this "manifest destiny." Surely there was a way to share America the Beautiful with the people who already lived here. We should remember what Jesus said were the two greatest commandments: to love God with all our hearts, souls, minds, and strength, and to love our neighbors as ourselves (Mark 12:28-31).

James K. Polk Elected President

Americans were tired of the economic difficulties that occurred while Democrat Martin Van Buren was President. The voters elected Whig candidates William Henry Harrison and John Tyler as President and Vice President in 1840. Four years later, the Whigs nominated Henry Clay and the Democrats nominated a young friend of Andrew Jackson, fellow Tennessean James K. Polk. During the campaign, the Democrats promised that America would expand into the West. The election was close, but Polk was victorious.

Events in American politics are important news in other countries. This was true in the 1840s, too. The illustration below of James K. Polk taking the oath of office was in the April 19, 1845, issue of the *Illustrated London News*.

Inauguration of James K. Polk

The Oregon Question

In the late 1700s, Great Britain claimed the area around the Columbia River as a British territory. Americans working for John Jacob Astor's fur trading company founded the settlement of Astoria near the Columbia River in 1811. During the War of 1812, the residents of Astoria learned that a British ship was coming to capture the settlement, so they sold it to a Canadian fur company. By the end of the War of 1812, America was also claiming Oregon country, saying that an American had discovered the Columbia River, Lewis and Clark had explored it, and Americans had settled in Astoria. The treaty ending the War of 1812 stated that both America and Great Britain would return any lands they had taken during the war. Astoria was returned to the United States. In 1818 Great Britain and America signed a treaty that they would hold the Oregon country jointly.

Oregon country extended southward to the northern border of California. In the north it reached the tip of Alaska, which was then controlled by Russia. Oregon country encompassed the present-day states of Idaho, Oregon, and Washington; portions of Montana and Wyoming; and parts of Canada. By the time James K. Polk was elected President, many Americans, especially Democrats, wanted America to control all of Oregon country. They were willing to go to war with Great Britain if necessary. The northern tip of Oregon country was at the 54° 40′ parallel of latitude, so their slogan was "54° 40′ or Fight." However, Great Britain and America came up with a peaceful solution in 1846. They divided Oregon country at the 49th parallel of latitude, which was already the border between the U.S. and Canada from east of Oregon to Lake Superior. America then extended from the Atlantic Ocean to the Pacific Ocean across its northern states and territories.

The Texas Question

Meanwhile, another territory problem loomed to the south in Texas. Texas had declared itself an independent country in 1836. Many Texians wanted to become part of the the United States. Mexico did not recognize the independence of Texas. At first America did not recognize it either. Two main problems caused American leaders to be uncertain about what to do. First, recognizing Texas as independent might cause war with Mexico. Second, taking Texas in as a territory would expand slavery into more of the United States.

The Polk Home in Columbia, Tennessee

Andrew Jackson waited as long as he could before recognizing the independent Republic of Texas. He recognized it on his last day in office. The Van Buren and Tyler administrations took little action on the Texas question. After the election of James K. Polk, Congress offered Texas the opportunity to become first a U.S. territory and later a state. Texians accepted the offer and Texas became the 28th state in December of 1845. After Texas became a part of the United States, the term Texan gradually replaced the term Texian, which was based on the Spanish word *Tejano*.

America then had two problems with Mexico. Mexico did not recognize Texas statehood, and the two countries did not agree on the location of the Texas border. America said the southern border of Texas was the Rio Grande, while Mexico said the border was farther north at the Nueces River. President Polk offered to pay Mexico for Texas, California, and the area in between. Mexico refused to negotiate.

The Mexican War

Polk sent troops to the area between the Rio Grande and the Nueces, believing he should defend American land. Mexico saw this move as an invasion and attacked the American soldiers. On May 13, 1846, the United States declared war on Mexico. Many Americans who lived in New England and most people belonging to the Whig Party opposed the war, calling it "Mr. Polk's War."

In June Americans in Sacramento, California, declared California to be an independent republic. In July the U.S. Navy took over the area and declared it to be a U.S. territory. In September of 1847, American troops invaded Mexico and captured Mexico City.

The telegraph was used to send Americans reports from the Mexican War. Some American officers who served in the war later fought in the Civil War, including Robert E. Lee, Thomas (later called Stonewall) Jackson, George Pickett, Ulysses S. Grant, and George McClellan.

The Mexican War ended when a treaty was signed in February of 1848, less than two years after the war had

Brady Daguerrotype of James K. Polk

started. The United States agreed to purchase Texas, California, and the lands in between. This area was about the same size as the Louisiana Purchase. The U.S. government paid fifteen million dollars for the land.

While Polk was President, America added two more states to the Union besides Texas. Iowa became the 29th state in 1846 and Wisconsin the 30th in 1848. The first U.S. postage stamp was issued during Polk's presidency and the Naval Academy was established.

In his 1844 campaign, James K. Polk promised to pursue westward expansion. In one term, he accomplished his goals. True to his word, he did not seek a second term. Voters were unhappy about the Mexican War, so Polk's Democratic Party lost the 1848 election to the Whig candidate. Read about Polk's life below.

New States Admitted

1845 Texas
1846 Iowa
1848 Wisconsin

JAMES K. POLK.
Eleventh President of the United States.

MRS J.K. POLK.

James Knox Polk
America's Eleventh President
March 4, 1845 - March 4, 1849

James Knox Polk was born in North Carolina in 1795. His father was a farmer and surveyor. When James was ten years old, the Polk family moved to Tennessee. Even though he lived on the rugged frontier, James was not physically strong. When he was seventeen years old, he required surgery, a rare event in that day.

Polk had only two and a half years of formal schooling, but he was able to enter the University of North Carolina as a sophomore. He graduated with honors in mathematics and the classics. Polk returned to Tennessee, studied law, and established a law practice in Columbia, Tennessee. The home of Polk's parents in Columbia is now a museum. It is pictured on page 310.

Polk was elected to the Tennessee legislature when he was twenty-seven years old. While serving in the legislature, he met the daughter of a prominent planter. Sarah Childress had been educated at a Moravian school in North Carolina. There she studied the Bible, drawing, English grammar, geography, Greek and Roman literature, music, and sewing. After marrying Polk, Sarah became a trusted advisor in both personal and political matters. She served as his secretary. The above illustrations of President and Mrs. Polk were created by Currier and Ives.

Polk was an ardent supporter of fellow Democrat and Tennessean Andrew Jackson. At age 29, Polk was elected to serve in the U. S. House of Representatives. He eventually served as its Speaker. After fourteen years in Washington, Polk returned to Tennessee and won election as Governor. He served one two-year term. Though he ran for Governor twice more, he did not win the governorship again. His Democrat friends in Washington did not forget him. When they needed a strong candidate for the 1844 election, they chose James K. Polk.

While in the White House, James and Sarah Polk honored their beliefs by forbidding alcohol and dancing in the White House. Sarah worked to enhance the beauty of the presidential home. She is given credit for having the song "Hail to the Chief" played to honor the President.

James K. Polk left the White House exhausted. Notice how much older President Polk looked in the photo on page 310 than Governor Polk looked in the drawing on page 308. President Polk died of cholera at age 53 a few months after leaving office. No other President has died at such a young age, except those who were assasinated. Polk's gravesite is pictured below.

Sarah Polk made her home at Polk Place in Nashville, Tennessee, where she was greatly admired. Soon after her husband's death, Sarah Polk's great niece was orphaned. Sarah became the child's guardian. Sally Polk Jetty remained with her great aunt the rest of Sarah's life.

In 1877 Sarah was given the first telephone in Nashville. President Hayes visited her in 1887. In 1888 she received a visit from President Cleveland and was also given the honor of turning on electric lights in Cincinnati. Sarah Childress Polk lived for forty-two years after the death of her husband. She died at Polk Place in 1891 at 87 years of age.

A Photograph of Polk's Grave, Taken While Union Forces Occupied Nashville During the Civil War

We may not agree with every decision that Polk made as President, but we can admire his personal consistency in doing what he believed to be right. Paul is an example to us in this as well:

> . . . I also do my best to maintain always
> a blameless conscience
> both before God and before men.
> Acts 24:16

Activities for Lesson 56

Map Study – Complete the assignments for Lesson 56 on Map 18 "The West" and Map 20 "The Lower 48" in *Maps of America the Beautiful*.

Timeline – In *Timeline of America the Beautiful* next to 1877, write: Sarah Polk is given the first telephone in Nashville, Tennessee.

Vocabulary – Look up each of these words in a dictionary: huddled, destiny, jointly, latitude, ardent. Write each word and its definition in your notebook.

Literature – Read "Hail to the Chief" in *We the People*, page 55, and chapter 1 in *Bound for Oregon*.

Creative Writing – In your notebook, write two or three paragraphs about your thoughts on "manifest destiny." Do you agree that America had the right to make Native Americans move from their land? Do you think America was right to insist on control over lands claimed by Mexico and Great Britain?

Student Workbook or Lesson Review – If you are using one of these optional books, complete the assignment for Lesson 56.

Moving West on the Oregon Trail

In 1836 Marcus and Narcissa Whitman and three other missionaries headed toward Oregon in a covered wagon. No white woman had ever crossed the Rocky Mountains before. They left from Liberty, Missouri. Soon they entered Western lands dotted only with Native American villages and a few fur trading posts. By the time they reached British Fort Vancouver, their wagon had long been abandoned, but they made it!

A Couple on the Oregon Trail

Just seven years later in 1843, one thousand pioneers set out on the same journey the Whitmans had accomplished. These pioneers were the beginning of "the great migration." Between 1843 and 1869, over 500,000 people traveled on the Oregon Trail. It was the best way to get across the Rocky Mountains. Many pioneers were bound for the rich farmland of the Willamette Valley in Oregon, while others went on to Washington. Look at the photo below. An Oregon Trail pioneer carved the year 1846 on this rock as he or she traveled through Wyoming that year. Some stopped when they reached Idaho, while others turned south there, taking the California Trail down to California, Nevada, or Utah.

One out of ten who set out to complete the two-thousand-mile journey died along the way. Most of these died from disease. Still, nine out of ten made it. They walked or rode through Kansas, Nebraska, Wyoming, and Idaho. These pioneers were brave, strong, and courageous. Look at the illustration above.

Those who wanted to reach California or the Northwest without taking the trail had only one alternative. They could go by ship. That is how many of the British got to Oregon country. The ship route was not easy. The Panama Canal had not yet been built. Travelers not taking the Oregon Trail to California or the Northwest had two choices: go around the tip of South America or sail to Panama, walk through the mosquito-infested jungles, and then wait for a ship to pick them up on the other side. The water route was not practical for many of the pioneers because they lived in the

Pioneer Carving in Wyoming, 1846

313

parents died. The Whitmans took them all into their home. They cared for a total of eleven children, including their nephew.

When a measles epidemic broke out among the Cayuse near the mission, Dr. Whitman could not cure them. Many of them died. According to Cayuse tradition, the Cayuse people had the right to kill a medicine man if he treated a patient and the patient later died. In 1847 a few Cayuse tribesmen killed Marcus and Narcissa Whitman and many immigrants who were staying at the mission.

Marcus and Narcissa Whitman are highly esteemed in the Pacific Northwest. The statue of Marcus Whitman at right is one of Washington State's two statues in the National Statuary Hall in the United States Capitol.

Marcus Whitman Statue in the United States Capitol

Waiting for Spring

Emigrants preparing to go west on the Oregon Trail headed for "jumping off" towns along the Missouri River each spring. Most went to Independence, Missouri. There they camped while waiting for spring grasses to grow. By April or May, the grass was usually ready and the travelers could head out. They would never make it to Oregon unless their oxen and mules had food to eat along the way. Oxen and mules were better suited to the Oregon Trail than horses were. Both types of animals had advantages and disadvantages. Oxen were gentle, but slow; mules were faster, but usually stubborn.

Covered Wagons

People heading out on the trail often rode up the Missouri River by steamboat and then prepared to head overland in covered wagons. They used farm wagons with front wheels that could be steered left or right. The coverings were made of cotton, and were treated with linseed oil in hopes that it would keep them from leaking. They still leaked.

Families purchased food to eat along the way. A family of four needed to take more than one thousand pounds of food on the journey. When farm implements and furniture were added to the food in the wagon, the weight often reached one ton. When it was time to head west, the wagons often got into traffic jams. Not everyone who decided to make

the trip had the necessary skills. Some didn't even know how to drive a wagon. It didn't take the travelers long to realize they had brought too much along, so they started throwing things out. Entrepreneurs from the jumping off towns rode out and picked items up along the trail and then took them back to town to sell to someone else. Families often carried so much cargo in their wagons that the people had to walk. Look at the drawing at left. Imagine going on a two-thousand-mile walk!

Trail Landmarks

When we travel today, we look for signs to help us know where we are. Oregon Trail travelers had to look for landmarks like rivers and geological formations. When travelers came to a large river, enterprising ferrymen were waiting to take them across—sometimes for a high price. Ferrymen could charge whatever they liked. One company earned $65,000 in one summer. After a time, so many travelers had passed over the trail that new pioneers didn't have trouble finding their way. They could see the ruts left by previous wagon trains, like those on pages 318 and 319. Still, the landmarks helped them know how far they

Emigrants enjoyed the spring near Scotts Bluff in Nebraska.

had come and how far they had to go. The landmarks also broke the monotony in landscapes when there was little in view besides ruts, sagebrush, and desert. A few geological formations found along the trail are pictured below. The pioneers looked forward to some landmarks in particular, like Soda Springs with its naturally-carbonated water. When they added a little of the sugar stored in their wagons to the water, they had a refreshing treat.

Rocks Avenue in Wyoming

Emigrants crossed the Snake River in Idaho.

The Oregon Trail passed by Wyoming's Devil's Gate.

The Oregon Trail in Idaho near Wild Horse Butte

317

A Day on the Trail

The schedule for most days on the trail was about the same. At night travelers circled their wagons, as shown in the illustration below. This was not to protect themselves from Native Americans, but to make a sort of fence or corral for their livestock. They gathered what wood they could find and started a fire for supper. The trail got more and more crowded over the years, so wood became harder to find. When

Ruts in the Desert Along the Oregon Trail

the emigrants couldn't find wood, they made fires with buffalo dung. Sometimes they were able to shoot quail or buffalo to add to their meals, but often the only things they had to eat were bread and bacon. Travelers often sang hymns around their campfires at night. Some families slept in tents and others slept under the stars. They rose before sunrise, cooked breakfast, and set out for the day. At midday, they took an hour lunch break. By six o'clock, they had traveled about fifteen miles since breakfast and it was time to circle the wagons again and fix supper.

Remembering the Oregon Trail

In 1852 Ezra Meeker traveled the Oregon Trail. In 1906 he drove an ox-drawn wagon back over the trail from west to east. He was seventy-six years old. His purpose was to raise money to place commemorative markers along the trail. Meeker gave lectures and wrote articles for magazines and newspapers. He sold booklets and postcards and asked people

This drawing from Harper's Weekly *of June 12, 1869 shows wagons circled. A pole sticking out of a wagon holds pots over a campfire. A woman on the left sits in a ladderback chair while she sews.*

Ezra Meeker

to make donations. At left is a photograph of Meeker. One of his markers is pictured below.

Today people continue what Meeker began. Modern travelers retrace portions of the Oregon Trail while on Western vacations. Wagon ruts can be found in many places in the West.

The journey on the Oregon Trail took about four to six months. We can admire the endurance of those travelers. The book of Hebrews teaches us about the importance of spiritual endurance when it tells about people in the Old Testament who endured:

Therefore, since we have so great a cloud of witnesses
surrounding us, let us also lay aside every encumbrance
and the sin which so easily entangles us,
and let us run with endurance the race that is set before us.
Hebrews 12:1

A Meeker Marker

Activities for Lesson 57

Thinking Biblically – Marcus and Narcissa Whitman left all to follow Jesus. Copy Luke 9:23-24 into your notebook.

Map Study – Complete the assignments for Lesson 57 on Map 18 "The West" in *Maps of America the Beautiful*.

Timeline – In *Timeline of America the Beautiful* next to 1906 write: Ezra Meeker retraces his journey on the Oregon Trail.

Literature – Read "First Woman on the Oregon Trail" in *We the People*, page 56, and chapter 2 in *Bound for Oregon*.

Student Workbook or Lesson Review – If you are using one of these optional books, complete the assignment for Lesson 57.

Wagon Train Ruts in the West

The Smithsonian Institution

British scientist James Smithson prepared his last will and testament in 1826. He left most of his estate to his nephew. He added the stipulation that if his nephew died with no heirs, the estate would then go to the United States of America. Smithson required that the U.S. use the money to found an institution to "increase and diffuse knowledge among men." Smithson stated that this institution should be called the Smithsonian Institution. No one knows why this scientist made this decision. He never visited the United States, and no record exists that he ever corresponded with anyone in America. James Smithson died three years after creating his will. After his death, the contents of his will became news in both America and Europe. Six years later his nephew died leaving no heirs.

Renwick's Smithsonian Castle

Who Was James Smithson?

James Smithson was born in France in 1765. His father was an Englishman who became the first Duke of Northumberland. His mother had royal blood. Smithson inherited his great wealth from her estate.

Smithson graduated from Pembroke College, a part of Oxford University. He studied mineralogy and chemistry. He was a diligent student and researcher. He published many scientific papers on chemistry, geology, and mineralogy. One was about the chemical structure of a lady's tear; another was about a better way to make coffee.

America Receives Her Bequest

The year that James Smithson's nephew died, President Andrew Jackson announced the gift to Congress. Jackson was unsure whether the Constitution gave him authority to accept this present, so he asked Congress to pass a law allowing him to do so. The prospect of the gift caused controversy. People were divided over whether America should accept it. Senator John C. Calhoun thought it was beneath the dignity of America to accept gifts. However, in 1836 Congress agreed to accept the generous endowment of James Smithson.

President Jackson chose diplomat and lawyer Richard Rush to go to England to retrieve the gift. The mother of Smithson's nephew tried to get the money, so Rush had to fight for it in the British Court of Chancery. America won the case, so Rush proceeded to sell Smithson's properties and convert his assets into British gold sovereigns (coins).

Today large sums of money can be transferred from one bank to another electronically. That was not possible in July of 1838 when Rush boarded a ship bound for America. With him were eleven boxes which contained 104,960 gold sovereigns, eight shillings, and sevenpence. Rush also brought Smithson's personal library of 213 volumes, his mineral collection, scientific notes, and personal belongings. After a voyage of six weeks, Rush arrived in New York. He sent a request to the U.S. Secretary of State, asking that he be allowed to rest after his long voyage before coming to Washington.

The gold sovereigns were deposited in the U.S. Mint in Philadelphia. When melted down, they yielded a value of $508,318.46. Other items in Smithson's estate became part of the Smithsonian Institution's collection. At right is a list of some of the possessions Mr. Smithson had at the time of his death.

> ### Personal Belongings of James Smithson, Esquire
>
> Carriage
> Silver forks, spoons, and ladles
> One pin with sixteen small diamonds
> One ring of agate
> One cameo ring
> One tortoise shell box
> Sixteen shirts
> Forty-four pocket handkerchiefs
> Thirteen pairs of stockings
> Three night caps
> Four pairs of gloves
> One telescope
> Silver-plated candlesticks
> Gun
> Two portraits in oval frames
> Landscape painting in gilt frame
> Teapot
> Milk jug
> Two plates
> Twelve cups and saucers
> Six coffee mugs
> *Travels through North America, Two Volumes*
> *Struggles Through Life*
> *Domestic Cookery*

What Should America Do With the Money?

With Smithson's gift safely in hand, America's leaders had to decide what to do with it. Congressmen, Senators, educators, and everyday citizens offered suggestions. Ideas included a national university, a teacher training college, and a school to promote better living conditions through science. A professor from the University of Virginia thought the Smithsonian Institution should teach chemistry, geology, and mineralogy, as Smithson himself had studied. The president of Brown University wanted a university that would teach only the classics, since science and technology were so often used to make war. Alexander Dallas Bache, great-grandson of Benjamin Franklin, wanted the Institution to support scientific research, believing it could do that better than universities could.

Since the Library of Congress was small at that time, one Massachusetts Senator wanted the Smithsonian to be a national library. Congressman John Quincy Adams introduced a bill that would establish the Smithsonian Institution as a national observatory where people could study astronomy. In 1840 a group of politicians began to talk about a national museum which would house objects from America's history, show America's technology, and tell about America's natural resources.

Founding of the Smithsonian Institution

After ten years of debate, Congress passed "An Act to Establish the Smithsonian Institution" in 1846. They dropped the idea of a national university, but the bill combined many other ideas that had been put forth. The bill stated that the Institution must be faithful to Smithson's desire for it to increase and diffuse knowledge. President James K. Polk signed the bill into law on August 10, 1846. Finally, Smithson's vision would become a reality.

The Smithsonian Institution Castle

In the Act establishing the Smithsonian, Congress declared that it should have an art gallery, lecture hall, library, chemical laboratory, natural history laboratory, and science museum. A Smithsonian Building Committee was formed to oversee the building of a structure that could house these components. The committee worked with architect James Renwick Jr., who later became the architect of Saint Patrick's Cathedral in New York City.

Renwick started to work on the building's design in 1846. He decided on a medieval style reminiscent of English universities. The design was asymmetrical, meaning that its two sides were not mirror images of each other. One end would be rectangular and the other would look like a chapel. He designed nine turrets, each with a distinct style.

The red sandstone building was constructed on the National Mall in Washington, D.C. It is pictured on pages 320 and 323. The National Mall is a large, open space, lined with many of Washington's most famous buildings and monuments. Renwick's building has been nicknamed the

The Smithsonian's N.R. Wood mounts a bird in 1916.

A Blackfeet Chief makes a phonograph record at the Smithsonian in 1916.

Transcribing Indian Music at the Smithsonian

Aerial View of the Smithsonian Castle and Other Facilities

"Castle." After it was finished in 1855, it housed all of the Smithsonian museums, plus an apartment for the Secretary and his family. The Smithsonian Institution had outgrown the Castle by 1881 and began to add additional facilities.

The Smithsonian Today

The Smithsonian Institution is the world's largest museum system. It now has sixteen museums. Among these are the National Air and Space Museum, the National Museum of American History, the National Museum of the American Indian, the National Portrait Gallery, and the National Museum of Natural History. Notice the man at the top of page 322. He was preparing a specimen for the natural history museum in 1916. Many Smithsonian museums are along the National Mall. Most are open to the public free of charge 364 days a year, every day except Christmas.

The Smithsonian has a research library with over one million volumes. Notice the woman pictured on page 322 who is recording a Native American chief and listening to a recording. The Smithsonian Institution sends traveling exhibits across the country. It publishes books and has a monthly magazine. The National Zoo is part of the Smithsonian.

The Smithsonian has millions of objects in its collections. It includes objects as diverse as the compass William Clark used on the Lewis and Clark expedition, the airplane Wilbur and Orville Wright flew at Kitty Hawk, a rock from the moon, the ruby red slippers Dorothy wore in *The Wizard of Oz*, the Hope Diamond, and a chair owned by Lafayette, pictured at left.

Chair Belonging to the Marquis de Lafayette Displayed in the Smithsonian in 1913

Today the Smithsonian Board of Regents includes the Vice President of the United States, the Chief Justice of the Supreme Court, three Senators, three members of the House of Representatives, and nine private citizens. The Board selects its Secretary, who is responsible for leading the Institution. In addition to the money supplied from the James Smithson Trust, Congress appropriates tax money for the Smithsonian Institution. Many foundations, corporations, and individuals also contribute to it.

The Smithsonian Institution does not openly honor God, but we can learn about God there because the Smithsonian showcases amazing things that God has created:

> For since the creation of the world His invisible attributes,
> His eternal power and divine nature, have been clearly seen,
> being understood through what has been made . . . .
> Romans 1:20

Activities for Lesson 58

Thinking Biblically – Read about Solomon's wisdom and scientific knowledge in 1 Kings 4:29-34.

Map Study – Complete the assignment for Lesson 58 on Map 3 "American Landmarks" in *Maps of America the Beautiful*.

Timeline – In *Timeline of America the Beautiful* next to 1846, write: The Smithsonian Institution is established.

Literature – Read "An Act to Establish the Smithsonian Institution" in *We the People*, page 57, and chapters 3-4 in *Bound for Oregon*.

Student Workbook or Lesson Review – If you are using one of these optional books, complete the assignment for Lesson 58.

God Created Niagara Falls

God created a breathtaking waterfall along the United States-Canada border. It is called Niagara Falls. As the Niagara River flows northward from Lake Erie, it descends 326 feet before reaching Lake Ontario. Over half of the drop happens at once, when the river plummets 188 feet over Niagara Falls. When the river reaches the falls, Goat Island divides it into two channels. Goat Island and the falls south of it are in the United States. The falls to the north of Goat Island are in Canada. Examine this photograph of Niagara Falls. It was taken from the American side.

American Falls begins just past Prospect Point. Next is tiny Luna Island, then Bridal Veil Falls. On the other side of Goat Island is Canada with its Horseshoe or Canadian Falls. Horseshoe Falls looks small in the photo because it is in the distance and most of it is hidden by Goat Island. Actually, it is the largest of the falls of Niagara. Look at more views of Horseshoe Falls on page 326. The crest of American Falls is 850 feet wide, Bridal Veil Falls is fifty feet wide, and Horseshoe Falls is 2,200 feet wide.

Three Views of Horseshoe Falls

Niagara Falls is one of the largest waterfalls in the world (notice its size in the NASA photo below), but it is not the tallest. God created about five hundred waterfalls that are taller than Niagara. One reason this falls is so beautiful and impressive is because so much water flows over it. The water going over Niagara Falls comes from four of the world's largest lakes: Lake Superior, Lake Huron, Lake Michigan, and Lake Erie (see Lesson 13). An average of 194,940 cubic feet of water flows over Niagara Falls every second. About ten percent flows over the American Falls and about ninety percent over Horseshoe Falls. The water has been known to travel as fast as sixty-eight miles per hour when it goes over the precipice, the edge over which the water flows. The deepest section of the Niagara River is below the falls, where the water is 170 feet deep.

Rainbow at Niagara Falls

NASA Image of Horseshoe Falls

When the water hits the rocks at the bottom of the falls, a mist rises, as you can see in the photos on pages 325-326. People are often reminded of God's promise to Noah when they visit Niagara Falls, because He displays many rainbows there, as seen in one of the photos on page 326. Two aspects of the falls that can't be experienced in pictures are the loud roar of the falling water and the cool spray of the mist. Maybe you can visit the falls someday to experience those for yourself.

The precipice at Niagara Falls is made of about ninety feet of hard limestone. Underneath the limestone is softer shale. The force of the Niagara River erodes the soil and rock that it passes over, so the water becomes rich with minerals. Approximately sixty tons of minerals go over Niagara Falls every minute. These minerals make the river green. Chunks of limestone sometimes fall off the top of the falls because of the force. These chunks of rock fall to the bottom of the falls. Ever since Europeans and their descendants have been observing the falls, its precipice has continued to recede. The rocks of Niagara contain fossils of sponges, fish, coral, and mollusks.

Down river from Niagara Falls, the Niagara River enters Niagara Gorge. Soon the river bends like an elbow. Just before the elbow are rapids. In the elbow is a large basin where the water travels counterclockwise in the Niagara Whirlpool.

The water from Niagara Falls is used by about one million people in America and Canada. It is used for drinking water, for the production of hydroelectric power, and for cooling purposes in industry. In 1950 the two countries agreed on how much water could be diverted from the river to make electricity. During the summer tourist season each year, the power plants divert less water during the daytime to make the waterfalls bigger.

Natives, Explorers, and Soldiers at Niagara Falls

Native Americans lived in the Niagara region for many years before the falls were first seen by Europeans. Samuel de Champlain and Ètienne Brûlé may have seen the falls in their explorations (see Lesson 13). The first European known to describe the falls was Catholic priest Louis Hennepin. Hennepin was a missionary who traveled with the French explorer Rene Robert la Salle. Hennepin wrote about the falls in his 1698 book, *A New Discovery of a Vast Country in America*. He is also credited with drawing the first illustration of the falls.

Hennepin also discovered St. Anthony Falls on the Mississippi River. A painting of that discovery hangs in the Minnesota State Capitol. He named the Falls of St. Anthony after his patron saint, St. Anthony of Padua. Minneapolis is in Hennepin County and has a Hennepin Avenue. In central Minnesota is Father Hennepin State Park.

The French built a fort on the American side of the falls in 1745. In 1759 the British captured the region. In 1809 Americans founded the town of Manchester, New York. Much fighting took place around Niagara Falls during the War of 1812. The British captured Manchester but returned it to America after the war. In 1848 Manchester was renamed Niagara Falls, New York. The town of Niagara Falls, Ontario, was originally called Elgin and later Clifton. It was named Niagara Falls in 1881.

Bridges Across Niagara Falls

Three bridges cross the Niagara River near the falls. The Whirlpool Bridge and the Rainbow Bridge cross between the towns of Niagara Falls, New York, and Niagara Falls, Ontario. The Lewiston-Queenston Bridge is nearby. These bridges are an important port of entry between the United States and Canada. A port of entry is a place where people travel between two countries. Besides flights into Kennedy International Airport in New York City, more people cross between the U.S. and Canada on these bridges than at any other point along the border.

1856 Currier and Ives Print of the Niagara Falls Suspension Bridge

The first bridge across Niagara was a roadway made of oak planks that hung from iron cables. In 1855 it was replaced by the Niagara Falls Suspension Bridge that had upper and lower decks. As seen in the print above, trains used the top deck, while pedestrians and carriages used the lower one. Can you imagine walking under those trains? Before the Civil War, many southern slaves escaped slavery by running away to Canada. Many crossed the Niagara Falls Suspension Bridge. In 1897 a steel arch bridge was built around and under the suspension bridge. Traffic continued across the suspension bridge while its replacement was under construction. The new bridge was named the Whirlpool Bridge.

The first Falls View Suspension Bridge was completed in 1867. A storm destroyed it in 1889. The second Falls View Suspension Bridge was completed in 1897. It was also known as the Honeymoon Bridge. It sometimes swayed in heavy winds and many worried about its stability. In January of 1938, a severe ice storm hit the area and the bridge fell into the Niagara River. Workers who had been trying to prevent a collapse had left their posts just ten minutes before it fell. Thousands watched it fall, but no one was hurt. The following year King George VI and Queen Elizabeth of England dedicated the site of its replacement. The new bridge built shortly thereafter is called the Rainbow Bridge. It was restored and improved at the turn of the 21st century.

The Lewiston-Queenston Bridge stretches 1,600 feet across the Niagara River. It connects Interstate 190 in Lewiston, New York, with a highway in Queenston, Ontario. This is the world's longest hingeless steel arch bridge. It was completed in 1962 and expanded in 2005. It is a copy of the Rainbow Bridge.

Niagara Attractions

Cave of the Wind. In 1834 a cave was discovered behind Bridal Veil Falls. At first, it was called Aeolus Cave. In Greek mythology Aeolus was the wind god. Guided tours of this cave, which came to be called Cave of the Wind, began in 1841. At the top of page 329 is an illustration that shows people walking down to the cave in 1875. Below it is a photo of the area in 1888. In 1920 the cave suffered a rock fall and became unsafe. The cave was destroyed in 1954 by a massive rock fall and by the use of dynamite to remove a dangerous overhang.

Tourists still take Cave of the Wind tours even though the cave is gone. They begin on Goat Island, which is accessible by two bridges which carry pedestrians, cars, and tourist trams. First, visitors enter an elevator that takes them down 175 feet into Niagara Gorge. In the summer, you can walk to Hurricane Deck, which is less than twenty feet from the waters of Bridal Veil Falls. The wooden decks taking visitors to Hurricane Deck are taken down each November and reassembled each spring. Otherwise winter weather would destroy them. The winds on Hurricane Deck reach as high as sixty-eight miles an hour, making you feel like you are in a tropical storm. People often see rainbows when they are on the Cave of the Wind tour.

Descent to Cave of the Wind, 1875

Journey Behind the Falls. In 1818 a staircase was built to take visitors to the bottom of Horseshoe Falls. For $1 visitors could see this "Sheet of Falling Water" attraction. Over the years improvements were made with the addition of elevators and tunnels to help people get to the bottom. Today the attraction is called Journey Behind the Falls.

Whirlpool Aero Car. Beginning in 1916, tourists could choose another Niagara adventure. They could ride high above the whirlpool rapids in an aerial cable car. Thirty-five tourists at a time can still climb aboard the same Whirlpool Aero Car and glide over the river, as seen at lower right on page 330.

Cave of the Wind Area, 1888

Maid of the Mist. As early as 1818, ferry service was available to take travelers across the Niagara River. In 1846 a steamboat began to ferry them across. It was named *Maid of the Mist*. Since 1846, seven boats have been used, all with the same name. Today these boats carry tourists close to the falls, where they can feel the rising mist. Five pictures of these boats are in this lesson. Can you find all five?

Tourists and Honeymooners at Niagara Falls

Thousands of couples choose Niagara Falls for their honeymoon, following a tradition begun in the 1800s. The first couple reported to have spent their honeymoon at Niagara was Theodosia Burr and Joseph Alston in 1801. Theodosia was the daughter of Aaron Burr, who served as Vice President with Thomas Jefferson. There is some evidence that Napoleon Bonaparte's brother and his bride honeymooned there in 1804.

Honeymooners were not the only people who enjoyed visiting Niagara Falls in the 1800s. By the time that James K. Polk served as President of the United States, tourists had been visiting Niagara Falls for several years. One way they learned about the falls was from

Above: Winter Tourists in Early 1900s
At Right: Harper's Weekly
Illustrations of Tourists from 1875

images artists had created. These hung in homes and public buildings. From 1825 to 1841, Theodore Wright published several editions of *The Northern Traveler*. When writing about Niagara, he said that public accommodations were excellent on both the American and Canadian sides. He said the Niagara River could be crossed safely at any hour of the day by ferry and noted that each side of the falls had a staircase down to the bottom of the falls. Wright said that throngs of visitors were there during the pleasant seasons of the year. He mentioned that stagecoaches could be hired to transport tourists in the falls area.

When the Erie Canal opened in 1825, people could get from New York City to Buffalo in only ten days. They could then easily travel from Buffalo to nearby Niagara Falls. The Niagara Falls Suspension Bridge, completed in 1855, made it possible for trains to cross the falls. Trains carried people from the east coast to Detroit and Chicago. Many people got to see the falls from their train. The top illustration above shows winter visitors in the early 1900s. Below it are two illustrations of Niagara visitors that appeared in *Harper's Weekly* in 1875.

Today millions of people visit Niagara Falls each year. On the American side they visit the city of Niagara Falls, New York, and Niagara Falls State Park, which opened in 1885. On the Canadian side they visit Niagara Falls, Ontario, and Queen Victoria Park, which opened in 1888.

Stunts Over Niagara

In October of 1829, Sam Patch jumped off the top of Horseshoe Falls. He survived the 175-foot leap and came to be called the Yankee Leaper.

Jean François Gravelet was a French acrobat, whose stage name was Charles Blondin. Born in 1824, Blondin began working as an acrobat when he was six years old. Even as a child Blondin was daring and he came to be called the Little Wonder. In 1859 and 1860, Charles Blondin

Whirlpool Aero Car

330

walked across Niagara Gorge on a 1,100 foot tightrope! The tightrope was 160 feet above the falls. Over the years Blondin went across the gorge several times. One walk is

Blondin Crossing the Gorge

illustrated at left. Once he pushed a wheelbarrow; once he was blindfolded; once he carried a man on his back; and once he crossed over on stilts.

In July of 1901, a schoolteacher in Michigan named Annie Edson Taylor read an article about the Pan-American Exposition in Buffalo, New York. The article described the growing interest in Niagara Falls. Annie's husband had died in the Civil War and she had been moving around the country for many years. She needed money and came up with an outlandish plan. Mrs. Taylor decided she would seek both fortune and fame by doing a spectacular stunt: she would go over Niagara Falls in a barrel!

On her birthday, October 24, 1901, Annie Edson Taylor got into a wooden pickle barrel that was five feet tall and three feet across. She nestled among cushions and strapped herself in with a leather harness. See illustration below. The barrel was tied to a small boat which towed her into the Niagara River. There her barrel was cut loose. The rapids tossed her about roughly and then she went over the falls. Amazingly, she survived. After a journey of about twenty minutes, she came ashore.

Diagram of Mrs. Taylor in Her Barrel

Mrs. Taylor claimed that she was in her forties, but actually she was 63 years old! Annie enjoyed a short time in the spotlight. For a while, people wanted to take photographs of her. See a stereoscopic photo of her below. She received a few requests to speak but she enjoyed no long-term financial success.

Over the next one hundred years, other people tried to go over the falls in various devices. One tried to go in a kayak and one in a jet ski! Only two-thirds of those attempting the plunge survived. Today these stunts are illegal in both the United States and Canada. Anyone who tries to go over the falls faces fines, as much as $10,000, because he puts rescue workers at risk.

Original caption reads: "Mrs. Taylor in Her Barrel to Make Her Daring Trip over Niagara Falls"

Tourists on the Maid of the Mist *in 1903 (left) and 1908 (right)*

Niagara Falls displays the mighty power of God:

> The floods have lifted up, O Lord,
> The floods have lifted up their voice,
> The floods lift up their pounding waves.
> More than the sounds of many waters,
> Than the mighty breakers of the sea,
> The Lord on high is mighty.
> Psalm 93:3-4

Activities for Lesson 59

Map Study – Complete the assignment for Lesson 59 on Map 2 "God's Wonders" in *Maps of America the Beautiful*.

Timeline – In *Timeline of America the Beautiful* next to 1846, write: The *Maid of the Mist* begins service at Niagara Falls.

Literature – Read "Over Niagara" in *We the People*, page 58-59, and chapters 5-6 in *Bound for Oregon*.

Vocabulary – Write a paragraph in your notebook about an imaginary thrilling adventure that uses all of these words: channel, precipice, diverted, accommodations, gorge.

Family Activity – Rehearse and perform the play, "Wild and Wonderful Niagara Falls." See pages 432-433 for directions.

Student Workbook or Lesson Review – If you are using one of these optional books, complete the assignment for Lesson 59.

John James Audubon, Artist and Naturalist

Summer Red Bird from Birds of America

Audubon painted this landscape while in Natchez.

John James Audubon traveled the American frontier painting its wildlife. In 1838 he completed *Birds of America,* a beautiful collection of 435 life-size engravings. Audubon inspired his sons to follow in his footsteps; they also became accomplished nature artists.

Audubon was born in Santo Domingo (now Haiti) in 1785. His father was a French naval officer. His mother worked as a servant. After his mother died, John James went to France to live with his father. He grew up there with his father and his stepmother, who adopted him. During his happy childhood, he collected birds' eggs and nests and drew them. He also studied fencing, geography, and mathematics.

At age eighteen, Audubon came to America to manage Mill Grove, his father's estate near Philadelphia. One of the commercial enterprises on the estate was a lead mine.

At Mill Grove, Audubon found the perfect place to continue his interest in nature and art. Even today the plantation is rich in wildlife. Over 175 species of birds and over four hundred species of plants have been identified there.

The year after Audubon arrived in America, he met and came to love Lucy Bakewell, the daughter of Englishman

William Bakewell, who owned the adjoining estate. After receiving approval from their fathers, Audubon married Lucy in 1808. They moved first to Louisville where Audubon established a general store. They later moved to Henderson, Kentucky. After several successful years in business, the American economy hit a difficult time, and the Audubon family lost all of their possessions. Audubon was even jailed for debt for a short time. Four children were born to the Audubons in Kentucky. Two sons survived to adulthood, Victor Gifford and John Woodhouse.

John James Audubon, 1826

In Search of Birds

In 1820, after working for a while as a taxidermist, Audubon took his gun, artist materials, and an assistant and began to travel along the Mississippi River, painting the birds of America. Audubon found many species because millions of birds migrate along the Mississippi flyway. Audubon painted each bird its actual size. His assistant was Joseph Mason, who became expert at painting the plants in Audubon's pictures. Mason worked with Audubon for about two years.

While traveling, Audubon painted chalk portraits to earn money for his venture. While he was away, Lucy contributed to the family income by working as a schoolteacher and tutor. One of the children she tutored was George Bird Grinnell, who later helped to found the first Audubon Society. It was Grinnell who chose the name Audubon for this society dedicated to protecting birds and their habitats.

Audubon spent time in Natchez, Mississippi, painting birds in the area (see Lesson 53). While there he taught at two schools and painted the landscape pictured on page 333. The original oil painting of this landscape hung at Melrose Plantation in Natchez for almost one hundred years. For a while, Lucy was able to join her husband in Natchez. They enrolled their sons in school there. It was in Natchez that Audubon received instruction in oil painting from traveling artist John Stein. Audubon used a variety of art materials to produce his paintings, including pastels, chalk, graphite, oil paint, egg whites, and more.

Though some birds that became part of *Birds of America* were painted in Natchez and other sites along the Mississippi, Audubon had many more places to go before his project was completed. He traveled as far south as the Florida Keys, as far north as Labrador in Canada, and as far west as Texas. While working on his paintings of birds, Audubon took notes about their characteristics and about his experiences in the wilderness.

In Search of a Printer

Audubon tried in 1824 to get the Academy of Natural Sciences in Philadelphia to help him publish engravings of his paintings. He was turned down. He went to England in 1826 with the paintings he had completed thus far. He displayed 250 paintings in England and in Edinburgh, Scotland. He found great success. People liked his life-size bird portraits and his descriptions of life in the American wilderness. In London he found an engraver for *Birds of America*. The engraver agreed to reproduce Audubon's paintings as hand-colored engravings. While in Great Britain, Audubon partnered with a Scottish ornithologist (a scientist who studies birds) to write life histories of the species that Audubon drew.

Audubon in the Wilderness

Customers did not receive the book all at one time. Instead, they purchased subscriptions. In 1830 the U.S. House of Representatives bought a subscription. That same year, Audubon dined at the White House with President Jackson.

Audubon continued to travel and paint. His son Victor accompanied him, while his son John stayed in England overseeing the printing and selling of the series. Victor and John painted the picture of their father at left.

In 1838 John James Audubon published the last engraving in the *Birds of America* series. Most customers purchased complete sets, which they received in eighty-seven installments of five hand-colored engravings each. Many of Audubon's paintings in *Birds of America* included more than one bird. When he completed his 435 life-size paintings of America's birds, he had included 1,065 birds from 489 species.

Audubon's prints are remarkable. He positioned the birds as they are found in creation. Unlike other nature artists of the day, he painted them in their natural surroundings. They are more than nature illustrations; they are works of art. The original prints of *Birds of America* bring large sums when they are auctioned today. Of the just over two hundred complete sets he sold, many are still intact.

Fame and Fortune

Birds of America brought Audubon financial success and fame. He and Lucy were able to purchase Minnie's Land, a thirty-five acre estate along the Hudson River in what is now upper Manhattan. Newspapers wrote about him, he gave lectures, and he socialized with well-known people. Between 1831 and 1839, he published the notes he had taken while drawing the birds of America. These notes were published in a five-volume set called *Ornithological Biography*. Between 1839 and 1843, a smaller version of *Birds of America* was also printed.

For six months in 1843, Audubon and his son John explored the Missouri River valley to research North American mammals. Audubon and his two sons completed the paintings for this project and published *Viviparous Quadrupeds of North America*. James Bachman, a minister, long-time family friend, and amateur naturalist, wrote its text. This work was printed by a process called lithography. After printing, the pages were hand-colored. It was one of the first books of its kind to be printed by that method in the United States.

For the last nine years of his life, Audubon and his wife made their home at Minnie's Land. Audubon died in 1851 at age sixty-five.

John James Audubon State Park in Kentucky has the largest collection of Audubon artifacts in the world. Audubon's works are found in many museums, including the National Gallery of Art. Audubon's first home in America, Mill Grove in Pennsylvania, is now managed by the National Audubon Society and is open to the public. Lucy Audubon sold her husband's original paintings for *Birds of America* to the New York Historical Society, which still owns them. Notice the examples at right, below, and on page 333.

Carolina Turtle-Dove

In the 1839 introduction to the smaller version of *Birds of America*, John James Audubon wrote that he never could cease "to admire and to study with zeal and the most heartfelt reverence, the wonderful productions of an Almighty Creator." Audubon helped people learn about and appreciate some of God's most beautiful creatures. Jesus taught:

> Look at the birds of the air, that they do not sow,
> nor reap nor gather into barns,
> and yet your heavenly Father feeds them.
> Are you not worth much more than they?
> Matthew 6:26

Activities for Lesson 60

Ivory-billed Woodpecker

Thinking Biblically – Jesus taught about about God's love by pointing out birds. Copy Matthew 6:26 into your notebook.

Timeline – In *Timeline of America the Beautiful* next to 1838, write: John James Audubon completes *Birds of America*.

Literature – Read "From Audubon's Journal" in *We the People*, page 60, and chapters 7-8 in *Bound for Oregon*.

Creative Writing – Go outside and observe a particular object of God's creation. It could be a tree, flower, bird, butterfly, or pet. In your notebook, write one or two paragraphs describing it in detail.

Student Workbook or Lesson Review – If you are using one of these optional books, complete the assignment for Lesson 60. If you are using the Lesson Review, take the quiz for Unit 12.

The Turbulent 1850s

As America entered the 1850s, Western growth caused more conflict over slavery. Four Presidents—Taylor, Fillmore, Pierce, and Buchanan—served the nation during this decade. None was able to lead the nation out of the conflict. However, America was having good times, too. Some miners discovered a beautiful lake in southern Oregon. Many lighthouses were built to protect sailors and their ships. Henry Wadsworth Longfellow wrote beautiful poetry. Stagecoaches carried passengers and cargo. As the decade of the 1860s began, Pony Express riders created a legend.

This American copper butterfly was photographed on an island off the coast of Maine.

Lessons in Unit 13

Books Used in Unit 13

- *Maps of America the Beautiful*

- *Timeline of America the Beautiful*

- *We the People*

- *Bound for Oregon* by Jean Van Leeuwen

A Growing Nation
Faces Growing Conflict

The American people and their elected representatives often have strong ideas about important issues. In the 1850s, the question of slavery became even more divisive as Americans held strongly differing views about it. Southerners held fast to the tradition of having slaves. They believed their economy depended on it. However, more and more people in the North were becoming abolitionists. Some brave abolitionists were even helping slaves escape to Canada.

The California Gold Rush

In the 1848 election, Whig candidate General Zachary Taylor won the presidency; but the Democrats won the most seats in Congress.

Between the time of Taylor's election and his inauguration, outgoing President James K. Polk made a surprise announcement in a speech to Congress: gold had been found at John Sutter's mill in California. Small numbers of emigrants had been moving to California; but in 1849, 80,000 people rushed to

James Marshall stands in front of Sutter's Mill in 1850.

California in the hope of finding gold and becoming rich. This event is called the Gold Rush; the people who went to California to find gold are called Forty-Niners.

Some reached California by ship, traveling 13,000 miles around Cape Horn at the tip of South America. Others also traveled by sea, but took the risky overland shortcut across the Isthmus of Panama. The total number that went by sea is estimated at 25,000. By far, most people used the wagons and mules or oxen they already had and headed out across the West. Most Forty-Niners were men. In 1850 only one in twelve Californians was female.

The Gold Rush brought out the worst in people. Greed does not bring about happiness. Mining was hard work. Few became rich. Even John Sutter himself and James Marshall, his employee who found the first gold, ended their lives in poverty. Notice Marshall in the foreground of the 1850 photo of Sutter's Mill above. Some entrepreneurs, like Levi Strauss and Philip Armour, earned a good living by selling products to the miners. Levi Strauss, a new immigrant from Bavaria, sold work pants. Philip Armour sold beef. Their businesses are still supplying customers today. Though many Forty-Niners returned home, many stayed in California.

The Compromise of 1850

The slave state versus free state controversy became more important because Western territories were getting enough people to become states. Would these states be slave or free? Western settlers who moved west from southern states wanted to take their slaves with them. People who opposed slavery wanted Western states to be free. Americans on both sides of the issue were afraid they would lose power if the number of free states and slave states got out of balance.

Kentucky Senator Henry Clay worked out a compromise to try to satisfy people on both sides of the issue. His Compromise of 1850 included these proposals: California would become a free state. Slavery would not be allowed there. Utah and New Mexico would be organized as territories and the people living in each one would decide whether they wanted to be a slave state or a free state. The slave trade would be outlawed in the District of Columbia. A new law would deal more harshly with fugitive slaves who had run away from their masters: northern states would have to return runaway slaves to their masters in the South.

People believed that President Taylor would not accept the compromise. However, President Taylor died in the summer of 1850 and Vice President Millard Fillmore became the new President. Fillmore signed the various laws that made up the Compromise, including the act that made California the thirty-first state in 1850. Though Clay and others hoped the compromise would help, it actually made matters worse. Northerners hated the law that required them to return runaway slaves. Many believed slavery was morally wrong, so some refused to obey the law. The compromise did not take care of the tension; it only increased it. Read about President Taylor at right and about President Fillmore on page 340.

Zachary Taylor
America's Twelfth President
March 5, 1849 - July 9, 1850

Zachary Taylor was born in 1784 into a wealthy Virginia family. In 1810 he married Margaret Mackall Smith. The Taylors had five daughters and one son. Margaret followed her husband from post to post as he pursued a military career. He became a general and also a wealthy slaveholder with land in Kentucky, Mississippi, and Louisiana.

Taylor gained a reputation as an Indian fighter. Though he fought Native Americans, he respected their rights to keep their own land. He believed the military should work to keep whites and Indians apart. Taylor became a popular hero after the Mexican War. He earned the nickname "Old Rough and Ready." His soldiers respected him because he was willing to suffer with them. His popularity helped him to be elected President.

On July 4, 1850, after just sixteen months in office, President Taylor became ill after attending ceremonies at the Washington Monument. Five days later, he called his wife to him. He asked her not to weep and said, "I have always done my duty. I am ready to die. My only regret is for my friends I leave behind." More than 100,000 people showed their respect for their beloved President at his funeral.

Millard Fillmore
America's Thirteenth President
July 9, 1850 - March 3, 1853

Millard Fillmore was born into poverty in New York in 1800. While working as an apprentice to a clothmaker, he taught himself to read. He borrowed money to pay his obligation to the clothmaker, and then returned home. He read every book he could. He managed to go to school for six months. Teacher Abigail Powers encouraged him. They later married. They had one son and one daughter.

Fillmore became a lawyer. He served in the New York legislature and in the U.S. House of Representatives. He became President during hard times. The country had just lost a President and it was in the midst of controversy concerning slavery. Fillmore made enemies by supporting the Compromise of 1850, which gave everyone something to hate. He was not nominated by his party for a second term. Shortly after that, his wife died, and also his only daughter. He ran for the presidency again in 1856, but lost.

Fillmore returned to the practice of law. In 1858 he married Mrs. Caroline C. McIntosh. He took two trips to Europe, served as the first chancellor of the Univeristy of Buffalo, and helped found the Buffalo General Hospital. He died in 1874.

Franklin Pierce Becomes President

In the 1852 election, Democrat and Mexican War veteran Franklin Pierce defeated another Mexican War veteran, the Whig Winfield Scott, for President. Pierce supported the right to own slaves.

Uncle Tom's Cabin

Also in 1852, Harriet Beecher Stowe published a book called *Uncle Tom's Cabin*. This work of fiction described the harsh realities of slave life. The book discussed issues related to slavery, including slaves running away. Mrs. Stowe wanted to see slavery ended. The book had a huge impact in America and in Europe. More people joined the antislavery movement after reading it.

The Kansas-Nebraska Act of 1854

At this time America's trade with Asia was growing, so many people wanted to build a railroad from the Midwest to the Pacific coast. The railroad would need to go through the lands west of Missouri and Iowa. This land needed to be organized into territories which could become states. People were divided over whether these states should have slaves. Back in 1820, the Missouri Compromise had stated that slavery would not be legal above the northern border of Missouri. Congress passed the Kansas-Nebraska Act in 1854. It repealed the Missouri Compromise and stated that these territories could decide for themselves about slavery.

America continued to be divided. The Democratic Party was especially divided. Most of Congress had been Democrat, but in the 1854 elections for the House of Representatives and the Senate, the Democrats lost many seats and were no longer in the majority. Some leaders who were opposed to slavery organized a new political party, the Republican Party.

Bleeding Kansas

Residents of Nebraska voted to ban slavery in their territory. Pro-slavery and anti-slavery settlers rushed into Kansas so that each side would have more people to vote on the issue in that territory. Some settlers attacked others who had different views. Two hundred people died during the conflict. People called the territory Bleeding Kansas. Americans were now fighting about slavery. Sadly, this would get much worse before the conflict was over.

Read about Franklin Pierce's life below.

Franklin Pierce
America's Fourteenth President
March 4, 1853 - March 4, 1857

Franklin Pierce was born in New Hampshire in 1804. He graduated from Bowdoin College in Maine, where he formed a lifetime friendship with author Nathaniel Hawthorne. After college, Franklin became a lawyer. While Franklin was in his twenties, his father became Governor of New Hampshire and Franklin was elected to the New Hampshire legislature. In 1832 Franklin Pierce was elected to the U.S. House of Representatives. Both Franklin and his father were avid supporters of Andrew Jackson.

Franklin Pierce married Jane Appleton in 1834. She was the daughter of the president of Bowdoin College. Jane was devoutly religious. Pierce was elected to the U.S. Senate in 1837. He became a strong defender of slavery.

Pierce left the Senate in 1841 and returned to New Hampshire with Jane. He became a famous lawyer and was well-known for his public speaking abilities. In 1844 he helped Polk win votes in New Hampshire. Pierce volunteered to fight in the Mexican War and Polk rewarded him with the title of Brigadier General.

Pierce was elected President in 1852. During the Civil War, he supported the North, but spoke openly against Abraham Lincoln. Franklin Pierce died in 1869.

The Election of James Buchanan

In the presidential election of 1856, James Buchanan was the Democratic nominee. He was a veteran of the War of 1812. The new Republican Party nominated John C. Fremont, a Western explorer who had fought in the Mexican War (see page 253). Buchanan won the presidency, but the Republicans won one-third of the Senate seats and almost half of the seats in the House of Representatives. Buchanan was inaugurated in March of 1857. During Buchanan's presidency, Minnesota became the thirty-second state in 1858 and Oregon the thirty-third in 1859. In 1861 Kansas entered the Union as a free state. Read about James Buchanan's life on page 342.

New States Admitted

1850 California
1858 Minnesota
1859 Oregon
1861 Kansas

James Buchanan
America's Fifteenth President
March 4, 1857 - March 4, 1861

James Buchanan was born in Pennsylvania in 1791, the last U.S. President born in the 1700s. He graduated from Carlisle College and then studied law. He moved to Lancaster, Pennsylvania. In his late 20s, he fell in love with Anne Caroline Coleman. Her family disapproved, and Anne broke off their engagement. She died soon after. Buchanan never married; he became America's only bachelor President.

Before the presidency, Buchanan served in the Pennsylvania legislature, the U.S. House of Representatives, and the U.S. Senate. He was Andrew Jackson's envoy to Russia and James K. Polk's Secretary of State. During the Pierce administration, he was Ambassador to England.

James Buchanan, at age 65, became the Democratic nominee for President in 1856. He gave few speeches and spoke little to the press. He let his supporters campaign for him. His nickname was Old Buck and his supporters were called Buchaneers. Before the election, he feared that the country was headed for war. As President he continued to believe that states should decide for themselves about slavery.

Though he supported the North, Buchanan, like Pierce, was condemned for his sympathies for the South. After leaving the presidency, he wrote a book defending his positions. Buchanan died in 1868.

The Supreme Court Decides the *Dred Scott v. Sanford* Case

Dred Scott and his wife were slaves. Scott sued for his freedom in Missouri. He believed he should be free since his master had moved him to places where slavery was illegal. The case went to the U.S. Supreme Court. Shortly after Buchanan became President, the U.S. Supreme Court issued its decision in the case entitled *Dred Scott v. Sanford*. The court declared that slaves were not citizens. It said that slavery was a state issue. The ruling was a victory for supporters of slavery. It angered those who opposed slavery.

John Brown's Attack at Harper's Ferry

John Brown was an abolitionist settler in Kansas. He was involved in the attacks on pro-slavery settlers there. In 1859 he led an attack on the Army arsenal in Harper's Ferry, Virginia (now in West Virginia). Evidently, he wanted to capture weapons and give them to slaves so they could revolt against their masters. Brown was captured by U.S. Army forces led by Robert E. Lee and Jeb Stuart. Brown was later executed for treason. Many northerners approved of Brown's actions.

Harper's Ferry is nestled in the Blue Ridge Mountains at the confluence of the Potomac and Shenandoah Rivers. When Thomas Jefferson visited the town in 1783, he stood on a rock now known as Jefferson Rock. In his *Notes of the State of Virginia*, he wrote: "This scene is worth a voyage across the Atlantic." Look at the pictures on page 343.

The National Park Service has preserved this tiny town in Harper's Ferry National Historical Park. The park is in West Virginia, Virginia, and Maryland. Here visitors learn about John Brown's raid and about life in Harper's Ferry during the 1850s. Harper's Ferry was an early manufacturing town. America's first successful railroad came through the town. It was home to one of America's first schools where blacks and whites learned together. The Appalachian Trail runs through Harper's Ferry.

Harper's Ferry with Railroad Bridge

The Underground Railroad

Throughout the 1850s, American abolitionists helped many runaway slaves escape. Hundreds of slaves gained their freedom each year. The Fugitive Slave Law that was part of the Compromise of 1850 put the abolitionists who helped the slaves in even greater danger.

As early as 1786, a society of Quakers was formed to help runaways. Over time others became involved in the movement. Around 1831 the effort was dubbed the Underground Railroad. People working in the Underground Railroad began to use railroad terms to describe their work. Homes and businesses

Jefferson Rock at Harper's Ferry

willing to feed or house slaves were called stations or depots. Owners of these stations were called stationmasters. Those who led slaves from one station to another were called conductors. When slaves reached a station, they were given food and allowed to rest in barns or in secret rooms before being conducted to the next station, which was usually ten to twenty miles away.

People who gave money to help the Underground Railroad were called stockholders. Sometimes slaves were able to use some of this money to travel by train or boat. Donated money also bought the slaves new clothes so they would look like free blacks and not like slaves. Volunteers on the Underground Railroad also helped runaway slaves get jobs and housing in their new homes in the North.

The Underground Railroad has many heroes, including former slave Harriet Tubman, who worked as a conductor. Traveling to the South nineteen times, she escorted three hundred slaves to freedom. John Fairfield, the son of a slave owner, also rescued many slaves. Quaker Levi Coffin helped more than 3,000.

Fashions of the Decade

In all of American history, women have enjoyed beautiful clothes. On page 344 are examples of clothing styles in the 1850s, as worn by the country's First Ladies. The top three ladies are wives of Presidents: Margaret Taylor, Abigail Fillmore, and Jane Pierce. At bottom is Harriet Lane Buchanan, niece of President Buchanan, who served as her uncle's First Lady since he was a bachelor.

Whites who worked in the Underground Railroad enjoyed their own freedom and used their freedom to help their fellow man. Paul told those who have spiritual freedom to serve one another:

> For you were called to freedom, brethren;
> only do not turn your freedom
> into an opportunity for the flesh,
> but through love serve one another.
> Galatians 5:13

Activities for Lesson 61

Thinking Biblically – Copy Galatians 5:13 into your notebook.

Map Study – Complete the assignments for Lesson 61 on Map 20 "The Lower 48" in *Maps of America the Beautiful*.

Timeline – In *Timeline of America the Beautiful* next to 1852, write: *Uncle Tom's Cabin* by Harriet Beecher Stowe is published.

Vocabulary – In your notebook, write each of the following words with its definition from the list below: divisive, entrepreneur, poverty, impact, condemned.

   a. declared to be wrong
   b. the state of being poor
   c. someone who starts a business
   d. causing opposition
   e. a direct effect

Literature – Read "Ho! For California" in *We the People*, page 61, and chapters 9-10 in *Bound for Oregon*.

Student Workbook or Lesson Review – If you are using one of these optional books, complete the assignment for Lesson 61.

First Ladies from Top to Bottom: Margaret Mackall Smith Taylor; Abigail Powers Fillmore; Jane M. Pierce; Harriet Lane Buchanan

344

God Created Crater Lake

God created the Cascade Mountain range in southern Oregon. At some time in the past, one of these mountains, called Mount Mazama by geologists, experienced a volcanic eruption. The eruption created a giant crater where the mountain had been. For many years God has sent precipitation into the crater, creating a beautiful sapphire-blue lake. Few places on earth are as clean as Crater Lake. Crater Lake lies one hundred miles from the Pacific Ocean. It is 6,164 feet above sea level. Its diameter varies from 4.54 miles to 6.02 miles. It is surrounded by lava cliffs that range from 507 feet to 1,978 feet high.

Wizard Island, Phantom Ship, and the "Old Man" of Crater Lake

Near the western edge of Crater Lake is Wizard Island, which rises 767 feet above the water's surface. Phantom Ship is the only other island in Crater Lake. When the lake is foggy or the light is low, the island resembles a ship. Look at the picture of Crater Lake below. Notice how the snow on its lava cliffs is reflected in the beautiful blue water. Find Wizard Island.

For over one hundred years, a mountain hemlock log has been floating upright in Crater Lake. It is called the "Old Man" of Crater Lake. Wind blows it from place to place around the lake.

Crater Lake with Wizard Island

Summer at Crater Lake

Summer days at Crater Lake are usually dry and mild with an average temperature of about sixty-seven degrees. They can be as cool as forty degrees or as hot as eighty or more. Summer skies are blue. Summer nights are cool, with temperatures sometimes falling below freezing. Thunderstorms are frequent at Crater Lake. Lightning displays are dramatic and winds can be high.

Winter at Crater Lake

Northern spotted owls live near Crater Lake.

Snow begins to fall in Crater Lake National Park in mid-October. The average yearly snowfall is 528 inches! In 1950, 903 inches fell. By early spring, ten to fifteen feet of snow is usually on the ground. In 1983 the snow depth was 21 feet. Think about how many snowflakes God has to make to create 528 inches of snow just at Crater Lake. He is making snow at many other places every year, too! Low visibility makes it difficult to see Crater Lake in the snowy winter weather, but people enjoy snowshoeing and skiing. It is June before the snow melts in most places, and sometimes snow is still on the ground in July. Even with all this winter weather, Crater Lake stores so much heat in the summer that it is rare for the lake to freeze. However, the weather was so cold in 1949 that the lake stayed frozen for three months.

The Water of Crater Lake

The snowfall at Crater Lake is very important. Except for two areas on the lake bottom that receive water from hydrothermal springs, all of the water in the lake comes from precipitation—five trillion gallons of it. Rain and snow fall directly into the crater. Rain and snow also enter the lake through runoff from its lava cliffs. Some of this water evaporates from the lake's surface, some seeps into the ground under the lake, and the remaining water keeps the lake at a depth of 1,943 feet at its deepest point. That is over one-third of a mile.

Crater Lake is the deepest lake in America and the seventh deepest lake in the world. God uses the depth of Crater Lake, the purity and clearness of its water, and the sunlight He sends on the lake to create the beautiful sapphire color of the water. Most lakes have particles in the water that make it look cloudy or dirty. Crater Lake is clear because no streams are bringing particles into it. Also, the volcanic rocks on the floor of the lake are hard. Therefore, the water is not dissolving many particles from them.

Large amounts of moss grow in Crater Lake at depths between one hundred and four hundred feet. This is possible because the water is so clear. Moss is not known to grow that deep anywhere else on earth. The lake is also home to 157 species of phytoplankton and twelve species of zooplankton. Communities of bacteria grow around the hydrothermal springs on the bottom. People stocked the lake with rainbow trout and kokanee salmon between 1888 and 1942. These fish thrive in Crater Lake.

People at Crater Lake

Archaeologists believe that people visited Mount Mazama before the volcano erupted. Sandals and other objects have been found under ash and pumice in the park. Klamath Indians tell legends about the eruption of the volcano. Look at the photo of a Klamath man at right. Native Americans told early settlers about some of America's amazing creations, but they did not tell them about Crater Lake because many viewed it as sacred. Some Native Americans today do not look at the lake because of this belief.

Klamath Man at Crater Lake in 1923

John Wesley Hillman, Isaac Skeeter, and other prospectors set out looking for a lost gold mine in 1853. While searching for it, they came upon Crater Lake. Twenty-one year old Hillman thought it was the bluest water he had ever seen. Skeeter thought they should name it Deep Blue Lake. The miners found no gold, so they left the area and the discovery was forgotten.

Another group of prospectors explored the area in 1862. The group's leader was Chauncy Nye. Nye wrote the first published description of the lake in an article for the *Oregon Sentinel* newspaper in Jacksonville, Oregon. He said that his party named it Blue Lake.

A road crew from Fort Klamath was building a wagon road in the area in 1863. Two of their hunters rediscovered the lake. Soon other soldiers and some civilians came to see it. Sergeant Orsen Stearns climbed down to the lakeshore, becoming the first person of European descent to do so. Captain F. B. Sprague also reached the shore and suggested Lake Majesty as a good name.

In 1869 James Sutton, editor of the *Oregon Sentinel,* and others went to the lake to explore in a canvas boat they had built. Five of them rode to Wizard Island. Sutton wrote an article for his newspaper, and called the lake Crater Lake. Look at the picture of boaters in 1912 at left.

Boating on Crater Lake in November, 1912

Young William Gladstone Steel

At a school in Kansas in 1870, young William Gladstone Steel unwrapped the newspaper that held his lunch. William read from the newspaper while he ate. The story about an unusual lake in Oregon fascinated him. He decided then that he would see that lake someday. He and his family moved to Portland, Oregon two years later; but it wasn't until 1885 that William made his way to Crater Lake.

When he saw its beauty, he decided that it should be preserved as a park. For the next seventeen years, Steel worked to make Crater Lake a national park. It became part of the Cascade Range Forest Reserve in 1893, but Steel was not satisfied.

He finally succeeded in 1902. That year Crater Lake and the 249 square miles around it became Crater Lake National Park. It is home to 680 species of plants. Animal species making their home there include seventy-four mammals, thirteen reptiles, thirteen amphibians, and 158 birds, including northern spotted owls, like the one on page 346. The park can be enjoyed by taking some of its ninety miles of hiking trails. Look at the hiker at left.

Tourist on the North Rim in 1962

The water of Crater Lake is pure. We have a responsibility to be pure. Jesus gave the pure in heart a wonderful promise:

Blessed are the pure in heart, for they shall see God.
Matthew 5:8

Activities for Lesson 62

Map Study – Complete the assignment for Lesson 62 on Map 2 "God's Wonders" in *Maps of America the Beautiful*.

Timeline – In *Timeline of America the Beautiful* next to 1950, write: Nine hundred and three inches of snow fall at Crater Lake.

Literature – Read "Letter from a Forty-Niner" in *We the People*, pages 62-63, and chapters 11-12 in *Bound for Oregon*.

Creative Writing – Do you think it is a good idea for the United States government to preserve certain places as National Parks? In your notebook, write two or three paragraphs giving your opinion and your reasons for it.

Student Workbook or Lesson Review – If you are using one of these optional books, complete the assignment for Lesson 62.

Portland Head Light and Other Lighthouses of Maine

The first explorers and settlers came to America in ships. Shipping has always been an important part of the American economy. Like coastlines around the world, America's shores have currents, reefs, rocks, and other hazards. Coastal weather is often foggy. Throughout American history, ships have needed lighthouses for guidance. Lighthouses help ship captains know their location, the presence of dangers, and that land is near. Lighthouses are built on coastlines, rocks, islands, and at the entrances to harbors and estuaries. Sometimes lighthouses are built right in the water. In addition to their role along America's coastlines, lighthouses are also important on the Great Lakes.

Seguin Light in Maine

Lighthouses project light at night and serve as markers during the daytime. Ship captains recognize where they are by looking at the distinct shape, size, and color of lighthouses. Some are cone-shaped, some round, some square, and some octagonal. Some have one tower; others have two. Some lighthouses have distinct designs painted on them.

Each lighthouse sends a series of flashes that is unique to that lighthouse. Ship captains use a Light List to know which lighthouse signal he is seeing. In addition to lights, many lighthouses have foghorns which help guide ships when the weather is foggy. A foghorn can be heard up to eight miles away. Some lighthouses have radio beacons that send out radio signals using Morse code. These radio beacons have a range of up to two hundred miles.

One of the world's first known lighthouses, Pharos of Alexandria, was in Egypt. It was one of the Seven Wonders of the Ancient World and stood for about 1,500 years. A famous Italian lighthouse was built in Genoa in 1161. Antonio Columbus was the lighthouse keeper there in 1449. His nephew was Christopher Columbus. When more people began sailing the world's seas after the time of Columbus, the need for lighthouses increased.

The first lighthouse in America was built in Boston Harbor in 1716. By 1800 there were twelve. America built many lighthouses during the 1800s. Many used Fresnel lenses, which French physicist Augustin Fresnel developed in 1822. The lens uses a collection of many glass prisms that bend almost all of the light into a bull's eye lens. By 1900 there were about 1,000 lighthouses in America. Sea-going vessels also used lightships for guidance in the 1800s. Lightships were placed offshore where lighthouses could not be built.

Now most lighthouses operate with automatic equipment, but early lighthouses were operated by a lighthouse keeper who lived at the lighthouse.

Baker Island Lighthouse

Bass Harbor Head Lighthouse

Boon Island Light

Maine Lighthouses of the 1850s

Many lighthouses were built during the 1850s. In this lesson, we concentrate on some of the ones built in Maine during that decade, plus a lighthouse that was ordered by George Washington. Notice the Sequin Island Lighthouse pictured on page 349. It was first established in 1795. The current tower and keeper's house were built in 1857. All of the lighthouse pictures in this lesson are from the collection of the U.S. Coast Guard.

Mount Desert Island in Maine has two lighthouses from the 1850s. In 1828 President John Quincy Adams had a wooden structure built on the highest point of the island. Its light was powered by whale oil. In 1855 it was replaced with the Baker Island Light, at left. It is made of brick; its light was once powered by lard.

An additional brick lighthouse, the Bass Harbor Head Lighthouse, was built on a Mount Desert Island cliff in 1858. At left is an aerial view of Bass Harbor Head Lighthouse.

Boon Island is nine miles east of York Beach, York, Maine. The first lighthouse on the island was built of wood in 1799. It was destroyed by a storm five years later. A second beacon was destroyed by a storm in 1832. The current granite lighthouse was first lit in 1855. It is 132 feet tall. The base is twenty-five feet across and the top is twelve feet across. A new lighthouse keeper's house was also built in 1855. In 1899 the keeper's house was mostly rebuilt and a second story was added. See the Boon Island Light at left.

Weather conditions on Boon Island are so harsh that keepers did not stay many years. Still,

Matinicus Rock Light's Twin Towers

it continued to be a manned lighthouse until a blizzard hit in 1978. The blizzard caused the keeper's home to be flooded with five feet of water. He had to seek protection in the lighthouse and was rescued by helicopter. Soon after the storm, the lighthouse was fitted with equipment so that it could run automatically without the need of a human lighthouse keeper to operate the lights.

Six miles south of Maine's Matinicus Island are the twin towers of the Matinicus Rock Light, pictured at left. Twin wooden towers were built here in 1827. In 1846 they were replaced with the current granite towers. A keeper's home was added that year. In 1855 a fog bell was added.

The Mantinicus Rock Light was made famous by a young heroine named Abbie Burgess. A violent storm hit Matinicus Island in 1856. Abbie's father, the lighthouse keeper, was away from home; and the storm kept him from coming home for several weeks. Abbie rescued her mother and younger sisters by getting them into one of the granite towers. The keeper's home washed away soon after. Abbie also kept the lighthouse lit for any ships in need. The story of Abbie Burgess' heroism is told in the book, *Keep the Lights Burning, Abbie*.

The towers were refurbished in 1857. The north light was permanently discontinued in 1924.

The Portland Head Light

Two years before becoming President, George Washington hired two masons from Portland, Maine, to take charge of building a lighthouse on Portland Head. Washington gave them detailed

Portland Head Light

instructions. He told them to take materials from the nearby fields and coastline, and he suggested they use oxen to haul the materials. Washington reminded them that the government was poor. He gave them four years to complete the work.

The first U.S. Congress, which began its work in 1789, appropriated money to complete the job these workmen had begun. The lighthouse was finished in 1790 and lit in January of 1791. The Marquis de Lafayette dedicated the Portland Head Light. Revolutionary War veteran Captain Joseph Greenleaf served as its first keeper.

As instructed by Washington, the Portland Head Light is built of rubble stone. It is lined with brick. Maine's oldest lighthouse still guides ships in the North Atlantic. It stands eighty feet above ground and 101 feet above the water. Its electric light can be seen sixteen miles away. It also has an air chime diaphragm horn that blasts for four seconds every 20 seconds during foggy weather. See picture above.

Lighthouse Facts

- The oldest original lighthouse in America still in service is in Sandy Hook, New Jersey. It was built in 1764.
- The U.S. Lighthouse Service was founded in August of 1789.
- The first lighthouses built on the Great Lakes were built in Buffalo and Erie, New York, in 1818.
- The first West Coast lighthouse built by the United States is the Alcatraz Lighthouse, built in 1854.
- The first lighthouse to use electricity is the Statue of Liberty, which was erected in 1886.
- The U.S. Lighthouse Service merged with the U.S. Coast Guard in July of 1939.
- America's newest lighthouse that stands on a shoreline was built in 1962 in Charleston, South Carolina. It is America's only triangular-shaped lighthouse and the only one with an elevator. It is the most powerful lighthouse in the Western Hemisphere.
- The tallest lighthouse in America is the 191-foot tall Cape Hatteras Light.

Lighthouses send out beacons of light to save ships from danger. Jesus sends out His light to save us from danger:

> While I am in the world, I am the Light of the world.
> John 9:5

Activities for Lesson 63

Thinking Biblically – Read John 3:19-21. Why do you think Jesus used light versus darkness to describe righteousness and truth versus evil? Write one or two paragraphs about this in your notebook.

Map Study – Complete the assignment for Lesson 63 on Map 3 "American Landmarks" in *Map of American the Beautiful*.

Timeline – In *Timeline of America the Beautiful* next to 1791, write: The Portland Head Light is lit for the first time.

Vocabulary – In your notebook, write a paragraph using all of these words: hazards, octagonal, beacon, physicist, triangular. Consult a dictionary if you need help with their definitions.

Literature – Read "Let the Lower Lights Be Burning" in *We the People*, page 64, and chapters 13-14 in *Bound for Oregon*.

Family Activity – Create a Lighthouse Painting. See the instructions on page 434.

Student Workbook or Lesson Review – If you are using one of these optional books, complete the assignment for Lesson 63.

Henry Wadsworth Longfellow, Poet

Young Longfellow

Amid the turmoil of the slavery question and the conflict between Northerners and Southerners, the calm, gentle voice of a Christian poet reminded his readers of the history they shared and of the wonder and beauty of their everyday lives. Henry Wadsworth Longfellow was a popular and influential American poet.

Longfellow was born in Portland, Maine, in 1807, when Maine was still part of Massachusetts. His father was a lawyer. While growing up, Henry enjoyed visiting the Portland Head Light. He became friends with its keeper. Henry began writing while still a child and published his first poem at age thirteen.

Henry Wadsworth Longfellow, pictured above, and his brother Stephen attended Bowdoin College, then a new college in Brunswick, Maine. The college is pictured below. Among the students there at the time were another future author, Nathaniel Hawthorne, and future President Franklin Pierce. Longfellow and Hawthorne became close friends. Hawthorne wrote prose (writing that is not poetry). Like Longfellow, he often wrote about American history. One of his most famous novels is *The Scarlet Letter*, which takes place in the colonial period of America.

Bowdoin College in Brunswick, Maine, 1902

When Longfellow graduated in 1825, Bowdoin College offered him a job as a professor if he would do further study in Europe. He toured Europe extensively and studied there for four years. Longfellow returned to Bowdoin in 1829. He taught French and Spanish from textbooks he wrote himself. He also served as the college librarian.

In 1831 Longfellow married Mary Potter. After teaching for six years at Bowdoin, he was offered a position at Harvard College in Cambridge, Massachusetts. Before taking the position, he and Mary went to Europe. While they were in the Netherlands, in late 1835, Mary died. Longfellow was devastated by her death. He continued his European travels to relieve his depression. In the Swiss Alps, he met the Appleton family from Boston and fell in love with their daughter Fanny. She did not return his love. The next year Longfellow came back to America and began a nineteen-year teaching career at Harvard. In 1839 he published his first book of poetry.

Longfellow continued to woo Fanny Appleton. After seven years, she married him in 1843. See Fanny's picture at right. Henry and Fanny had six children, including the three girls pictured on page 355. In 1854 Longfellow left Harvard to concentrate on writing. He and his family continued to live in Cambridge. Longfellow was perhaps the first American who made his living as a full-time author. His family supplied him with loving support.

Fanny Appleton Longfellow

Fanny died after suffering burns in an accident at home in 1861. Longfellow was heartbroken. A month after her death, he wrote these words to her sister: "I thank God hourly—as I have from the beginning—for the beautiful life we led together, and that I loved her more and more to the end." Longfellow's own face was badly burned as he tried to help his wife during the accident. He grew a beard to conceal his injuries, as seen on page 356.

Longfellow's poetry was loved by his countrymen. He became famous in America and in Europe. Both Oxford and Cambridge Universities in England gave him honorary degrees. One of the highest honors Longfellow received came after his death in 1882. His bust was placed in Poet's Corner in Westminster Abbey in London. Edward the Confessor began Westminster Abbey in 1050. It is here that Great Britain has crowned each of its kings and queens beginning with William the Conqueror in 1066. Famous poets and scientists are buried in Westminster Abbey, and it has many monuments to famous people. The section called Poet's Corner has tributes to famous writers such as William Shakespeare. Henry Wadsworth Longfellow was the first American to be honored in Poet's Corner.

Longfellow wrote with humor and with an understanding of people's deepest feelings. He made Americans feel good about their history. He penned some of the most famous lines of American poetry.

In *The Courtship of Miles Standish*, Longfellow writes about one of the early Pilgrims (see page 80). In this fictionalized poem, he tells of an encounter between young Priscilla and her suitor, John Alden:

> Archly the maiden smiled, and, with eyes overrunning with laughter,
> Said, in a tremulous voice, "Why don't you speak for yourself, John?"

The phrase, "Why don't you speak for yourself, John?" became a popular American saying.

Longfellow's poem *Evangeline* tells of French Canadians whom the British exiled from Canada in 1755. Many Acadians went to Louisiana, the closest French-speaking colony. The Acadians there became known as Cajuns. *Evangeline* begins with these beautiful words:

This is the forest primeval.
The murmuring pines and the hemlocks . . . .

Longfellow's "Paul Revere's Ride" carries us back to the beginning of the American Revolution. It reminds us that Revere hurried "through every Middlesex village and farm" to call colonial militiamen to gather their arms and fight the British. It begins:

Listen, my children, and you shall hear
Of the midnight ride of Paul Revere.

Longfellow helped people appreciate the sounds of Native American speech in his epic poem, *Song of Hiawatha*. The poem is set in Minnesota. It mixes various native cultures. The story is based on an Ojibwe legend. Many words in the poem are Ojibwe and Dakota Sioux. Longfellow based his poem on the research of Henry Rowe Schoolcraft and his wife, who was half Ojibwe (see page 287). The *Song of Hiawatha* sold 50,000 copies during the first two years after it was published. Famous lines from that poem are:

By the shores of Gitche Gumee,
By the shining Big Sea-Water,
Stood the wigwam of Nokomis,
Daughter of the Moon, Nokomis.
Dark behind it rose the forest,
Rose the black and gloomy pine-trees,
Rose the firs with cones upon them;
Bright before it beat the water,
Beat the clear and sunny water,
Beat the shining Big Sea-Water.

"Gitche Gumee" is the Ojibwe term for Lake Superior.

Besides historic themes, Longfellow's poems also portray the intimacy of family life. In "The Children's Hour," he writes:

Between the dark and the daylight,
When the night is beginning to lower,
Comes a pause in the day's occupations,
That is known as the Children's Hour.

Daughters Alice, Edith, and Anne Allegra

He teaches us about the integrity and hard work of a father in "The Village Blacksmith." It begins:

Under a spreading chestnut tree
The village smithy stands;
The smith, a mighty man is he,
With large and sinewy hands;
And the muscles of his brawny arms
Are strong as iron bands.

When Longfellow turned seventy years old in 1877, America celebrated with him. The children of Cambridge, Massachusetts, presented him with a chair. A plaque on the chair read:

> To the author of "The Village Blacksmith." This chair made from the wood of the spreading chestnut tree is presented as an expression of grateful regard and veneration by the children of Cambridge, who with their friends join in the best wishes and congratulations on this anniversary.

Henry Wadsworth Longfellow

Longfellow experienced personal sadness in his life with the loss of both of his wives. Still, he hung on to his faith and to hope as Jesus taught us to do:

> These things I have spoken to you, so that in Me you may have peace.
> In the world you have tribulation, but take courage; I have overcome the world.
> John 16:33

Activities for Lesson 64

Timeline – In *Timeline of America the Beautiful* next to 1877, write: Henry Wadsworth Longfellow is honored on his 70th birthday.

Vocabulary – In your notebook, copy each of the following sentences. Fill in each blank with the correct word from this list: turmoil, devastated, honorary, penned, culture.

1. Hawthorne _____ *The Scarlet Letter* long after the colonial days when it is set.
2. Even though Tommy couldn't finish the race after he was injured, he was given an _____ medal.
3. I learned a lot about the _____ of Italy while we had an Italian exchange student last year.
4. Our family was in _____ when our flight was cancelled on Christmas Eve.
5. The village was _____ by the long battle fought there.

Literature – Read "Poems of Longfellow" in *We the People*, pages 65-66, and chapter 15 in *Bound for Oregon*.

Creative Writing – In your notebook, write a poem of ten or more lines. (Rhyming dictionaries are helpful when writing poetry.)

Student Workbook or Lesson Review – If you are using one of these optional books, complete the assignment for Lesson 64.

Stagecoaches and the Pony Express

With so many people moving west, Americans had an increasing need for better ways to travel and a faster way for easterners and westerners to communicate. Businessmen formed stagecoach companies to transport people and mail in the west. For a short time, the Pony Express carried mail.

Stagecoaches

Stagecoaches had been popular in England. Settlers began using them soon after they formed colonies in America. A stagecoach was an enclosed wagon that carried passengers between stages. A stage was a stop where passengers found food and lodging and where the driver could get fresh horses. Look at the photo below.

Stagecoaches used in the American West had two bench seats attached to the outside of the coach, one in front and one in back. A driver and a guard sat on the front seat. Additional guards or travelers sat on the back seat. On top of the coach was a space for luggage and packages. Six to nine passengers sat inside the coach. Underneath was a suspension system that made the ride more comfortable on the rough Western roads than older coaches had been.

A typical coach weighed about 2,500 pounds. Stagecoaches often carried mail in the cargo space on top. Roads that carried mail were sometimes called post roads. A team of four to six horses could pull the weight of the coach, the passengers, and the baggage between five and twelve miles per hour. By the end of the nineteenth century, stagecoaches were replaced by railroads, which were faster, safer, and more reliable.

A California Roadside Inn and Stagecoach in the 1850s

Wells Fargo

In 1852 the Wells Fargo company began providing banking and shipping services in the West. It opened offices first in San Francisco and then in many new towns and mining camps. Wells Fargo used whatever shipping method was fastest. In the 1860s, the company became involved in the stagecoach business.

357

Wells Fargo used Concord Coaches, designed by carriage maker Stephen Abbot and master wheelwright Lewis Downing. A carriage maker and a wheelwright are pictured on pages 122-123. Concord Coaches used strips of thick bull hide to keep the coach from jarring the horses. It also gave passengers a gentler ride. Author Mark Twain called the Concord Coach, "an imposing cradle on wheels."

Wells Fargo stagecoaches carried a green treasure box under the driver's seat. The boxes were

Wells Fargo Warehouse as Seen in Harper's New Monthly Magazine

Wells Fargo Employee with Shipments

made of Ponderosa pine, oak, and iron. Coins, checks, gold bars, gold dust, and legal papers were transported in them. As a result, they were highly prized by highway bandits. Shotgun messengers protected the green treasure boxes. One of the West's most famous sheriffs was Wyatt Earp; he once worked as a shotgun messenger. A masked bandit called Black Bart managed to rob twenty-seven stagecoaches. After detectives working for Wells Fargo caught him, he was placed in San Quentin prison. He is pictured at right.

Notice the Wells Fargo employee at left and a Wells Fargo warehouse above.

The Pony Express

Before the Pony Express began, mail headed for California was carried over a 2,800 mile southern route around South America or it was shipped to Panama, taken across the isthmus, and then shipped to California. With fears of a Civil War, leaders began to search for an alternate route. The Federal government offered to give a contract to a company that could provide this service. Businessmen William Russell, Alexander Majors, and William Waddell formed the Central Overland California & Pike's Peak Express Company. They won the contract and the Pony Express was born.

In 1860 railroads could carry mail as far as St. Joseph, Missouri. The Pony Express offered to carry it between St. Joseph and Sacramento, California, in ten days. The company purchased four hundred horses, mostly thoroughbreds, Morgans, mustangs, and pintos. They built stables along the route. See the Fort Bridger, Wyoming, stables on page 359.

An advertisement in a California newspaper solicited riders. It asked for young, skinny, wiry fellows, who were expert riders, under eighteen, and willing to risk death daily. When hired, riders were given a Bible. They had to agree to no drinking, gambling, or swearing.

The Pony Express had 165 stations that were ten to fifteen miles apart. A rider and his horse left a station, carrying a leather mail bag called a mochila. At the next station, the

Black Bart

Pony Express Stables at Fort Bridger, Wyoming

rider switched horses. After about seventy-five miles, the rider rested and a new rider continued the journey. On one occasion, Bob Haslam rode for 380 miles through Nevada.

The route was dangerous, but according to legend, the Pony Express only lost one bag of mail. At first they carried mail once a week, but later they carried it twice a week. Pony Express riders carried mail from east to west and from west to east. The route was dry and dusty in summer. Riders battled ice and snow in the winter. Pony Express riders carried twenty pounds of mail and twenty-five pounds of equipment. The charge was $5.00 per half ounce, so people began using thinner paper for letters and newspapers.

The first delivery was big news. Riders started out from both St. Joseph and Sacramento on April 3, 1860. The last rider on the eastbound run arrived in St. Joseph ten days after the first rider had left Sacramento. The last rider on the westbound run arrived in Sacramento after eleven days. During the last few miles, bands played and crowds cheered. While the Pony Express was in business, the average length of a run was ten days in summer and twelve to fourteen days in winter.

One hundred eighty-three men served as Pony Express riders. The oldest rider was in his mid-forties, but most were about twenty. Most of them weighed about 120 pounds. Their salary was $25 per week. One Pony Express rider was William Frederick Cody, who became known as Buffalo Bill. Cody was fourteen years old when he rode for the Pony Express. He later formed the Buffalo Bill Cody's Wild West Show.

Broncho Charlie Miller was an actor in the Wild West Show. (Bronco is the correct spelling for an untrained horse, but Charlie spelled his name Broncho.) Miller claimed to have ridden for the Pony Express when he was eleven years old. He died in New York in 1955.

Wells Fargo took over during the last few months the Pony Express was in business. The Pony Express had worked well, but it was not financially successful. It operated for only eighteen months, ending in late October of 1861. The Pony Express had carried 34,753 letters. During its existence, the use of telegraphs was increasing. On October 24, 1861, the work of putting up telegraph lines from the east coast to the west coast was completed. At right is an illustration of a Pony Express rider passing a man putting up telegraph poles. With the telegraph in use, the Pony Express was no longer needed.

Pony Express Rider and Telegraph Installers,
Harper's Weekly *Illustration, November 2, 1867*

Pony Express Rider

The Pony Express played an important role during its short history. These young men carried the news in 1860 that Abraham Lincoln had been elected President. They carried the text of his Inaugural Address the next year in just seven days and seventeen hours, the fastest run the Pony Express ever achieved! The Pony Express ran long enough to inform California that the Civil War had begun.

Though the Pony Express was not the first mail delivery company in the West, it is the most famous. In the 1950s, a portion of the original Pikes Peak Stables that the Pony Express used in St. Joseph, Missouri, became the Pony Express Museum. In 2010, the museum celebrated the 150th anniversary of the founding of the Pony Express.

The Pony Express is an American legend. It represents American determination and courage. Every year, riders honor those brave men by retracing the route of the Pony Express. We also must be courageous:

> Be stong and let your heart take courage,
> All you who hope in the Lord.
> Psalm 31:24

Activities for Lesson 65

Thinking Biblically – Read Job 39:19-25, which praises God for his amazing creation of the horse.

Map Study – Complete the assignments for Lesson 65 on Map 18 "The West" in *Maps of America the Beautiful*.

Timeline – In *Timeline of America the Beautiful* next to 1852 write: The Wells Fargo company begins providing banking and shipping services in the West.

Literature – Read chapter 16 and "Author's Note" in *Bound for Oregon*.

Creative Writing – In your notebook, write a story of at least one page about an adventure of a Pony Express rider. Include some historical details you learned in this lesson.

Student Workbook or Lesson Review – If you are using one of these optional books, complete the assignment for Lesson 65. If you are using the Lesson Review, answer the questions on *Bound for Oregon* and take the quiz for Unit 13.

A Nation Divided

Abraham Lincoln was President during the hard times of America's Civil War. Lincoln delivered his Gettysburg Address when a cemetery was created as a burial ground for the thousands of soldiers who died during the Battle of Gettysburg. Confederate General Robert E. Lee is considered one of the greatest generals in American history. He consistently led his men to victory against superior forces. Women played an important role in the Civil War, on the home front and on the battlefield. The First Ladies of the Union and the Confederacy served alongside their husbands for the causes they believed in.

President Abraham Lincoln and his Wife Mary Todd Lincoln, with Sons Thomas, at Left, and Robert Todd, at Center

Lessons in Unit 14

Lesson 66 – Our American Story: The Civil War

Lesson 67 – An American Landmark: Gettysburg Battlefield and Cemetery

Lesson 68 – An American Biography: Robert E. Lee, Gentleman from Virginia

Lesson 69 – Daily Life: Women in the Civil War

Lesson 70 – Daily Life: Two First Ladies

Books Used in Unit 14

- *Maps of America the Beautiful*

- *Timeline of America the Beautiful*

- *We the People*

- *Across Five Aprils* by Irene Hunt

The Civil War

The conflicts over slavery that had brewed throughout the 1850s were about to erupt. America was about to divide. The election of 1860 was a major turning point in the conflict between North and South.

Election of 1860

As the 1860 election drew near, Democrats could not agree on a candidate. Northern Democrats nominated Stephen Douglas from Illinois, while southern Democrats nominated John C. Breckenridge from Kentucky. Former Whigs formed a new party called the Constitutional Union. They nominated John Bell from Tennessee.

The Republican Party was new, less than ten years old. Many Republicans thought the obvious choice was William Seward, a Senator from New York. However, he was strongly anti-slavery; and many Republicans believed that would keep him from winning. They wanted someone more moderate. In the end they chose Abraham Lincoln, a lawyer from Illinois, and Hannibal Hamlin from Maine, as their presidential and vice-presidential candidates. The Republicans adopted a written

*Lincoln and Hamlin
Campaign Button*

statement of their beliefs called a party platform. In it, they stated three main points: John Brown was wrong to raid the Harper's Ferry arsenal; states can make their own decisions without the Federal government telling them what to do; and slavery should not extend into new territories.

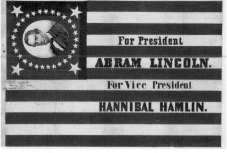

Lincoln and Hamlin Campaign Banner

At left is a large cloth banner used in the Lincoln-Hamlin campaign. It was designed in the style of a United States flag with stars representing thirty-three states. Lincoln also used the new technology of photography to become known to the public. Above is a campaign button with a photograph of Lincoln on one side and Hamlin on the other. After a hard campaign, Lincoln and Hamlin won the election.

Secession Meeting in South Carolina, Frank Leslie's Illustrated Newspaper, *December 1, 1860*

Secession

Between the election and the inauguration, Lincoln tried to reassure the South that he would not interfere with slavery there. Southerners were not convinced. States began to secede. President James Buchanan announced that secession was wrong, but he did not believe he could prevent it. By the time Lincoln was inaugurated, seven states had seceded from the Union, in this order: South Carolina, Mississippi, Florida, Alabama, Georgia, Louisiana, and Texas. Notice illustration at left.

Confederate States of America

In February of 1861, representatives of the seven seceded states met in Alabama to form a new country, the Confederate States of America. They adopted a Constitution similar to the U.S. Constitution. Representatives from these states elected Jefferson Davis, a former U.S. Senator from Mississippi, to be their President. Georgia Senator Alexander Hamilton Stephens became Vice President. The Confederates seized Federal property within their states, including post offices, arsenals, and forts.

Lincoln's First Inauguration

At right is an illustration of President-elect Lincoln and President Buchanan (tipping his hat) on their way to the inauguration. When Lincoln gave his inaugural address on March 4, 1861, he again said that he would not interfere with slavery where it already existed. He said that the Union was permanent, secession was wrong, and if war began it would be the South's fault.

Lincoln's First Inauguration, Harper's Weekly

The First Shots Are Fired at Fort Sumter

Federal troops remained at Fort Sumter which is on an island near Charleston, South Carolina. South Carolinians refused to let supplies be brought into the fort. Lincoln decided to send them anyway and informed the South Carolina Governor of his decision. Confederate General P. G. T. Beauregard demanded that the Federals at Fort Sumter surrender. They refused, and the Confederates opened fire early on the morning of April 12. The cannon fire lasted twenty-six hours. Finally the Federal troops surrendered. During the surrender ceremony, one Union soldier died and one was mortally wounded when a cannon accidentally exploded. They were the first two casualties of the Civil War.

Americans Fight One Another

On April 13, 1861, Abraham Lincoln asked for 75,000 volunteers for the Union Army. See at right a soldier serving in the 22nd New York state militia in 1861. Lincoln announced that southern ports would be blocked. As a result, four more states decided to leave the Union: Virginia, Arkansas, North Carolina, and Tennessee. Not only was the country divided, but northerners and southerners were divided among themselves. Some counties in

Soldier from 22nd New York State Militia, 1861

western Virginia seceded from Virginia to remain in the Union. About 100,000 southerners fought for the Union and many people in northern states went south to fight for the Confederacy. Many families were divided. J. E. B. Stuart served as a general for the Confederacy, but his father-in-law fought with the Union.

Both the North and the South thought the war would be over soon and that it would be easy to win. In reality it lasted four long years. Three million Americans served either in the Union Army or the Confederate Army. Over 600,000 people died. The war cost $6.5 billion.

The National Park Service has identified 384 significant battles fought in twenty-six states. Of those battles, 294 were in Confederate states. The chart at right tells how many battles were fought in each state.

As the war progressed, northerners and southerners even called battles by different names. Northerners often named them for nearby bodies of water, while southerners often named them for nearby towns or landmarks. In this lesson, the northern battle name is given first and the southern battle name is in parentheses.

Number of Battles by State	
Virginia	123
Tennessee	38
Missouri	29
Georgia	28
Louisiana	23
North Carolina	20
Arkansas	17
Mississippi	16
West Virginia	15
Kentucky	11
South Carolina	11
Alabama	7
Maryland	7
Oklahoma	7
Florida	6
North Dakota	5
Texas	5
Kansas	4
Minnesota	2
New Mexico	2
Ohio	2
Pennsylvania	2
Colorado	1
Idaho	1
Indiana	1

The First Battle of the Civil War

After Union forces surrendered at Fort Sumter, Confederate forces gathered in July at Manassas, Virginia, near Bull Run Creek, about twenty-five miles from Washington, D.C. Hundreds of residents of Washington, D.C., rode out in carriages to watch the battle. They thought Union soldiers would easily defeat the Confederates. When the Confederate Army won, Union soldiers and spectators quickly retreated back to Washington. No other major battles took place until 1862.

1862

Early in 1862, Union forces began taking control of Confederate rivers and railroads in Tennessee and Mississippi. They defeated

Confederate troops at Fort Donelson and Fort Henry on the Tennessee and Cumberland Rivers in Tennessee, and then they captured the city of Nashville, Tennessee. The next Union goal was to take control of the major railroad center at Corinth in northern Mississippi. Before northern forces reached Corinth, Union and Confederate forces fought in southwestern Tennessee in the Battle of Pittsburg Landing (also called Shiloh). Both sides lost over 10,000 men, but the Union was victorious and continued south to capture Corinth. Southerners named the battle for a small nearby church. Though the building was destroyed in the weeks after the battle, the Shiloh church is still an active congregation. At right are illustrations of Shiloh Church and a scene from Pittsburg Landing on the Tennessee River.

Shiloh Church

The Confederates were stronger in Virginia and won the second Battle at Bull Run (also called Manassas) in August of 1862. In September southern General Robert E. Lee attempted an invasion of the North. Though neither side won a decisive victory in the Battle of Antietam (also called Sharpsburg) in Maryland, the Confederate Army retreated after one day of fighting.

Union forces stationed in Nashville headed southeast toward a major railroad center at Chattanooga, Tennessee. Confederate forces moved to defend the city. As the Union armies advanced toward Chattanooga, they defeated a Confederate force at Murfreesboro, which lies between Nashville and Chattanooga.

Scene from Battle of Pittsburg Landing, Sunday, April 6, 1862, from
Frank Leslie's Illustrated Newspaper

1863

On January 1, 1863, President Lincoln issued the Emancipation Proclamation, freeing all slaves in the areas still in rebellion. Slaves in Kentucky, Maryland, Missouri, and the portions of the Confederacy controlled by Union forces remained in bondage. Lincoln believed that this would give the North a moral reason to keep fighting. At left is a picture of Lincoln and his cabinet at the first reading of the proclamation.

On June 20, 1863, the counties that seceded from Virginia joined the Union as the new state of West Virginia. It was the 35th state.

Lincoln, third from left, and His Cabinet at the First Reading of the Emancipation Proclamation

The Confederates tried again to invade the North, but Union forces defeated them at the Battle of Gettysburg in Pennsylvania on July 1-3. On July 4, Union forces in the South won the Battle of Vicksburg in Mississippi. Vicksburg is on the Mississippi River. A few days later, Union forces captured Chattanooga and headed for Atlanta, Georgia.

1864

In March Lincoln made Ulysses S. Grant commander of all Union forces. Since he had led the Union victories at Shiloh, Vicksburg, and Chattanooga, Lincoln hoped he could defeat the Confederates in Virginia, too. In September Union forces under General William T. Sherman gained control of Atlanta, Georgia. He headed toward Savannah on the southeast Georgia coastline. His troops destroyed a wide path through Georgia as they headed southeast. In November Lincoln was re-elected for a second term as President. His Vice President was Andrew Johnson, a Democrat from Tennessee. Late in 1864, Confederates tried to recapture Nashville, but were soundly defeated. In December General Sherman reached the Georgia coastline, capturing Savannah.

New States Admitted

1863 West Virginia
1864 Nevada

Throughout the war, the Federal government continued to conduct other business such as the addition of Nevada as the 36th state in 1864.

1865

On March 4, Abraham Lincoln delivered his second inaugural address. Just over a month later, on April 9, General Robert E. Lee's Army of Northern Virginia surrendered to General Ulysses S. Grant at Appomattox Court House, Virginia. Other Confederate forces surrendered during the next few months.

A Soldier's Life

Most men in the Civil War were not professional soldiers. Most had volunteered or had been drafted by either the Union or the Confederacy. A drafted soldier has been told by his government that he must serve as a soldier. Sometimes a wealthy man paid a poorer man to fight for him. Most soldiers on both sides of the war were from small towns or farms.

Battles were actually rare occurrences in a soldier's life. They spent a great deal of time marching and camping. Soldiers usually slept outdoors. When it rained, there was usually

Confederate Buttons and Buckles

Confederate Mess Articles, Used for Eating

Confederate Diary and Other Belongings

no dry place to go. Southern soldiers were often without adequate food, clothing, and shelter. Though Union soldiers had better equipment and food than Confederate soldiers, both suffered hardships. Notice Confederate artifacts in the photos on page 366 and Union officers at right.

Officers from the Seventeenth New York Battery, 1863

A soldier lived a regimented life. A typical day might go something like this: the soldier awoke when he heard the bugle sounds of reveille and then had breakfast, cleaned up the camp, and found firewood. Before and after lunch, he and his fellow soldiers practiced skills needed in battle. This was called drill. Late in the afternoon, he tidied up his uniform and cleaned his weapons, to be ready for roll call and inspection, after which he

Confederate Bugle

participated in a dress parade. After receiving his supper rations, he had free time until the evening tattoo, which was a final roll call for the day. He went to bed after the tattoo, unless he was serving on picket duty, which meant he would guard the camp while others slept.

During free time, soldiers relieved boredom by playing marbles, jackstraws (a form of pick-up sticks), checkers, cards, and chess. Soldiers also wrote in diaries or wrote letters home. Notice the diary on page 366. Soldiers who were illiterate at the beginning of the war sometimes learned how to write from fellow soldiers and officers so that they could communicate with their loved ones at home.

Soldiers had to obey orders from superior officers or they would be punished. Sometimes they would be humiliated or lose some of their pay. Soldiers could even be executed for the most serious crimes, like secretly leaving the Army without permission. This was called desertion.

Soldiers used many of their pre-war skills while serving in the military. Musicians might be called upon to play the fife or bugle. Look at the bugle above. Young boys often served as drummers. A blacksmith could serve the Army by shoeing horses and repairing things made of iron. Doctors served by caring for the sick and wounded. See the surgeon illustration and photograph of a blacksmith below.

"A Surgeon at Work," by Winslow Homer, Published July, 1862

Union Blacksmith Shop at Petersburg, Virginia, 1864

"Pickets Trading Between the Lines" by Edwin Forbes   Civil War Drawing by Waud

Southerners called Union soldiers and other northerners "Yankees." Yankee soldiers wore blue uniforms. Northerners referred to southerners as "Rebels." Confederate soldiers were called Johnny Rebs. Though the Civil War is often talked of as a conflict between "The Blue and the Gray," southern soldiers often wore whatever they could get. Notice the Confederate buckles and buttons at the bottom of page 366. Sometimes Yankees and Rebels didn't act like enemies. At night, neighboring camps of Yankees and Rebels might sing together in the darkness. Notice the drawing above where Union and Confederate picket guards are trading with one another.

Of course, soldiers were also called upon to fight. Many former slaves and free blacks fought bravely for the Union. The *Harper's Weekly* illustration at right is entitled "A Negro Regiment in Action."

Civil War News and Civil War History

We learn a great deal about the Civil War through letters and diaries kept by soldiers and civilians. A civilian is a person who is not serving in the military. We can also learn about it through illustrations, photographs, memoirs, books, and articles. The war was constantly reported in newspapers at the time. Illustrators, like Winslow Homer, Thomas Nast, and Alfred R. Waud drew for *Harper's Weekly*. Edwin Forbes drew for *Frank Leslie's Illustrated Newspaper*. Notice the illustration by Homer at

"A Negro Regiment in Action"
by Thomas Nast

"Soldier Reading" by Edwin Forbes
September, 1863

368

1864 Thomas Nast Illustration for Harper's Weekly: *"The Press. The Field. The Sketchbook."*

bottom left on page 367 and those by Waud, Nast, and Forbes on these two pages.

In 1864 Thomas Nast created "The Press. The Field. The Sketchbook." At top are scenes showing how *Harper's Weekly* reporters and artists gathered information in the camp and on the battlefield. At the bottom of the illustration are a family reading a newspaper at home and soldiers reading a newspaper in camp, with an open sketchbook in between.

Matthew Brady in July, 1861, After Photographing the Battle of Bull Run

By the time the war began, Matthew Brady was a well-known photographer. He felt it was his responsibility to photograph the war. Brady and his employees traveled with the Union Army to do so. He is the most famous Civil War photographer. Photos taken by his employees were also labeled "Photo by Brady," so it is not always possible to know which ones Matthew Brady actually took. Above is a photograph of Matthew Brady taken after he photographed the Battle of Bull Run.

A Final Sadness

Five days after Lee's surrender, while the Union was celebrating victory, President Lincoln was killed by an assassin. He died the following day on April 15, 1865. Read about Lincoln's life on pages 370-371.

Abraham Lincoln
America's Sixteenth President
March 4, 1861 - April 15, 1865

Abraham Lincoln was born in a log cabin in Kentucky in 1809. His parents were Thomas and Nancy Hanks Lincoln. When he was seven years old, his family moved to southern Indiana. His mother died when he was nine years old. His father later married Sarah Bush Johnston, who had three children. Abraham's only sister died when he was nineteen years old. Two years later, Lincoln's family, including his stepmother's children, moved to Illinois.

In the spring of 1830, Lincoln set out on his own. A businessman hired him to take a load of produce down the Mississippi River to New Orleans on a flatboat, something he had done once before while in Indiana. These experiences gave him insight into the terrible impact of slavery on human lives. When he came back to Illinois, he settled in New Salem. There he tried several occupations, including co-owning a store, serving in the militia during the Black Hawk war, serving as a postmaster, and surveying.

Lincoln's political career began in 1832. He ran for a seat in the Illinois legislature, but lost. In 1834 he tried again and was elected. While in the legislature, he studied law. He became an attorney in 1837. Soon he moved to the state capital in Springfield, Illinois, to practice law.

In Springfield, Lincoln built his career. He met and married Mary Todd from Kentucky. After the birth of their first son, Robert, Lincoln and his wife purchased a home in Springfield. It was the only home they ever owned. Their second son, Edward, called Eddie, was born there in 1846, the same year that Lincoln was elected to the U.S. House of Representatives. Lincoln served for one two-year term. His family joined him in Washington for part of the term, but they lived mainly in Springfield. Early in 1850, little Eddie died after an illness. He was almost four years old. That December, William, called Willie, was born. In 1853 Mary gave birth to Thomas, whom Lincoln called Tad.

In 1858 Lincoln was chosen as the Republican candidate to run against Democrat Stephen Douglas for a seat in the U.S. Senate. When he accepted the Republican nomination, he gave his now-famous "House Divided" speech. In it he quoted Jesus' words, "a house divided against itself cannot stand." During the campaign, Lincoln and Douglas had seven public debates. Lincoln lost the election to Douglas.

Two years later in 1860, Lincoln ran for President of the United States. In November he was elected as America's sixteenth President. Abraham and Mary Lincoln and their sons Willie and Tad left home on February 11, 1861 (Robert was already living away from home at college). One thousand people came to the Springfield depot. They stood in the drizzling rain to say goodbye to a good friend. It took twelve days to get to Washington. Along the way, Lincoln gave speeches.

Even powerful people like the President of the United States can learn from children. A few weeks before the election, Abraham Lincoln got a letter from an eleven-year-old girl from New York. She told him he should grow a beard. When Lincoln was inaugurated, he became America's first President with a beard.

While Abraham Lincoln was President, he served as Commander-in-Chief of the armed forces as they fought in a civil war against people who had formerly been fellow citizens. His

family had a personal tragedy during the war. Eleven-year-old Willie died when Lincoln had been in office less than a year.

At left is a photograph of Lincoln with his son Tad. It was taken during Lincoln's presidency. The photgraph of Mary Todd Lincoln on page 370 was also taken while the family lived in Washington. It is a Brady photograph.

Lincoln was elected to a second term in 1864. Soon after his inauguration the next year, the war ended. On April 14, 1865, he and his wife Mary went to see a play at Ford's Theatre in Washington, D.C. While they watched the play "Our American Cousin," actor John Wilkes Booth shot the President. Lincoln died the next morning at a nearby boarding house. Lincoln was fifty-six years old. The photograph of Lincoln on page 370 is thought to be his last. It was probably taken in February of 1865. The original hangs in the Smithsonian's National Portrait Gallery in Washington, D. C.

A funeral service for Lincoln was held at the White House. A funeral train then took Lincoln's body from Washington to Springfield, Illinois, where he was buried. Hundreds of thousands of mourners came to pay their respects during the two-week journey.

Though these words from 2 Samuel tell about Israel's King Saul, they are an appropriate summary of what happened in America in 1865.

How have the mighty fallen,
And the weapons of war perished.
2 Samuel 1:27

Activities for Lesson 66

Map Study – Complete the assignments for Lesson 66 on Map 19 "The Civil War" and on Map 20 "The Lower 48" in *Maps of America the Beautiful*.

Timeline – In *Timeline of America the Beautiful* next to 1861, write: Union and Confederate forces meet at the first Battle of Bull Run.

Literature – Read "Letters from Abraham Lincoln" in *We the People*, page 67, and chapter 1 in *Across Five Aprils*.

Student Workbook or Lesson Review – If you are using one of these optional books, complete the assignment for Lesson 66.

Gettysburg Battlefield and Cemetery

Confederate Prisoners After the Battle of Gettysburg

In the summer of 1863, General Robert E. Lee and his Army of Northern Virginia invaded the North. On July 1, Union and Confederate troops converged near the little town of Gettysburg, Pennsylvania. On July 1 and 2, the Confederates were winning, but on July 3, Union forces gained control of the battle. Lee ordered his Army to withdraw to Virginia. At left are Confederate prisoners the Union Army captured. This battle is called the "High Water Mark of the Rebellion." Never would the South have the upper hand again. Hopes for an independent Confederate States of America ended, though the war raged on for almost two more years.

The battle was devastating to little Gettysburg and the farms around it. Wounded soldiers filled churches, public buildings, and many homes. The Union Army soon set up a hospital nearby. The wounded were taken there before being carried to hospitals in Baltimore, Philadelphia, and Washington, D.C. The Sanitary Commission and another benevolent group, the Christian Commission, helped treat over 20,000 wounded soldiers from both the Union and Confederate armies.

Thousands of Union soldiers who had died in the battle were buried in temporary graves around Gettysburg. Residents of Gettysburg wanted to provide them a better burial ground. They appealed to the Governor of Pennsylvania, asking that the state purchase

Gettysburg National Military Park

part of the battlefield for a proper cemetery. The state appointed a local lawyer to coordinate the effort and hired a landscape architect to design it. The Soldier's National Cemetery was dedicated in November of 1863.

The Gettysburg Address

An elaborate dedication ceremony was held on November 19, 1863. It included prayers, songs, and a speech by a famous orator, Edward Everett. He spoke for two hours; President Abraham Lincoln spoke for two minutes. It is his Gettysburg Address that is remembered from that day.

Lincoln began by reminding the assembled crowd what Americans had done "fourscore and seven years" before when they "brought forth on this continent a new nation,

Abraham Lincoln, November, 1863

conceived in liberty and dedicated to the proposition that all men are created equal." He told them that they were there to dedicate a portion of the battlefield as a "final resting-place for those who here gave their lives that that nation might live." He called on the North to renew their own devotion to the "cause for which they gave the last full measure of devotion." Lincoln expressed his hope "that these dead shall not have died in vain, that this nation under God shall have a new birth of freedom, and that government of the people, by the people, for the people shall not perish from the earth." Above is a photo of Lincoln taken around the time of the dedication.

Remembering Gettysburg

The Gettysburg Battlefield Memorial Association was formed in 1864 to honor the Union soldiers who fought there by preserving the battlefield. In 1895 General Daniel Sickles sponsored legislation in Congress to create the Gettysburg National Military Park. See photo at left. Sickles fought in the Battle of Gettysburg. He lost a leg in the battle, thus ending his military career. A commission of Civil War veterans managed the park as a memorial to both the Union and Confederate armies who fought there. In 1933 the park became part of the National Park Service.

Sunset at Gettysburg National Military Park

Gettysburg Camp 50th Anniversary, July, 1913

*Stone Union Infantryman Statue
at Gettysburg National Military Park*

*The sun rises over Gettysburg's Cemetery Ridge with
the North Carolina monument in the foreground.*

Bronze Statue of Union Soldier

*Monument of the
42nd New York Infantry*

Gettysburg National Military Park includes many monuments that individual states erected to honor their citizens who served in the Civil War. See monuments and statues at left and above.

On page 375 are a photograph of Alfred R. Waud making a sketch at Gettysburg, a Gettysburg battle scene that appeared in *Harper's Weekly*, and a sketch Waud drew of a Union general at Gettysburg.

In July of 1913, over 50,000 veterans of both the Union and Confederate armies gathered at Gettysburg to commemorate the fiftieth anniversary of the battle. See the photograph of that encampment on page 374. Each year thousands of visitors from around the world visit Gettysburg. They drive through the huge battleground and see strategic places where brave soldiers on both sides fought for what they believed to be right.

Learning about the battles of the Civil War can remind us of the blessings of peace and make us want to live lives of peace. Remember Paul's words:

Alfred R. Waud creates Harper's Weekly *illustrations at Gettysburg.*

> If possible, so far as it depends on you,
> be at peace with all men.
> Romans 12:18

Activities for Lesson 67

Thinking Biblically – Even in the midst of terrible battles, God is sovereign. Copy Proverbs 21:31 into your notebook.

This Gettysburg Battle Scene created by Waud appeared in Harper's Weekly *on August 8, 1863.*

Map Study – Complete the assignment for Lesson 67 on Map 3 "American Landmarks" in *Maps of America the Beautiful*.

Timeline – In *Timeline of America the Beautiful* next to 1913, write: Over 50,000 Union and Confederate veterans gather for the fiftieth anniversary of the Battle of Gettysburg.

Vocabulary – Look up each of these words in a dictionary: converge, rebellion, temporary, elaborate, veteran. Copy each word and its definition in your notebook.

Literature – Read "The Gettysburg Address" in *We the People*, page 68, and chapters 2-3 in *Across Five Aprils*.

Student Workbook or Lesson Review – If you are using one of these optional books, complete the assignment for Lesson 67.

Waud Sketch from Gettysburg

Robert E. Lee, Gentleman from Virginia

Robert Edward Lee was an excellent military officer who won the respect of his men as well as the enemy. Many believe he was the best general on either side of the Civil War. Lee was born in 1807 in Virginia. His parents were Henry Lee and Anne Hill. Henry Lee was nicknamed "Lighthorse Harry," because of his service as a cavalry officer in the American Revolution. It was he who said that George Washington was "First in war, first in peace, and first in the hearts of his countrymen." Anne was a descendant of Martha Washington. When Robert was a child, the family moved to Arlington, Virginia, just outside of Washington, D. C.

Arlington House

Family Life

When Lee was a boy, he often visited Arlington House, the home of George Washington Parke Custis and his wife Mary. The house stood along the Potomac River in Arlington. Mr. Custis was the grandson of Martha Washington. She and her husband George Washington adopted him when he was six months old, following the death of his father Parke Custis, who was Martha's son (see page 178). Mr. Custis built the home in 1802 as a tribute to his beloved adoptive father, George Washington.

When Lee grew into a strong and handsome young man of five feet, ten inches tall, he proposed to the Custises' only daughter, Mary Anna Randolph Custis. Not only had Lee visited her as a child, they went to the same church, Christ Episcopal in Arlington. They were married in 1831; and Lee moved into Arlington House. Though his military career took him and his family to many places around the country, they considered Arlington House their home. Robert and Mary had seven children. Six were born in Arlington House. Robert E. Lee was a good father, firm and kind to his sons and gentle with his daughters.

General Lee was a warm and friendly man who enjoyed social gatherings. He loved children. When he was at home, he sometimes gathered rosebuds before breakfast and laid one at the place of each lady. The smallest rosebud was laid at the place of his youngest daughter, Mildred. His wife Mary was deeply religious and longed for her husband to become a devout believer. At age 46, he was confirmed in the Episcopal Church at the same time as two of his daughters. After this, he took great interest in church matters and religious literature.

The family especially enjoyed Christmas at Arlington House. They celebrated in English fashion with holly, ivy, mistletoe, myrtle, and pine and with a yule log on Christmas Eve. On Christmas Day, they gave gifts to family, friends, and servants. The Lee children received gifts like books, boots, dolls, and skates. They had morning prayers and breakfast and took the carriage to Christ Episcopal. After visiting friends, they returned home for a Christmas feast.

Robert E. Lee loved his wife's family and their home. In the 1850s, he began to help his father-in-law with financial affairs. When Mr. Custis died in 1857, Mary inherited the home. Lee took leave from his military responsibilities and came home to Arlington to be the executor of Mr. Custis' estate and to become the manager of his properties.

Lee at Chancellorsville, Virginia, on May 2, 1863

Military Career

Lee was educated at the United States Military Academy at West Point, New York, like his father before him. He graduated in 1829, second in his class. For the first twenty-three years of his military career, he served in Georgia, Virginia, New York, Texas, and Mexico. He was wounded during the Mexican War.

Lee became Superintendent at West Point in 1852. He was in Washington, D.C., in 1859 when John Brown raided the arsenal at Harper's Ferry. Lee commanded the troops that captured Brown and those who conspired with him. See pages 342-343. From February of 1860 to February of 1861, Lee was responsible for the U.S. Army's Department of Texas.

As southern states began to secede from the Union, Lee had to decide whether he would be loyal to the Union or to his home state of Virginia. He did not agree with secession, but he felt the greatest loyalty to Virginia, the ancestral home of his family. In April 1861, he had to make a choice. On the 18th, he was offered the field command of the United States Army. On the 19th, he learned that Virginia had seceded. In the wee hours of the morning of April 20, 1861, Lee wrote his resignation from the United States Army in his bedroom at Arlington House. On April 23, he accepted command of the Virginia forces.

Lee's tent is displayed at the Museum of the Confedracy in Richmond, Virgina. On display are his bed, boots, field glasses, saddle, and his unusual table with legs made from a tree branch.

Lee was made commander of The Army of Northern Virginia in 1862. He was named General-in-Chief of All Confederate Armies in February of 1865. After serving in that capacity for only a few weeks, Lee surrendered his armies to General Ulysses S. Grant at Appomattox Court House on April 9, 1865. Look at the drawing above of an early victory and the photo at left of objects Lee used during the war.

General Lee and his wife had abandoned Arlington House during the Civil War. The Federal government confiscated it in 1864. Part of the estate became Arlington National Cemetery. At Arlington today are America's Tomb of the Unknown Soldier, the grave of President John F. Kennedy with its eternal flame, and graves of thousands of men and women who have served in the armed forces. Arlington House was later returned to the Lee family after Robert E. Lee's son George Washington Custis Lee sued the Federal government for the property.

Robert E. Lee, President of Washington College, 1869

After the War

After the Civil War, Robert E. Lee became president of Washington College in Lexington, Virginia. See his photo at left. He served there until his death in 1870 at age 63. General Lee was known as a kind gentleman. He was loved by those who knew him, especially his soldiers. He embodied character traits Paul wrote about to the Christians of Colossae:

So, as those who have been chosen of God, holy and beloved,
put on a heart of compassion, kindness, humility, gentleness and patience.
Colossians 3:12

Activities for Lesson 68

Thinking Biblically – Read Matthew 5:1-12 and think about how Robert E. Lee was an example of some of these attributes.

Timeline – In *Timeline of America the Beautiful* next to 1852, write: Robert E. Lee becomes Superintendent of West Point.

Vocabulary – In your notebook, write your own definition for each of these words: respect, tribute, career, devout, executor. Look in the lesson for clues for the meaning of the words. When you are finished, look in a dictionary to check your definitions.

Literature – Read "Recollections of General Robert E. Lee" in *We the People*, page 69, and chapter 4 in *Across Five Aprils*.

Student Workbook or Lesson Review – If you are using one of these optional books, complete the assignment for Lesson 68.

Women in the Civil War

While their husbands, fathers, and brothers suffered on the battlefield, wives, mothers, and sisters suffered at home. First, they said farewell to their loved ones. Then, they had to take care of the day-to-day tasks, all the while fearing for the men they loved. They prayed, they worked, they served, and they waited. They wrote letters to their loved ones. They received letters from them. They rejoiced when they heard good news and cried when the news was bad. They cherished their loved ones' photographs. Some women never saw their loved ones again; others saw them come home wounded, maimed, or sick from disease. Others welcomed their loved ones safely home after the war and began new chapters in their lives, filled with relief and thankfulness to God.

While terrible pain was endured in both North and South, southern women—black and white—faced even greater hardships, because the war was fought on their own lands. The

In this Harper's Weekly *illustration from September 6, 1862, women sew, wash laundry, write a letter for a wounded soldier, and offer comfort.*

Union Army occupied much of the South. Though declared free during the war, black women in the South were faced with the reality of taking care of their families without many resources. Notice the slave women and children at right.

Women in the North and the South got personally involved in the war. Some women were able to earn a living because of their involvement in the war. Some worked in factories. Many worked in hospitals, tenderly caring for the sick and wounded. Examine the *Harper's Weekly* illustration from 1862 on page 379.

Slave Women and Children

Fighting Battles

Women were not officially allowed in either the Union or Confederate armies, but a few disguised themselves as men and joined anyway. Sometimes their true identity was found out, and they were discharged. One woman wrote that she was glad she was free to go into the Army rather than stay at home and weep. A handful of women worked as spies.

Some women joined so they could be with their husbands who were also serving. A Mrs. S. M. Blaylock joined the Confederate 26th North Carolina Infantry, Company F. She dressed in men's clothes, received a bounty (a payment used to encourage men to join), and began to do all the work her fellow soldiers did. However, when her husband was discharged two weeks later, she informed the Army that she was a woman and returned the bounty. She was quickly discharged. On the Union side, Florina Budwin and her husband joined the Army together. They fought side by side. When captured by the Confederates, they went to the horrible prison at Andersonville, Georgia. Florina's husband died in the stockade. She also died after being transferred to another prison.

Facing Financial Hardships

Southerners had constant financial difficulties. The government had little money; families lost their fortunes; husbands and fathers couldn't earn money or raise crops because they were away fighting the war. Many southern women had to find ways to provide for their families. The South suffered greatly from inflation of prices. One Virginia

A Beloved's Photograph

lady complained to her sister that bacon was forty-five cents per pound and calico fabric cost one dollar. The economy was better in the North. One Virginia woman received a letter from her brother-in-law in Maryland, a slave state that did not secede. He bragged about how much better things were in the North, writing about parties and the latest fashions. In January 1865, a southern woman wrote in her diary that the country was desperate for food for both people and animals. She said the people seemed demoralized.

Mothers, wives, sisters, and sweethearts worked to supply the needs of their beloved soldiers; they also helped the Army. Old women and little girls worked together for their cause. They donated food to feed soldiers. Southern women sewed uniforms and battle flags by hand.

In this illustration by Thomas Nast from Harper's Weekly, *a Southern woman speaks with a Yankee soldier who has stopped at her home during the time Union forces were marching through Georgia.*

Suffering Under Union Occupation

Southern women never knew when Yankee soldiers might come to their homes and farms and take whatever they wanted. Many of the men in their families and neighborhoods were away fighting in the war, so they felt vulnerable. Confederate soldier Nehemiah Atwood tried to reassure his mother and sisters. He told them that he did not believe the enemy would hurt them, and that they must not be scared. Some women kept moving farther and farther south to stay ahead of the advancing Union troops. Others stayed at home and tried to hide family valuables. In a letter written by the wife of a Confederate general, she mentioned that a friend's home had been searched about fifty times and that the Yankees took everything they could lay their hands on. Some Union soldiers were compassionate. See the illustration above. Once a woman talked to a Yankee while hiding her silverware under her skirt. As they talked, it fell onto the floor. He helped her pick it up and left it with her.

As more and more of the South was occupied by the Union, southern women could not move freely from town to town. They had to receive passes from the U.S. Army before they could visit loved ones in other places.

Caring for the Sick and Wounded

At the beginning of the Civil War, there were no nurses in America who had medical training. Hospitals were set up in mansions, small homes, and even in fields. One Confederate hospital was set up on the lawn of the University of Virginia. The terrible medical needs suffered during the war caused people to realize the need for improvements in medical care. Conditions in northern hospitals began to improve. Women in both North and South participated in fund raising drives to improve conditions for patients. Mrs. Juliet Opie Hopkins from Alabama made great sacrifices for the Confederacy. When the war began, she sold estates she owned in Alabama, Virginia, and New York. She gave the

Medical Supplies from the Civil War Era

money to the Confederate government to found hospitals for soldiers. She went to the Confederate capital in Richmond, Virginia, to volunteer. Twice she was shot on the battlefield while helping the wounded. Mrs. Hopkins' picture was on Alabama's Confederate money. See the Civil War era medical supplies at left.

In 1865 the Confederate Congress discussed a bill to establish fair wages for women who worked in hospitals. The bill included a commitment to give them firewood and rations. Besides the paid nursing staff, volunteers went daily to the hospitals. They encouraged patients and helped in practical ways, like writing letters to their dear ones at home. Louisa May Alcott served in a Union hospital in Washington, D.C. She caught typhoid while there. She wrote *Hospital Sketches* based on her experiences. In her fictional book *Little Women*, Alcott wrote about how women lived during the war. The character Marmie goes away from her "little women" to take care of her husband who became ill while serving as a chaplain for the Union Army. The girls left at home made great sacrifices while she was away.

The best remembered medical volunteer of the Civil War was Clara Barton, pictured below. She began her work in Washington, D.C., where soldiers were temporarily housed in the U.S. Capitol Senate Chamber. There Miss Barton gave them supplies from her own home. She asked others to provide more supplies for the soldiers. Many responded to her request. For the rest of the war, Clara Barton organized the collection of supplies and worked to distribute them to those in need. She also attended to wounded Union soldiers on battlefields, took care of wounded Confederate soldiers who had been captured, prepared soldiers to be taken by train to hospitals, helped educate former slaves, and helped establish field hospitals. Once she was nearly killed when a bullet passed through the sleeve of her dress. Once she discovered that a wounded soldier was a woman. Barton convinced the woman to let the Army know and to go back home.

After the war, Clara Barton helped locate 22,000 men who were missing. She helped identify the graves of men who died in the Confederate prison at Andersonville. She traveled and lectured about her Civil War experiences. In Europe she learned about the International Red Cross. After she returned home, she helped organize the American Red Cross in 1881 and became its first president.

Susie King Taylor was born in Georgia, the daughter of slaves. As a girl, she attended two secret schools taught by African American women. She received further education from two white youths, who taught her even though it was illegal to do so.

Clara Barton

During the Civil War, she and other slaves escaped to St. Simons Island which was occupied by the Union Army. There Union officers encouraged her to start a school for black children. She married black officer Edward King who was stationed on the island. When the regiment left St. Simons, Susie traveled with them. Both her husband and her brother were members of the regiment. While serving as nurse and laundress for the soldiers, she taught many of them to read and write during their off-duty hours. Edward died after the war. Susie later married Russell Taylor and lived the remainder of her life in Boston. Her *Reminiscences of My Life in Camp with the 33rd United States Colored Troops, Late 1st S. C. Volunteers* was published in 1902.

Susie King Taylor

Former slave women in the South were jubilant when the war was over. Nearly seventy years after the Civil War, one remembered what happened when slaves around her had learned about their freedom. She said they sang, "You are free. You are free." Women in the North were also jubilant. Southern women were relieved the war was over, but they were also sad.

Many American women on both sides of the conflict had to face life after the war without beloved husbands, fathers, brothers, and sons. Many turned to God for comfort:

Blessed be the God and Father of our Lord Jesus Christ, the Father of mercies
and God of all comfort, who comforts us in all our affliction so that we will be able
to comfort those who are in any affliction with the comfort
with which we ourselves are comforted by God.
2 Corinthians 1:3-4

Activities for Lesson 69

Timeline – In *Timeline of America the Beautiful* next to 1881, write: Clara Barton helps organize the American Red Cross.

Literature – Read "Childhood Reminiscences" in *We the People*, pages 70-72, and chapter 5 in *Across Five Aprils*.

Creative Writing – Imagine that you work in a Civil War hospital as a nurse or doctor. In your notebook, write a letter to your family telling about your day-to-day experiences.

Student Workbook or Lesson Review – If you are using one of these optional books, complete the assignment for Lesson 69.

Two First Ladies

Two southern women supported the men who led the Union and the Confederacy during the Civil War. Mary Todd Lincoln was born in Kentucky and Varina Howell Davis was born in Mississippi. Both served the people their husbands led.

Mary Todd Lincoln

Like her future husband, Mary Todd was born in the slave state of Kentucky. She was born in 1818. Her father was a merchant, lawyer, member of the Kentucky legislature, and veteran of the War of 1812. Her mother died when she was six years old, leaving behind six children. Her father remarried the following year. He and his second wife had nine children.

Mary Todd had thirteen years of schooling, much more than most people of her day, especially girls. When she was twenty-one years old, she visited a sister in Springfield, Illinois. There she met Abraham Lincoln, whom she married two years later. See their home below.

Mary Todd Lincoln, 1861

The Lincoln Home in Springfield, Illinois

Mary had a strong interest in politics, and she became an active participant in Abraham's political career. The couple had four sons, all born in Springfield. Edward, the second son, died in 1850 at age four.

When Mary Todd Lincoln and her husband entered the White House in 1861, she was 42 years old. See her photo above. She was a staunch supporter of the Union, though she was often called a southern sympathizer. Indeed, her brother, her three half-brothers, and one brother-in-law were in the Confederate Army. The brother-in-law was a Confederate general. He and two of her half-brothers were killed in the war and the other half-brother was wounded.

Mary Todd Lincoln watched as the Union was falling apart and tried to do what she could to help. Though strongly criticized for spending great amounts of money on clothes and redecorating the White House, she believed this would make the Union look stable to France and England, since either of these countries could side with the Union or the Confederacy. Mrs. Lincoln volunteered as a nurse in Union hospitals. With her husband, she toured Union Army camps. She believed that slaves should be freed. She used her influence to encourage the President to make the Emancipation Proclamation of 1863. She participated in fundraising for the Sanitary Commission, which was formed to provide for the needs of Union soldiers.

Mary Todd Lincoln's dressmaker was Elizabeth Keckly, a former slave. As a result of their friendship, Mrs. Lincoln got involved with the Contraband Relief Association, which raised money to help former slaves find housing and jobs and obtain clothing and medical care.

Mary Todd Lincoln suffered a great personal tragedy during the war, when another son died at almost eleven years of age. Then, when the Union was still celebrating victory, her husband was tragically murdered by an assassin.

Mary Todd Lincoln suffered tragedies similar to many other women in the Union and the Confederacy: the loss of a son and a husband and the division of her family between North and South. After her husband's death, she suffered severe mental health problems and the loss of another son when he was 18. Mary Todd Lincoln died in 1882 at the home of her sister in Springfield, Illinois.

Varina Howell Davis

Varina Howell was born on her family's plantation near Natchez, Mississippi. When she was seventeen years old, she made a two-month visit to the home of an old family

Varina Howell Davis, about 1860

friend, Joseph Emory Davis. "Uncle Joe's" younger brother Jefferson Davis, a widower, was visiting also. Jefferson's first wife, Sarah, the daughter of President Zachary Taylor, had died ten years before.

At the end of the visit, Varina and Jefferson were unofficially engaged. At first her mother disapproved; but she finally relented. The couple was married when Varina was nineteen. Davis was thirty-four.

Jefferson Davis was soon elected to the U.S. House of Representatives and later to the U.S. Senate. By the time the Civil War began, Varina had spent most of her adult life in Washington, D.C. She had enjoyed Washington society.

Jefferson Davis resigned his Senate seat in June of 1861, and the couple returned to Mississippi. Soon he was elected President of the Confederate States of America. See the picture of the Confederate White House below. As Confederate First Lady, Varina knitted clothing for soldiers and made shoes for them. She donated blankets and spent hours visiting soldiers in Confederate hospitals. She did not serve as a nurse, since her husband asked her not to do so.

President Davis was arrested at the end of the war. Varina and their children went to Savannah, where she was kept almost a prisoner. Her children were harassed by Union supporters, so she sent them to Canada under the care of her mother. She worked hard to get her husband out of prison. He was released in 1867. They eventually moved to Biloxi, Mississippi, to a home left to them in a friend's will. After her husband died, Varina lived there a few more years and then donated the house as a home for Confederate veterans. She moved to New York and supported herself as a writer until her death.

Mrs. Lincoln and Mrs. Davis learned firsthand about the sadness and horror of war. They learned what God taught many years before in His word:

Entrance to the Confederate White House in Richmond, Virginia

For the whole Law is fulfilled in one word, in the statement,
"You shall love your neighbor as yourself." But if you bite and devour one another,
take care that you are not consumed by one another.
Galatians 5:14-15

Activities for Lesson 70

Timeline – In *Timeline of America the Beautiful* next to 1867, write: Jefferson Davis is released from prison.

Literature – Read "Camp Songs of the Civil War" in *We the People*, pages 73-74, and chapter 6 in *Across Five Aprils*.

Creative Writing – In your notebook, write one or two paragraphs about how people can live in peace even when they have different beliefs and opinions.

Family Activity – Dance the Virginia Reel. See the instructions on page 435.

Student Workbook or Lesson Review – If you are using one of these optional books, complete the assignment for Lesson 70. If you are using the Lesson Review, take the quiz for Unit 14.

15 America Begins to Heal After the Civil War

When the Civil War ended, strong leadership was needed to put the nation back together. President Abraham Lincoln and his successor, Andrew Johnson, favored a gentle approach while Congress promoted a harsh one. President Johnson met strong opposition and came close to being removed from office. The next President was Civil War hero Ulysses S. Grant. While Grant was President, the Yellowstone area became Yellowstone National Park; the transcontinental railroad was completed at Promontory Point, Utah; Fanny J. Crosby was writing many of her beautiful Christian hymns; and cowboys were driving cattle from Texas to Kansas.

Frozen Spray from the Africa Geyser in Yellowstone National Park, 1979

Lessons in Unit 15

Lesson 71 – Our American Story: Putting America Back Together
Lesson 72 – God's Wonders: God Created the Wonders of Yellowstone
Lesson 73 – An American Landmark: Promontory Point, Utah
Lesson 74 – An American Biography: Fanny J. Crosby, Hymn Writer and Poet
Lesson 75 – Daily Life: Cowboys, Cattle Drives, Wild West Shows, and Rodeos

Books Used in Unit 15

- *Maps of America the Beautiful*

- *Timeline of America the Beautiful*

- *We the People*

- *Across Five Aprils* by Irene Hunt

Putting America Back Together

When Abraham Lincoln died, Vice President Andrew Johnson became President. The cruel war had ended, but America still needed to heal. Many questions needed to be answered. What should be done to help former slaves who had no food, clothing, or shelter? What must Confederate states do before being admitted back into the Union? Should Confederate leaders and soldiers be punished? Who should serve as officials in the former Confederate states? People had different ideas about what should happen. Some people wanted to forgive the southern Rebels and get the country moving forward quickly. Others wanted to punish the South.

Helping Former Slaves

Before Lincoln died, Congress created the Freedmen's Bureau to help freed slaves with food, housing, medical care, and education. Even with this help, life for former slaves was difficult. Many slaves left the farms and plantations where they had lived and headed for cities that were not ready to handle so many refugees. Other slave families began working for farmers. They became sharecroppers who received a share of the money earned when the farmer sold his crop. They did the same kind of hard work they had done as slaves.

FRANK LESLIE'S ILLUSTRATED NEWSPAPER.

MENDING THE FAMILY KETTLE.

COLUMBIA—" Now, Andy, I wish you and your boys would hurry up that job, because I want to use that kettle right away. You are all talking too much about it."

Many sharecroppers continued to be poor and went deeply in debt to their employers.

Many whites did not want blacks to participate in government. Southern states passed laws that prevented blacks from voting and owning property. Some whites were violent toward blacks. They did this to intimidate blacks to try to keep them from voting or participating in politics.

Southern States Return to the Union

President Lincoln thought the President had the authority to allow Confederate states back into the Union. He wanted to make it easy for them to become part of the United States again.

New President Andrew Johnson was from Tennessee, a state which had seceded. He agreed with Lincoln and began to carry out that policy. During the summer and fall of 1865, President Johnson began to readmit southern states to the Union. These states began to elect men to serve in the U.S. Senate and House of Representatives. Most of the men elected were Democrats who had been southern leaders before and during the Civil War.

At this time in American history, Congress met in Washington, D.C., for only a few months each year. They did not meet during the summer and fall of 1865. When northern Senators and Representatives returned to Washington in December of that year, they refused to let the newly-elected southern Senators and Representatives serve. These northern Republicans began to pass laws to "reconstruct" the southern states. Congress said that former Confederate leaders could not vote or hold office, but they passed a law that allowed former slaves to vote. Army troops were sent to the South to maintain order and to show the southern states who was in charge. This period of American history is called Reconstruction. Johnson did not agree with what Congress was doing. The cartoon on page 388 is from a June 1866 issue of *Frank Leslie's Illustrated Newspaper*. It shows Johnson holding a kettle that needs mending. The broken kettle represents the South.

Carpetbaggers and Scallywags

Many northerners moved to the South during Reconstruction. Some came to help by working in the Freedman's Bureau, teaching in the new schools set up for former slaves, or doing other good works. Others came to take advantage of the southerners who were having hard times. With blacks able to vote and Confederates unable to vote, many Republicans were elected to office. They appointed their friends to various positions. Sometimes they appointed newly-arrived northerners. Southerners resented these people. They called them carpetbaggers, because their luggage often was made of a material like carpet. Southerners who cooperated with Republicans and carpetbaggers were called scallywags. Notice the carpetbagger cartoon below.

In the 1866 Congressional elections, the Republicans gained even larger majorities in the House and Senate. President Johnson did not agree with the rules that Congress made for readmitting the states, but he was not able to stop what Congress was doing.

Harper's Weekly *Cartoon of a Carpetbagger, Drawn by Thomas Nast, November 1872*

White House Visitors

Though he had many stresses, President Johnson also had pleasant experiences in the White House. In 1866 Johnson entertained the Queen of Hawaii, which was then called the Sandwich Islands. It was the first time a queen had visited the White House. She gave him an ivory basket, which is now in the Andrew Johnson home in Greeneville, Tennessee. He also entertained British author Charles Dickens. President Johnson enjoyed children. He was the first President to host an Easter Egg Roll on the lawn of the White House. When he turned sixty years old, he invited 300 children to his birthday party at the White House.

Johnson Impeached

Congress took aim even at President Johnson in their harsh policies. In 1867 it passed laws limiting presidential powers. One took away his role as Commander-in-Chief of the Army. Another stated that he could not fire a cabinet member without the permission of Congress. These laws were unconstitutional, so Johnson disobeyed them. The House of Representatives responded by impeaching Johnson. Impeachment is the term used when a government official is accused of doing something so bad that he should no longer hold his office. According to the Constitution, when the House of Representatives impeaches someone, the Senate must hold a trial to see if the person is guilty. When the Senate held the trial for President Johnson in May of 1868, he was found not guilty by one vote. Notice the illustration at right.

Formal Notice of Johnson's Impeachment in the House of Representatives, Frank Leslie's Illustrated Newspaper, *March, 1868*

The Purchase of Alaska

In 1867 Nebraska became the 37th state. That same year, Johnson's Secretary of State William Seward encouraged the government to purchase Alaska from Russia. The government paid $7.2 million. Many people thought it was a giant frozen wasteland. They called the purchase "Seward's Folly" or "Seward's Icebox." Alaska has turned out to be a bargain. It eventually became America's 49th state.

During the Johnson administration, a telegraph cable was laid across the Atlantic Ocean between America and Europe, so that people could communicate quickly.

Read about President Johnson's life below.

Andrew Johnson
America's Seventeenth President
April 15, 1865 - March 4, 1869

Andrew Johnson was born in North Carolina on December 29, 1808. When he was almost three years old, his father Jacob saved some people he knew from drowning in a river. This act of heroism weakened his health, and he died soon after. Because they were poor, Andrew's mother Mary (called "Polly") apprenticed him and his brother William to a local tailor. Andrew ran away after getting into trouble. In 1826 Andrew moved with his mother and stepfather to Greeneville, Tennessee. Family tradition says that they arrived with a cart pulled by a blind pony.

In Greeneville, Johnson opened his own tailoring shop. In 1827 he married Eliza McCardle. Mordecai Lincoln, a relative of Abraham Lincoln, performed the ceremony. Andrew and Eliza had three sons and two daughters. Johnson had little education, so his wife became his teacher. He also paid people to read to him while he worked.

At age 21, Johnson was elected to his first political position. He served as a Greeneville alderman. In 1834 he was elected mayor. Johnson continued to move up the political ladder. He served first in the Tennessee House of Representatives and later in the Tennessee Senate. It was then that he bought his first slave, a fourteen-year-old girl named Dolly. He soon bought her half brother Sam.

Sam Johnson

Dolly Johnson with Andrew Johnson's Grandson, Andrew Johnson Stover

In 1843 Johnson was elected to represent Tennessee's first district in the U. S. House of Representatives. After serving ten years, he was elected Governor of Tennessee. In 1857 he was elected to the U.S. Senate. In 1859 Andrew Johnson's son Robert followed in his father's footsteps and became a member of the Tennessee legislature.

When the Civil War began, Johnson remained loyal to the Union and continued to serve in the U.S. Senate even though Tennessee had seceded. In 1862 the Union Army captured his home state's capital city, Nashville. Johnson was appointed to serve as a military governor over the state. His son Charles served as an assistant surgeon with the Union Army. During the war, Charles died after falling off a horse. Since Tennessee was under Union control at the time of the Emancipation Proclamation, slaves in the state were not freed. Johnson freed Tennessee slaves in October of 1864. When Mrs. Johnson gave their slaves the news that they were free to go or free to stay, they all chose to stay. See the photos above.

In 1865 Johnson became Vice President of the United States when Lincoln was inaugurated for his second term. When President Lincoln died, Johnson became President. When Johnson left the presidency in 1869, he returned to Tennessee. That same year he ran for another term as a United States Senator but was defeated. His son Robert died that year. Greeneville, Tennessee, hosted a celebration on August 8, 1871, to commemmorate the day when Andrew Johnson freed his personal slaves eight years before. Andrew Johnson's former slave Sam led the parade and Johnson gave an address. African Americans in Tennessee have continued to recognize August 8 as a holiday, as have some in surrounding states.

Johnson was defeated in 1872 when he ran for a seat in the U.S. House of Representatives. Finally, in 1875, he was elected again to the U.S. Senate. He served briefly before dying of a stroke. Large crowds came to Greeneville to pay their respects to a beloved man. Notice the photo of his house at right. Johnson's former slave Sam told people where his former master had requested to be buried.

Closed shutters and black ribbons marked Johnson's home in Greeneville, Tennessee, on the day he died.

General Grant Becomes President

In 1868, the Republicans turned to Civil War hero Ulysses S. Grant as their presidential candidate. He defeated the Democratic nominee, Horatio Seymour, who had once served as Governor of New York. President Grant became the eighteenth President in 1869. Though he served honorably and honestly himself, Grant appointed some people to serve in his administration who did not follow his example. Several of these men committed crimes. Sometimes his officials took bribe money from people wanting favors. Grant did not do much to stop them.

General Grant

Congress passed a law in 1872 that pardoned tens of thousands of former Confederates. This made it possible for them to regain political power. Many blacks did not participate in politics. Sometimes whites made threats that made them afraid to do so. Though conditions were better for blacks who lived in the North, neither northern nor southern whites gave complete equal rights to blacks. It was not until the Civil Rights movement of the 1950s and 1960s that they would receive equal rights.

New States Admitted

1867 Nebraska
1876 Colorado

Though President Grant was criticized for the corruption of his officials, he was elected to a second term in 1872. In 1876 during his second term, Colorado became the 38th state. Read about President Grant's life below.

Ulysses Simpson Grant
America's Eighteenth President
March 4, 1869 - March 4, 1877

Hiram Ulysses Grant was born in 1822 in a cottage near Point Pleasant, Ohio, along the banks of the Ohio River. His father Jesse was a leather tanner. His mother was Hannah Simpson Grant. His parents called him Ulysses or "Lyss." He loved horses and was breaking and training them by the age of nine. When Grant entered West Point, he was accidentally listed as Ulysses Simpson Grant and the name stuck. He graduated from West Point in 1843. In 1848 he married Julia Dent, to whom he was always devoted.

Grant fought in the Mexican War, serving under General Zachary Taylor. After the war, he was assigned to various military posts east of the Mississippi River. In 1852 he was assigned to a position on the west coast. Since Grant was a loving husband and father, he found this very difficult. He hated leaving his wife while she was expecting their second child. Communication was slow, so he had to wait months to find out his second son had been born. He continually tried to raise money to move his family to be with him but was unable to do so. Though he had reached the rank of captain, Grant resigned and went home to be with his family.

The Grant family moved to St. Louis, where Grant became first a farmer and then a real estate agent. Wanting to be nearer his parents, he moved to Galena, Illinois, where he worked in his father's leather store. After the Civil War began, Grant left his father's shop and became commander of a volunteer regiment. He rose to the rank of Brigadier General. Grant commanded the troops that defeated the Confederates at Fort Donelson in Tennessee. When the Confederate commander asked Grant for his terms of surrender, Grant said: "No terms except an unconditional and immediate surrender can be accepted." People began to call U. S. Grant Unconditional Surrender Grant.

Lincoln promoted Grant to Major General. Though some complained about Grant's abilities, Lincoln defended him. He said, "I can't spare this man—he fights." In 1864 Lincoln made him General-in-Chief of the Union Army. Grant ordered General Sherman to march through Georgia to the Atlantic Ocean. Meanwhile, Grant worked from his headquarters in Virginia, where he directed Union troops across the country. For four months, Julia and their youngest son stayed with him. Lincoln visited

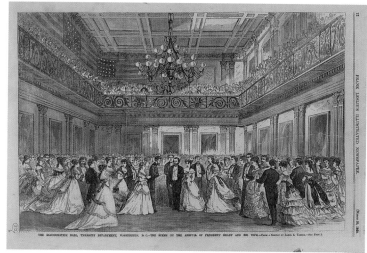

Grant's Inaugural Ball, 1869, as Illustrated in Frank Leslie's Illustrated Newspaper

Grant there. They discussed the final strategies the Union would use to finish the war and how to reunite the country after the war. In April of 1865, Lee surrendered to Grant at Appomattox Court House in Virginia.

Grant resigned his commission as General of the United States Army the day he was inaugurated as President of the United States. Above is an illustration of his inaugural ball. He took part of his Army staff to the White House. He supported the oppressive Reconstruction laws passed by Congress, sometimes even using the Army to make the South comply. Grant was well-respected in the North. Union veterans cheered when they saw him in public.

Ulysses, Jesse, and Julia Grant, 1872

well-respected in the North. Union veterans cheered when they saw him in public.

Personally Grant was gentle and shy. He read widely and spoke intelligently on many topics, but his favorite subject was horses. He wrote beautiful letters to his wife Julia. At left is an 1872 photograph of Grant at his cottage by the sea with his wife Julia and their son, Jesse.

When Grant left the presidency, he became a partner in a business that went bankrupt. After learning that he had throat cancer, he began to work very hard to write his memoirs. He wanted to earn money to pay his debts and leave money for his family. In his last days his family gathered around him. He died shortly after writing the last page of his memoir. The book earned almost $450,000.

Grant loved his family. As a young man, he left his army career to be with his wife and children and also moved to be near his parents. As he suffered illness late in his life, he worked to help his family financially. God calls every man to honor his family:

A good man leaves an inheritance to his children's children.
Proverbs 13:22

Activities for Lesson 71

Thinking Biblically – After the Civil War, many people needed to give and receive forgiveness on both sides. Copy Colossians 3:12-13 into your notebook.

Map Study – Complete the assignments for Lesson 71 on Map 20 "The Lower 48" in *Maps of America the Beautiful*.

Timeline – In *Timeline of America the Beautiful* next to 1867, write: The U.S. government purchases Alaska from Russia.

Vocabulary – In your notebook, copy the following sentences. Fill in each blank with the correct word from this list: intimidate, authority, ivory, wasteland, administration.

a. Before controls and limitations, thousands of elephants were killed to make valuable _____ items from their tusks.
b. I didn't know you had the _____ to tell us what we have to do!
c. Most of the people in the President's _____ agreed with his decision.
d. Our farm looked like a _____ before we started cleaning up and planting crops.
e. I try not to let his angry words and expressions _____ me.

Literature – Read chapters 7-8 in *Across Five Aprils*.

Student Workbook or Lesson Review – If you are using one of these optional books, complete the assignment for Lesson 71.

God Created the Wonders of Yellowstone

When God created Yellowstone, He made a beautiful landscape with spraying geysers, bubbling mud pots, lakes, waterfalls, and a great canyon with yellow stone walls. Yellowstone is like a giant water park created by God Almighty. He painted the park in beautiful colors and filled it with animals, such as bison, wolves, moose, elk, and grizzly bears. The Federal government set the region aside as Yellowstone National Park in 1872 so that all Americans could enjoy what early visitors called a "wonderland."

Beehive Geyser

Hot Water Under the Ground

The rock that God placed deep inside the earth is very hot. He also put water underground. From this rock and water, He creates what scientists call hydrothermal features. Many are in Iceland and on the Kamchatka Peninsula of Russia, but about half of the hydrothermal features on earth are in Yellowstone—over 10,000! Three are pictured on this page.

Geysers form when volcanic rock underground heats water to the boiling point. Pressure underground causes steam and water to shoot upward. Some geysers erupt every few minutes; for others, years pass between eruptions. Yellowstone has over three hundred geysers. One hundred fifty of them are within one square mile.

A Hot Spring on the Seven Mile Hole Trail

Morning Glory Pool

Fumaroles are like geysers, but instead of sending up water, they send up hot gases and steam. They are the hottest hydrothermal features in Yellowstone. When they erupt, they make a loud hissing sound.

Old Faithful

Old Faithful

The most famous creation in all of Yellowstone National Park is Old Faithful, a geyser that shoots steam and hot water as high as 180 feet into the air. Though the length of its eruption, the height of its eruption, and the amount of time between eruptions vary from day to day and year to year, it is famous because it is fairly dependable. Tourists who come to see it can be sure they will see a geyser in action. That is why it is called Old Faithful! In 2010 it erupted about every ninety minutes. The eruptions lasted between one and a half and five minutes. The water rose between 106 and 180 feet, averaging 130 feet. Just before it erupts, the water temperature is 204 degrees Fahrenheit. Old Faithful is pictured at left. Notice Great Fountain Geyser and Castle Geyser on page 397. Beehive Geyser is pictured on page 395.

Minerva Terrace

Hot Springs of Yellowstone

Most of Yellowstone's hydrothermal features are hot springs. Hot springs are like geysers, but they bubble at the surface instead of erupting. They have less underground pressure than geysers. Minerva Terrace, shown on page 396, is a hot spring which produces ornate formations. Most of the rock at Minerva Terrace is limestone. When water rises through the limestone, it creates a chalky white rock called travertine. These formations change constantly.

Great Fountain Geyser

Notice the Chromatic Pool shown below. Different species of microorganisms thrive at different temperatures. Water at Chromatic Pool has various temperatures. Microorganisms of different colors give the Chromatic Pool its variety of colors. Microorganisms harvested at Yellowstone helped scientists develop DNA testing. The National Park Service plans to use money earned through microorganism research at Yellowstone to protect the park's future.

Punch Bowl Spring, shown below, is surrounded by a ring of mineral deposits called a sinter. Notice that Punch Bowl Spring, Chromatic Pool, and Castle Geyser on this page, and the two hot springs on page 395, look like they are surrounded by snow. The white is actually mineral deposits from evaporated water. Morning Glory Pool is shaped like another of God's creations—the morning glory flower.

Castle Geyser

Mud pots are hot springs that have a high volume of acid and not much water. When hydrogen sulfide rises from deep within the earth, some microorganisms use it for energy. They convert this hydrogen sulfide into sulfuric acid, which breaks down rock into clay. When gases escape through the wet clay, it bubbles. It is amazing to watch these ever-changing blobs of bubbling mud.

Chromatic Pool

Punch Bowl Spring

The Grand Canyon of the Yellowstone

The Yellowstone River begins south of Yellowstone National Park and ends six hundred miles away in North Dakota, where it empties into the Missouri River. It is America's longest river that has not had a dam built across it.

While in the park, the river enters the Grand Canyon of the Yellowstone, shown at right, with its beautiful yellow stone walls. The canyon is about twenty miles long. It varies from eight hundred to 1,200 feet deep and is from 1,500 to 4,000 feet wide.

Falls on the river include the Upper Falls at 109 feet high and the Lower Falls at 308 feet high. It is more than twice as high as Niagara Falls, but it has much less water.

Yellowstone Lake

Yellowstone Lake, at right, is about twenty miles long and fourteen miles across. Because the lake is so big and deep, in certain windy conditions the surface can be as tempestuous as an ocean. Since the lake sits at an elevation of 7,733 feet, the water is very cold. It is so cold that people cannot swim in it for long. People can only survive for twenty to thirty minutes in water that cold. The lake freezes over completely in winter. Ice thickness varies from a few inches to two feet.

The Grand Canyon of the Yellowstone

Ice on the Shore of Yellowstone Lake

The bottom of Yellowstone Lake is similar to the land around it. It has canyons, geysers, hot springs, and fumaroles. In those areas, the water is very hot. One spot at Mary Bay is 252 degrees Fahrenheit. Parts of the lake support amazing animal communities with bacteria, sponges, and earthworms.

Native Americans at Yellowstone

A small, peaceful tribe of Native Americans once lived in the Yellowstone area. They were known as the Sheep Eaters. In 1871, when they went to live at Wind River Reservation with their relatives the Shoshone, they still maintained their traditional lifestyle. Unlike other tribes in the region, they did not use horses.

Fur Trappers at Yellowstone

The Governor of the Louisiana Territory mentioned the "River yellow Stone" in an 1805 letter. He later sent Thomas Jefferson a map showing the river. Native Americans had drawn the map on a beaver pelt. President Jefferson hung the pelt in the entrance hall at Monticello. There is no evidence that Lewis and Clark explored the area or that Native Americans told them about the thermal features there.

The fur trapper John Colter is the first known white man to see the geothermal features in the Yellowstone region. He had been a member of the Lewis and Clark expedition, but he set out on his own before they returned to St. Louis. He explored the Yellowstone area in the winter of 1807-1808. He discovered Jackson Lake, Yellowstone Lake, and an area he called the Hot Spring Brimstone. We learned about John Colter on page 253.

After the Lewis and Clark expedition, William Clark continued to keep notes about the Louisiana Territory, learning from others who visited there. At some point he wrote the following note, probably after 1809. The capitalization and punctuation are Clark's:

> At the head of this river the natives give an account that there is frequently herd a loud noise, like Thunder, which makes the earth Tremble, they State that they seldom go there because their children Cannot sleep—and Conceive it possessed of spirits, who were averse that men Should be near them.

A group of fur trappers came close to the Teton Mountains in 1818. They probably came into the Yellowstone area because one of them wrote: "Boiling fountains having different degrees of temperature were very numerous; one or two were so very hot as to boil meat." In 1881, after Yellowstone became a national park, the park superintendent and others were exploring there. They found a tree with J.O.R. AUG. 29, 1819 carved into it. On the other side were wooden pins like ones fur trappers used to dry pelts. This was the first confirmed evidence that fur trappers had been in the park. Around 1900 a Frenchman by the name of Roch who lived in Michigan claimed to have worked as a fur trapper in the Yellowstone region when he was a young man. He said that he had carved his initials in a tree. When he was identified, Roch was between one hundred and 109 years old.

Daniel Potts wrote the first detailed description of the geothermal features of Yellowstone in 1826. With his original spelling and punctuation, he tells of:

> A number of hot and boiling springs some of water and others of most beautiful fine clay and resembles that of a mush pot and throws its particles to the immense height of from twenty to thirty feet in height The Clay is white and of a pink and water appears fathomless as it appears to be entirely hollow under neath. There is a also a numer of places where the pure suphor

is sent forth in abundance one of our men Visited one of those wilst taking his recreation there at an instan the earth began a tremendious trembing and he with dificulty made his escape when an explosion took place resembling that of thunder. During our stay in that quarter I heard it every day.

Soldiers, Missionaries, and Prospectors in Yellowstone

Among those who visited the Yellowstone area in the 1850s and early 1860s were members of the U.S. Army, as well as Jesuit missionary Pierre-Jean De Smet, who had come to the West as a missionary to Native Americans. They called him Blackrobe. In 1851 mountain man Jim Bridger (see pages 252 and 253) drew a map of the Yellowstone area for De Smet. De Smet researched the area, visited it, and added to Bridger's map.

After the California Gold Rush of 1849, miners began to find gold in other Western lands. Prospectors came to the Yellowstone area beginning in 1863. By 1867 news about the wonders of Yellowstone were spreading. A journalist predicted that someday thousands of pleasure seekers and sightseers would come to Yellowstone. Some descriptions were exaggerated, like the one that said that Yellowstone Lake was "so clear and so deep, that by looking into it you can see them making tea in China."

Explorers in Yellowstone

Another Catholic missionary among Native Americans was Francis Xavier Kuppens. He visited Yellowstone with Blackfeet Indians in the spring of 1865. That October, Kuppens was at St. Peter's Mission when a group of government officials took refuge there during a snowstorm. Kuppens told the officials about his visit to Yellowstone. A local Canadian who was married to a Blackfeet squaw came to the mission and also gave a graphic description of the area. None of the visitors had ever heard of Yellowstone, but the descriptions made one of them say that it should be reserved as a national park.

After the Civil War, three groups explored the Yellowstone region. In 1869 David Folson and two others explored it. They met the peaceful Sheep Eaters. The threesome saw many of the area's geological and geothermal features. They were awed by its beauty. When they returned, Folson was afraid to publicize what they found for fear that people would think he was making it up. An acquaintance tried to get their accounts published in *Harper's*, but the editors replied that they did not want to risk their reputation "with such unreliable material." Parts of their story were finally printed in a Chicago magazine.

Photo of the Upper Falls of the Yellowstone River by Jackson

Photo of Hot Springs on the Gardiner River by Jackson

Canyon of the Yellowstone by Thomas Moran

Folsom got a job in the office of Henry Washburn, Surveyor-General of the Territory of Montana. There he helped create an accurate map of the region. In 1870 Washburn led another threesome in an exploration of Yellowstone.

In 1871 the U. S. government sent a group of scientists into the region. The group's leaders were Ferdinand V. Hayden from the U.S. Geological Survey of the Territories and Captain John W. Barlow, chief engineer of the Army's Division of Missouri. Artist Thomas Moran and photographer William Henry Jackson joined them. The images they created helped other Americans begin to understand something of the wonders of Yellowstone. On page 400 are two stereoscopic photographs by Jackson. Notice the painting by Moran above.

Hayden's experience convinced him that the Yellowstone area should become a national park. With the encouragement of Hayden and others, Congress passed a law to make it a park. Most of the park is in Wyoming, but parts are in Montana and Idaho. President Grant signed the law on March 1, 1872. Now the wonderland of Yellowstone would be protected for the people of America and their visitors from around the world.

At Yellowstone people can see many examples of God's creative power.

Give thanks to the Lord of lords, for His lovingkindness is everlasting.
To Him who alone does great wonders, for His lovingkindness is everlasting;
To Him who made the heavens with skill, for His lovingkindness is everlasting;
To Him who spread out the earth above the waters, for His lovingkindness is everlasting.
Psalm 136:3-6

Activities for Lesson 72

Thinking Biblically – In your notebook, write one or two paragraphs about how the wonders of Yellowstone that God made bring glory to Him.

Map Study – Complete the assignment for Lesson 72 on Map 2 "God's Wonders" in *Maps of America the Beautiful*.

Timeline – In *Timeline of America the Beautiful* next to 1872, write: The Yellowstone area becomes a national park.

Literature – Read "The Discovery of Yellowstone Park" in *We the People*, page 75, and chapter 9 in *Across Five Aprils*.

Student Workbook or Lesson Review – If you are using one of these optional books, complete the assignment for Lesson 72.

Promontory Point, Utah

Railroad corporations in America had built 35,000 miles of track by the end of the Civil War, but Americans still had no fast way to travel from coast to coast. In the 1850s, leaders began to talk seriously about building a transcontinental railroad. Southerners wanted it to

Railroad workers lay track across the Great Plains in this Harper's Weekly *illustration.*

be built from New Orleans, across Texas, and across the deserts of the Southwest. Northerners never gave this route serious consideration, since it would have benefited the South and possibly aided the spread of slavery.

The Civil War slowed the dream of a transcontinental railroad, but some progress continued. In 1862 Congress passed a law giving the Union Pacific Railroad authority to build a line west from Omaha, Nebraska, and the Central Pacific Railroad authority to build a railroad line east from Sacramento, California. The two companies were to meet somewhere between Omaha and Sacramento.

Work began during the Civil War. See the illustration of the construction above. As the two companies laid track toward one another, the growing railroad connected a few towns along the way and created many more. Construction was difficult because crews had to build across canyons and rivers and through mountains. Weather was a problem, too.

Each company hired up to 15,000 workers. The Union Pacific hired many Irish immigrants and Civil War veterans. As many as ninety percent of the Central Pacific workers were Chinese immigrants to California. In May of 1869, the crews finally came together at Promontory Point, Utah.

One crew member had a unique job. Former Civil War photographer Andrew J. Russell worked as an official Union Pacific Railroad photographer. He recorded this historic construction project. See Russell's photograph of the Promontory Point railroad trestle on page 403.

Look closely. Notice the steam locomotive pushing railroad flatcars. Would you want to ride a heavy train across this wooden trestle?

Digital photographs are a modern invention. Making photographs in the 1800s was a slow process. To make one photograph, a photographer put glass plates and chemicals into his camera. The camera had no button to make the camera shutter open and close. Instead, the photographer simply took off the lens cap and guessed how long to wait. After this, he took the glass plate to a portable

Railroad Trestle at Promontory Point, Utah

structure nearby. The structure was sealed so that no light could come in. In this "darkroom," he used more chemicals to create a picture. Russell used this process to make 650 ten-by-thirteen-inch glass plates of the Union Pacific Railroad. When you see old photographs in *America the Beautiful,* think about the hard work involved in creating these images. Today we can take photographs easily, but each photograph taken in the 1800s represents a great deal of work.

Golden Spike Ceremony

When the work was nearing completion in 1869, officials planned a Golden Spike Ceremony to take place at Promontory Point. By the time it was held, the Union Pacific had laid 1,086 miles of track; the Central Pacific had laid 689 miles.

On May 10, 1869, one thousand people gathered to celebrate the completion of the transcontinental railroad. Among them were railroad and government officials; members of the 21st U.S. Infantry Regiment; and railroad construction workers.

Four special spikes were created for the ceremony. Two were gold; one was silver; and one was iron, gold, and silver. One golden spike was presented on behalf of the Central Pacific Railroad. San Franciscan David Hewes gave $400 worth of his own gold to make it. A foundry in San Francisco cast the five and five-eighths inch golden spike. On one side was engraved: "May God continue the unity of our country as the railroad unites the two great Oceans of the world. Presented David Hewes San Francisco." Engraved on the top was "The Last Spike."

The owner of a San Francisco newspaper donated a five-inch long spike made from $200 worth of gold. Its engraving stated: "With this spike the San Francisco News Letter offers its homage to the great work which has joined the Atlantic and Pacific Oceans. This month-May, 1869."

Nevada presented a silver spike. It was forged by a blacksmith. The rough, unpolished spike barely made it to the train in time to make it to the ceremony. Arizona territory contributed an iron spike, plated with gold on the head and silver on the shaft. Its engraving said: "Ribbed with iron clad in silver and crowned with gold Arizona presents her offering to the enterprise that has banded a continent and dictated a pathway to commerce. Presented by Governor Safford."

The company that made ties for the Central Pacific Railroad hired a billiard table manufacturer to make a highly-polished railroad tie out of California laurel wood. A silver plaque on the tie read: "The last tie laid on completion of the Pacific Railroad, May, 1869." Four holes were drilled into it so that the commemorative spikes could be placed in the tie during the ceremony. A shipping company presented a special spike hammer. A tool maker made it, and a San Francisco company plated it heavily with silver.

As part of the ceremony, workers placed the special tie on the grade and then laid the last rail sections across it. A wealthy Sacramento banker served as emcee. A minister from Massachusetts led a prayer. After a speech, Central Pacific President Leland Stanford and Union Pacific Vice President Thomas Durant used the silver-plated hammer to gently tap the four spikes into the tie. The special tie was then removed and replaced with a pine one. Workers then drove in three iron spikes. A fourth spike of iron and a hammer, like those usually used to drive in spikes, were handed to Stanford. The spike and hammer were wired to the transcontinental telegraph line, so that Americans far away could "hear" the actual completion of the transcontinental railroad. Stanford took a swing. He hit the tie, but missed the spike. Durant tried. He even missed the tie. A regular railroad worker had to drive in the last spike. The telegraph operator sent out the message "D-O-N-E." The massive project at last was completed.

Chief Engineer Montague of the Central Pacific and Chief Engineer Dodge of the Union Pacific shook hands. Two trains, the Central Pacific's *Jupiter* and the Union Pacific's *No. 119*, were run up to Promontory Point until they almost touched. Look at the photograph at right.

Photograph Taken on May 10, 1869, During the Golden Spike Ceremony

The *Jupiter* and the *No. 119*

Two steam locomotives pulled railroad cars that brought Mr. Stanford, Mr. Durant, and their guests to Promontory Point for the ceremony. The *Jupiter* brought Mr. Stanford and the *No. 119* brought Mr. Durant. The *Jupiter* had been built in New York in September of 1868. Like all Central Pacific locomotives built before 1870, it was taken apart and loaded on a ship, which went around Cape Horn at the tip of South America and up to San Francisco. There its parts were placed on a barge and towed to Sacramento, where the *Jupiter* was reassembled. In March of 1869, it was placed into service as a Central Pacific locomotive.

Central Pacific President Leland Stanford had chosen a different locomotive to pull his train to Promontory Point. As he and his guests traveled east toward the ceremony, the

Reproduction of the Jupiter

locomotive was badly damaged when it hit a log on the tracks. The *Jupiter* was nearby, and though it had been in service less than two months, it was chosen to pull the cars bringing the dignitaries.

During the *Jupiter's* active service, she was repainted, converted to a coal-burning system, and sold to another railroad company. This historic locomotive was sold for scrap in the early 1900s.

The Union Pacific's *No. 119* was built in New Jersey in November of 1868. The *No. 119* was also a last minute fill-in. As Durant headed for the ceremony at Promontory Point, his chosen locomotive pulled into a little town in Wyoming where four hundred laid-off railroad workers had been waiting for three months to get their pay. The workers chained his car to a side track for two days as they waited for their pay to come. During the delay, waters in the Weber River rose, removing some of the supports holding up the Devil's Gate Bridge. The engine pulling the train was then too heavy to go across the bridge. The engineer pushed each of the lighter passenger coaches so they could coast across the bridge, but now they had no engine.

The *No. 119* was sitting in a nearby town. Workers there received a telegraph message telling about the problem, so the *No. 119* headed for the bridge. It safely pulled the train of dignitaries to the ceremony. This historic locomotive also continued in service until it was sold for scrap in the early 1900s.

Between 1975 and 1979, a California engineering firm worked to reproduce the *Jupiter* and the *No. 119*. They used a locomotive design engineer's handbook from 1870 and enlarged photographs from 1869. Trucks brought the reproductions eight hundred miles to Promontory Point. They were christened with water from the Atlantic and Pacific Oceans and commissioned on May 10, 1979, 110 years after the Golden Spike ceremony. Look at the photos of the reproductions on this page and on page 406.

You can learn more about the transcontinental railroad and the ceremony that celebrated its completion by visiting the Golden Spike National Historic Site. There you can see the reproductions of the *Jupiter* and the *No. 119*.

Reproduction of the No. 119

People used the intelligence that God gave them to find a way to build a railroad to connect east and west. It was God Who created America the Beautiful for them to cross.

From the rising of the sun to its setting
The name of the Lord is to be praised.
Psalm 113:3

Activities for Lesson 73

Map Study – Complete the assignment for Lesson 73 on Map 3 "American Landmarks" in *Maps of America the Beautiful.*

Timeline – In *Timeline of America the Beautiful* next to 1869, write: The transcontinental railroad is completed at Promontory Point, Utah.

Vocabulary – Write five sentences in your notebook, using one of these words in each: trestle, darkroom, homage, clad, massive. Refer to a dictionary if you need help with their definitions.

Literature – Read "Dedication Prayer" in *We the People*, page 76, and chapter 10 in *Across Five Aprils*.

Student Workbook or Lesson Review – If you are using one of these optional books, complete the assignment for Lesson 73.

This modern photo shows reproductions of the Central Pacific Jupiter *and the Union Pacific* No. 119 *meeting at Promontory Point, Utah.*

Fanny J. Crosby, Hymn Writer and Poet

Frances Jane Crosby was born in Putnam County, New York, in 1820. Though blinded at six weeks of age, she became a teacher, a poet, and a hymn writer. She wrote over 8,000 hymns, including some of the most beloved hymns ever written. One of the most famous is "Blessed Assurance." This is the only lesson in *America the Beautiful* that is not illustrated. Sit and listen as an adult reads it to you and imagine what it was like not to be able to see and yet to have the faith and love that Fanny J. Crosby had for the Lord.

Once a preacher offered sympathy to Fanny, telling her that it was a pity that God did not give her sight. She said, "Do you know that if at birth I had been able to make one petition, it would have been that I should be born blind?" When he asked why, she said, "Because when I get to heaven, the first face that shall ever gladden my sight will be that of my Savior!"

When Fanny was 83 years old, she wrote *Fanny Crosby's Life-Story*. This is the story in her own words of how she became blind and of how she felt about it.

> It seemed intended by the blessed Providence of God, that I should be blind all my life; and I thank Him for the dispensation. I was born with a pair of as good eyes as any baby ever owned; but when I was six weeks of age, a slight touch of inflammation came upon them: and they were put under the care of a physician.
>
> What he did to them, or what happened in spite of him, I do not know, but it resulted in their permanent destruction, so far as seeing is concerned; and I was doomed to blindness all the rest of my earthly existence.
>
> I have heard that this physician never ceased expressing his regret at the occurrence; and that it was one of the sorrows of his life. But if I could meet him now, I would say, "Thank you, thank you—over and over again—for making me blind, if it was through your agency that it came about."
>
> This sounds strangely to you, reader? But I assure you I mean it—every word of it; and if perfect earthly sight were offered me tomorrow, I would not accept it. Did you ever know of a blind person's talking like this before?
>
> Why would I not have that doctor's mistake—if mistake it was—remedied? Well, there are many reasons: and I will tell you some of them.

One is, that I know, although it may have been a blunder on the physician's part, it was His intention that I should live my days in physical darkness, so as to be better prepared to sing His praises and incite others so to do.

Fanny's Childhood

John and Mercy Crosby were Fanny's parents. One of Fanny's grandfathers fought in the War of 1812 and her great-grandfather fought in the American Revolution. Her more distant ancestors were Pilgrims. As a child, Fanny enjoyed listening to family stories about Enoch Crosby, another relative who was a hero in the American Revolution.

Fanny's father died when she was very young. Her mother was only twenty-one years old and had to work as a maid to support the family. As a child, Fanny was blessed to have many godly relatives around her. She spent many hours with her grandmother. As an adult, she wrote a poem called "Grandmother's Rocking Chair."

As a child, Fanny learned to knit. Adults spent many hours reading to her from the Bible. She had a wonderful memory. It was said that by age ten, she could recite Genesis, Exodus, Leviticus, Numbers, Matthew, Mark, Luke, and John. The family also enjoyed reading poetry aloud, and adults read her many books.

Fanny enjoyed playing like other children. She climbed trees and rode horses. One of Fanny's favorite pastimes was to sit and listen. She would either fold her hands or knit. She loved to listen to rain, storms, and other sounds of nature. While sitting, Fanny would imagine that she was a sailor, a general, the leader of a choir praising God, or a preacher pleading with people to come to Christ.

Sometimes people would tell her that she would not be able to do certain things because she was blind. This made her sad and depressed, so she would go off alone and ask God if He did not have some place for her. She often felt as if she heard Him say that she would someday be useful and happy, even in her blindness. She would then go back to her friends and family, feeling that someday she would be just that. Gradually she lost her sadness at being blind. She took comfort in the Scriptures and in hymns. As a child, she wondered if someday she could make hymns, too. Fanny wrote her first poem when she was eight years old. In it she talked about her refusal to feel sorry for herself because she was blind. Fanny's grandfather was especially encouraging about her poetry.

New York Institute for the Blind

Not long after the New York Institute for the Blind (now the New York Institute for Special Education) was founded, Fanny traveled there by steamboat when she was fifteen to live and to go to school. Teachers taught students by reading to them and by giving lectures. Braille had not yet become a popular way for blind people to learn. Though a little homesick at first, Fanny was thrilled to be in school. She had longed for knowledge and prayed for it fervently. God had answered her prayer. She enjoyed all subjects except one. About that subject, she wrote:

> I loathe, abhor, it makes me sick,
> To hear the word, Arithmetic.

At school Fanny became known as a poet. People at the school praised her work. One day Fanny learned a very special lesson. The school superintendent came to her classroom and asked for her to come to his office. She thought that perhaps he wanted her to write a special poem. Instead, he said, "Fanny, your *attempts* at poetry have brought you into prominence here in the school, and a great deal of flattery has been the result. Shun a flatterer, Fanny, as you would a snake!" He went on to say, "The flattery and laudation of the world, Fanny, is a very fragile thing upon which to depend. . . . Remember that the very air you breathe—the very food you eat—all the ability or talent you may develop come from God. Remember you are always in His presence: and who has any right to be vain for a moment, when standing before the great Owner and Creator of all things?" He talked to her kindly, but firmly, for about five minutes.

Something told Fanny that his words were true and that it was all for her benefit. Tears came to her eyes and she felt pain, but she went behind his chair, put her arms around his neck, and kissed his forehead. She said, "You have talked to me as my father would have talked, were he living, and I thank you for it over and over again. You have given me a lesson that I might have had to learn through bitter experience and I shall profit by it." Fanny learned to give God the credit for anything she accomplished in her life.

Fanny the Teacher

Fanny Crosby became a teacher at the school when she was twenty-two years old, teaching grammar, rhetoric, ancient history, and modern history. Her mother had married again when Fanny was nineteen years old. Mercy and her new husband had three children. The first died in infancy, but Fanny became very close to her two half sisters. They spent many joyous hours together when she went home for vacations. When Fanny was an elderly woman, she lived with one of them.

While Fanny taught at the New York Institute for the Blind, some of the teachers and students went on a goodwill tour for the school. They traveled on a boat up the Erie Canal, stopping in towns along the way. They sang, gave speeches, recited from memory, and described their school. They went all the way to Buffalo on the canal and then went on to visit Niagara Falls. They stood on Goat Island, hearing the rush of the waters, while a teacher described Horseshoe Falls to them.

In 1844 Fanny and others from the school went to Washington, D.C., to raise awareness about blind people. Fanny gave a poetical address to a joint session of the U.S. Senate and House of Representatives. In the audience were two future Presidents, James Buchanan and Andrew Johnson. While in Washington, she met and received a hand clasp from seventy-six-year-old member of the House of Representatives and former President John Quincy Adams. She heard him give a speech about the Smithsonian Institution.

Fanny met many famous people while teaching at the Institute. Among them were the poet William Cullen Bryant, newspaper editor Horace Greeley, popular singer Jenny Lind, and Presidents James K. Polk and John Tyler. When Horace Greeley heard one of Fanny's poems, he asked her to write for his newspaper. Fanny's grandfather walked four miles to buy a paper with his granddaughter's poem in it.

At one time, Grover Cleveland's brother William was the head teacher at the school. When their father died, William brought the sixteen-year-old to work at the school. He became a clerk. William encouraged Fanny to visit Grover from time to time to encourage him, since he was taking his father's death so hard. Fanny and Grover Cleveland became good friends. Young Grover Cleveland enjoyed helping others. He often copied Fanny's poems for her. Their friendship continued even after he became President of the United States.

Fanny the Author

When Fanny was 24 years old, she had her first book of poetry published, *The Blind Girl and Other Poems*. It included her first published hymn. During her lifetime, she wrote two other books of poetry, a book of short stories and poems, and an autobiography. She also wrote several secular songs that sold well.

Fanny the Wife

At the Institute, Fanny met her future husband, Alexander Van Alstyne. Like Fanny, he was first a student and later a teacher. However, he went to college and studied Greek, Latin, and theology, before returning as a teacher. Fanny and Alexander married in 1858, when she was 38 years old. It was then that Fanny left her life at the Institute, where she had spent eight years as a student and fifteen as a teacher. "Van" insisted that she continue to write under her maiden name. They had one daughter, who died as a baby. Alexander and Fanny were married for forty-four years.

Alexander was one of the best organists in New York. He also played cornet and taught music. He often taught students free of charge if they could not pay. He was a composer who wrote music for many of Fanny's songs. Though Fanny herself played guitar, harp, piano, and other instruments, she rarely wrote the melodies for her songs.

Fanny the Hymn Writer

In 1864, at age 44, Fanny met William B. Bradbury, a composer of hymn melodies. He told her that he had wanted her to write songs for him for many years. For four years, until his death in 1868, Fanny wrote many songs for him. He knew that he would not live long and encouraged her to continue writing after his death. Fanny did just that.

Fanny did not want credit for all of the hymns she wrote, so many of her hymns were published under a pseudonym, a made-up name. Over the years, she used about one hundred different pseudonyms. A few of the most common ones were James Apple, Henrietta E. Blair, Robert Bruce, Lizzie Edwards, Victoria Frances, and Mrs. C. M. Wilson.

Believing that one must be in a proper mood to write a hymn, Fanny would sit alone and pray for thoughts and feelings. Fanny said that she never attempted to write a hymn without asking the Lord to be her inspiration. She kept hymns for a while before publishing them, going back over them to "cut, trim, or change" them. Life sometimes inspired Fanny. Once when she needed something in particular, she asked God for it and He supplied it. After that answered prayer, she wrote "All the Way My Savior Leads Me."

Tunes sometimes helped Fanny to write hymns. When she wrote "Blessed Assurance," she set it to a tune that a friend had already written. Fanny thought it was one of the sweetest tunes she had heard in a long time.

Once American hymn composer William Doane came to see Fanny. He asked her to put words to a tune he had written. He was in a hurry because he had to catch a train in forty minutes. He played the tune for her. She told him that his music said, "Safe in the Arms of Jesus." She scribbled out some words and told him to read it on the train. That hymn became one of Fanny's most famous and was one of her personal favorites.

Fanny's mother, who had sacrificed so much for her little blind daughter, was blessed to live into her nineties and to enjoy her daughter's fame. Fanny also lived to an advanced age. When she wrote her autobiography at age 83, she was traveling around the country visiting churches, speaking, and reciting her poems to audiences. She believed herself still in the prime of life and believed that hymn writing was her true life's work. She wrote, "I seem to have been led, little by little, toward my life-work," and "My work grows sweeter and grander to me each day."

Fanny J. Crosby died just before her ninety-fifth birthday. Her tombstone says simply, "Aunt Fanny" and "Blessed assurance, Jesus is mine. Oh, what a foretaste of glory divine."

I will sing to the Lord as long as I live;
I will sing praise to my God
while I have my being.
Psalm 104:33

Activities for Lesson 74

Thinking Biblically – Read these verses about singing songs of praise to God: Psalm 100:2; Psalm 107:22; Ephesians 5:19; James 5:13. Choose one to copy into your notebook.

Timeline – In *Timeline of America the Beautiful* next to 1858, write: Fanny J. Crosby and Alexander Van Alstyne are married.

Literature – Read "Hymns of Fanny J. Crosby" in *We the People*, pages 77-78, and chapter 11 in *Across Five Aprils*.

Creative Writing – In your notebook, write two or three paragraphs about Fanny's decision to accept her blindness with thankfulness to God. Write about how her life would have been different if she was angry or bitter.

Family Activity – Gather some friends for a Fanny J. Crosby Hymn-Singing. See the instructions on page 436.

Student Workbook or Lesson Review – If you are using one of these optional books, complete the assignment for Lesson 74.

Cowboys, Cattle Drives, Wild West Shows, and Rodeos

In the years following the Civil War, Texas cattle ranchers had more cattle than they could use. They needed to find a way to get their beef to the East Coast where it was in high demand. Railroads were a good way to transport beef, but the nearest ones were in Kansas and Missouri. As usual, the free enterprise system found a way for supply to meet demand.

Texas Becomes Cattle Country

Spanish ships brought cattle to the New World. The first cattle ranches in America were begun on missions run by Spanish priests in Texas. Priests in Texas hired Indians to take care of their cattle. When Americans began to move into Texas, they brought English breeds of cattle with them. The Texas longhorn is a cross between Spanish and English breeds. When cattle spread out in the vast Texas countryside, some became wild. Settlers could find wild cattle and start their own ranches. After the Civil War, this became more common.

At Top: Cowboys Branding Calf; At Bottom: Cattle Brand Designs

Ranchers decided to hire strong young men to drive their cattle north. Young veterans of the Civil War and freed slaves were ready to take the jobs. They were ready to become cowboys. Many American Indians and Hispanics found work as cowboys, too.

Ranchers branded their cattle so they could tell which cattle belonged to them. A brand is a symbol burned on the cow's skin to identify its owner. Brands helped ranchers find their own cattle when they were stolen or lost. Each rancher had his own iron brand design. Designs were simple and easy to identify. A rancher or his ranch hand heated a branding iron in a fire. When it was hot enough, he held it against a cow's hide until the brand's design was burned into it. The cowboys in the picture above are branding a calf. Modern ranchers still brand their cattle. They are proud of their brands and often name their ranches after them. See examples of brands above.

Cowboys

Cowboys worked hard. They had an important job that helped ranchers earn money and easterners have beef to eat. In cowboy movies, they spend a lot of time chasing outlaws and fighting with Indians; but real cowboys spent their time taking care of cattle and herding them to the end of the trail. Many didn't even carry a gun.

Cowboys wore special clothing. They wore suspenders with their canvas pants that were black, brown, or tan. They wore long-sleeved shirts made of cotton or wool, which protected their arms and kept them cool. Cowboys wore vests, which were usually made of wool. Vest pockets held a watch, money, and maybe a sweetheart's photograph.

Cowboy hats are a variation of the Spanish sombrero. The cowboy hat's wide brim kept off rain and protected the cowboy's face from the sun. He used it to fan the campfire and to gather food and water. At night, cowboys used them to cover their faces.

Cowboys tied large bandanas around their necks. They were made of cotton or silk. Some were a solid color and some were calico prints. Bandanas protected cowboys from dust, wind, rain, and sun. They could also be used to filter water or make a bandage. Cowboys could wet them to cool off their necks.

At Top: Cowboy Boot with Spur in Stirrup; At Bottom: Cowboy Wearing Chaps with Lasso Hanging from Saddle

Some parts of a cowboy's attire were made of cowhide. Cowboy boots, like those at left above, had pointed toes which were easy to get into their stirrups and high heels which kept them from sliding forward in the stirrup. Leather chaps covered cowboys' pants to protect them from thorn bushes, rocks, and the longhorns of the cattle. See chaps above. The cowboy's fringed gloves were also made of leather. They helped keep the cowboy's hands from getting blisters from ropes and reins, burns from hot branding irons, and cuts from cow hooves. Long cuffs on the gloves kept their sleeves clean.

When riding, cowboys often wore oilskin dusters, a kind of coat with an extra flap around the shoulders. The coats had a long slit in the back, to make it easy to wear when riding a horse. These coats were made of cotton treated with rubber to make them waterproof. They protected the cowboy from dust storms, rain, and wind. Cowboys wore heavier coats in the winter.

Cowboys had special tools. Hanging from the saddle in the lower picture is a lasso, a long rope with a sliding knot, used to catch and guide cattle. They also used spurs to urge their horses on as they rode. Notice the spur in the top photo.

Chow was served from a chuck wagon, which carried food and cooking supplies. Texan Charles "Chuck" Goodnight invented the chuck wagon in 1866. It was drawn by mules or oxen. It carried food, utensils, and a water barrel. The chuck wagon had drawers, shelves, and a fold-out counter. It was covered with a canvas top. Common chow included beef steaks, bison steaks, bacon (called chuck wagon chicken), beans (called Pecos strawberries), biscuits (called sourdough bullets), cowboy coffee, and a stew made from cow parts. See chuck wagon at right.

A cowboy traveled light. His only luggage was a leather saddlebag, which held books, clothing, food, a map, money, tools, and utensils. He carried water in a canteen, since cattle drives went through hot, dry places with few watering holes. He drank

Chuck wagon and Cookie

the water himself and sometimes shared it with his horse. Cowboys tied their bedrolls behind their saddles. A bedroll was a piece of canvas covered with a blanket or quilt. He could roll extra clothes in the bedroll. See cowboy tying a bedroll below.

Like workers in other jobs, cowboys developed a special vocabulary, which is still used today. An animal that has not yet been branded is a maverick. A corral is a fenced-in place where horses and cattle are kept. A rough or wild horse is a bronco. A stray animal is a mustang. Many cowboy words came from Spanish.

The golden era of the cattle drives only lasted about thirty years. The peak year was 1871, when 700,000 cattle were driven to Kansas alone. After the cattle drives, cowboys continued to work on ranches. Modern cowboys still do. Though they occasionally use horses, they usually use trucks. Sometimes they even use helicopters and airplanes to keep up with the cattle. The modern cowboy doesn't have to sleep night after night on the open range. Instead, he can live in a home with his family.

Cowboy Tying Bedroll

Cattle Drives

Texas ranchers took good care of their cattle, trying to raise as many calves as possible. When the calves were one to two years old, it was time to drive them north. When the cattle reached northern ranges, cowboys helped them find adequate pasture to get fattened up quickly. The cattle were then put on a train and taken to market. In between the ranch and the train station was the cattle drive.

"The Horse Wrangler,"
Photographed by Erwin Evans Smith, 1910, Bonham, Texas

A cattle drive included about one thousand cattle, a dozen men, and eight to ten horses per man. The crew included a trail boss; a cook, called a cookie; a wrangler; and about nine drovers. Wranglers took care of the horses. See cookie on page 414 and wrangler at left.

During the daytime, cowboys drove cattle along a trail. The cattle would spread out in a column up to a mile and a half long. Pairs of drovers rode on either side of the herd. The crew communicated with one another using hat signals or hand signals learned from the Plains Indians. Before noon they would lead the cattle off the trail so they could graze. After a couple of hours, they would head northward again. They usually covered ten to fifteen miles a day. A drive from Texas to western Kansas could take twenty-five to one hundred days. Calves born on the drive were placed in a special wagon. At night they were allowed to be with their mothers. When rivers were low enough, both the cattle and the cowboys' horses swam across. When rivers were high, they waited for the water to go down.

At night the cattle were herded into an area called the bed ground. Two cowboys guarded the bed ground by riding in circles around the cattle, passing each other twice as they made the circle. The other cowboys slept on their bedrolls. If they had a little free time, they might play a game, as illustrated below.

One of the most famous trails used in cattle drives was the Chisholm Trail, which went from near Brownsville, Texas, on the Rio Grande to Dodge City and Abilene, Kansas. It passed through Waco, Texas. Businessmen there built a toll suspension bridge across the Brazos River. Thousands of cattle crossed over the bridge during cattle drives for a charge of five cents each. Most drovers made their cattle swim across instead.

Many cowboys loved their life in the great outdoors. They saw canyons at sunrise; they listened to the mockingbirds, owls, and the howl of the coyote. They cared about the cattle and knew how to take care of them. They even learned to sing to them when the cattle were scared. Being a cowboy required bravery. Sometimes herds were startled and began to stampede. Often the cause was lightning. Whether this happened in the daytime or the nighttime, the cowboys took off after them, trying with all their might to calm them down and bring them back together. Sometimes this took many hours.

Rodeos

In the late 1800s and early 1900s, easterners and even Europeans became fascinated with the lifestyles of cowboys,

Cowboys Playing a Game

415

Indians, outlaws, and lawmen. Entrepreneurs gathered cowboys, Indians, sharpshooters, and actors together to create Wild West Shows. William "Buffalo Bill" Cody organized one of the best known of these shows. Zack Mulhall from Guthrie, Oklahoma, had a show, which toured from 1900 to 1915. His daughter Lucille starred in it as the "world's first cowgirl." She was a favorite of President Theodore Roosevelt.

Oklahoma rancher Gordon William Lillie helped Pawnee Indians survive during a harsh winter. He became their "white chief." For a while he and some Pawnees worked in Buffalo Bill's show, but from 1888 to 1913, he led his own Pawnee Bill Wild West Show. Lillie was married to a proper lady from Philadelphia. His wife learned to sharp shoot and to ride broncos sidesaddle and began to perform in his show.

Cowboys needed particular skills to perform their jobs. Ranches began having competitions to see who could best perform these skills. Wild West shows showed these skills to audiences around the country. Eventually, the Wild West shows disappeared, but contests involving cowboy skills continued. Modern rodeos have competitions in calf roping, steer wrestling, bronco riding, bull riding, barrel racing, and other skills. Cowboys and cowgirls compete in rodeos. Native Americans also host rodeos.

Cowboy culture has continued to be popular in America. People who have never been near a Texas ranch like to dress up in cowboy boots and cowboy hats. Today there are even cowboy churches that reach out to ranchers, farmers, horsemen, rodeo contestants, and, of course, cowboys.

For every beast of the forest is Mine,
The cattle on a thousand hills.
Psalm 50:10

Activities for Lesson 75

Map Study – Complete the assignments for Lesson 75 on Map 18 "The West" in *Maps of America the Beautiful*.

Timeline – In *Timeline of America the Beautiful* next to 1871, write: Western cattle drives peak during this year.

Vocabulary – In your notebook, write your own definition for each of these words: transport, demand, canvas, stirrup, outlaw. Look in the lesson for clues to the meaning of the words. When you are finished, look in a dictionary to check your definitions.

Literature – Read "Cowboy Songs" in *We the People*, pages 79-80, and chapter 12 and the Author's Note in *Across Five Aprils*.

Creative Writing – In your notebook, write a one-page story about a cowboy adventure. Use some of the details about cowboy life that you learned in this lesson.

Student Workbook or Lesson Review – If you are using one of these optional books, complete the assignment for Lesson 75. If you are using the Lesson Review, answer the questions on *Across Five Aprils* and take the quiz for Unit 15.

Iroquoian Longhouse

Supplies

- 250 gumdrops
- 300 toothpicks
- 5 pieces white paper
- tape
- 3 cotton balls
- liquid glue

Instructions

Look at the drawing above of an Iroquoian longhouse. Build a model of this structure using toothpick and gumdrop construction, as illustrated in the photo below. Each gumdrop is a joint where the toothpicks come together. Use these dimensions:

12 toothpicks long
5 toothpicks wide (minus a door on each end, 1 toothpick wide and 2 toothpicks tall)
3 toothpicks tall
3 toothpicks per side of the roof, coming to a peak in the center

You won't be able to move your structure once you begin, so build on a surface that won't be needed for anything else for a while. Roll and tape the pieces of paper lengthwise into tight rolls. Use these as supports for the roof. They should fit snugly under 5 of the gumdrops at the peak of the roof. Toothpick and gumdrop construction is not easy! You will encounter various challenges that will require careful thinking and imagination.

To make "smoke" come from the longhouse smoke holes, look at the photo below. Unroll the cotton balls. Cut each roll in half. Spread liquid glue on one side of the strips of cotton. Twist and glue cotton around five toothpicks until the toothpicks are completely covered except for one point. Carefully stick the points of the five covered toothpicks in the places for the five smoke holes. At right is a photo of a finished longhouse.

Some children may be allergic to ingredients in gumdrops. Make sure your child is safe.

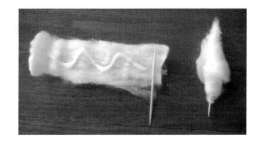

Navajo Flatbread

Ingredients

- 5 cups all-purpose flour, plus extra for dusting
- 1 teaspoon salt
- 2 tablespoons baking powder
- 1/2 cup oil, plus extra for frying
- 1 1/2 cups warm water

Instructions

Mix flour, salt, and baking powder in a large bowl. Add oil and water and mix with a fork until dough starts to combine. Wet your hands and work the dough by hand until it is well-mixed and consistent. Do not over-mix or your bread will be tough.

Knead the dough in the bowl for three minutes by repeating this process: push the dough flat, stand it on its end, then push it flat again. After kneading, let the ball of dough rest for 10 minutes.

Divide the ball of dough into ten equal pieces. Roll the dough with a rolling pin to make circles about 1/8" inch thick, or about 6" across. Dust your work surface with flour if dough is sticky.

Heat a skillet on the stove on medium-low for 7 minutes, then add a few drops of oil and spread around with spatula. Place a flatbread in the skillet and fry for 2 minutes on each side, adding a few drops of oil to skillet for each side. Bread should have dark brown spots on both sides when it is done. You may need to adjust your stove temperature so that the flatbreads don't cook too fast or too slow. Eat while they are fresh and warm! You can eat them with butter and honey, or pile with what you would put in a taco.

> ## Parental Supervision Required
>
> This recipe uses the stove and hot oil.
>
> **Please Note:** Be careful. Some children may be allergic to recipe ingredients.

Pocahontas Museum

Supplies

- multi-color package of construction paper
- ten pieces of white paper
- stapler
- colored pencils, crayons, or markers
- scissors

> **Parental Supervision Required**
>
> This project uses scissors and a stapler.

Instructions

For this activity, you will create a museum to educate visitors about the life of Pocahontas. You will make or collect objects and label them. Look at Lesson 12 to remind yourself of details of the life of Pocahontas. You can set up your museum on a large table.

Exhibit 1: Stones and Clubs Cut two identical club shapes from brown construction paper. Staple them together around the edge, leaving them open at one end. Stuff with wads of crumpled paper and staple shut. Make paper rocks using the same method. On a sheet of white paper, write a short description of how Pocahontas and John Smith first met. Explain that John Smith was made to lie on stones while men stood over him with clubs, and that Pocahontas rescued him.

Exhibit 2: Furs and Corn If possible, find anything in your house made of real or artificial animal fur. If you don't have anything made of fur, draw short hairs on a piece of brown paper. Make ears of corn out of yellow and green paper and place them inside a real basket. Make a sign explaining that Pocahontas often came to the Jamestown settlement to visit John Smith and to bring furs and corn to trade.

Exhibit 3: Held for Ransom On a white piece of construction paper, draw three Englishmen, some corn, and a pile of guns. Make a sign about the kidnapping of Pocahontas and explain that the pictured items were demanded of Chief Powhatan in exchange for his kidnapped daughter.

Exhibit 4: Learning About Jesus Place a Bible next in your museum. Make a sign explaining how Pocahontas was taught English and about God and Jesus, decided to become a Christian, and changed her name to Rebecca.

Continued on the following page.

Exhibit 5: Marriage to John Rolfe On a piece of paper, write April 5, 1614 and draw a heart around it. Cut two 1-inch wide strips of construction paper. On one strip, write "Rebecca." On the other strip, write "John Rolfe." With a stapler, join the strips together like a paper chain. Place the links next to the date of their wedding. Make a sign describing the marriage of John Rolfe and Rebecca.

Exhibit 6: Thomas Rolfe Wrap a doll in a plain blanket. If you don't have a doll available, draw a picture of baby. Make a sign explaining that John Rolfe and Rebecca had a son named Thomas.

Exhibit 7: Trip to England Cut two identical boat-shapes out of brown paper and staple them together around the bottom and sides. Slide a pencil, stick, or straw for the mast between the sides of the ship. Tape a white napkin or tissue onto the mast for a sail. Make a sign telling about the Rolfe family's trip to England in 1616.

Exhibit 8: Death of Pocahontas Write "Pocahontas" at the top of a gray piece of paper, cut to look like a tombstone. Also write on it where she was born, to whom she was married, where she died, and how old she was when she died. Make a sign explaining how Pocahontas died.

Exhibit 9: Remembering Pocahontas On white paper, draw or paint a picture of Pocahontas like the painting below that now hangs in the National Portrait Gallery. Make a sign telling what you think are the most significant contributions of Pocahontas.

Make a sign for your museum. When your museum is complete, invite family members to visit your museum and learn about the life of Pocahontas. Stand near your exhibits so you can answer any questions.

Colonial Printing

Supplies

- 1 sheet of craft foam, 9" x 12" or larger (available at craft stores)
- liquid glue
- scrap cardboard (such as the side of a cereal box, cut to 8 1/2" x 11")
- black non-toxic craft paint
- sponge paintbrush
- heavy 8 1/2" x 11" paper or cardstock
- heavy book (8 1/2" x 11" or larger, covered in waxed paper to keep it clean)
- newspaper
- paper plate or bowl

> **Parental Supervision Required**
>
> This project uses scissors.

Instructions

For this activity, you are going to recreate the basic printing method used for the Bay Psalm Book. Remember that the Bay Psalm Book, and every book or newspaper printed at the time, contained thousands of letters and required many hours to create. You are going to print the phrase TRUST IN THE LORD AND DO GOOD from Psalm 37:3. We recommend that you wear an apron just like a colonial printer would have! Some steps must be done quickly, and you will need to know what is coming next. Carefully familiarize yourself with all the instructions before you begin.

Step 1: Make movable type. Write TRUST IN THE LORD AND DO GOOD in bubble (outline) letters about 1.5 inches tall on the craft foam. Make all of the letters the same height. Cut out all of the letters. This is your movable type.

Step 2: Set type. In colonial times, the person who set movable type to form words and sentences was called a *compositor*. The rack that held the set type was called a *galley*. You can use a piece of cardboard for a galley. Place your letters in the correct order to spell the phrase BACKWARDS. That means you need to start on the top right side and spell to the left, placing every letter facing backwards. On the second line, start on the right side again. When all of your "type" is "set," put two or three dots of glue on the underside of each to letter to hold it in place. Give the glue about twenty minutes to dry while you prepare your ink and cover your work surface with newspaper.

Step 3: Ink the letters. This job was done by the *beater*. He used a leather covered ball on a wooden handle to put ink on the letters. You can use a sponge paintbrush. Put black paint in a paper plate or bowl (about as much as if it was ketchup for your fries). Stir in 3 or 4 drops of water to thin the paint. Dampen your paintbrush with water and squeeze it out completely. Dip the brush into the "ink" and brush over all your letters. Make sure all the letters are neatly and evenly covered. Work quickly so the paint does not begin to dry. Immediately lay a piece of heavy paper evenly over the letters.

Step 4: Pressing the platen. In colonial printshops, the *pressman* lowered the *platen* to make the impression of the letters on paper. You can use a heavy book (covered with wax paper to keep it clean) for a platen. Carefully set the book on top of the paper and press down hard with your hands. Don't let anything slide! Hold the book firmly for 20-25 seconds, making sure there is pressure on the whole surface. Lift the book and set it aside. Starting with one corner, slowly peel off the paper and lay it flat on the table.

Step 5: Proofread and Improve. Look at your printing carefully. Did the ink make a good impression of all the letters? Are there any smudges or dry spots? Are there any spelling mistakes? Make any changes that are needed and print three more copies of the page. Re-ink your letters each time. Colonial printers used this basic method to create multiple copies of the pages of books, newspapers, stationary, posters, and pamphlets.

You will become a better printer with practice. Now that you know the printing process, you can print anything! Your foam letters are reusable (just pull them gently off the cardboard), and you can make more letters. What else would you like to print? Your name perhaps? You can also cut shapes and pictures to print. Colonial printers used pictures carved in wood called *woodcuts* to print illustrations. Remember that everything must be set backwards to come out forwards!

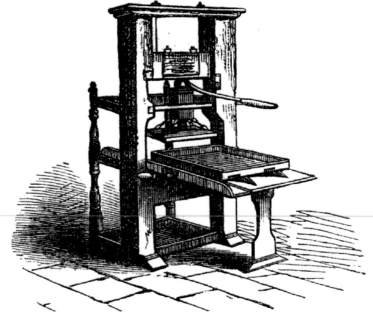

Boston Tea Party

Supplies

- 2 square pieces of craft wood, approximately 6" x 6" x 1/4" (available at craft stores)
- 12 strips of craft wood, approximately 3/4" x 8" x 1/4" inches (ruler-shaped)
- ruler
- wood or craft glue
- black permanent marker
- herbal tea of your choice and cookies

Instructions

Build a miniature tea crate from the East India Company, which shipped the tea to Boston that angry colonists dumped into the harbor.

1. Line up your ruler with one edge of the square piece of wood. Make a mark at 1 inch, 2 inches, 2 1/2 inches, 3 1/2 inches, 4 inches, and 5 inches. Repeat on each edge of both wood squares (see top photo).

2. Glue 3 long strips of wood to each edge of the square pieces of wood, lining up the strips in between the three pairs of marks. Make sure your wood squares are lined up so your crate will be level. Let dry 15 minutes. (You will need to balance the wood squares upright, as shown in the middle photo.)

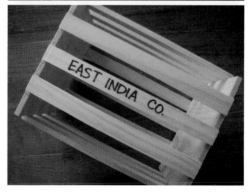

3. Repeat with the rest of the wood strips, gluing them to the sides of the wood squares. Let dry between each side.

4. When the glue is completely dry, write "East India Co." on each side of the crate with a black permanent marker (see bottom photo). At the end of each wood strip, make two small marks to look like the slats were nailed on.

Put the crate in the center of your dining table as a centerpiece. Put a paper plate of cookies on top of it. Enjoy cups of hot herbal tea (which Bostonians were encouraged to drink instead of British tea) and cookies around the table.

Colonial Marbles and Bag

Supplies

- 3 colors of polymer clay (the kind that can be baked)
- 1 felt rectangle (9" x 12") in any color
- scissors
- yarn or string

> **Parental Supervision Required**
>
> This project uses scissors.

Instructions for the Marbles

1. Roll each color of clay into a snake shape.

2. Twist the three clay snakes together, then rub together gently in your hands until you have a single, smooth, thicker snake with swirled colors. (Don't rub so long that the distinct colors disappear.)

3. Break off a piece from the snake about the size of a large grape. Roll it gently in your hands until it is a sphere. Repeat with the rest of the clay, making some slightly larger and some slightly smaller.

4. Bake marbles according to the directions on the clay package and let them cool.

Instructions for the Bag

1. Find the largest plate or bowl that will fit on the felt rectangle and trace around it, making a circle.

2. Cut out the circle of felt. With a marker, trace another circle about one inch from the edge. See photo at right.

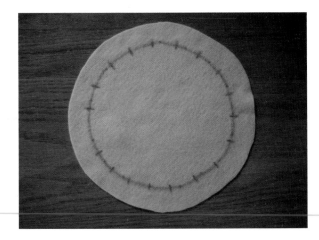

3. Mark approximately 1-inch increments around the second circle you have drawn. You need to have an even number of marks. Carefully make a tiny snip with scissors on each of these marks. Be careful not to cut your finger with the tips of the scissors!

4. Cut a piece of yarn or string 3 1/2 feet long. Wind tape around one end for a "needle." Pull the string in and out of the holes until you have string coming out the same direction of 2 holes that are next to each other. When you start, leave about

eight inches of string hanging outside from your first hole. When you finish, you should have several inches of string hanging from the hole next to it on the same side of the felt. See photo at right. The side that the strings are hanging from is the outside of your bag. Snip off the hanging strings to about 4 inches each.

5. Place your cooled marbles in the middle on the inside of the felt circle. Gently pull the outside strings at the same time until the top of the bag is closed. Tie the hanging strings in a bow you can easily untie. Now you have a favorite colonial toy!

How to Play

To play a game with your marbles, draw a 3-foot diameter circle on your driveway with chalk. Choose one larger marble to be your shooter, and scatter the rest inside the circle. With your pointer finger, make a hook. Put the shooter marble in the hook of your finger. Place the two knuckles of your hooked finger next to the edge of the chalk circle. Use your thumb to flick the marble out of the hook. See if you can knock other marbles out of the circle. Keep practicing and you will get better!

Liberty Bell Mosaic

Supplies

- 1 piece white poster board
- 2 sheets each, red, white, and blue construction paper
- liquid glue or glue stick
- scissors
- black marker
- pencil
- ruler

> **Parental Supervision Required**
>
> This project uses scissors.

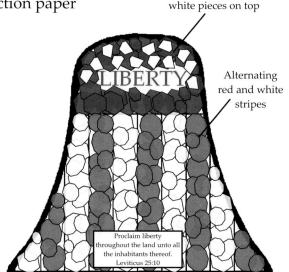

Blue with thirteen white pieces on top

Alternating red and white stripes

Proclaim liberty throughout the land unto all the inhabitants thereof. Leviticus 25:10

Instructions

1. Look at the illustration at right to see the shape of the Liberty Bell. Using one of the shorter edges of the poster board as the bottom, draw a bell shape with a pencil on the poster board. Cut out the bell.

2. Tear each piece of construction paper into small pieces of various sizes and shapes. No piece should be larger than a postage stamp.

3. With a black marker, write "LIBERTY" in large letters all the way across near the top of your bell. Draw a horizontal line below the word as pictured at right.

4. From the top of the bell to the line you drew, glue pieces of torn blue paper around the word "LIBERTY." (Spread glue on a small section of the poster board, attach pieces of construction paper, then repeat on another section.)

5. Glue thirteen pieces of torn white paper on top of the blue along the top of the bell. These represent the first 13 states.

6. With a pencil and ruler, mark up-and-down lines about two inches apart down the rest of the bell.

7. Make alternating red and white stripes on the bottom of the bell with the torn paper, as you did with the blue paper.

8. Cut a small rectangle out of a scrap piece of the poster board about the size of an index card. Write on it neatly: "Proclaim liberty throughout the land, unto all the inhabitants thereof. Leviticus 25:10" Glue it in the center bottom of your bell.

Supplies for the Voyage of Discovery

Supplies

+ 60 index cards
+ 5 dice

Instructions

Make two index cards for each of the supplies listed at right. Write the name of each item on the card, or for more fun, draw a picture of each item and label it. You will have two cards with a compass, two with a telescope, two with books, etc. Number the two sets of supply cards 1-30. Shuffle the cards and place them in a stack.

The game is for two people or two teams. The first player or team to collect all the supplies for the Voyage of Discovery is the winner. Roll one die each to determine who goes first.

Items to Put on Cards	
compass	syringes
telescope	hand saws
books	hatchets
paper	chisels
ink	pocket mirrors
crayons	sewing needles
fish hooks	scissors
fishing lines	sewing thread
guns	silk ribbons
ammunition	brightly-colored
clothes	fabric
blankets	face paint
knapsacks	beads
tent fabric	keelboat
mosquito curtains	peace medals
medicine	

On each turn, begin by rolling all five dice. Your points are ten times the total number of the dice. If you roll 1/2/3/4/6, those equal 16 so you get 160 points. If you want to, you may re-roll up to four of the dice to try to get a higher number. You may do this as many times as you want to, but if you roll a 4 on any of the dice after your first roll, your turn ends immediately with 0 points. When you decide to stop rolling, total all five dice, multiply the number by 10, and draw one supply card for every 100 points you have earned. If you get 220 points, you draw two supply cards. Lay the cards you draw face-up on the table. If you roll a 4 on any roll after your first roll, you don't get any cards.

Here is an example turn: The player rolls all five dice and gets 1/1/2/3/4. Those total 11, so the player has 110 points. He decides to set aside the highest number (4) and roll the other 4 dice again. On his second roll, he gets 1/2/3/6. Adding these the 4 he set aside, the total is 16. He sets aside the 6 and rolls the remaining three dice, this time getting 2/5/5. He decides to stop rolling. He has 6/5/5/4/2. Those total 22. That makes 220 points, so he draws two supply cards.

Sometimes you will end up with duplicate supply cards. If you get 200 points or more on a turn, after you draw your two cards, you may trade any one of your cards for any one of your opponent's cards.

If the game continues until all the cards have been drawn but neither player has a complete set of supplies, players continue to roll the dice as above. If a player reaches 200 or more points on a roll, he may take any two cards from his opponent. The player may not take any cards if he rolls less than 200 points.

Before and After the Erie Canal

Supplies

- ◆ 2 shoe box lids
- ◆ blue marker or crayon
- ◆ 2 batches clay (2 cups flour, 1 cup salt, 1 cup water, and 1 tablespoon oil for each batch)
- ◆ toothpicks
- ◆ clippings from bushes

Instructions

This project demonstrates why it was easier to transport people and freight after the construction of the Erie Canal. You will create a model of the Erie Canal and a portion of Lake Erie and the Hudson River. As you shape the canal with clay, think about the difficulties of the actual construction when the builders had to dig or blast the earth and rock away. And remember that the actual canal was 364 miles long!

> Some children may be allergic to ingredients in the clay. Make sure your child is safe.

1. On the first shoe box lid, color a 2-inch wide stripe on one short end for the Hudson River. Color a semi-circle on the other end for Lake Erie. Repeat this on the second lid, and add a 2-inch wide stripe connecting Lake Erie and the Hudson River down the middle for the Erie Canal.

2. Mix the batches of clay one at a time. Knead each batch for a few minutes with your hands to make it soft and consistent.

3. Mold the land area around the water in each shoe box lid. Make hills, mountains, and valleys.

4. Make signs for the bodies of water and tape them to toothpicks. Place them in the clay.

5. Use clippings from bushes to represent forests in your diorama.

6. If you wish, you can embellish your dioramas with towns, roads, boats, and overland and canal travelers. The clay will harden by the next day. You can color with markers on the clay after it hardens.

Sharing God's Word

Supplies

- clean, empty container with plastic lid (coffee can, large yogurt tub, etc.)
- paper
- scissors

> **Parental Supervision Required**
>
> This project uses scissors.

Instructions

For this activity, you get to follow the example of John Jay and help people have access to God's word.

Carefully cut a slit large enough for coins in the lid of your container. Cut a piece of paper to make a label for the container. Write "Share God's Word" on the label and a Bible verse of your choice. Suggested verses are Psalm 40:8, Psalm 119:105, and Isaiah 26:8. Add any other decorations to the label you wish. Tape the label on the outside of the container.

Tell your family that this container is to collect change to help people have access to God's word. Invite everyone to participate. Leave the container in a prominent place in your house. When the container is full, dump out the change and count it. Ask a parent to help you send this as a donation to an organization that distributes Bibles. Among the many options are the American Bible Society, Love Packages, and Gideons International.

World War II sailor James Lee Frazer took time every day to read the Bible.

Plantation Dinner

Wealthy Natchez plantation families had grand feasts for themselves and their guests, prepared and served by slaves. The inspiration for our menu is from the book *Plantation Sketches* by Margaret Devereux, who wrote about life on plantations of the Old South so that her grandchildren would know what it was like. Here is how Mrs. Devereux described plantation dinners: "In times of peace, both before and after the war, the social life at the table, with family and always welcome friends, was a source of much pleasure. For a dinner of ten or twelve persons, including ourselves, there would be a ham at the head, a large roast turkey at the foot, a quarter of boiled mutton, a round of beef *à la mode* [roast beef], and a boiled turkey stuffed with oysters. In the middle of the table would be celery in tall cut-glass stands, on the sides cranberries in molds and various kinds of pickles. With these would be served either four or six dishes of vegetables and scalloped oysters, handed hot from the plate-warmer. The dessert would be a plum pudding, clear stewed apples with cream, with a waiter [serving piece] in the center filled with calf's-foot jelly [flavored gelatin], syllabub [flavored whipped cream] in glasses, and coconut or cheesecake puddings at the corners."

Linden Mansion in Natchez

You can make a scaled-down version of this plantation dinner. If you wish, use fancy dishes and serving pieces and set the table with a tablecloth and cloth napkins. If possible, invite another family over in the style of traditional southern hospitality.

Menu

- one of these meats: ham, roast turkey, or roast beef
- raw celery (served standing in glasses in the center of the table)
- molded cranberry sauce
- pickles
- two or three hot vegetables (suggestions: creamed corn, mashed potatoes, lima beans, green beans, yellow squash, or turnip greens)
- stewed apples with cream for dessert (recipe on the next page)

> ### Parental Supervision Required
>
> This project uses a knife and a stovetop.
>
> **Please Note:** Be careful. Some children may be allergic to dinner ingredients.

Stewed Apples with Cream

Ingredients

- 6 firm apples
- water
- ½ teaspoon cinnamon
- ¼ teaspoon ground cloves
- ¼ teaspoon ground ginger
- 2/3 cup brown sugar
- 1 pint heavy cream

Directions

Peel the apples if desired, cut in half, and remove the core. Place 2 cups of water in a large pot or saucepan. (Your pot should be large enough that all the apple halves can touch the bottom. Use two pots if needed. If you use two pots, use two cups of water per pot.) Stir spices and sugar into the water. Place the apples in the saucepan. Bring the liquid to a boil.

As soon as it boils, turn the heat down to low and put the lid on the saucepan. Let simmer 20 minutes (15 minutes for peeled apples). Watch carefully to make sure the pot does not boil dry. If you have to add water, add only enough to keep the apples from sticking. After 15-20 minutes of simmering, stick a fork in an apple half. If the fork goes in easily, the apples are done. If not, simmer longer, testing every 2 minutes. Your apples should be soft, but not mushy. You can make stewed apples before dinner, turn the heat off, leave the lid on, and then simmer again for a few minutes to warm before serving.

To serve, place two apple halves in a small bowl. Pour about ½ cup of the cooking liquid and 3 tablespoons warmed cream over the apple halves. Makes 6 servings.

Wild and Wonderful Niagara Falls

In this activity, you will produce a short play about Niagara Falls. Your audience will learn about Niagara Falls and some of the notable events that have happened there. Your play can have one performer or many; give parts to as many people as you have participating. Ask someone to be the narrator and read the lines. We have provided the lines for the play and some staging instructions. You fill in the rest! Think about how to make your play run smoothly and entertain and educate your audience. Practice several times so everyone knows what to do, including a bow at the end. You might want to make tickets and programs. Even if you have only one person in the audience, put on a great play!

Stage Instructions

1. Welcome! While this line is read, an actor sprays the audience with a light mist of water from a spray bottle. An actor dressed as a tour guide or tourist smiles and enthusiastically holds up a sign that says "This way to Niagara Falls!"

2. First Recording: One or two actors, dressed as explorers walk around the stage silently looking, pointing, and exclaiming. One of them pulls out a pad and pencil and furiously writes on the paper.

3. Bridges: One or more actors walks across the stage, pretending to walk on the lower deck of the suspension bridge. They wear helmets and cover their heads with their hands, walking in a crouched, fearful position, continually looking up with frightened faces.

4. Honeymooners: Someone dressed up as a bride or a groom (or two people dressed as both) walks across the stage carrying suitcases. They look happy, shy, and embarrassed.

Narrator's Lines

1. Welcome to Niagara Falls! Niagara Falls is between Lake Erie and Lake Ontario on the border between Canada and the United States of America. The beautiful falls sends 194,940 cubic feet of gushing, rushing water 188 feet over the edge every second!

2. Louis Hennepin made the first known description and drawing of the falls. He visited Niagara with French explorer René Robert Cavelier and wrote about it in his book *A New Discovery of a Vast Country in America* published in 1698.

3. The first bridge across Niagara Falls was made of oak planks hung from iron cables. The first bridge was replaced by the Niagara Falls Suspension Bridge in 1855. The suspension bridge had an upper deck for trains and a lower deck for carriages and pedestrians.

4. Niagara Falls is a popular destination for honeymooners. This tradition goes back to the early the 1800s. Aaron Burr's daughter and Napoleon's brother are reported to be some of the first Niagara Falls honeymooners.

5. Hurricane Deck: One or more people stand as if they are being blown by furious winds and can barely remain standing. Meanwhile, they point and silently admire the scenery.

6. *Maid of the Mist*: One or more people hold a donut-shaped life-preserver (cut out of poster board) that says MAID OF THE MIST in large black letters. All of them duck under umbrellas and rock back and forth as if they are on the deck of a boat.

7. Jumpers and Divers: One or more people stand in a silly diving position, wearing inflatable floaters, goggles, and towels wrapped around their waists.

8. Annie Edson Taylor: Someone stands in a large empty garbage can in a dress, carrying a purse, with a pillow tied on his or her head. The actor looks scared and keeps his or her eyes closed.

9. Charles Blondin: A rope or jump rope is laid across the floor. An actor walks across it, gingerly taking one step at a time and wobbling precariously, all the while waving to the audience with confidence.

10. Come see Niagara Falls! An actor walks across the tightrope, this time wearing a blindfold. He or she holds a sign facing the audience that reads "Follow me to Niagara Falls!"

5. Platforms that allow visitors to reach Hurricane Deck are built every spring and removed every November. On Hurricane Deck, visitors can stand less than 20 feet from the waters of Bridal Veil Falls, which is part of Niagara Falls. At Hurricane Deck, winds can reach 68 miles per hour!

6. In 1846 a steamboat began taking tourists across the Niagara River. It was called *Maid of the Mist*. Since then, seven different boats have been used, all called *Maid of the Mist*. On the boat, visitors can get close to the bottom of the falls where they get drenched from the rising mist.

7. In October 1829, Sam Patch jumped over Niagara Falls and survived! He earned the nickname "Yankee Leaper." People have tried going over the falls in various ways, including a kayak and a jet ski. Today, going over the falls is illegal in Canada and the United States, and an attempt could earn you a $10,000 fine.

8. In 1901 a Civil War widow named Annie Edson Taylor who had fallen on hard times went over Niagara Falls in a barrel, hoping to gain attention and make money from her fame. She claimed to be 40 years old, but was really 63! She fixed up a wooden pickle barrel with accessories suited for the stunt, and over the falls she went. She survived the exciting journey, but didn't make much money for her trouble.

9. Charles Blondin got started in the acrobat trade when he was only six years old. In 1859 he made his first trip across Niagara Falls—not on a boat or a bridge, but on a tightrope! His tightrope was 1,100 feet long and hung 160 feet above the falls. That was the first of many trips across the falls. On his various trips across the falls, Blondin pushed a wheelbarrow, carried a man on his back, and walked on stilts. Once he crossed blindfolded!

10. We invite you to see for yourself one of America the Beautiful's most famous attractions! Catch the mist, hear the roar, feel the wind, and see a rainbow! THE END

Lighthouse Painting

Supplies

- a few sheets of watercolor paper
- watercolor paint set
- watercolor brush

Instructions

Find a beautiful photograph of a lighthouse. You might look on the Internet or in travel or photography books at the library. First, make a light pencil sketch on watercolor paper. Use the watercolors according to the package instructions to create a beautiful lighthouse painting. Take your time and make one or two practice paintings first so you can try some of your ideas and see how colors look together. Be careful to rinse and pat dry your brush well before changing colors.

Dance the Virginia Reel

Learn this fun dance that was popular during the Civil War! The more the merrier! Try to gather up at least six people to dance. The folk tune "Turkey in the Straw" is a perfect accompaniment to the "Virginia Reel." Many free midi files are available online. Try searching for "Turkey in the Straw Midi." (Never use the Internet without a parent's permission.)

Instructions

1. Divide into two lines facing each other, everyone directly across from a partner. Stand far enough apart that you can reach out your arms and grasp hands. Begin with your hands at your sides.

2. (Music count: 1-2-3-4) Take four small steps forward.

3. (1-2-3-4) Take four small steps backward.

4. (1-2-3-4) Take four small steps forward.

5. (1-2-3-4) Take four small steps backward.

6. (1-2-3-4-5-6-7-8) Join right hands with your partner and walk in a circle back to place.

7. (1-2-3-4-5-6-7-8) Join left hands with your partner and walk in a circle back to place.

8. (1-2-3-4-5-6-7-8) Join both hands with your partner and walk in a circle back to place.

9. (1-2-3-4-5-6-7-8) Do-si-do with your partner (make a circle around each other, passing back-to-back, without turning around, ending where you started).

10. (1-2-3-4-5-6-7-8-9-10-11-12-13-14-15-16) The couple at one end of the lines (the head couple) joins both hands and gallops between the other couples eight counts down and eight counts back to place.

11. (1-2-3-4-5-6-7-8-9-10-11-12-13-14-15-16) The head couple makes an arch with their hands. The other couples join both hands and in turn walk under the arch, drop hands, walk around the back of the arch on their side, and get back in line. After all the couples have passed under the arch, the head couple walks to the bottom of the lines.

12. The dance begins again. The couple now at the top of the line will be the new head couple.

Hymn-Singing

Instructions

This activity is to organize a time for a group singing of hymns written by Fanny J. Crosby and other hymns. This can involve just your family or may include extended family and friends. Discuss as a family how you want to organize your hymn-singing. You might want to invite another family from your church to your home for dessert and a hymn-singing.

Fanny J. Crosby

You need one copy of the words to the hymns for at least every two people that will be at your hymn-singing. With a parent's help, you can find words for Fanny J. Crosby hymns on the Internet. Copy and paste them into a document and print out enough copies for your group. Design a cover with the title "Fanny J. Crosby Hymns" and staple together the booklets to hand out at your hymn-singing. Visit www.notgrass.com/ablinks.php for a link to the words and MIDI files of the tunes for many of Fanny J. Crosby's hymns. (Never use the Internet without a parent's permission.) If you do not have Internet access at home you might be able to borrow hymnals from your church. Many hymnals have a section in the back where you can look up hymns by author.

Here are some of Fanny J. Crosby's best-known hymns. Choose five to seven for your hymn-singing.

A Wonderful Savior	Jesus, Keep Me Near the Cross
All the Way My Savior Leads Me	Praise Him! Praise Him!
Blessed Assurance	Redeemed, How I Love to Proclaim It!
He Hideth My Soul	Rescue the Perishing
Hide Me, O My Savior	Safe in the Arms of Jesus
I Am Thine, O Lord	Take the World, But Give Me Jesus
Jesus Is Tenderly Calling	To God Be the Glory!

Write down some information on the life of Fanny J. Crosby you learned in Lesson 74. Share some details about her life, her relationship with God, her perspective on her blindness, and any other information you wish before your group begins singing. After singing hymns by Fanny J. Crosby, sing some other familiar hymns that you have chosen ahead of time. You can also ask those present for requests.

Ask someone ahead of time to conclude your hymn-singing with a prayer. Let people keep their copy of the Fanny J. Crosby Hymns booklet.

Sources

Answers in Genesis
Amherst University
Architect of the Capitol
Colonial Williamsburg
Columbia University
The Hermitage
James K. Polk Ancestral Home
John James Audubon State Park, Kentucky
Lewis and Clark Fort Mandan Foundation
Library of Congress
Maine Historical Society
Massachusetts Institute of Technology
Meriam-Webster, Incorporated
Microsoft Encarta
Monticello
Mount Vernon
Minnesota Department of Natural Resources
National Audubon Society
National Geographic
National Park Service
Native Languages of the Americas
Nebraska Department of Education
Nebraska State Historical Society
New York Institute for Special Education
New York State Canals
Noah Webster House and West Hartford Historical Society
Princeton University
Public Broadcasting System
Smithsonian Institution
Texas State Historical Association
United States Army Corps of Engineers
United States Coast Guard
United States Department of Agriculture Natural Resources Conservation Service
University of Virginia American Studies Project

Image Credits

Note: Numbers indicate the page numbers of images. The meanings of the letters t, m, b, l, and r are as follows: t - top of page; m - middle; b - bottom; l - left; r - right.

Architect of the Capitol 70, 316t

Bethany Poore 417bl/br, 423, 425, 428

Boston Public Library (Flickr, CC-BY-2.0) 303

Bureau of Land Management 313b, 315, 317 (except t), 318t, 319m, 347

cvilletomorrow/Brian Wheeler (Flickr, CC-BY-2.0) 211

Department of the Interior 264t (Tami Heilemann)

Dover Publications 67, 68t/m, 71a, 121mr, 122tl/bl, 123tr/br, 124m/b, 125, 129m, 153br, 154tr, 156m, 202, 203b, 344

El Frito (Flickr, CC-BY-2.0) 434

fdtate (Flickr, CC-BY-2.0) 277

Fearless Fred (Flickr, CC-BY-2.0) 161br

Joe Shlabotnik (Flickr, CC-BY-2.0) 229

Library of Congress front cover (soldier, steamboat, Native American), 7b, 9tr, 12b, 13, 15, 16 (except br), 17, 18, 19, 20, 27 (Sauk and Fox), 31t, 34b, 44b, 45, 46t, 47, 48ml/br, 49br, 51m, 52, 57b, 58tr, 58br, 59, 60, 72, 73b, 79br, 80tr, 83, 85t, 94tl, 96tr, 100b, 101t, 104t, 105t/bl, 108b, 111m/bl, 113, 116b, 128b, 131t, 133b, 134, 135m/b, 143b, 144, 146, 147b, 148, 151, 153tr/bl, 156t, 159tl, 164, 165mr, 166, 169, 172tl, 176b, 177, 178, 179, 180, 181, 182t, 190, 199, 203 (Magpie), 204, 209b, 210, 213t/m, 214 (except t), 215, 216 (except b), 217t/m, 219, 220, 221, 227, 231, 232, 234b, 235tr/b, 236, 238, 239, 240t, 245, 247t, 248t, 253b, 254, 257t, 259t/bl, 277, 278, 279t, 282t, 283tr, 284mr/b, 286t/m, 288tl/ml, 288bl (Carol M. Highsmith's America), 289, 290, 291, 292, 293t, 295t, 296, 297, 298, 299, 300, 301, 302, 305, 306t, 308, 309, 310, 311bl/br, 312, 318b, 320, 322, 323, 325 (Carol M. Highsmith's America), 329t, 330t/m, 331t/bl/br, 332, 333t, 338, 339, 340, 341t, 342, 347, 353b, 354, 359, 361, 362, 363, 364, 365, 367t/bl/br, 368, 369t, 370, 371, 372t, 373t, 374t, 375, 377t, 379, 381, 384t, 385, 388, 389, 390t, 392t/bl/br, 393, 400, 401, 402, 403, 404, 412t, 413, 414, 415, 430, back cover (stagecoach)

Mev McCurdy author photo

NASA 326b

National Archives and Records Administration 404, 429

National Park Service front cover (train, lighthouse), 6b, 54b, 61, 255, 343, 372b, 373b (Bill Dowling), 374 (except t, Bill Dowling), 384b, 387 (E. D. White), 390bl/br, 391, 395t, 395bl (R. Robinson), 395br (Jim Peaco), 396t, 396b (J. Schmidt), 397t (J. Schmidt), 397m/bl/br (Jim Peaco), 398t, 398b (J. Schmidt), 405, 406

Paul Lowry (Flickr, CC-BY-2.0) 351b

Photos.com front cover (bear)

RightIndex (Flickr, CC-BY-2.0) 223b

U.S. Coast Guard 349, 350, 351t

U.S. Fish and Wildlife Service 1t (Tom Nebell), 1b (Carolina Vasconcelos), 3tr, 206tm, 207t (Dave Menke), 207b, 287b, 337, (Brette Soucie), 346

U.S. Geological Survey 5ml, 152, 206tl, 241, 265m, 265b (Heather Henkel), 271b

Wikimedia Commons 71b, 145, 257bl/br, 306b, 328, 334, 336, 378, 383, 436, back cover (Independence Hall)

All other images are from **JupiterImages**.

Note: Images marked CC-BY-2.0 are licensed through the Creative Commons Attribution 2.0 Generic License. For more information, visit http://creativecommons.org/licenses/by/ 2.0/deed.en